VEGAN HANDBOOK

Over 200 Delicious Recipes,
Meal Plans, and Vegetarian Resources for All Ages

Edited by Debra Wasserman & Reed Mangels, Ph.D., R.D.

The
VR**g** VEGETARIAN
Resource Group

From The Vegetarian Resource Group
Baltimore, Maryland

A NOTE TO THE READER

This is the second book in our *Vegetarian Journal Reports series.* The Contents of *Vegan Handbook* are not intended to provide personal medical advice. Medical Advice should be obtained from a qualified health professional.

Library of Congress Cataloging-in-Publication Data
Vegan Handbook -- Over 200 Delicious Recipes,
Meal Plans, and Vegetarian Resources for All Ages /
Edited by Debra Wasserman & Reed Mangels, Ph.D, R.D.
Library of Congress Catalog Card Number: 96-60113

ISBN 0-931411-17-3

Printed in the United States of America
10 9 8 7 6 5 4 3 2 1

TABLE OF CONTENTS

Acknowledgements

This book contains the work of many dedicated writers, health professionals, cooks, and others. Each in his or her own special way has contributed greatly to this huge project. First I'd like to thank Reed Mangels, Ph.D., R.D. who not only provided the nutritional analysis for over 200 recipes but also added her insight to the health-related articles and helped edit the entire manuscript. Her dedication to the vegetarian movement is tremendous!

This book would not be complete without the terrific artwork produced by Vonnie Crist, Denise Drasata-Peters, and John Peters. They are all quite talented.

I greatly appreciate the number of hours Michele Cagan and Israel Mossman volunteered to proofread and edit the entire book. Ashley Pound and Eva Mossman also proofread parts of this book and their work is appreciated also.

Finally, special thanks to the following authors who originally contributed one or more articles to *Vegetarian Journal* and they now appear in this book. I'm sure a lot of hard work and research went into producing each and every one of the pieces appearing in *Vegan Handbook*. Many thanks to Ruth Blackburn, M.S., R.D.; Nanette Blanchard; Cindy Blum; Stuart Cantor; Mary Clifford, R.D.; Jacqueline Dunnington, Ph.D.; Dez Figueira; Mary Franz, M.S., R.D.; Marilyn Haldane; Suzanne Havala, M.S., R.D.; Bobbie Hinman; Betty Jahn; Larry Kaiser; Michael Keevican; Stephen Knutson; Enette Larson, M.S., R.D.; Jay Lavine, M.D.; Reed Mangels, Ph.D., R.D.; Donna Maurer; John McArdle, Ph.D.; Mark Messina, Ph.D.; Virginia Messina, M.P.H., R.D.; Judith Grabski Miner; Israel Mossman; Bobbi Pasternak, R.N.; Karna S. Peterson, M.P.H., R.D.; Craig D. Reid, Ph.D.; Mark Rifkin; Lisa Rivero; Habeeb Salloum; Amy Shuman, R.D.; Wayne Smeltz, Ph.D.; Amy South; Susan Stafursky; Charles Stahler; Eve Shatto Walton, R.D.; and Debra Wasserman.

Introduction

I started editing and laying out the manuscript for this book on a hot summer day and completed the long task during a blizzard. Like the changing seasons, this book contains a wide variety of recipes and fascinating articles you're sure to enjoy. We've tried to include information that will be useful to the beginning vegetarian as well as those who have been following this lifestyle for a long time. Many of the over 200 vegan recipes can be prepared with ingredients found in supermarkets. In some cases, you are encouraged to visit a natural foods store to purchase products. Most of the recipes in this book are lowfat; however, there are a few exceptions. A nutritional analysis is provided for each recipe and in many cases variations are suggested in case you do not have a particular ingredient on hand.

While using this book you may want to keep the following information in mind. First, to keep the sodium content down in each dish try to use salt-free or low-sodium vegetable broth, tomato products, and canned beans when included in a recipe. Second, if nutritional yeast is listed as an ingredient, be sure not to use brewer's yeast which is bitter in taste. Nutritional yeast, on the other hand, is grown on a molasses medium and has a sweet, "cheesy" taste. It can be found in natural foods stores. Third, when you have the time you can prepare beans from scratch and freeze them in small containers to use in recipes calling for canned beans. When strawberries, blueberries, and other fruit are in season, you may want to freeze batches of these items in containers or bags for later use. Lastly, my motto is "fresh is best" and cooks should use seasonal ingredients. For example, if available, use fresh herbs. And finally, don't forget to enjoy life!

-- *Debra Wasserman*
Co-Director of The Vegetarian Resource Group

VEGAN MEAL PLAN

This is a modified version of a meal plan originally created by Ruth Blackburn, M.S., R.D., for The Vegetarian Resource Group. Like any food plan, this should only serve as a general guide for adults. The plan can be modified according to your own personal needs. Individuals with special health needs should consult a registered dietitian or a medical doctor knowledgeable about vegetarian nutrition.

A. <u>PROTEIN FOODS</u>: 1-2 SERVINGS PER DAY
(Each of the following equals one serving.)

1-1/2 cups cooked dried beans or peas
8 ounces tofu*
4 ounces tempeh
2 cups calcium fortified soy milk*
1/2 cup almonds*, cashews, walnuts, pecans, or peanuts
4 Tablespoons peanut butter

B. <u>WHOLE GRAINS</u>: at least 6-8 SERVINGS PER DAY
(Each of the following equals one serving.)

1 slice whole wheat, rye, or other whole grain bread
1/2 whole grain bagel or English muffin
1 buckwheat or whole wheat pancake or waffle
1 two-inch piece cornbread
1 whole grain muffin or biscuit or whole grain tortilla
2 Tablespoons wheat germ
1 ounce wheat or oat bran
1/4 cup sunflower, sesame*, or pumpkin seeds
3/4 cup wheat, bran, or corn flakes
1/2 cup cooked oatmeal or farina
1/2 cup cooked brown rice, barley, bulgur, or corn
1/2 cup cooked whole wheat noodles, macaroni, or spaghetti

C. <u>VEGETABLES</u>: at least 4-6 SERVINGS PER DAY

1. Two servings per day of any of the following: 1/2 cup cooked or 1 cup raw broccoli*, Brussels sprouts, collards*, kale*, chard, spinach, romaine lettuce, cabbage, carrots, sweet potatoes, winter squash, or tomatoes.

2. Two servings per day (one serving equals half cup cooked or one cup raw) of any other vegetable.

D. FRUITS: 4-6 SERVINGS PER DAY

1. Two servings per day of any of the following: 3/4 cup berries, 1/4 cantaloupe, 1 orange, 1/2 grapefruit, 1 lemon or lime, 1/2 papaya, 4-inch x 8-inch watermelon slice, or 1/2 cup orange, grapefruit, calcium-fortified orange*, or vitamin C enriched juice.

2. Two to four servings per day of other fruits: 1 small piece fresh fruit, 3/4 cup grapes, 1/2 cup cooked fruit or canned fruit without sugar, or 2 Tablespoons raisins, dates, or dried fruit.

E. FATS: 0-4 SERVINGS PER DAY
(Each of the following equals one serving.)

1 teaspoon vegan soft margarine or oil
2 teaspoons vegan mayonnaise or salad dressing
1 Tablespoon soy cream cheese or gravy

F. STARRED (*) FOOD ITEMS: 2, 3, OR MORE SERVINGS PER DAY

1. Men should include 2 choices daily

2. Women should include 3 choices daily

G. ADDITIONAL COMMENTS:

1. Pregnant and lactating women, persons under 18 years of age and persons with bone or muscle trauma or other special needs may require additional servings.

2. Vegans (people who do not consume any animal products such as dairy and eggs) need to include a vitamin B12 source regularly. Sources include some vitamin B12 fortified breakfast cereals and soy milks (check labels) and Red Star T-6635+ nutritional yeast (1-2 teaspoons supplies the adult RDA).

On the next page is a sample one-week vegan menu to give you an idea as to what a vegan may eat on a daily basis. Of course, this meal plan can be modified.

ONE WEEK VEGAN MENU

	BREAKFAST	LUNCH	DINNER	SNACK

MONDAY	banana pancakes
	orange juice
	calcium fortified soy milk
		bean tacos
		  with lettuce
		  and tomato
		applesauce
		  with cinnamon
			lentil/tomato loaf
			wheat rolls
			broccoli and
			  cauliflower
			pineapple
				soy ice cream

TUESDAY	peanut butter
	raisin bagels
	strawberries
		bean spread
		whole grain bread
		mushroom soup
		tangerine
			tofu burgers
			  on whole grain buns
			sweet potatoes
			green beans with
			  almonds
			pear slices
				air-popped
				  popcorn
				grape juice

WEDNESDAY	oatmeal with dried fruit
	wheat toast
	cantaloupe
		carrot cream soup
		peanut butter crackers
		banana
			layered vegetable and
			  bean casserole
			brown rice
			tomato and lettuce
			peach halves
				nuts/seeds/raisins
				  mixture

THURSDAY	eggless French toast
	orange juice
	calcium fortified soy milk
		tofu/spinach spread
		wheat bread or
		  crackers
		potato salad
		apple
			rice stuffed peppers
			steamed kale
			corn
			fruit salad
				crackers with
				  peanut butter

FRIDAY	scrambled tofu
	vegan biscuits
	orange and grapefruit
	  sections
		vegan chili
		corn muffins
		cole slaw with
		  crushed pineapple
			carrot cutlets
			mashed potatoes
			green and yellow beans
			blueberries or other fruit
				soy milk shake

SATURDAY	grits
	wheat toast
	grapefruit juice
		chickpea spread
		rye bread
		raw vegetables
		chocolate chip
		  cookies
			vegetable/nut loaf
			steamed greens
			baked sweet potato
			baked apple
				air-popped
				  popcorn

SUNDAY	potato pancakes apple sauce calcium fortified soy milk	pasta salad pita bread vegetable juice	baked beans Spanish rice carrots pear	nuts/seeds/raisins mixture

30 DAY MENU
FOR THOSE WHO DON'T LIKE TO COOK

By Charles Stahler

It is easy to have a different vegetarian meal every day of the month with little or no cooking.

1. Potlucks -- Many local vegetarian groups sponsor potluck dinners in homes or at parks. You can bring juice and have a wonderful meal full of variety. There is always plenty for those who don't use animal products.

2. Organize your own potluck at you house one day a month -- Let your friends know about the potlucks and put a note in a local vegetarian group's newsletter or your community newsletter. You can supply juice, the plates, etc. Let others bring delicious dishes. There are members of other environmental and animal groups who you could invite to the potluck.

3. Purchase *Vegetarian Journal's Guide to Natural Foods Restaurants in the U.S. and Canada* -- This way when you travel you will always be able to find places offering vegetarian meals. Send $14 to VRG, PO Box 1463, Baltimore, MD 21203.

4. Purchase *Meatless Meals for Working People* from The Vegetarian Resource Group -- You can find out which foods are vegetarian in fast food chains. Send $6 to VRG, PO Box 1463, Baltimore, MD 21203.

5. Purchase a vegetable pot pie from a natural foods store or supermarket.

6. Attend vegetarian and animal rights activities, and get invited to a friend's home for a vegetarian dinner.

7. Lightlife's Smart Dogs or other veggie "hot dogs" and vegetarian baked beans -- Warm up these items that are readily available in health food stores and many mainstream supermarkets.

8. Legume brand stuffed tofu manicotti -- a quick frozen TV dinner without cheese, available in your local health food store. (Other types of entrees also available.) Add a tossed salad and Italian bread and you've got yourself a terrific meal.

9. Supermarket salad bar -- A good source of a meal. If you had this once or twice a month, you wouldn't get bored with it. Try to choose lowfat dressings.

10. Gourmet takeout -- For one or more days, gourmet markets make a great takeout. Today there are more choices than you could imagine for a complete vegetarian meal.

11. Ethiopian food -- Relatively inexpensive and luckily there are usually several Ethiopian restaurants in urban areas. Eat there or takeout delicious vegetarian stews (consisting of legumes and vegetables) with Injera (Ethiopian bread).

12. Vegetable lo mein and steamed mixed vegetables from a local Chinese restaurant -- Request brown rice instead of white rice.

13. Spicy eggplant with vegetables or other such dish from a Szechuan-style Chinese restaurant -- Choose different items from the menu for variety.

14. Moo Shu Vegetable -- A great vegetarian version of Moo Shoo Pork found in Chinese restaurants.

15. Middle Eastern food -- Order hummus, falafel, baba ghanuj, tabbouli, and much more. Good variety and may contain high-calcium tahini. You almost never see dairy in Chinese or Middle Eastern restaurants since they generally obtain their calcium from vegetable sources.

16. A quick meal -- Open a can of chickpeas, mash them lightly, and prepare it like you would tuna salad. Put on bread, and you're ready to eat. If you don't like the salt, you can rinse the chickpeas. Try eggless mayonnaise from a natural foods store.

17. Indonesian Restaurants -- They sometimes offer vegetarian tempeh dishes.

18. Thai Food -- It's sort of like Chinese cuisine, but slightly different. You can get spicy food if you wish. Thai restaurants will usually substitute tofu for meat. Specify that you do not want oyster sauce and that they can substitute garlic sauce. The curry dishes are especially delicious.

19. Vegetable chow fon in Chinese restaurants -- A wide noodle made out of rice flour. This is almost always on the menu in New York, and several other cities. You may have to ask for it. Sometimes the staff eats it in an authentic Chinese vegetarian restaurant.

20. Indian food -- Many, many vegetarian dishes are found in Indian restaurants. If you don't like spicy food, ask them to make it mild. Usually served with rice. I like masala dosa, which is an eggless crepe made out of lentil flour wrapped around potatoes.

21. Appalachian Trail Stew -- I ate this mostly while hiking on the Appalachian Trail. It's easy to prepare: put all into one pot and boil until done -- lentils, a little macaroni, barley, and maybe a cut-up potato. For flavoring you can add garlic powder or tomato sauce for a different dish. For a little more variety, add some cut up broccoli or frozen vegetables.

22. Vegetable mixture -- Frozen corn, peas, Brussels sprouts, and whatever veggies you like. Add to cooked pasta or serve over rice. This is a quick meal.

23. Purchase quick vegetarian cup of soups in a supermarket or natural foods store -- Serve with a whole-grain bread and perhaps a salad.

24. Mexican food -- Try a veggie taco, burrito, tostada, etc. You can get take out or frozen or packaged. Most Mexican restaurants and fast food chains no longer put lard in their beans, but you should always ask to make sure.

25. From your frozen food case -- Purchase potato pancakes, potato blintzes or pierogis, and frozen vegetables.

26. Vegetable burgers -- Archer Daniels Midland, one of the largest food companies in the world, is now making a veggie burger that is called the Harvest Burger and is packaged under the Pillsbury Green Giant label. There are plenty of other packaged varieties in natural foods store.

27. Tempeh -- Get some from a health foods store. Fry in non-stick pan. Make a sandwich with tempeh, bread, and any veggies you like. There are also tempeh burgers.

28. Gluten or seitan -- This is made from wheat and has the texture of meat. You can buy it from a health food store or in a can from an Oriental grocery store (less expensive.) Cook it with a starch and some green veggies. For example, macaroni, seitan, and peas and corn. The gluten or seitan is already cooked, so it is a matter of adding it in with the other ingredients and heating it up.

29. Take-out pizza without the cheese -- Try a variety of veggies on top.

30. Vegetarian chili -- Prepare your own quickly from cans or get take out. You don't need to cook beans from scratch.

Charles Stahler is Co-Director of The Vegetarian Resource Group and leads a very busy life.

Luscious Vegetarian Pasta Sauces

By Jacqueline Dunnington

Pasta without sauce would be dismal fare. The vegetarian can enjoy a wide variety of traditional or adventuresome sauces that incorporate the flavors of worldwide cuisines. Bon Appetit!

TRADITIONAL ITALIAN TOMATO SAUCE
(Salsa di Pomodoro)
(Makes 4 cups)

Many versions of this recipe exist, but this is a basic one.

1 Tablespoon olive oil
1 cup white onions, finely chopped
1 clove crushed garlic
1/2 cup shredded carrots
2 pounds fresh, peeled, chopped tomatoes or 4 cups low-sodium canned crushed tomatoes
2 Tablespoons crushed dried basil leaves or 1/4 cup snipped fresh basil leaves
1 teaspoon salt or salt substitute
1 teaspoon freshly ground black pepper

In a deep pot, sauté onions in oil until transparent. Add garlic, carrots, tomatoes, and all seasonings. Cover. Simmer for an hour or until sauce is quite thick. Stir often.

TOTAL CALORIES PER 1 CUP SERVING: 106
TOTAL FAT AS % OF DAILY VALUE: 6%   FAT: 4 gm
PROTEIN: 3 gm   CARBOHYDRATES: 17 gm
CALCIUM: 77 mg   IRON: 2 mg   SODIUM: 600 mg
DIETARY FIBER: 4 gm

CURRIED EGGPLANT SAUCE
(Makes 3-1/2 cups)

An exotic yet simple sauce adapted from a recipe discovered in New Delhi. The eggplant liquefies to form a healthy vegetable "cream."

1 Tablespoon vegetable oil
1 cup chopped white onions
3 cups peeled eggplant, cut into 1/2-inch cubes
3 cups fresh tomato wedges, diced
1/2 cup green onions, finely chopped
1/2 cup seedless raisins
3/4 cup water
1 teaspoon salt or salt substitute
1 teaspoon cayenne pepper
2 Tablespoons curry powder

Heat oil in deep pot, add onions and sauté until soft. Stir often. Add tomatoes, eggplant, green onions, and raisins. Mix well. Stir in broth (or water) into which the spices have been blended. Cover and simmer about 8 to 10 minutes. Remove pot from stove and let stand another 5 minutes.

TOTAL CALORIES PER 1 CUP SERVING: 184
TOTAL FAT AS % OF DAILY VALUE: 9%   FAT: 5 gm
PROTEIN: 4 gm   CARBOHYDRATES: 36 gm
CALCIUM: 59 mg   IRON: 3 mg   SODIUM: 679 mg
DIETARY FIBER: 5 gm

CAJUN-STYLE GUMBO SAUCE
(Makes 4 cups)

A virtually fat-free sauce based on New Orleans cuisine.

3/4 cup vegetable broth
1/2 cup chopped onion
1 large tomato, peeled and chopped
2 Tablespoons fresh parsley, finely
    chopped
1/2 teaspoon salt or salt substitute
1 teaspoon cayenne pepper
1 herb bag with sprig of thyme, basil
    and a bay leaf (optional)
1 cup diced red bell pepper
1 cup sliced fresh or frozen okra
1 cup fresh or canned corn kernels

Bring broth to a boil in deep pot. Add onions and peppers and all seasonings. Cover. Simmer for an hour. Add okra (If fresh okra is used, blanch first and slice into very thin rounds.), corn, and the tomato. Stir well, cook for 10 minutes covered. Add a bit more broth to desired consistency. Remove herb bag. Great with pasta shells.

TOTAL CALORIES PER 1 CUP SERVING: 80
TOTAL FAT AS % OF DAILY VALUE: 2%   FAT: 1 gm
PROTEIN: 3 gm   CARBOHYDRATES: 10 gm
CALCIUM: 40 mg   IRON: 1 mg   SODIUM: 337 mg
DIETARY FIBER: 2 gm

GREEN CHILI PESTO SAUCE
(Serves 8)

A zesty recipe in which the Mediterranean meets the Rio Grande.

4 garlic cloves
1 cup fresh basil leaves, snipped very
    fine
1/2 cup pine nuts or walnut pieces
3 peeled, seeded, roasted green chiles
    (about 2/3 cup of canned chiles)
1 teaspoon salt or salt substitute
Cayenne to taste
1/4 cup olive oil

In a mortar or food processor, grind all ingredients but oil. Reduce to a paste. Then add oil very gradually, mixing into paste with a spatula. Stir vigorously into 1 pound of cooked, drained, piping-hot pasta.

TOTAL CALORIES PER 1 CUP SERVING (WITHOUT PASTA): 113
TOTAL FAT AS % OF DAILY VALUE: 17%   FAT: 11 gm
PROTEIN: 2 gm   CARBOHYDRATES: 2 gm
CALCIUM: 18 mg   IRON: <1 mg   SODIUM: 420 mg
DIETARY FIBER: 1 gm

GRAPE AND RED PEPPER SAUCE
(Makes 3 cups)

An unusual sauce invented from summer's bounty.

1 Tablespoon olive oil
3 Tablespoons water
3 large red peppers, cut in 1/4-inch
    strips
3 red onions, cut in 1/4-inch slices
1 cup seedless grapes (red or green),
    cut in halves
2 large cloves of garlic, crushed
1/2 teaspoon salt or salt substitute
1/4 cup fresh basil leaves, snipped
    very fine (or 2 Tablespoons dried
    leaves)
Freshly ground pepper to taste

Heat oil and water in deep pot. Add peppers and onions. Cook until soft, stir often.
    Add grapes and all seasonings. Mix well. Cover pot, reduce heat, and simmer for 20 minutes. Add a few drops of water if needed.

TOTAL CALORIES PER 1 CUP SERVING: 126
TOTAL FAT AS % OF DAILY VALUE: 9%   FAT: 5 gm
PROTEIN: 2 gm   CARBOHYDRATES: 21 gm
CALCIUM: 48 mg   IRON: 1 mg   SODIUM: 388 mg
DIETARY FIBER: 4 gm

SICILIAN SWEET-SOUR SAUCE
(Salsa Agrodolce)
(Makes 3 cups)

A zesty, out-of-the-ordinary sauce from Italy.

1 Tablespoon olive oil
3 Tablespoons water
1 cup chopped white or yellow
   onions
1 cup chopped green bell peppers
2 cups fresh tomato wedges or 1-1/2
   cups canned crushed tomatoes
1/2 cup parsley, finely chopped
2 Tablespoons liquid sweetener
1/2 teaspoon salt or salt substitute
1 teaspoon freshly ground black
   pepper
1 teaspoon powdered cinnamon
1 teaspoon crushed basil leaves
3 Tablespoons apple cider vinegar

Heat oil and water in deep pot. Add onions
and peppers. Cook until soft, stir often. Add
tomatoes, parsley, and other seasonings. Mix
well and cover pot. Simmer on low heat for
at least 20 minutes. Stir often to keep mixture cooking evenly.

TOTAL CALORIES PER 1 CUP SERVING: 147
TOTAL FAT AS % OF DAILY VALUE: 9%   FAT: 5 gm
PROTEIN: 3 gm   CARBOHYDRATES: 26 gm
CALCIUM: 58 mg   IRON: 2 mg   SODIUM: 405 mg
DIETARY FIBER: 4 gm

MULTICOLOR SAUCE
(Makes 3-1/2 cups)

*Colors from a Picasso painting inspired this
sauce's name.*

1 Tablespoon olive oil
3 Tablespoons water
1 cup red bell peppers, chopped
1 cup green bell peppers, chopped
1/2 cup white onions, chopped
1/2 cup raw carrots, shredded
1 cup yellow squash, finely diced
1/2 teaspoon salt or salt substitute
1 teaspoon freshly ground pepper
1 teaspoon crushed dried oregano
   parsley sprigs for garnish
2 or 3 Tablespoons cooked black
   beans for garnish (optional)

Heat oil in deep pot. Add peppers and
onions, cook until soft. Drain off excess oil.
Add other vegetables, cover pot, reduce heat,
and add seasonings. Stew over low heat for
about a half hour. Pour over pasta and
garnish with parsley and black beans.

TOTAL CALORIES PER 1 CUP SERVING: 90
TOTAL FAT AS % OF DAILY VALUE: 6%   FAT: 4 gm
PROTEIN: 2 gm   CARBOHYDRATES: 11 gm
CALCIUM: 28 mg   IRON: 1 mg   SODIUM: 337 mg
DIETARY FIBER: 2 gm

*Jacqueline Dunnington is a freelance writer
from Santa Fe, New Mexico.*

PASTA PERFECT

By Nanette Blanchard

According to the National Pasta Association, Americans eat approximately 19 pounds of pasta per capita every year. While that isn't as much as Italians eat, pasta really is becoming an American food. We've come a long way from eating overcooked spaghetti drowning in tomato sauce. Now Americans eat pasta in salads and soups and even for dessert. Many people even know the difference between fettuccine and linguine, and more home cooks are now making their own homemade pasta with the use of a pasta machine.

The types of dried pasta available are increasing rapidly.

October is National Pasta Month and the types of dried pasta available are increasing rapidly. Frozen tofu ravioli, amaranth spaghetti, whole wheat couscous, and Jerusalem artichoke noodles are just some of the more unusual types currently available. Pasta may be colored with beets or spinach and flavored with garlic or chili powder.

Food historians are still debating who invented pasta -- the Romans or the Chinese. It is even possible they both invented it simultaneously. Most pasta experts generally agree that the legend about Marco Polo introducing pasta into what is now Italy is a myth.

There are at least 300 different types of pasta: long, short, thick, thin, and pasta shaped like tubes, bows, shells, wheels, and even butterflies. Pasta is served in almost every country in the world in some form.

The proper way to cook pasta is to bring a large stock pot of water to a rolling boil. It isn't necessary to add either salt or oil to the pasta cooking water. Stirring the pasta immediately after it is added to the boiling water is the best way to keep pasta from sticking. Cover the pot until the water returns to a boil and then remove the lid. Test pasta along the way to see if it is tender. Drain pasta as soon as it has cooked enough and toss with the sauce. Be sure to check the package instructions before cooking a new shape or type of pasta.

PASTA WITH ROASTED VEGETABLES AND BALSAMIC VINEGAR
(Serves 4)

Roasting vegetables is easy and delicious. The balsamic vinegar added to the roasting vegetables cooks down into a rich sauce.

1 bunch scallions, cut into 1-inch
   lengths
1 bell pepper, coarsely chopped
1 zucchini, coarsely chopped
4 tomatoes, chopped
3 cloves garlic, chopped
3 Tablespoons balsamic vinegar
1 Tablespoon olive oil
1/2 pound bow-tie or wheel pasta

Combine chopped scallions, bell pepper, zucchini, tomatoes, garlic, balsamic vinegar, and olive oil in a shallow baking dish. Bake at 400 degrees for about 30 minutes, stirring once, or until vegetables are soft. Meanwhile, cook pasta in boiling water according to package directions. Drain hot cooked pasta and toss with vegetables. Serve in a warmed bowl or dish.

TOTAL CALORIES PER SERVING: 296
TOTAL FAT AS % OF DAILY VALUE: 8%   FAT: 5 gm
PROTEIN: 9gm   CARBOHYDRATES: 55 gm
CALCIUM: 37 mg   IRON: 4 mg   SODIUM: 20 mg
DIETARY FIBER: 3 gm

TEX-MEX CORN MACARONI
(Serves 6)

Corn pastas are really wonderful with southwestern foods. They are a little trickier to cook properly; so be certain to follow the instructions.

1 pound corn macaroni (found in
    natural food stores)
2 Tablespoons vegetable oil
1 onion, chopped
3 cloves garlic, minced
1/2 cup peeled, chopped green chile
    peppers (frozen or canned)
2 green peppers, chopped
1 Tablespoon chili powder
1 teaspoon dried oregano
2 cups chopped fresh tomatoes
1 cup corn kernels, fresh or frozen

Cook pasta in boiling water according to package directions. Sauté onion and garlic in oil over medium-high heat in large skillet about 5 minutes, or until tender. Add both types of peppers and cook an additional 3 minutes, stirring. Add chili powder, oregano, tomatoes, and corn and cook another 5 minutes, stirring occasionally. Drain pasta and add to vegetables in large pan. Cook over low heat until warm.

TOTAL CALORIES PER SERVING: 339
TOTAL FAT AS % OF DAILY VALUE: 11%   FAT: 7 gm
PROTEIN: 7 gm   CARBOHYDRATES: 61 gm
CALCIUM: 19 mg   IRON: 1 mg   SODIUM: 156 mg
DIETARY FIBER: 5 gm

BAKED SPINACH-PASTA CASSEROLE
(Serves 8)

This dish makes terrific leftovers and can be assembled several hours in advance. Frozen chopped spinach can also be used to save time; just thaw and add when the fresh spinach is added to the recipe.

1 pound pasta shells
1 pound spinach, chopped and
    steamed until tender
2-1/2 cups low-sodium tomato sauce
1/2 cup soy milk
3 cloves garlic, minced
1 Tablespoon fresh chopped basil (or
    1 teaspoon dried)
Salt and freshly ground black pepper
    to taste
1/4 cup bread crumbs

Cook pasta in boiling water according to package directions. Drain. In large casserole dish, toss hot pasta with spinach, tomato sauce, soy milk, garlic, and basil. Season to taste. Top with bread crumbs. Bake at 350 degrees, uncovered, for 30 minutes or until bubbly. Serve hot.

TOTAL CALORIES PER SERVING: 276
TOTAL FAT AS % OF DAILY VALUE: 2%   FAT: 1 gm
PROTEIN: 11 gm   CARBOHYDRATES: 55 gm
CALCIUM: 91 mg   IRON: 5 mg   SODIUM: 112 mg
DIETARY FIBER: 3 gm

COLD PEANUT NOODLES
(Serves 6)

This simple dish should be made in advance and is quite welcome at a buffet or dinner party. Add steamed snow peas or broccoli for a heartier dish.

1 pound whole wheat spaghetti
2 Tablespoons sesame oil

2 cloves garlic, crushed
1 Tablespoon ginger root, minced
3 Tablespoons peanut butter
2 Tablespoons soy sauce
2 Tablespoons rice vinegar
1 Tablespoon lemon juice
5 scallions, chopped
1 cup sliced radishes
1 cucumber, sliced

Cook spaghetti in boiling water according to package directions. Drain. Whisk together sesame oil, garlic, ginger root, peanut butter, soy sauce, vinegar, and lemon juice. Mix dressing with hot cooked pasta. Add scallions, radishes, and cucumber and mix together gently. Chill in the refrigerator for several hours, covered, before serving.

TOTAL CALORIES PER SERVING: 337
TOTAL FAT AS % OF DAILY VALUE: 15%   FAT: 10 gm
PROTEIN: 13 gm   CARBOHYDRATES: 55 gm
CALCIUM: 48 mg   IRON: 3 mg   SODIUM: 385 mg
DIETARY FIBER: 7 gm

QUICK TOMATO-NOODLE SOUP
(Serves 6)

A nice main dish soup when you're too busy to spend time in the kitchen.

1 onion, chopped
1 green pepper, chopped
3 cloves of garlic, minced
2 ribs of celery, chopped
2 Tablespoons vegetable oil
46-ounce can low-sodium tomato juice
Salt and black pepper to taste
2 cups small pasta (orzo or acini di pepe)

Sauté onion, green pepper, garlic, and celery in oil in large stock pot over medium heat for 10 minutes or until soft. Add tomato juice and season to taste. Add pasta and simmer over low heat 20 minutes or until pasta is tender.

TOTAL CALORIES PER SERVING: 281
TOTAL FAT AS % OF DAILY VALUE: 9%   FAT: 6 gm
PROTEIN: 9 gm   CARBOHYDRATES: 51 gm
CALCIUM: 43 mg   IRON: 3 mg   SODIUM: 40 mg
DIETARY FIBER: 4 gm

EASY BEAN THREAD SOUP
(Serves 4)

Bean threads are noodles made out of mung beans. They cook quickly and become transparent when tender. Look for them in the Oriental section of your grocery store.

1 Tablespoon minced ginger root
2 carrots, halved and thinly sliced
1 Tablespoon vegetable oil
4 scallions, sliced
4 cups vegetable broth
2 ounces bean threads (about a handful or one bunch)
1 cup fresh or frozen peas or corn kernels
1 Tablespoon soy sauce

Sauté ginger and carrots in oil for 5 minutes over medium heat or until soft. Add scallions and broth, stirring, bring to a boil. Break up bean threads slightly while adding them to the boiling broth. Cover and cook until bean threads are tender, about 10 minutes. Add peas or corn and cook another 3 minutes. Stir in soy sauce and serve hot.

TOTAL CALORIES PER SERVING: 150
TOTAL FAT AS % OF DAILY VALUE: 8%   FAT: 5 gm
PROTEIN: 3 gm   CARBOHYDRATES: 35 gm
CALCIUM: 26 mg   IRON: 1 mg   SODIUM: 482 mg
DIETARY FIBER: 2 gm

Nanette Blanchard is a freelance food writer from Durango, Colorado.

POTATO POWER

By Jacqueline Dunnington

The potato made its worldwide debut after the Spaniards discovered the plant in Peru in the 1530's. The ancient Peruvian natives, the Incas, named the 5,000 or so varieties of the plant, the "papa." Conquistadores brought the "papa" back to Europe where it became a gourmet treat long before becoming a staple foodstuff.

The humble potato has a long and unusual history. Scholars have followed its global travels, scientists have probed its properties, and gourmets have savored its tasty charms. The spud has even perched on a royal head; Queen Marie Antoinette of France wove potato plant blossoms into her hair during an era when Continental cooks were busy creating recipes featuring the native-American spud.

The potato made its worldwide debut after the Spaniards discovered the plant in Peru in the 1530's. Columbus also encountered the tuber a few decades earlier. The ancient Peruvian natives, the Incas, named the 5,000 or so varieties of the plant -- the "*papa*." Conquistadores brought the "*papa*" back to Europe where it became a gourmet treat long before becoming a staple foodstuff. One of the ironies of history is that the global potato crop is worth about a billion dollars today, which makes it worth many times the price of gold and silver taken from the Americas. Europeans brought the spud to the United States.

Botanically, potatoes are of the *Solanum tuberosum* family that includes such plants as the tomato, eggplant, pepper, and petunia. The sweet potato and its cousins are of the *Ipomoea batatas* family that includes the morning glory.

The potato, an energy-packed complex carbohydrate, is an excellent source of dietary fiber, vitamin C, potassium, and other minerals. Not only is the friendly tuber easy on the budget, it is a versatile and edible gem fit to be set on any table. Enjoy the following potato recipes!

POTATO-VEGETABLE CHOWDER
(Serves 8)

A thick soup that welcomes the substitutions of a creative cook. Produce a chowder as thick or thin as desired by adjusting the liquid.

2-1/2 cups vegetable broth
2-1/2 cups water
1 cup low-sodium tomato or vegetable juice
1 cup peeled tomatoes, chopped
1 cup carrots, chopped
1 cup green beans or yellow wax beans
1 cup onions, finely chopped
1 cup zucchini or yellow squash, thinly sliced
1 cup leek, chopped
2 cups unpeeled red potatoes, diced
1 cheesecloth bag of fresh herbs of choice (parsley, basil, etc.)

Bring liquid to boil in a deep soup kettle. Add all vegetables and seasonings. Turn down heat to simmer and partially cover the pot. Simmer until vegetables are tender. Serve hot with crusty whole wheat bread and a light fruit dessert.

Variation: Almost any vegetable but onions, tomatoes, and the potatoes can be substituted for another vegetable. Don't use the cabbage family because the flavor is too radically changed. Green peas and baby lima beans are a great addition, as are corn kernels (about half a cup).

TOTAL CALORIES PER SERVING: 97
TOTAL FAT AS % OF DAILY VALUE: 2%   FAT: 1 gm
PROTEIN: 3 gm   CARBOHYDRATES: 22 gm
CALCIUM: 40 mg   IRON: 1 mg   SODIUM: 89 mg
DIETARY FIBER: 3 gm

POTATO-STUFFED GREEN PEPPERS
(Serves 4)

This dish is great with corn on the cob.

4 large green bell peppers
1/2 cup onions, finely chopped
1/2 cup red peppers, finely chopped
2 teaspoons olive oil
Salt and pepper to taste
1 Tablespoon dried crumbled chives
2 cups mashed potatoes
2 cups low-sodium tomato sauce

Preheat oven to 350 degrees. Slice away pepper tops below stems. Remove seeds and interior spines. Gently parboil peppers about 5 minutes. Drain upside down. Set peppers aside.

Sauté onions and red pepper in oil until soft. Add seasonings to mashed potatoes. Carefully stuff peppers, set them in a deep-sided baking dish. Pour tomato sauce around base of peppers. Bake at 350 degrees for

about 20 minutes, covered. Uncover, and bake 5 minutes longer. Serve warm.

TOTAL CALORIES PER SERVING: 164
TOTAL FAT AS % OF DAILY VALUE: 5%   FAT: 3 gm
PROTEIN: 4 gm   CARBOHYDRATES: 34 gm
CALCIUM: 38 mg   IRON: 2 mg   SODIUM: 39 mg
DIETARY FIBER: 5 gm

POTATO AND LEEK CASSEROLE
(Serves 4)

Serve with a tossed green salad.

3 cups well-scrubbed leeks, cut into
    1/2-inch pieces
1/2 cup carrots, shredded
2 Tablespoons olive oil
Salt and pepper to taste
1 teaspoon powdered dry rosemary
1 cup vegetable broth
2 pounds unpeeled red potatoes,
    sliced in thin rounds
1/4 cup parsley or chives (or mixed),
    finely chopped

Preheat oven to 375 degrees. In deep skillet, coat leeks and carrots with olive oil. Cover and simmer over low heat until soft. Add seasonings. Mix well. Layer a well-oiled 2-1/2- to 3-quart casserole (with cover) with 1/3 of the potatoes, then 1/2 the seasoned vegetables. Repeat and finish with last 1/3 of potatoes. Pour broth evenly into casserole. Cover and bake for 50 minutes covered at 375 degrees. Uncover and bake for another 10 minutes. Garnish with parsley and chives.

Carrots can be substituted with zucchini. Half of leek can be chopped yellow onions.

TOTAL CALORIES PER SERVING: 312
TOTAL FAT AS % OF DAILY VALUE: 12%   FAT: 8 gm
PROTEIN: 7 gm   CARBOHYDRATES: 57 gm
CALCIUM: 109 mg   IRON: 6 mg   SODIUM: 101 mg
DIETARY FIBER: 6 gm

POTATO SALAD SUPREME
(Serves 6)

Serve this salad with guacamole and crackers.

4 cups potatoes, chopped in cubes
1 cup broccoli flowerets, steamed
   and cooled
1 cup peeled tomato wedges
1 cup celery, finely chopped
1/2 cup green onions, chopped
1 cup vegan fat-free salad dressing
Seasonings to taste
1/2 cup pitted ripe olives, sliced

Mix all ingredients in a large bowl, saving olives for garnish. Serve at room temperature for best flavor.

TOTAL CALORIES PER SERVING: 188
TOTAL FAT AS % OF DAILY VALUE: 2%   FAT: 1 gm
PROTEIN: 5 gm   CARBOHYDRATES: 39 gm
CALCIUM: 45 mg   IRON: 3 mg   SODIUM: 388 mg
DIETARY FIBER: 4 gm

POTATO APPETIZERS
(Serves 10)

Delightful, easy-to-serve appetizers.

1 pound potatoes
2 Tablespoons olive oil
Salt and pepper to taste
1/2 cup chives or green onions,
   finely chopped
1/2 teaspoon paprika
1/2 cup wheat germ

Peel and chop potatoes. Place potatoes in a pot and cover with water. Boil until soft.

   Mash cooked potatoes with oil, then add seasonings. Meanwhile, heat oven to 375 degrees. Shape mixture into 1-inch balls.

Mix the paprika and wheat germ together in a dish. Roll potato balls in paprika and wheat germ mixture until coated. Place on oiled baking sheet. Bake at 375 degrees for about 20 minutes. Let stand on folded paper towels before serving with toothpicks.

TOTAL CALORIES PER SERVING: 79
TOTAL FAT AS % OF DAILY VALUE: 5%   FAT: 3 gm
PROTEIN: 3 gm   CARBOHYDRATES: 10 gm
CALCIUM: 10 mg   IRON: 1 mg   SODIUM: 3 mg
DIETARY FIBER: 1 gm

POTATO AND RED ONION ROAST
(Serves 4)

A delight from the oven. Serve with a green bean salad and whole wheat bread sticks.

4 pounds small red potatoes, halved
   but unskinned
2 large red onions cut into 1/2-inch
   pieces
2 Tablespoons olive oil
1 Tablespoon crushed dried parsley
1 Tablespoon crushed dried rosemary
Salt and pepper to taste

Preheat oven to 400 degrees. Coat uncooked potato halves and onions with oil and seasonings. Spread in a deep-sided roasting pan and roast for about 40 minutes. Turn the onion/potato mixture several times while roasting until all pieces are light brown.

TOTAL CALORIES PER SERVING: 421
TOTAL FAT AS % OF DAILY VALUE: 11%   FAT: 7 gm
PROTEIN: 11 gm   CARBOHYDRATES: 81 gm
CALCIUM: 85 mg   IRON: 7 mg   SODIUM: 35 mg
DIETARY FIBER: 8 gm

Jacqueline Dunnington is a freelance writer from Santa Fe, New Mexico.

RICE: THE GLOBAL GRAIN

By Jacqueline Dunnington

Rice is a cereal from the grass plant *Oryza sativa*; it is an annual crop raised in warm climates worldwide. The plant was originally native to the deltas of Asian rivers such as the Euphrates, the Ganges, the Mekong, and the Yangtse. The Chinese started to cultivate the plant at least 4,000 years ago, and their word for rice is the same as their word for agriculture. Rice cultivation migrated west to India before coming to the United States in the mid-17th century. At least half the world's population subsists on rice as a primary complex carbohydrate; there are over 40,000 known varieties.

Rice is inexpensive, adaptable to a variety of cuisine, and highly nutritious. It is an ideal staple food for the vegetarian.

The following recipes, along with basic cooking methods, feature brown rice: long-grain, short-grain, or brown Basmati. If commercially-prepared rice mixes are used, follow directions on package.

<u>Conventional preparation:</u> Bring 2-1/2 cups of water for every one cup of brown rice to full boil in a pot. Add salt or salt substitute if desired and stir in brown rice. Return mixture to a boil and immediately turn to lowest heat, cover tightly, and cook 45-50 minutes or until all water is absorbed. (High altitudes demand more time.) Stir grains with a fork.

<u>Open-pot method:</u> Bring at least 3 cups of water to every cup of brown rice to a full boil. Add salt or substitute if desired. Stir in rice and cook to desired tenderness, normally short of an hour. (High altitudes demand more time.) Drain and stir grains with fork.

<u>Microwave:</u> In a microwave-suitable container, combine 2 cups water with each cup of brown rice. Add salt or salt substitute if desired. Cover well, cook on HIGH for 5-6 minutes, reduce oven setting by half and cook about 30 minutes longer. Cooking time will vary depending on oven's power. (Altitude affects microwave cooking very slightly.) Uncover carefully, let steam escape, then stir grains with a fork.

Soaking is not necessary for any of the above cooking methods. One cup of uncooked brown rice yields 3 cups of cooked rice, regardless of the cooking method used.

MEXICAN RICE CASSEROLE
(Serves 4)

Enjoy this hearty dish!

1 cup yellow onions, chopped
2 teaspoons olive oil
1 cup raw brown rice
2-1/4 cups water or vegetable broth
1/2 cup whole kernel corn
1/2 cup green pepper, finely chopped
1 small tomato, cut into very thin wedges
1 small yellow squash, cut into very thin slices
Salt and pepper to taste
1 to 2 Tablespoons chili powder
2 Tablespoons fresh cilantro, finely chopped

In a deep, large pot with tight-fitting lid, sauté onions in oil until soft. Add rice and water or broth. Cover pot, reduce heat, simmer slowly. After 35-40 minutes, add corn, green pepper, tomato, squash, and all seasonings. If mixture seems dry, add more liquid.

TOTAL CALORIES PER SERVING: 246
TOTAL FAT AS % OF DAILY VALUE: 6%   FAT: 4 gm
PROTEIN: 6 gm   CARBOHYDRATES: 44 gm
CALCIUM: 35 mg   IRON: 2 mg   SODIUM: 27 mg
DIETARY FIBER: 2 gm

RISI E BISI
(Serves 5)

An Italian classic. Serve with grilled tomatoes for a perfect side dish.

1 cup yellow onions, chopped
2 teaspoons olive oil
2-1/2 cups strong vegetable broth
1 cup raw brown rice
Salt to taste
2 cups freshly shelled green peas
1/4 cup fresh parsley, finely chopped

In a large, deep pot, sauté onions in oil. Add broth, rice, and salt. Bring to boil, reduce heat to simmer, cover pot. Cook 35 minutes then add peas and more broth if needed. Cover and cook to desired firmness, about another 15 minutes. This delicate dish needs a light touch and occasional stirring. Garnish with parsley before serving.

TOTAL CALORIES PER SERVING: 223
TOTAL FAT AS % OF DAILY VALUE: 6%   FAT: 4 gm
PROTEIN: 6 gm   CARBOHYDRATES: 42 gm
CALCIUM: 38 mg   IRON: 2 mg   SODIUM: 115 mg
DIETARY FIBER: 3 gm

RICE AND TWO BEAN SALAD
(Serves 5)

A tasty combination of several food items. Serve with corn muffins.

2 cups pre-cooked brown rice
1 cup pre-cooked kidney beans
1 cup pre-cooked green or yellow
   string beans
1 medium peeled tomato, diced
1/4 cup finely chopped chives
1 Tablespoon prepared mustard
Pepper to taste
3/4 cup vegan fat-free salad dressing
2-3 cups shredded salad greens

Place rice, beans, tomato, and chives in large salad bowl. (All vegetables should be at room temperature.) Mix mustard and pepper into the dressing. Pour over the vegetable medley, mix well, and serve on beds of shredded salad greens.

TOTAL CALORIES PER SERVING: 188
TOTAL FAT AS % OF DAILY VALUE: 2%   FAT: 1 gm
PROTEIN: 6 gm   CARBOHYDRATES: 37 gm
CALCIUM: 40 mg   IRON: 2 mg   SODIUM: 333 mg
DIETARY FIBER: 4 gm

QUICK CANTONESE RICE AND SNOW PEAS
(Serves 4)

A touch of the Orient. Delicious when served with crispy rice cakes.

1 large garlic clove, minced
1 Tablespoon oil
17-ounce box frozen snow peas

1 cup sweet (red) onion, finely
  chopped
1 teaspoon freshly ground pepper
1 teaspoon ground ginger
2 cups slightly undercooked brown
  rice
Soy sauce to taste

In skillet or wok, heat oil with garlic. Add
peas and onions, stirring constantly for 4-5
minutes and being careful not to burn ingredients. Stir in seasonings, fold in rice, and heat
thoroughly. Add soy sauce.

TOTAL CALORIES PER SERVING: 219
TOTAL FAT AS % OF DAILY VALUE: 8%   FAT: 5 gm
PROTEIN: 7 gm   CARBOHYDRATES: 38 gm
CALCIUM: 92 mg   IRON: 4 mg   SODIUM: 8 mg
DIETARY FIBER: 6 gm

LEEK, CARROT,
AND RICE SOUP

(Serves 5)

*This is adapted from a recipe my Swiss grand-
mother created. No fat is used to prepare the
soup. Serve with toasted slices of whole grain
bread.*

2 leeks
1/2 cup thinly sliced onion
3 cups vegetable broth
1 cup shredded carrots
Salt and pepper to taste
2 cups pre-cooked brown rice
1 cup vanilla soy or rice frozen lowfat
  dessert
1/4 cup finely chopped chives

Trim and scrub leeks, cut into tiny slivers.
Steam leeks and onions until soft and transfer

to soup pot. Add broth and carrots. Season
and simmer about 35 minutes. Stir in rice
and frozen dessert. If a creamy soup is
preferred, purée in blender before a final
heating. Top with chives.

TOTAL CALORIES PER SERVING: 189
TOTAL FAT AS % OF DAILY VALUE: 3%   FAT: 2 gm
PROTEIN: 4 gm   CARBOHYDRATES: 40 gm
CALCIUM: 57 mg   IRON: 2 mg   SODIUM: 26 mg
DIETARY FIBER: 3 gm

RICE AND FRUIT
DELIGHT

(Serves 4)

*A dessert or main dish from California. Serve
with banana nut bread.*

1/2 cup dried currants
1/4 cup warm water
1-1/2 cups pre-cooked brown rice
1/2 cup pineapple cubes
1/2 cup seedless grape halves
1/2 cup maple syrup
Juice of 1 lemon or lime, seeds
  removed
Juice of 1 orange, seeds removed
1/4 teaspoon ground cinnamon

Place currants in warm water and then drain.
In a serving bowl, mix rice with all fruits.
Blend maple syrup into juices, stir in cinnamon, pour liquid over rice and stir well. Chill
before serving.

TOTAL CALORIES PER SERVING: 272
TOTAL FAT AS % OF DAILY VALUE: 2%   FAT: 1 gm
PROTEIN: 3 gm   CARBOHYDRATES: 67 gm
CALCIUM: 73 mg   IRON: 2 mg   SODIUM: 7 mg
DIETARY FIBER: 3 gm

BOMBAY RICE CURRY
(Serves 5)

A spicy dish from Asian Indian traditional cooking adapted for the Western kitchen. Serve with lentil or rice crackers, or side dishes of red or green lentils. Adding chutney is almost a must!

This is a several-step recipe. Don't be timid about the spices -- use your imagination and taste for special flavors. Remember cooking is not mathematics, it is artistry in the kitchen.

1 cup onion, finely chopped
1/4 cup water
1 cup peeled eggplant cubes
1/2 cup raw nuts (peanuts, cashews or pecans)
1 cup peeled fresh tomato cubes
1 cup peeled apple cubes
2 large garlic cloves, peeled
1/2 teaspoon ground turmeric
1/2 teaspoon ground cinnamon
1/2 teaspoon ground coriander
1 teaspoon freshly-ground pepper (more to taste, if desired)
1 teaspoon salt
1 teaspoon cumin seeds
1 teaspoon mustard or dill seeds
2 teaspoons ground red pepper or chili powder
Water as needed
4 cups pre-cooked (still warm) brown rice (brown Basmati is best)
1/2 cup raisins (optional)
1/2 cup shredded coconut (optional)

Sauté onions in water in a skillet. Meanwhile, crush eggplant, nuts, tomato, apple, and garlic on a slab or pound into a paste with mortar and pestle, adding water if needed to form a soft mass. (Tiny lumps are fine.) Blend spices into the paste, and then stir all into the soft onions. Taste and adjust spice level -- it is easy to add at this point. Quickly whisk in enough water to make the spiced vegetable sauce like thick soup. Pour over warm rice. Garnish with raisins or coconut if desired.

TOTAL CALORIES PER SERVING: 303
TOTAL FAT AS % OF DAILY VALUE: 14%   FAT: 9 gm
PROTEIN: 8 gm   CARBOHYDRATES: 50 gm
CALCIUM: 47 mg   IRON: 2 mg   SODIUM:469 mg
DIETARY FIBER: 6 gm

Jacqueline Dunnington is a freelance writer from Santa Fe, New Mexico.

LENTIL MANIA

By Jacqueline Dunnington

Humans have been dining on lentils for centuries. These lens-shaped edible seeds, scientifically classified as the *Lens esculenta* or *Lens culinaris,* have been discovered in Bronze Age dwellings on St. Peter's Island in Switzerland. The Bible (Genesis 25:34) records that Esau sold his birthright for a "pottage of lentils."

There are two popular varieties of lentils: the "French" or brownish-green type, which is usually cooked whole, and the smaller, orange colored "Egyptian" variety, which is invariably split.

Orange lentils are found in India, Africa, and the Middle East. Botanists are still hunting for clues about the origin of the plant. Meanwhile, vegetarians delight in the flavor and nutritional benefits of its seeds.

LENTIL SALAD
(Serves 5)

A classic salad for all seasons. Serve with crusty whole wheat bread.

1 cup pre-cooked green lentils
1 cup pre-cooked orange lentils
1/2 cup celery, finely chopped
1 cup steamed green beans, finely cut
1/4 cup freshly chopped parsley

Dressing:
1 Tablespoon mild, prepared mustard
Salt and pepper to taste
Dash of lemon juice
1/2 cup reduced fat Italian dressing

Small head of lettuce, shredded
1 ripe tomato, cut into wedges
1/4 cup finely chopped chives

In a salad bowl, mix cooked lentils, celery, green beans, and parsley. Combine dressing ingredients in a small bowl. Toss lentil mixture with dressing and serve on shredded lettuce. Garnish with tomato wedges and chives.

TOTAL CALORIES PER SERVING: 130
TOTAL FAT AS % OF DAILY VALUE: 2%   FAT: 1 gm
PROTEIN: 9 gm   CARBOHYDRATES: 22 gm
CALCIUM: 50 mg   IRON: 4 mg   SODIUM: 398 mg
DIETARY FIBER: 5 gm

LENTIL AND LEEK RISOTTO
(Serves 4)

Enjoy this delicious dish.

2 cups well-scrubbed leeks, chopped
1 clove garlic, minced
1/2 cup red pepper, finely chopped
1 Tablespoon olive oil
3 cups vegetable broth or water
1-1/4 cups brown rice
Salt and pepper to taste
Pinch of basil
1 cup pre-cooked lentils
1/4 cup freshly chopped parsley
1/4 cup finely grated carrots

In a 4-quart deep pot with cover, sauté leeks, garlic, and red pepper in oil. When soft, add broth or water, and stir in rice along with seasonings. Reduce heat and simmer covered for about 40 minutes or until rice is done. Uncover, stir in cooked lentils and reheat until piping hot. Garnish with parsley and grated carrot before serving.

TOTAL CALORIES PER SERVING: 358
TOTAL FAT AS % OF DAILY VALUE: 8%   FAT: 5 gm
PROTEIN: 10 gm   CARBOHYDRATES: 65 gm
CALCIUM: 69 mg   IRON: 4 mg   SODIUM: 19 mg
DIETARY FIBER: 5 gm

LENTIL SOUP
(Serves 4)

Enjoy this delicious soup.

2 shallots, finely chopped
1 small yellow onion, finely chopped
2 teaspoons olive oil
3 cups water
1 cup dry green lentils

1 red potato, peeled and finely diced
1 large tomato, peeled and diced
1 small stalk celery, diced
1 small carrot, slivered
1/4 cup freshly chopped parsley
Salt and pepper to taste
Dry croutons or chopped chives

In a deep soup pot, sauté shallots and onions in heated oil. Add water and lentils and bring to a boil. Reduce heat and simmer, adding more water if needed to keep the three-cup level of liquid. Cook lentils until barely tender. Add all other vegetables and seasonings. Continue cooking at least 20 minutes longer. Fork-mash or purée mixture. Serve warm, garnished with croutons or chives.

TOTAL CALORIES PER SERVING WITHOUT CROUTONS: 221
TOTAL FAT AS % OF DAILY VALUE: 5%   FAT: 3 gm
PROTEIN: 11 gm   CARBOHYDRATES: 40 gm
CALCIUM: 45 mg   IRON: 5 mg   SODIUM: 25 mg
DIETARY FIBER: 7 gm

SPICY LENTIL AND PEPPER SAUCE FOR PASTA OR RICE
(Serves 4)

A healthy and unusual gourmet treat.

1 Tablespoon olive oil
1 large onion, finely chopped
2 cloves garlic, minced
1 cup green and red bell pepper, finely chopped
1 large tomato, diced
1 cup no salt added vegetable juice
1 cup pre-cooked lentils
2 cooked, peeled hot chilies, finely minced (canned or fresh)
Pinch of basil
Salt and pepper to taste

In a deep pot, sauté onions, garlic, and peppers in heated olive oil. Stir often. Cover and reduce heat to low, add tomato and juice, and simmer for 20 minutes. Add cooked lentils and seasonings (including chilies). Heat thoroughly before serving. If the mixture seems too dry at any time, add a few spoonfuls of water. Serve sauce over cooked pasta or brown rice.

TOTAL CALORIES PER SERVING (SAUCE ONLY): 134
TOTAL FAT AS % OF DAILY VALUE: 6%   FAT: 4 gm
PROTEIN: 6 gm   CARBOHYDRATES: 21 gm
CALCIUM: 31 mg   IRON: 2 mg   SODIUM: 285 mg
DIETARY FIBER: 4 gm

LENTIL AND FIVE VEGETABLE STEW
(Serves 4)

A lowfat stew loaded with flavor.

1 large leek stalk, finely chopped
1 large carrot, shredded
2 cups water
1-1/2 cups canned crushed tomatoes
1 cup yellow corn kernels
1/2 cup broccoli florets, lightly
  steamed
1 cup pre-cooked lentils
2 teaspoons dried red pepper flakes
Salt and pepper to taste

In a stew pot, boil well-cleaned chopped leek and shredded carrot in water until tender. Drain well and add remaining ingredients. Cook until well heated. You may want to add a bit of pre-cooked brown rice or your favorite herb seasoning.

TOTAL CALORIES PER SERVING: 147
TOTAL FAT AS % OF DAILY VALUE: 2%   FAT: 1 gm
PROTEIN: 8 gm   CARBOHYDRATES: 22 gm
CALCIUM: 62 mg   IRON: 3 mg   SODIUM: 167 mg
DIETARY FIBER: 6 gm

LENTILS CURRIED WITH RHUBARB AND POTATOES
(Serves 4)

An unusual recipe from India. Serve with chutney and a big bowl of brown rice.

1 cup dry orange lentils
1 very large sweet potato, peeled and
  sliced
1 Tablespoon oil
1 cup rhubarb, diced
2 Tablespoons liquid sweetener
1 Tablespoon curry powder
1 teaspoon ginger root, grated
1 teaspoon hot red chili powder
Salt and pepper to taste
1/4 cup shredded coconut

Cover lentils with water in a deep pot. Bring to a boil, reduce heat, and add raw sweet potato slices. Simmer until soft (about an hour). Remove from heat, drain, and set aside.

   Preheat oven to 400 degrees. Heat oil in a skillet. Once hot, add rhubarb. Reduce heat and cook until tender. Stir in sweetener and seasonings. Mix with drained cooked lentils and potatoes that have been mashed together with a fork. Pour into a oven-proof dish and bake at 400 degrees until piping hot (about 20 minutes). Garnish with coconut.

TOTAL CALORIES PER SERVING: 256
TOTAL FAT AS % OF DAILY VALUE: 9%   FAT: 6 gm
PROTEIN: 10 gm   CARBOHYDRATES: 42 gm
CALCIUM: 77 mg   IRON: 4 mg   SODIUM: 31 mg
DIETARY FIBER: 8 gm

Jacqueline Dunnington is a freelance writer from New Mexico.

CARROT CUISINE

By Jacqueline Dunnington

The extended carrot family (*Daucus carota*) includes such edibles as celery, fennel, all parsnips, parsley, dill, caraway, coriander, and other herbs. There are dozens of varieties and hybrids of the common orange carrot with which we are most familiar (*Daucus carota satvia*) ranging from long and thin to short and stubby. Carrot culture most probably started in the western reaches of Asia near the Kyber Pass and Afghanistan. Also, the pretty plant, Queen Anne's Lace, is now considered to have been the recent parent to our nutritious vegetable.

In addition to being crunchy, colorful, and inexpensive, carrots are an outstanding source of natural fiber and a valuable source of vitamin A.

CARROT-STUFFED CABBAGE LEAVES
(Serves 4)

Serve this dish with rye bread.

1 head green cabbage, about 2-1/2 pounds
2 medium yellow onions, finely chopped
1 clove garlic, crushed
1 Tablespoon oil
1-1/2 cups raw carrots, scrubbed and finely grated
2 cups cooked mashed potatoes
1/2 cup raisins
1/4 cup fresh parsley, finely chopped
Salt or salt substitute and pepper to taste
3 cups carrot or tomato juice

Remove cabbage core, plunge cabbage in pot of boiling water, cover, bring to full boil, and then remove from heat. Allow cabbage to stay in covered pot about 20 minutes, drain, and allow cabbage to cool. (Reserve a bit of cooking water.) Peel off 16 large leaves, trim coarse center ribs and set aside.

Sauté onions and garlic in oil until clear but not brown. Pour into deep bowl and add grated carrots, potatoes, raisins, and seasonings and combine well. Spoon mixture into center of each leaf, fold leaf edges over stuffing (envelope style), roll into cigar-shapes fastened with wooden toothpicks (plastic ones will melt). Arrange in two layers at bottom of deep, flame-proof dish. Pour juice over stuffed leaves, cover, and simmer for half an hour. Add more liquid if needed.

TOTAL CALORIES PER SERVING: 333
TOTAL FAT AS % OF DAILY VALUE: 8%   FAT: 5 gm   PROTEIN: 8 gm
CARBOHYDRATES: 71 gm
CALCIUM: 218 mg   IRON: 4 mg
SODIUM: 128 mg
DIETARY FIBER: 13 gm

CARROT-STUFFED BAKED POTATOES
(Serves 4)

Accompany with a steamed green vegetable.

4 large baking potatoes, scrubbed
2 cups raw carrots, scrubbed and finely diced
1 cup onions, finely diced
2 teaspoons olive oil
Pinch of dried crumbled basil
1/4 cup fresh parsley, freshly snipped
Salt or salt substitute and pepper to taste
Fresh chives, finely chopped (optional)

Preheat oven to 400 degrees. Scrub potatoes well, dry, and pierce with fork in several places (prevents bursting). Set potatoes in 400 degree oven to bake.

Meanwhile, scrub (don't peel) carrots, dice, and simmer in water until tender. While carrots cook, sauté onion in oil in skillet. When clear, pour onions into deep bowl, set aside. Remove carrots from heat when tender, drain very well (save a bit of liquid), and mash. Pour into bowl with onions. When potatoes are soft to squeeze, remove from oven (don't turn off heat), slice off a length of top skin, scrape flesh into bowl with vegetables, add basil, and fork mix. If mix is too dry, add a little carrot juice or soy milk. Season to taste and add parsley. Refill potato shells, set on cookie sheet and reheat. Serve topped with chives if desired.

TOTAL CALORIES PER SERVING: 279
TOTAL FAT AS % OF DAILY VALUE: 5%   FAT: 3 gm   PROTEIN: 6 gm
CARBOHYDRATES: 60 gm
CALCIUM: 48 mg   IRON: 3 mg
SODIUM: 39 mg
DIETARY FIBER: 7 gm

SPICY BRAISED CARROTS
(Serves 4)

Enjoy this delicious dish.

4 cups thin raw carrots, cut extra thin julienne
1 cup red onions, finely chopped
1 cup green bell pepper, finely chopped
2 teaspoons oil
1 clove garlic, crushed
1/4-inch fresh ginger, grated
1/2 cup hot water
1 teaspoon curry powder
Large pinch dried orange peel
Salt or salt substitute and pepper to taste
Juice of one lime

Parboil carrots for 5 minutes, drain well. Meanwhile, braise onions and green pepper in oil with garlic and ginger in wide shallow pot until vegetables are soft. Stir often and rapidly. Turn heat to low. Combine hot water, spices, and lime juice. Slowly add the carrots and water to the onions. Cover the pot and simmer for about 30 minutes or to desired tenderness.

TOTAL CALORIES PER SERVING: 105
TOTAL FAT AS % OF DAILY VALUE: 5%   FAT: 3 gm   PROTEIN: 2 gm
CARBOHYDRATES: 20 gm
CALCIUM: 46 mg   IRON: 1 mg
SODIUM: 42 mg
DIETARY FIBER: 5 gm

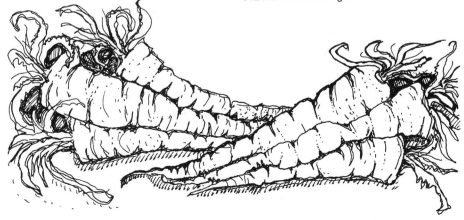

ROASTED CARROTS AND JULIENNE VEGETABLES
(Serves 4)

Serve over cooked kasha, brown rice, or pasta for a main dish.

4 long and thin raw
    carrots, scrubbed
1 potato (about 4
    ounces), scrubbed
1 small zucchini (5 to 6
    inches long),
    scrubbed
1 small yellow squash
    (5 to 6 inches long),
    scrubbed
1 large yellow onion,
    chopped
3 Tablespoons orange
    marmalade
2 Tablespoons oil
Salt or salt substitute
    and pepper to taste
2 Tablespoons un-
    toasted sesame seeds

Preheat oven to 400 degrees. Cut carrots and potatoes into short shoestrings (1-1/2-inches long) of equal thickness. The squash should be chopped into chunks twice as thick as onions, potatoes, and carrots.

In a large plastic bag, mix all ingredients (except the sesame seeds) then spread in roasting pan about 7 x 12-inches and cover with foil. Bake at 400 degrees for 25 minutes covered and then 25 minutes uncovered or to desired tenderness. Sprinkle with water if dry; turn often. Sprinkle on sesame seeds before serving.

TOTAL CALORIES PER SERVING: 206
TOTAL FAT AS % OF DAILY VALUE: 14%   FAT: 9 gm   PROTEIN: 3 gm
CARBOHYDRATES: 30 gm
CALCIUM: 86 mg   IRON: 2 mg
SODIUM: 32 mg
DIETARY FIBER: 5 gm

CARROT CONFETTI SALAD
(Serves 4)

Accompany with baked russet potatoes or yams.

2 cups raw carrots,
    scrubbed and
    slivered
1 cup red cabbage,
    trimmed and
    shredded
1 cup raw zucchini,
    scrubbed and
    slivered
1/2 cup scallions,
    finely chopped

Dressing:
4 Tablespoons lowfat
    vinaigrette
Pinch dried dill weed
Salt or salt substitute
    and pepper to taste

Toss all vegetables in large salad bowl with dressing. Chill and serve.

TOTAL CALORIES PER SERVING: 50
TOTAL FAT AS % OF DAILY VALUE: 3%   FAT: 2 gm   PROTEIN: 1 gm
CARBOHYDRATES: 9 gm
CALCIUM: 32 mg   IRON: 1 mg
SODIUM: 140 mg
DIETARY FIBER: 3 gm

QUICK CARROT NUT SPREAD
(Serves 12 as sandwich filling)

Serve with shredded lettuce or as spread for breads with a green salad.

1 cup raw carrots,
    scrubbed and
    slivered
2/3 cup chunky pea-
    nut or cashew
    butter
1 teaspoon lime juice
3/4 cup ripe banana,
    peeled and sliced
1/2 cup dried currants
Salt or salt substitute
    to taste

Combine all ingredients in blender, adding about a quarter of the ingredients at a time.

TOTAL CALORIES PER SERVING: 115
TOTAL FAT AS % OF DAILY VALUE: 11%   FAT: 7 gm   PROTEIN: 14 gm
CARBOHYDRATES: 10 gm
CALCIUM: 13 mg   IRON: 1 mg
SODIUM: 71 mg
DIETARY FIBER: 2 gm

Jacqueline Dunnington is a freelance writer from Santa Fe, New Mexico.

BEAN BAG

A Primer of Easy Bean Recipes

By Mary Clifford R.D.

Beans, beans, the musical fruit...

Talk about an image problem. Let's get it over with now: Among common bean-bashing complaints are: a) they cause gas; b) they take too long to cook; and c) they're boring.

But that's only if you don't know what to do with beans or how to handle them. The ease and versatility of beans makes them an invaluable staple in any kitchen cabinet. The recipes presented in this article are easy, inexpensive, and quick. Try the recipes and follow our tips as we introduce you to the basics of bean cookery. You'll need only a few kitchen successes with legumes before you'll be wondering where they've "bean" all your life.

Keep in mind that these recipes call for some of the more common types of beans, but you can easily substitute a different variety in almost all recipes with good results. Since there are hundreds of varieties, you don't ever have to eat the same dish twice!

And while most of us are familiar with the dried form of beans, many are available fresh as well (which will cook faster than dried). Cans or jars of beans can be a real time- and labor-saver for those who aren't fond of spending long hours in the kitchen. But even preparing dry beans takes little effort past pre-soaking and then putting them on the stove to simmer. Pressure-cooking is another method that will allow you to make beans in record time. Since beans freeze very well, you can also cook a double batch whenever you make them, then drain and freeze the extra beans in portion-size containers.

Soaking:

Except for split peas and lentils, beans should be soaked before cooking. If you have problems with gas, change the soaking water frequently. That will help to remove the oligosaccharides, the complex natural sugar that is indigestible and can lead to gas. As a dietitian, I have also heard many of my clients swear by BEANO brand drops, a liquid which the manufacturer, AKPharma, Inc., says will prevent gas problems by making indigestible sugars available for digestion. (Consequently, diabetics should discuss this with their physician or dietitian prior to using.) For more information on BEANO, call (800) 257-8650.

⇒ **Quick soak method:**
Boil the legumes in enough water to cover by 2 or 3 inches for 2 minutes. Remove from heat and let sit one hour. Cook according to package or recipe directions.

⇒ **Traditional soak method:**
Combine beans and enough water to cover by 2 or 3 inches and soak in refrigerator overnight. Discard soaking water and cover with fresh water. Cook according to package or recipe directions.

General Cooking Directions:

Heat beans to boiling point; boil 10 minutes. Reduce heat to low, cover, and simmer. Most beans require between 1-1/2 to 2-1/2 hours' cooking time, but large or older beans may take longer. Black-eyed peas cook quickly, and lentils and split beans cook quickest of all, needing only about 30 minutes.

Avoid adding additional ingredients, such as molasses, salt, tomatoes, lemon juice, vinegar, or wine, until the beans are almost done. Otherwise, the beans may toughen or take longer to cook.

One cup of dry beans will yield 2 to 3 cups cooked. A one-pound package of dry beans is about 2 cups dry, or 5 to 6 cups cooked.

Storing:

Dried, packaged beans will keep indefinitely in a cool, dry place, as will cans or jars. Cooked, cooled beans can be stored covered for a day or so in the refrigerator. For longer storage, freezing works very well.

QUICKEST-EVER BEAN STEW
(Serves 6)

Serve with garlic bread for additional raves. This stew is best served the same day, which shouldn't be a problem since it takes only minutes to prepare.

Any leftover vegetables will work, as will a combination of beans.

4-1/2 cups vegetable broth
1 Tablespoon tamari
One 2-pound package frozen stew vegetables, or 6 cups chopped vegetables (such as potatoes, carrots, celery, onions, or turnips)
1/2 teaspoon oregano
1/2 teaspoon thyme
2 cups cooked chickpeas
1/3 cup flour
1/2 cup red wine (or 1/2 cup vegetable broth)
2 cups chopped greens (try spinach or kale)
Salt and pepper to taste

In large saucepan, combine all ingredients except flour, wine, greens, and salt and pepper.

Heat vegetable mixture to boiling over high heat. Reduce heat to low and simmer stirring occasionally, until vegetables are hot (about 20 minutes).

In a cup or small bowl, combine flour and wine. Stir into stew and reheat to boiling. Stir in greens and cook about 5 minutes longer. Add salt and pepper to taste. Serve.

TOTAL CALORIES PER SERVING: 264
TOTAL FAT AS % OF DAILY VALUE: 5%   FAT: 3 gm   PROTEIN: 11 gm
CARBOHYDRATES: 47 gm
CALCIUM: 111 mg   IRON: 4 mg
SODIUM: 419 mg
DIETARY FIBER: 4 gm

BLACK BEANS AND RED PEPPERS
(Serves 4)

Black beans are a staple food in Asia and Latin America. They are absolutely wonderful with cumin added, and are a good bean for soups. They're also good in dips; so be sure to try them the next time you're making a bean dip. Because of their intense dark color, some pretty garnishes are in order. Here, red peppers provide a flash of color and flavor.

1 teaspoon olive oil
1 medium red onion, coarsely chopped
1/2 teaspoon ground cumin
3/4 pound red peppers, thinly sliced
3 cups cooked black beans
2 cups vegetable broth
2 Tablespoons cornstarch
Salt and pepper to taste

In large saucepan, heat oil over medium heat. Add onion and sauté, stirring, until lightly browned. Add cumin and peppers and cook, stirring occasionally, until tender.

Set aside 1/4 cup of broth. Stir beans and remaining 1-3/4 cups of broth into onion mixture. Heat to boiling.

In cup or small bowl, stir together reserved broth and cornstarch. Stir into boiling mixture and cook, stirring, until sauce is thickened and clear. Add salt and pepper to taste. Serve immediately.

TOTAL CALORIES PER SERVING: 238
TOTAL FAT AS % OF DAILY VALUE:
5%   FAT: 3 gm   PROTEIN: 13 gm
CARBOHYDRATES: 43 gm
CALCIUM: 49 mg   IRON: 3 mg
SODIUM: 111 mg
DIETARY FIBER: 6 gm

SPICY HOPPIN' JOHN
(Serves 4)

A traditional Southern dish, often served for good luck on New Year's Day. Black-eyed peas are great any time of year!

1 teaspoon hot chili oil
　　or other spicy oil
1/4 cup chopped onion
1 small green pepper,
　　coarsely chopped
1 cup vegetable broth
Salt and pepper to taste
3 cups cooked black-eyed
　　peas
2 Tablespoons flour

In 2-quart saucepan, heat oil over medium heat. Add onion and sauté, stirring, until browned. Stir in green pepper and cook until brightly colored and just tender.

Set aside 1/4 cup of broth. Add remaining broth and black-eyed peas, and add salt and pepper to taste. Heat to boiling over high heat, then reduce heat to low and simmer about 5 minutes.

In cup or small bowl, stir together reserved broth and flour. Add to Hoppin' John and cook, stirring until mixture thickens. Serve immediately.

TOTAL CALORIES PER SERVING: 171
TOTAL FAT AS % OF DAILY VALUE:
3%   FAT: 2 gm   PROTEIN: 11 gm
CARBOHYDRATES: 28 gm
CALCIUM: 38 mg   IRON: 2 mg
SODIUM: 60 mg
DIETARY FIBER: 12 gm

CURRIED SPLIT PEAS AND VEGETABLES
(Serves 4)

Split peas or lentils would work very nicely here. Lentils are often a favorite of non-vegetarians, since they have a sort of "meaty" texture in dishes like this. I chose to use split peas, though, since so many people don't know what to do with them beyond the traditional split pea soup.

3/4 cup dry split peas
4 cups vegetable broth
1-2 Tablespoons curry
　　powder, to taste
2 cups chopped vege-
　　tables (try peas,
　　eggplant, zucchini,
　　and green beans)
2 cups pre-cooked,
　　peeled, and cubed
　　sweet potatoes
1/3 cup raisins

In large saucepan, combine split peas, broth, and curry powder. Heat to boiling over high heat.

Reduce heat to low and simmer, covered, until peas are tender -- about 30 minutes.

Add remaining ingredients. Reheat to boiling and cook, stirring until vegetables are hot, about 10 minutes longer.

TOTAL CALORIES PER SERVING: 323
TOTAL FAT AS % OF DAILY VALUE:
3%   FAT: 2 gm   PROTEIN: 13gm
CARBOHYDRATES: 67 gm
CALCIUM: 77 mg   IRON: 3 mg
SODIUM: 236 mg
DIETARY FIBER: 7 gm

TAMALE PIE
(Serves 4)

What recipe article about beans would be complete without a variation on chili? Here we've topped a very simple chili with a cornmeal batter for a filling one-dish meal.

Chili:
One 28-ounce can low-
　　sodium, crushed
　　tomatoes
1 cup whole-kernel corn
2 cups pre-cooked kid-
　　ney beans
2-4 Tablespoons chili
　　powder, to taste
Pepper to taste

Topping:
3/4 cup cornmeal
3/4 cup flour
2 teaspoons baking pow-
　　der
3/4 cup water
2 Tablespoons melted
　　soft margarine

Preheat oven to 425 degrees. Lightly oil a shallow 2-quart baking dish.

In large bowl, combine chili ingredients. Pour into baking dish.

In small bowl, combine cornmeal, flour, baking powder, and salt. Add water and margarine, stirring until dry ingredients are just moistened; do not overbeat.

Spoon cornmeal mixture over chili (don't worry if chili is not completely covered; batter will spread during baking). Bake tamale pie about 25 minutes or until bubbly and cornbread is golden.

TOTAL CALORIES PER SERVING: 435
TOTAL FAT AS % OF DAILY VALUE: 12% FAT: 8 gm PROTEIN: 16 gm
CARBOHYDRATES:70 gm
CALCIUM: 264 mg IRON: 7 mg
SODIUM: 317 mg
DIETARY FIBER: 11 gm

PINTO PURÉE
(Serves 4 --
4 sandwiches or 8 patties)

I stumbled on this versatile dish when I had a lot of leftover pinto beans, but it will also work with any extra beans you have. Serve the spread cold on hearty bread or crackers for a change from hummus or other sandwich fillings. Add some oatmeal for body (instructions below), then pan-fry or bake it, and you have a soft patty that's great with mustard, ketchup, or steak sauce -- kind of like a salmon patty without the salmon, good hot or cold. (I also rolled some into

"meatballs" and served them as a cold hors d'oeuvre with a hot-and-sweet mustard dip.)

4 cups cooked pinto
 beans
2 Tablespoons dried
 minced onion
3 Tablespoons relish
2 teaspoons prepared
 mustard
1/4 teaspoon paprika
1/4 teaspoon ground
 cumin
Salt and pepper to taste

In food processor, blender, or large bowl with potato masher, combine all ingredients until smooth.

Note: To make patties, stir 1-1/4 to 1-1/2 cups rolled oats into mixture, depending on how moist your purée is. The mixture should be firm enough to form, but not dry and crumbly. Form into 8 patties. Bake in 400 degree oven on lightly oiled baking sheet, or pan fry until golden. Serve hot or cold.

TOTAL CALORIES PER SERVING
(Puree): 252
TOTAL FAT AS % OF DAILY VALUE:
2% FAT: 1 gm PROTEIN: 14 gm
CARBOHYDRATES: 48 gm
CALCIUM: 85 mg IRON: 5 mg
SODIUM: 158 mg
DIETARY FIBER: 13 gm

TOTAL CALORIES PER SERVING
(Burgers): 174
TOTAL FAT AS % OF DAILY VALUE:
2% FAT: 1 gm PROTEIN: 9 gm
CARBOHYDRATES: 32 gm
CALCIUM: 49 mg IRON: 3 mg
SODIUM: 80 mg
DIETARY FIBER: 7 gm

BUTTER BEAN AND CORN CHOWDER
(Serves 4)

Butter beans are large lima beans. (Often, you will find baby lima beans in the frozen section of your market.) They are mellow, with a creamy flavor that makes them perfect for soup.

1 cup vegetable broth
2 cups cooked butter
 beans
One 15-ounce can
 creamed corn
1 small carrot, coarsely
 chopped
1/4 cup finely chopped
 celery
1/2 teaspoon oregano
Salt and pepper to taste

In 2-quart saucepan, combine all ingredients. Heat to boiling over high heat. Reduce heat to low and simmer, covered, until carrots and celery are tender, about 15 minutes.

TOTAL CALORIES PER SERVING: 197
TOTAL FAT AS % OF DAILY VALUE:
2% FAT: 1 gm PROTEIN: 9 gm
CARBOHYDRATES: 41 gm
CALCIUM: 26 mg IRON: 3 mg
SODIUM: 370 mg
DIETARY FIBER: 8 gm

Mary Clifford is a Registered Dietitian in Roanoke, Virginia.

COOKING WITH
GREENS

By Debra Wasserman

Vegetarians, especially vegans, who are looking for non-dairy sources of foods high in calcium should turn to greens. Too often, dark green leafy vegetables are avoided because they have the reputation of being bitter or unappetizing. I hope that you will give the following good-tasting recipes a try. For variety, you can easily substitute different greens in each recipe. (See below.)

TYPES OF GREENS AND THEIR COOKING TIMES

BEET TOPS	4 MINUTES
BOK CHOY	5 MINUTES
CABBAGE	6 MINUTES
CHARD	3 MINUTES
COLLARDS	7 MINUTES
DANDELION	5 MINUTES
ESCAROLE	4 MINUTES
KALE	6 MINUTES
LETTUCE	3 MINUTES
SPINACH	1 MINUTE
TURNIP	5 MINUTES

Note: The greens listed above can be prepared easily by simply chopping them up, steaming them in a steamer over some water for the time indicated above, and then sprinkling a little lemon juice on them, as well as salt and pepper if desired. Home grown greens when just picked tend to be more tender and have a less bitter taste. Greens make a wonderful late fall crop in gardens. They will thrive through the first snowfall in colder climates.

CINDY'S HEARTY LEMON SOUP
(Serves 6)

Enjoy this delicious soup!

1 cup long grain brown rice
2 cups water
1/4 teaspoon each garlic powder, onion powder, black pepper, turmeric, and thyme
10 cups reduced-sodium vegetable broth
1 teaspoon tamari or soy sauce (optional)
5 scallions, sliced
2 cups finely shredded greens (kale, collards, etc.)
1 cup nutritional yeast (not Brewer's)
Juice of 2 lemons

Cook rice and spices in water. When done, add vegetable broth, tamari or soy sauce, and scallions. Simmer for 10 minutes. Add greens and simmer another 5 minutes. Add yeast and lemon juice before serving.

TOTAL CALORIES PER SERVING: 291
TOTAL FAT AS % OF DAILY VALUE: 9%   FAT: 6 gm
PROTEIN: 19 gm   CARBOHYDRATES: 44 gm
CALCIUM: 138 mg   IRON: 4 mg   SODIUM: 270 mg
DIETARY FIBER: 6 gm

SCRAMBLED TOFU
AND BOK CHOY
(Serves 4)

Serve hot with whole wheat toast for breakfast.

1-1/2 teaspoons oil
1/2 pound bok choy, chopped
12 snow peas (optional)
Small onion, chopped finely
Pinch of black pepper
1 teaspoon turmeric (optional)
1 pound tofu, crumbled
1 Tablespoon tamari or soy sauce

Sauté all the ingredients except the tofu and tamari or soy sauce for 3 minutes over a medium-high heat. Add the tofu and tamari or soy sauce. Sauté for another 2 minutes.

TOTAL CALORIES PER SERVING: 120
TOTAL FAT AS % OF DAILY VALUE: 11%   FAT: 7 gm
PROTEIN: 11 gm   CARBOHYDRATES: 5 gm
CALCIUM: 170 mg   IRON: 7 mg   SODIUM: 270 mg
DIETARY FIBER: 1 gm

CABBAGE DELIGHT
(Serves 5)

A combination of spices adds to this unique dish.

1 Tablespoon oil
1 large onion, chopped
1/4 teaspoon mustard seed
Small head cabbage, chopped
1/4 teaspoon each of turmeric,
    coriander, cumin, garlic powder,
    and pepper
1/2 cup tomatoes, chopped
1/2 lemon, squeezed (2 Tablespoons)

Heat mustard seeds and onion in oil in a covered pan until seeds pop. Add cabbage and spices. Sauté 15 minutes. Add tomatoes and lemon juice. Heat 3 to 5 minutes longer.

TOTAL CALORIES PER SERVING: 98
TOTAL FAT AS % OF DAILY VALUE: 5%   FAT: 3 gm
PROTEIN: 3 gm   CARBOHYDRATES: 17 gm
CALCIUM: 121 mg   IRON: 2 mg   SODIUM: 46 mg
DIETARY FIBER: 5 gm

SAUTÉED COLLARD GREENS
AND TOMATOES
(Serves 4)

This side dish is absolutely delicious.

1 teaspoon oil
1 pound collards, chopped
2 ripe tomatoes, chopped
2 teaspoons lemon juice
1/2 teaspoon garlic powder
1/4 teaspoon mustard powder

Sauté all the ingredients together over medium-high heat for 7 minutes. Serve hot.

TOTAL CALORIES PER SERVING: 54
TOTAL FAT AS % OF DAILY VALUE: 3%   FAT: 2 gm
PROTEIN: 2 gm   CARBOHYDRATES: 10 gm
CALCIUM: 94 mg   IRON: 1 mg   SODIUM: 24 mg
DIETARY FIBER: 3 gm

BOK CHOY AND APPLES
(Serves 3)

Serve this side dish with brown rice.

1-1/2 teaspoons oil
1/2 pound bok choy, chopped
1 apple, cored and chopped
1 teaspoon cinnamon
1/4 teaspoon nutmeg

Sauté all the ingredients in a large frying pan over medium-high heat for 5 minutes.

TOTAL CALORIES PER SERVING: 59
TOTAL FAT AS % OF DAILY VALUE: 5%   FAT: 3 gm
PROTEIN: 2 gm   CARBOHYDRATES: 8 gm
CALCIUM: 65 mg   IRON: 1 mg   SODIUM: 13 mg
DIETARY FIBER: 1 gm

***Debra is the author of* Simply Vegan.**

THE GREEN SCENE

By Mary Clifford, R.D.

Popeye ate spinach; collards have something to do with the South; and kale is the garnish at deli counters; stuffed in between bowls of macaroni salad and coleslaw. Does anyone really eat this stuff?

Yes, and they actually enjoy it! To be sure, greens do have a strong flavor. If your favorite vegetable is iceberg lettuce, greens may take some getting used to. But kale, mustard greens, spinach, and other dark green leafy vegetables deserve much more respect than they currently command. The following recipes and information will get you started on experimenting with greens.

GENERAL INFORMATION ON GREENS:

- ◆ **AVAILABILITY:** Fall through spring are peak times.
- ◆ **STORAGE:** Keep unwashed in refrigerator crisper until ready to use.
- ◆ **CHOOSING:** For best quality, purchase greens the same day, or at most, a day before you're going to use them, since they wilt quickly. Choose greens that have firm, uniformly-colored leaves -- avoid wilted, yellowing or brown bunches. A small amount of discolored leaves can be removed prior to cooking.
- ◆ **PREPARATION:** Wash carefully before using. The sandy soil in which they are grown often clings to the leaves, and careful rinsing in several changes of water is needed to remove this grit. If the stalks are especially woody, either discard them, use them to flavor vegetable stock, or peel them, cooking as you would broccoli stalks or asparagus.
- ◆ **COOKING:** Cooking times depend on the green. (Kale is tough; mustard greens and spinach can be eaten raw.) A general rule of thumb is that greens can be cooked in a covered pot in the water that clings to the leaves after washing -- no need to add extra. They should be cooked until tender, but not mushy. (Microwaving or steaming works well, also.) As for cooking times, many cookbooks instruct you to boil the greens for 45 minutes or more, rendering them into the slimy mush many of us remember as our first encounter with greens. However, 5-8 minutes is usually sufficient, depending on your tastes. In general, most greens can be substituted for one another in most recipes.

GREENS GLOSSARY:

Bok choy: Often used in Chinese cooking, bok choy resembles Swiss chard, and, as with Swiss chard, the ribs can be used as a celery substitute.

Collards: A favorite of ancient Greece and Rome, collards are now primarily associated with soul food and the southern United States.

Kale: Quite possibly the first cultivated cabbage, kale is popular in Scotland and Germany, where the chilly climates are perfect for its cultivation. Somewhat tougher than other greens, kale is more suitable to eat in cooked dishes than raw.

Mustard greens: Like mustard seeds, the greens of the mustard plant have a strong, but pleasant taste. They have a peppery bite that goes well with other rich flavors.

Spinach: The origins of this well-known green are obscure; it may be a latecomer to the vegetable scene, becoming well known only a mere 700 or so years ago. If you were ever tortured with overcooked, slimy spinach, you owe it to yourself to try it raw in a crunchy salad.

Swiss chard: The ribs can be cooked or eaten like celery; use the leafy part as you would any other greens.

Turnip Greens: The commonplace turnip, and thus its greens, probably originated in Asia Minor. It has been so widely consumed throughout history (particularly before it ran into competition from potatoes) that it is generally overlooked, or considered "poor people's food."

Please note: Other leafy vegetables are also considered to be greens; this list includes the more common ones.

WARM CURRIED GREENS AND PASTA
(Serves 4)

Try this the next time you have leftover pasta.

2 teaspoons oil (try grapefruit, orange, or other fruit-infused oil, or a fruity olive oil)
2 teaspoons curry powder
1/3 cup vegetable broth
4 cups cooked pasta (macaroni, shells, radiatore, or other small pasta)
3/4 pound greens, rinsed and finely shredded
1/3 cup dark seedless raisins
Salt and pepper to taste

In non-stick saucepan, heat oil over medium heat. Add curry and cook about 1 minute, until sizzling. Carefully add broth and remaining ingredients. Cover and cook, stirring occasionally, until greens are crisp-tender and pasta is hot, about 8 minutes.

TOTAL CALORIES PER SERVING: 254
TOTAL FAT AS % OF DAILY VALUE: 5%   FAT: 3 gm
PROTEIN: 8 gm   CARBOHYDRATES: 48 gm
CALCIUM: 74 mg   IRON: 4 mg   SODIUM: 98 mg
DIETARY FIBER: 4 gm

COUNTRY-STYLE GREENS
(Serves 4)

Most of the recipes that exist for greens call for bacon, bacon grease, or ham bones. This recipe is a nod to that basic preparation style, but of course we left out the meat.

1/2 teaspoon flavored oil (try sesame or chili oil)
2 green onions, finely chopped
3/4 cup vegetable broth
1-2 drops liquid smoke
3/4 pound greens, rinsed and coarsely chopped
2 teaspoons vegetarian bacon bits
1 to 2 drops hot red pepper sauce (optional)

In large saucepan, heat oil over medium heat. Add onions and sauté a few minutes until bright green. Add vegetable broth, liquid smoke, and greens. Cover and simmer 6-8 minutes, or until greens are tender. Stir in bacon bits and pepper sauce, if desired. Serve immediately.

TOTAL CALORIES PER SERVING: 31
TOTAL FAT AS % OF DAILY VALUE: 2%   FAT: 1 gm
PROTEIN: 2 gm   CARBOHYDRATES: 4 gm
CALCIUM: 71 mg   IRON: 2 mg   SODIUM: 146 mg
DIETARY FIBER: 2 gm

GREENS AND APPLES
(Serves 4)

Tart, sweet apples go very nicely with tangy greens. This dish is especially nice with mustard greens or kale.

2 teaspoons soft margarine
2 medium-size Granny Smith apples, coarsely chopped
1/3 cup frozen apple juice concentrate

1 pound greens, rinsed and finely chopped
Salt and pepper to taste

In large saucepan, melt margarine over medium heat. Add apples and cook, stirring, until lightly browned.

Add remaining ingredients. Cover and cook, stirring occasionally, until greens are tender. Serve immediately.

TOTAL CALORIES PER SERVING: 122
TOTAL FAT AS % OF DAILY VALUE: 3%   FAT: 2 gm
PROTEIN: 3 gm   CARBOHYDRATES: 25 gm
CALCIUM: 93 mg   IRON: 2 mg   SODIUM: 121 mg
DIETARY FIBER: 4 gm

BRAISED BOK CHOY WITH MUSHROOMS
(Serves 4)

Serve this super-fast dish over brown or wild rice for a simple gourmet meal.

1 teaspoon sesame oil
2 cups sliced mushrooms
1/2 teaspoon ground ginger
Salt and pepper to taste
3/4 cup vegetable broth
2 pounds bok choy, diagonally sliced into 1-inch pieces

In non-stick saucepan, heat oil over medium heat. Add mushrooms. Cover and cook, stirring occasionally, until mushrooms collapse and give up their liquid. Uncover and continue cooking until lightly browned.

Add remaining ingredients. Simmer uncovered about 8 minutes, until bok choy is crisp-tender and most of liquid has evaporated.

TOTAL CALORIES PER SERVING: 59
TOTAL FAT AS % OF DAILY VALUE: 3%   FAT: 2 gm
PROTEIN: 5 gm   CARBOHYDRATES: 6 gm
CALCIUM: 188 mg   IRON: 2 mg   SODIUM: 80 mg
DIETARY FIBER: 2 gm

CREAMY RICE AND GREENS CASSEROLE
(Serves 4)

Tim Lavezzo is a classical guitarist and an excellent cook, and he was kind enough to share this hearty dish with me. Well, almost. Actually, he's one of those excellent cooks who doesn't work from recipes and never writes anything down. This recipe is a close re-creation of one of his dishes.

One 10.5-ounce package silken firm tofu
Pinch of turmeric (optional, for color)
Salt and pepper to taste
1-1/4 cups vegetable broth
2 Tablespoons teriyaki sauce
1 pound greens, rinsed and finely chopped
3 cups cooked rice

Coat a 2-quart casserole with vegetable cooking spray. Set aside. Pre-heat oven to 400 degrees.

In food processor or blender, process tofu, turmeric, salt and pepper, if desired, broth, and teriyaki sauce until smooth.

In large bowl, combine tofu mixture, greens, and rice. Spoon into greased casserole. Bake at 400 degrees about 30 minutes or until top is lightly browned.

TOTAL CALORIES PER SERVING: 259
TOTAL FAT AS % OF DAILY VALUE: 5%   FAT: 3 gm
PROTEIN: 11 gm   CARBOHYDRATES: 47 gm
CALCIUM: 109 mg   IRON: 5 mg   SODIUM: 531 mg
DIETARY FIBER: 2 gm

add tuna balsamic

GREENS QUICHE
(Serves 6)

A tofu-spinach quiche that long-time vegetarians Irene and Ron Malakowski made for a potluck picnic last summer disappeared like magic. Their wonderful dish inspired this version, which has less tofu and more greens (to reduce the fat content), but will nonetheless make for a satisfying meal. If you like, and can spare the fat, add a homemade or prepared crust.

Two 10.5-ounce packages silken firm tofu
1/8 teaspoon garlic powder
1 small onion, coarsely chopped
Pinch of turmeric (optional, for color)
2 Tablespoons prepared mustard
1 cup vegetable broth
1/2 teaspoon cumin
Salt and pepper to taste
1 pound greens, rinsed, finely chopped, and cooked (drain well)

Coat a 9-inch pie plate with vegetable cooking spray. Set aside. Pre-heat oven to 450 degrees.

In food processor or blender, process all ingredients except greens until smooth. In large bowl, combine with greens. Spoon into greased pie plate.

Bake quiche about 65 minutes in 450 degree oven, or until golden and knife inserted in center comes out clean.

TOTAL CALORIES PER SERVING: 86
TOTAL FAT AS % OF DAILY VALUE: 5%   FAT: 3 gm
PROTEIN: 8 gm   CARBOHYDRATES: 6 gm
CALCIUM: 89 mg   IRON: 2 mg   SODIUM: 197 mg
DIETARY FIBER: 1 gm

Mary Clifford is a Registered Dietitian from Roanoke, Virginia.

LINKAGES BETWEEN BUSINESS, ETHICS, AND THE ENVIRONMENT
AS THEY RELATE TO FOOD PRODUCTION

By Wayne Smeltz, Ph.D.

Back on March 29, 1989, in a *New York Times* article by Marian Burros, a report on pesticides in food had caused a near state of panic among consumers. The study done by the Natural Resources Defense Council, a private environmental group, reported that children's exposure to pesticides in food resulted in six to twelve times greater impact than that for adults and that pesticide intake is strongly suspected to be linked to higher incidence of cancer.

This study was then highlighted by a *60 Minutes* report and was even given more media attention because Meryl Streep had become the chief spokesperson for the Council's grassroot offshoot, *Mothers and Others for Pesticide Limits*.

The immediate outcome of this furor was a boom in demand for foods grown without pesticides, referred to as *organically grown food*. For example, Burros' *New York Times* article refers to a natural foods market in the SoHo section of Manhattan where people lined up each morning waiting to buy organic produce. Demand outstripped supply and price seemed to be of little consequence.

As this article will document, for many years there have been numerous social activist groups and small businesses addressing the environmental and ethical issues associated with producing our food supply. An examination into these various organizations reveals broad philosophical differences and strategies to deal with the issues of food and environmental concern. This may be the reason that these issues have only recently attracted the attention of the general public and big business.

After interviewing over 40 business people in the natural foods industry, I have noted a fairly strong linkage between philosophical beliefs, diet, and environmental concerns. In particular, the philosophies of Ahimsa, macrobiotics, and vegetarianism seem to be strongly connected to a concern for the environment and other living beings.

HISTORICAL BACKGROUND

Historically, the most persistent task facing people has been finding enough to eat. It is only recently and in select parts of the world that this is no longer a primary activity. Large scale farming and livestock production in these areas result in an abundance of food. For many years, the external costs of these activities were ignored or not considered important. As evidenced by the *New York Times* article, the external costs of potentially unsafe foods and environmental blight are no longer being ignored by all people. Neither is the fact that in many parts of the world there remain food shortages and that these parts of the world are also paying environmental costs to export foods to wealthier nations.

As civilization has developed, each society has adopted its own food regimen. Partially guided by the pragmatics of geographical location, societies began to instruct their citizens on what to eat and what not to eat. Well-known and ancient examples of this practice were the Kosher rules of the Jewish religion and the Ahimsa philosophy of some Eastern cultures. Kosher rules dictating that certain foods should not be eaten, and that certain foods should not be eaten in combination with other foods, are the word of G-d and appear to be motivated by health and ethical concerns.

Altman (1988) (see bibliography) notes that the philosophy of Ahimsa is thousands of years old and traces from the Jain forefather Lord Mahavira (599 - 527 B.C.E.), Buddha, and Lao Tao (both sixth century B.C.E.). Ahimsa is described as "dynamic harmlessness," which encompasses the renunciation of the will to kill or the intention to hurt any living being through hostile thought, word, or deed.

The essence of Ahimsa, according to Altman (1988), is the realization of dynamic compassion. Dynamic compassion is explained by Altman as acting in ways that (1) heal instead of harm; (2) respect and further life instead of destroying it; and (3) serve as an active channel for compassion. Carson (1972) notes that this tradition has greatly impacted the vegetarian and animal rights movements, while Altman (1988) notes that this ethic is highly compatible with environmental concern. Altman further notes that this ethic promotes social activism and is not as passive as believed by most Westerners. For example, Altman points to the many small businesses started by Jains and the many organic and sustainable agriculture businesses based on the tenets of dynamic compassion.

THE MACROBIOTIC ETHIC

The followers of macrobiotics are another group practicing the ethic of dynamic compassion in food production. Kotzch (1986) notes that macrobiotics was begun in Japan in the late 1800's by Sagen Izhizuka in reaction to shifts in Japanese diet caused by increased trade with other countries. Izhizuka felt that Japan's growing health problems could be attributed to the use of additives and processed foods. He argued that only foods that were grown regionally without pesticides and which could be eaten fresh were healthy.

A disciple of Izhizuka, George Ohsawa, left Japan to promote macrobiotic principles in other countries. Returning to Japan for a visit, he found that it had become almost impossible to find traditional organic foods. As a result, he urged followers to develop small businesses that adhered to the macrobiotic diet. Farms, food processing, and marketing businesses were started under this ethic. Today the network remains, with many small farms specializing in a few organic products and sending them to the Ohsawa -- Japanese processors. These processors operate in a labor intensive tradition, with many products processed totally by hand. A current executive remarks that the combine's mission remains the same: "Our main aim has been to promote the health of individuals and of society, not to make a lot of money." And, he added with a laugh, "We have been fairly successful."

Kotzsch (1986) concludes that this method of food delivery has also been environmentally rewarding as each farmer prizes the small amount of land he or she has to grow on and treats it with respect and care. Some families have been farming on the same land for over four hundred years, preserving its tenuous growing potential.

ORGANIC BUSINESS
AND ETHICS

The roots of the organic movement in the United States appear to grow from the writings of Dr. Rudolph Steiner, an Austrian renaissance man who wrote in the 1920's. Steiner's writings argue for a systems perspective on the relationship of humans with non-human animals and the environment. Termed "biodynamics," Steiner calls for a special preparation of the soil through compost to maximize the life and nutrients in the soil and the food grown in it. Smith (1988) notes that biodynamic farming is actually a more restrictive technique than organic and that through the late 1980's only nineteen farms in the United States were certified by the biodynamic certification program.

Burros (1989) points out that prior to World War II, most agriculture was essentially organic (see chart at the end of this article), which means without the use of pesticides and chemicals. Chemical pesticides became a staple of mass production agriculture around 1950, and worry about this technique of food production began in the sixties. Concern also focused on the concentration of land ownership, whose objective was to maximize yield, with seeming disregard for the land, environment, and quality of life. It was at this time that many alternative food stores and businesses began. The motivations of these businesses were varied, but almost all were in reaction to the environment and the health neglect of large scale food production.

One example is the experience of Gordon Bennett, a founder of Westbrae Natural Foods. Bennett began selling organic pears at a roadside stand in Berkeley, California, after dropping out of Harvard University a few weeks before graduation. This lifestyle was one that he, his wife, and another couple felt was ethically correct and one that brought them back into touch with the environment. The couples soon added more organic products, and as demand increased, they developed a natural granola. The group had no previous business experience and learned as they went, looking on it as an experience and an adventure.

The business grew into a complete natural foods product line with sales over $10 million; it was bought out in the 1980's. Mr. Bennett then assumed the presidency of the SoyFoods Association, where he hoped to promote soy-based products that are healthy alternatives which do not damage the environment.

Another early organic entrepreneur was Barbara Jaffe, who in 1971 at the age of 17, quit school to start baking organic breads. Jaffe had became disenchanted with the "establishment" and wanted to make a contribution to a more ecological and healthier world. Her father persuaded Jaffe at least to build a business with her baking skills and thus Barbara's Bakery was born. The business was highly successful and was sold in 1985 to Weetabix, a British food conglomerate. The reason for the sale was that Ms. Jaffe had little interest in running a mature business and wanted to devote more time to socially oriented activities.

A similar experience is voiced by Stan Lessens, founder of Green Earth, a natural foods store in Baltimore. Lessens relates that in the sixties, he was looking for a path to serve the earth. He believes in the Ahimsic view of dynamic compassion and that it is people's responsibility to serve the earth that we have obviously been neglecting. His mission was to sell foods that were not only nutritional but that did not harm the environment. His first store was located in a cellar in a deteriorating part of Baltimore city. In time, the area gentrified and the store was moved and expanded. Lessens has since sold this store and started another New Age-type store. Lessens also believes that being ethical in business is a competitive plus and is the best hope for the earth.

A concern for the earth and the environment was the driving force for the start-up of Whole Earth, a food cooperative in Princeton, New Jersey. After returning from Earth Day celebrations in 1970, a group of environmentally concerned citizens were trying to decide how they could contribute to a better earth. Their decision was to open a food cooperative that would provide products and education for a healthier lifestyle. After some rocky financial times, the cooperative is now very profitable, with excess funds going to environmentally oriented projects.

Another example of the relationship between ethics, business, and the environment is the experience of *The Farm* in Summertown, Tennessee. Part of the folklore of the alternative lifestyle promoting dynamic compassion, *The Farm* began in the sixties to offer communal living with a focus on ethical and environmental concerns. *The Farm* grew significantly and developed operations in construction, foods, and publishing, as it was concerned with environment and health issues. During the seventies, *The Farm* went through internal conflict and was broken up into independent cooperative operations. While trying to retain their alternative outlook, each operation was to survive financially on its own. In an interview with the president of the book publishing and press operation, Robert Holzapfel, he noted that each opera-

tion of *The Farm* had become financially self-sufficient and that he felt like an entrepreneur running a business. Holzapfel also feels a strong commitment to the ethical standards that *The Farm* stands for and will publish only material that contributes to the well-being of the earth. Holzapfel believes strongly in the link between environmental awareness, dynamic compassion, and vegetarianism.

VEGETARIANISM, BUSINESS, AND ETHICS

The link between dynamic compassion, environmental concern, and vegetarianism is one that my research has consistently found. This is interesting because Akers (1983) notes that the link between individual vegetarians is not nearly as strong. This is no doubt due to the significantly different philosophical and religious backgrounds that lead people to vegetarianism. Carson (1972) notes that the word vegetarian dates from 1842, even though groups advocating a meatless diet predate that time. These groups were motivated by religious concerns and were seeking to live a purer, ethical life.

Several early, well-known vegetarians began businesses because of their concern over the healthiness of food. The Reverend Mr. Sylvester Graham invented the "Graham Cracker" to assist people in digestion. Akers (1983) notes that Graham's writings often examined the relationship between nature, ethics, and vegetarianism and that this motivated his entrepreneurship.

Dr. J.H. Kellogg's motivation to be a vegetarian was spurred by his belief in the Seventh-day Adventist religion. After graduating

from the church-related medical college, Kellogg became the head of the Adventist health sanitarium in Battle Creek, Michigan. Kellogg was so successful in his promotion of the sanitarium that it became known as Kellogg's Sanitarium.

Spurred on by the guiding light of the Adventist movement's Ellen White to promote vegetarian fare, Kellogg began experimenting to develop tasty alternatives to meat. After several years of experimentation, Dr. Kellogg and his brother W.K. perfected a flake breakfast food. Through W.K.'s business savvy, the product was distributed and consumed nationally. "Me-too" companies soon followed, and Battle Creek became the breakfast food capital of the world. The vegetarian emphasis was soon dropped.

The Vegetarian movement experienced a gradual decline until the 1960's. The aforementioned search for a more natural and ethical lifestyle led people back to vegetarianism, as the ethic switched from a religious perspective to ecological and health motivations. Akers (1983) provides the best synthesis that exists between nutrition, ethics, and ecology of a vegetarian diet. One may call this synthesis slanted, but it is drawn from reputable sources and gives one pause for thought.

One factor in favor of vegetarian agriculture is that it requires significantly fewer land resources than livestock agriculture. Estimates are that it takes 8 to 10 times more land and energy to produce one pound of meat than one pound of grain or vegetable. As a result of this need for land, many forests are being cleared to provide grazing land to feed livestock. Forests provide many passive benefits to the environment, such as preventing floods and absorbing carbon dioxide, thus moderating climates. Forests also help to minimize soil erosion and induce steady

rainfalls. As more countries adopt our methods of food raising, it is feared that deforestation will significantly increase and problems such as the greenhouse effect and acid rain will be exacerbated.

In addition, Akers (1983) points out that livestock agriculture requires tremendous amounts of water. This threatens the depletion of groundwater, which lowers the water table, creating many problems such as shortages, flooding, and the decreased safety of the water supply. Livestock agriculture and chemical agriculture also produce pollution that seeps into the water supply. This fact has been recognized by the many people who will not drink water coming from the general water supply and has spurred a boom in the bottled water and seltzer industry (which may or may not be any better.)

The organic foods and bottled water examples are strong indications that the problems associated with our present methods of agriculture are being recognized by the general public. The extent of the problem is debatable, but many are becoming convinced that drastic changes are needed. Akers (1983) and others argue that a vegetarian ethic will help promote an environmentally sound ecosystem. While the ethic may not be embraced by the general public, many are beginning to follow aspects of the diet.

There are many examples of current entrepreneurs who are motivated by this ethic and concern for the environment. One example is Greg Caton, who developed Lumen, which is a soy analog for meat. Caton calls his product "the food for a new age." Caton (1988) argues that the environmental and health costs of raising livestock are so great that it is inevitable that meat substitutes will develop into a viable market. He even goes so far as to predict that most people will cease eating meat by 2010 as a result of epidemics caused by chemicals in foods.

Another business basing its product lines on a vision of a better environment is 21st Century Foods. Their mission is to introduce fresh foods that are low on the food chain and cause little environmental harm. This firm argues that people must change their diet so that a transformation of our philosophical, biological, and environmental attitudes can be realized. The company has had a rocky financial history, but current demand for organic products should buoy sales. Their all-organic foods include various soy products, corn masa, and algae.

THE LINKAGES BETWEEN BUSINESS ETHICS AND ENVIRONMENTAL CONCERN

There are many more examples of how individuals are translating their ethical and environmental concerns into entrepreneurial activities. Among this group, there is a strong feeling that if we do not radically alter the way that we feed ourselves, we will face the rather rapid destruction of our ecosystem. There is consensus that there has already been so much destruction that even stabilizing the situation requires drastic measures.

Whether this perception is correct or not is debatable, but it is beginning to mobilize more businesses into considering this ethic in their strategic decision making. Another obvious change is that many individuals who would normally voice their concerns through social activism or political channels are now seeing the economics-commerce route as potentially the most powerful.

A cover story in the late 1980's by *Utne Reader*, an alternative magazine with a huge paid circulation, was devoted to "Ethical Business." The caption below this was entitled "Oxymoron? Our Last Best Hope for Planet Earth?" Kelly (1989) states that

business is presently destroying the earth with unsound practices, but argues that there are signs that a new life-affirming paradigm is emerging. One dimension of this paradigm is straight out of Milton Freedman, with firms being started to clean up pollution caused by the wastes of other firms. Another writer in this volume, Hawken (1989), believes that entrepreneurs are now the real cultural revolutionaries in our society, arguing that through ethical entrepreneurship ventures, the earth can be rebuilt with dynamic compassion.

The environmental stewardship role of entrepreneurship is not only being promoted to consumers, but also to prospective entrepreneurs. The April 1989 editon of *In Business* is devoted to "Entrepreneuring for a Healthy USA." Representative articles in this edition are entitled "Making the Earth Safe for Optimism," "Biodegradable Breakthroughs," and "Growing Big on Natural Food." The magazine's editorial stresses that the ethical environment we create for business is strongly connected with the physical environment in which we live. Again the message is that if we do not incorporate environmental concerns into our business practices, our quality of life will significantly deteriorate.

The link between the ethics of dynamic compassion, environment, and business is being drawn together. At recent Natural Foods Expos, the talk was not so much about the food, but the environmental consequences of the packaging. Consumers are beginning to understand the negative eternalities caused by their consumption and are beginning to be willing to pay upfront to minimize later damage.

There appears to be a growing sense that by practicing dynamic compassion with our earth and with other living beings, the ultimate recipient is ourselves. Our history of uncontrolled consumption in what we thought to be maximization of efficient production has resulted in many environmental and health problems. While many of these problems have been solved with subsequent business innovation, the gap appears to be widening and the cost of resolving these problems staggering. The resolution seems to be more in prevention than in innovative solutions to problems caused by business methods.

There are a growing number of entrepreneurs who see their enterprise as a means to further their ethical and environmental concerns. The examples presented in this article are a cross-section of entrepreneurs driven by the ethics of dynamic compassion and/or vegetarianism that also promotes environmental protection. There is also a growing awareness and acceptability by social groups to promote and utilize entrepreneurship as a means to push for the ethical positions that they strongly believe in.

The long-term impact of this social activist-based entrepreneurship remains to be seen. Several of these businesses have grown significantly and have become highly profitable. Others have grown and then have been acquired by food giants. Certainly large companies hold the capital and power necessary to implement significant change. Their concerns are certainly more market driven than driven by ethics and/or environ-

mental concerns. However, if these smaller firms can establish that there are markets for organic products and the like, then the food giants will step in.

To date, examples of acquisitions besides the ones mentioned in this article already, are Heinz' acquiring Near East Foods, and Castle and Cooke's acquiring several organic raisin growers. Nazario (1989) notes that other large food producers such as Sunkist are starting to produce organic produce and 20 large supermarket chains have begun to stock organic produce.

The purpose of this article has been to examine the linkages between business, ethics, and the environment as they relate to food production. Certainly the linkages exist and have recently received much greater scrutiny. While it is not expected that the general public will completely embrace the philosophies of dynamic compassion and/or vegetarianism, certain aspects of these ethical arguments are being more accepted. Proponents of movements have also come to realize that business may be their most effective source for achieving meaningful change in behavior. The ultimate impact of these movements presents some very interesting research opportunities.

BIBLIOGRAPHY

Akers, Keith, *A Vegetarian Sourcebook*, Vegetarian Press, 1993.

Altman, Nathaniel, *The Nonviolent Revolution*, Element Books: Great Britain, 1988.

Burros, Marian, "A Harvest of Organic Produce, In the Wake of Pesticide Fears," *New York Times*, March 29, 1989, p. C-1.

Carson, Gerald, *Men, Beasts and Gods*, Charles Scribner: New York, 1972.

Caton, Greg, *Lumen: A Food for a New Age*, CNCAISIEV GRAPHICS: Louisiana, 1988.

Goldstein, Jason, ed., "Entrepreneuring Today for a Healthy USA," *In Business*, April, 1989.

Hawken, Paul, "Entrepreneurs: The Real Cultural Revolutionaries," *Utne Reader*, Jan./Feb., 1989, pp. 72 -73.

Kelly, Marjorie, "Revolution in the Marketplace," *Utne Reader*, Jan./Feb., 1989, pp. 54 - 63.

Kotzch, Ronald, "The Pioneering Spirit of Ohsawa Japan," *East-West Journal*, October, 1986.

Nazario, Sonia, "Big Firms Get High on Organic Farming," *Wall Street Journal*, March 21, 1989, B-1.

Smith, Patti, "Whole Earth Farming," *East-West Journal*, October, 1988, pp. 80 - 85.

INTERVIEWS

Caton, Greg, C.E.O. Lumen Foods

Dreuling, Denny, Manager, Whole Earth Food Cooperative

Hozapfel, Robert, President, The Book Publishing Company

Lessens, Stanford, President, Green Earth Foods

Posner, Howard, Former C.E.O., 21st Century Foods

Pritchard, Gil, Barbara's Bakery

ETHICAL ENTREPRENEURS WITH A MISSION

By Wayne Smeltz, Ph.D.

Researchers who study organizations have different methods for classifying them. For example, one researcher may group together all businesses which sell food to stores and then group together all businesses which retail the food to the public.

Henry Mintzberg, an organizational researcher, developed classifications based on how authority and power are set up and used within the organization. Five of his organizational types have been readily verified by analyzing and classifying ongoing organizations. A sixth configuration, *the missionary form* (ethical for our purposes), is an organization centered on a <u>cherished</u> <u>mission</u> which dominates all organizational activity, preempting systems of authority, expertise, and politics.

However, the missionary configuration is not as well documented as the other forms, nor is it easily recognizable, especially when classifying business organizations. Yet, Mintzberg (1988) maintains that this configuration may be the prevailing business structure of the future. In a related article, Quinn, Mintzberg, and James (1988) argue that many businesses are currently trying to implement elements of the missionary form because it is thought to enhance the culture and the subsequent success of the organization.

The ability to incorporate missionary elements into existing organizations is also seen as important because of its close tie-in with business ethics and codes. The increased concern over ethics is not only being voiced by large businesses (for example, Business Roundtable, 1988), but also by social activist groups, which advocate a form of missionary entrepreneurship to encourage meaningful social change.

Mintzberg hypothesizes that a missionary organization works best when the mission is clear and focused, distinctive, and inspiring to all members. *The objective of each member is to preserve, extend, and/or perfect the mission.* As a result, the organizational leaders can trust that employees will make decisions in the organization's interest. Impact from influences outside the organization seems to be minimal since the organization's members either avoid external influence or aggressively pacify any would-be influence as part of the process of imposing the firm's mission on selected targets. Survival is important only to sustain the mission, not the organization. The missionary organization consists, essentially, of a group of people who know what they have to do and do it with a minimum of supervision, work standards, action plans, performance controls, and all the other formal paraphernalia of structure. Mintzberg believes that members have every incentive to cooperate, because they share common goals and seek no personal rewards.

Mintzberg identifies three main variations of the missionary configuration (with many in-between):

1. THE REFORMER: This form of organization attempts to bring about significant change in society. The nature of the attempted change can range from the social activism of a Ralph Nader (or animal rights and vegetarian groups) to the revolutionary change envisioned by the Bolsheviks. The dilemma faced by this form is how to keep members loyal and unadulterated by external forces while they are out working among these forces. Selznick (1952) points out that typical responses to this dilemma are assimilation within society or isolation from society.

2. THE CONVERTER: This form seeks to change society by attracting members to join their movement and embrace its ideology. It is not as open as the reformer, and the issue of assimilation and isolation are of even greater concern among Converters. For example, Niv (1978) classified communes as Converters and notes that their failure rate has been high.

3. THE CLOISTER: This form intentionally seeks to isolate itself from society.

Mintzberg concedes that it may be difficult to classify a given organization or movement neatly into one of these three categories. There are inherent pulls that any organization experiences which often place it between any pure organizational types. Mintzberg presents several hybrid types that combine elements of the missionary type and the other five he developed.

One such form is called the *quasi-missionary*, which is an organization that for all intents and purposes should not be missionary, but evolves into one. This variation begins with a typical mission with employees seeking promotion, political power, and material rewards. However, as the firm evolves, the ideology of the firm begins to replace typical objectives, and employees are recruited who believe in this ideological basis. This type of firm is evidenced by many Japanese firms and "excellent" firms described by Peters and Waterman in the popular book, *In Search of Excellence.*

Another hybrid is the evolution from a missionary configuration to a typical one which Mintzberg calls the *pseudo-missionary*. On the surface, this form appears to operate with a missionary thrust, but in actuality it operates as a tool for its members to acquire prestige or power. Social service agencies and charities are seen to be prone to this type of evolution.

The final hybrid is actually an autocracy that is being manipulated by its leader (usually an entrepreneurial figure) to operate under a missionary guise. This approach is often taken by individuals who seek to make a quick profit (economic or name recognition) by seizing on opportunities previously identified by reformers who seek to make meaningful change. These individuals will either develop a "me-too" product or a product or service that claims to satisfy a significant unfulfilled need.

If Mintzberg's theoretical missionary organization exists, one should be able to identify it from a sample of organizations. All of Mintzberg's missionary examples are social activist, religious, or communal-type organizations. The only exception is Japanese firms which are not pure missionary types, but are described as quasi-missionary types. I am looking to see if his theory can be applied to a business population.

The clearest distinction among organizations should be found in the importance of the mission and use of ideology by the organization. I developed four hypotheses to differentiate the groups.

HYPOTHESIS 1: The pursuit of a cherished mission will be a significantly more important start-up and managerial factor for missionary entrepreneurs than for other entrepreneurs.

HYPOTHESIS 2: Missionary entrepreneurs will choose employees based on a desired match of ideological beliefs, while other executives will choose employees on professional and cost considerations.

HYPOTHESIS 3: Missionary organizations are less likely to have business plans and formalized goals than other organizations.

HYPOTHESIS 4: Missionary types will perceive environmental factors such as competition to be less important than will other types of organizations.

STUDY

Data was collected by survey and structured interviews conducted by the author (Wayne Smeltz, Ph.D.) as part of a study examining the role of ethics in the start-up and management of entrepreneurial firms in the natural foods industry. The subjects consisted of 42 entrepreneurs who were also the chief executive officer and five individuals who were either running the firm for the entrepreneur(s) or who had bought out the firm. Forty-one of the 47 respondents were in charge of for-profit organizations, 2 were in charge of food co-ops with a profit tax status, and 4 were in charge of non-profits.

To test the first hypothesis mentioned above, an eight-item scale was utilized that asked respondents to rank their rationale for starting up or taking over this type of business. Four additional items asked respondents to rate, on a five-point scale, how much effect the importance of serving a social good and contributing to social change had on their choice of mission.

To test the second hypothesis, respondents were asked whether employees were hired based on a belief in the firm's ideology or based on traditional factors such as expertise or cost considerations. Respondents were also asked whether compatible employees and organizational values enhanced performance as well as whether they were satisfied with the performance of their employees.

To test the third hypothesis concerning the use of formalized control mechanisms, items were developed to determine when and if the firm had instituted a formalized business plan, growth objectives, and mission statement. To test the fourth hypothesis concerning perceived environmental impact, items were developed to indicate the executive's perception of the level of competition and the impact that competition had on the firm. Another question asked respondents to indicate their level of apprehension over the prospect of large firms entering and taking over the market.

RESULTS

Survey results showed a strong relationship between respondents' answers and whether the businesses were missionary or traditional firms. Through analysis of the responses, organizations were correctly identified 87% of the time, or 41 out of 47 cases. Three of the six cases were missionary forms that had been taken over by traditional owners while two cases were missionary forms (food co-ops) managed by traditional managers. Overall, analysis of the survey provided support for the idea of a separate concept of a missionary business.

Results for hypothesis 1 provided support for the importance of mission as a cornerstone of a missionary organization. The first test, a comparison of reasons for entering this type of business, provides strong support of the greater importance placed on the mission by missionary entrepreneurs. Wealth, as expected, was less important to missionary leaders than for traditional leaders. However, both groups were motivated by serving a need in society and also believe that small business is a significant force in achieving needed social change.

Analysis of data on hypothesis 2 showed only partial support. One significant supporting difference was that missionary executives believed that a match of employees' values with the firm's values enhances performance. One reason for the lack of support for the difference in the two types of organizations was that many missionary entrepreneurs found it very difficult to hire workers with similar values. Another factor which applied to both groups was the extreme difficulty they had finding good workers.

For hypothesis 3, answers tended to be in the same direction. Only one item, formalized business planning, was statistically different. Perhaps it is not surprising that there is no significant difference for the existence of a formalized mission, given the nature of a mission-driven firm, which may balance the tendency towards informality. The same may be said for all types of businesses that are trying to grow either for profit or to spread a mission.

For hypothesis 4, there was significant statistical support for two of the three items. Traditional entrepreneurs note a significantly higher level of competition and see this competition as having a great deal of impact on how they do business. Missionary entrepreneurs do not seem to consider competition as having an impact on their operations. This latter perception was reinforced during the interviews.

DISCUSSION

In this study there was strong support for the idea that a segment of entrepreneurs begin organizations to serve a cherished mission and that this factor distinguishes them from typical entrepreneurs. These "ethical entrepreneurs with a mission" see themselves as part of a social movement and see entrepreneurship as a means for expressing and extending their missionary beliefs.

The findings obtained in this research suggests that there is an entrepreneurial personality, regardless of the philosophy behind the start-up of the business. This entrepreneurial personality may develop over time (the result of being in a competitive situation which modifies the founder's outlook) or this perspective may exist from the onset. The former perspective is supported by an analysis which indicated that several firms that started as missionaries then adopted traditional organization attributes.

BUSINESS ETHICS SURVEY RESULTS

Total number interviewed of traditional cases = 20
Total number interviewed of missionary cases = 27

ATTEMPTING TO CLASSIFY ORGANIZATIONS BY TYPE

CASES	# OF CASES	SURVEY CORRECTLY PREDICTED
TRADITIONAL	20	17
MISSIONARY	27	24

ORDER OF REASONS MOST GIVEN FOR ENTERING NATURAL FOOD INDUSTRY

TRADITIONAL	MISSIONARY
1. Autonomy and independence	1. Be creative
2. Be creative	2. Cherished mission
3. Implement own ideas	3. Autonomy and independence
4. Pride in workmanship	4. Pride in workmanship
5. Wealth	5. Implement own ideas
6. Cherished mission	6. Wealth
7. Acclaim of others in same business	7. Acclaim of others in same business
8. Acclaim and notoriety	8. Acclaim and notoriety

COMPARISON OF BELIEFS AND TRAITS OF TRADITIONAL AND MISSIONARY ENTREPRENEURS

(Statistically there was not enough difference in results to make conclusions about all items.)

IMPORTANT TO TRADITIONAL	MORE IMPORTANT TO MISSIONARY SAMPLE
1. Serving a significant societal need.	1. Natural Foods Industry can make significant social change.
2. Small businesses can make a significant change.	2. Feel more part of a movement than an entrepreneur.
3. Formalized growth objectives.	3. Compatible values enhance performance.
4. Formalized mission.	4. Formalized business planning less important.
5. Fear of large firms entering market.	5. Impact of competition less important.

Research on non-profit entrepreneurs (e.g. Young, 1983) also reinforces the notion of an entrepreneurial orientation, which when combined with a missionary sense will be the necessary catalyst for organizational formation.

The missionary-motivated organization is seen to be an important member of the organizational population because of the vision of its entrepreneurial leader and also because of the vitality noted by Mintzberg in persisting toward the accomplishment of a cherished mission. These entrepreneurial types appear to be willing to take on risky, almost unpopular, ventures because of belief in what they are doing. Often their ventures are involved in controversial businesses which operate within hostile environments. However, these entrepreneurs are also closely tied into social activist networks which provide support and guidance.

BIBLIOGRAPHY

Corporate Ethics: A Prime Business Asset. The Business Roundtable, 1988.

D. Miller and H. Mintzberg, "The Case for Configuration," Working Paper, McGill University, 1980.

H. Mintzberg, *The Structuring of Organizations.* Englewood Cliffs: Prentice Hall, 1979.

_____, *Power In and Around Organizations.* Englewood Cliffs: Prentice Hall, 1983.

_____, "The Structuring of Organizations," in *The Strategy Process*, Quinn, Mintzberg, and James (eds.), Englewood Cliffs: Prentice Hall, 1988, pp. 276-304.

_____, *Mintzberg on Management.* New York: The Free Press, 1989.

A. Niv, "Survival of Social Innovation: The Case of Communes," Working Paper, The Jerusalem Institute of Management, 1978.

T. Peters and R. Waterman, *In Search of Excellence.* New York: Harper and Row, 1982.

J. Quinn, H. Mintzberg, and R. James (eds.), *The Strategy Process.* Englewood Cliffs: Prentice Hall, 1988, pp. 344-345.

A. Selznick, *The Organization Weapon: A Study of Bolshevik Strategy and Tactics.* New York: McGraw-Hill, 1952.

D. Young, *If Not For Profit, For What?* Lexington: Lexington Books, 1983.

Dr. Smeltz is writing a book about ethical entrepreneurs, focusing on the natural foods industry. This article and the previous article are excerpted from his research.

DON'T GET BUGGED BY INSECTICIDES

By Craig D. Reid, Ph.D.

In 1963, while Rachel Carson strolled through the lush spring woodlands of Indiana, with her feet crunching through what appeared to be a wispy layer of late winter snow, she wanted to absorb the sights and sounds of nature. However, that layer of snow was the residues of haphazard applications of DDT. Rachel saw and heard no birds, bees, or animals. It was a silent spring.

Because of her classic book, *Silent Spring*, Rachel Carson gave birth to the anti-pesticide movement. She was one of the first to recognize that even though there was no immediate danger, consumption of pesticide-contaminated food products over a lifetime could lead to future health problems.

In 1987, the Environmental Protection Agency (EPA) warned that pesticide residues in food were one of the most serious health hazards facing the American public. Pesticides, such as insecticides and herbicides, are compounds used to kill specific organisms. However, because of the careless use of pesticides, humans have inadvertently become a target. Insecticides are the most dangerous because they attack basic physiological processes such as nerve transmission which are common to insects and humans.

Three federal government agencies share responsibility for pesticides and monitoring their residues in the U.S. food supply. The EPA registers or approves the use of pesticides based on evidence that their use will not cause an unreasonable risk to health or the environment. They also set tolerances (maximum amount of a residue permitted on food) for pesticide use that may lead to residues in food. The U.S. Department of Agriculture (USDA) monitors meat, poultry, and egg products for pesticide residues and the Food and Drug Administration (FDA) monitors produce and enforces tolerances on imports and interstate-shipped domestic foods. Ironically, there is no mandatory inspection system for fish unless the product was raised on a fish farm.

As more Americans learn about the association between good health and increased consumption of fruits and vegetables, they will eat more of these products. This also implies that consumers will be ingesting more pesticide residues. The National Academy of Sciences (NAS) has reported that children eat more insecticide residues than adults because they consume more fruits and vegetables per pound of body weight. The 1989 Natural Resources Defense Council (NRDC) report showed that 34% of a preschooler's diet was fruit, compared to 20% of an adult's. For example, the average preschooler eats six times more grapes, five times more apples and oranges, and three times more broccoli than the average adult.

Furthermore, the NRDC contends that more than 50% of a person's lifetime cancer risk from exposure to cancer-causing pesticides in foods is incurred during the first 6 years of life. Moreover, the average preschooler consumes five times more cow's milk than an adult woman. The EPA estimates that at least 60% of a preschooler's exposure to captan (a probable carcinogen which cows receive from contaminated feed) comes from milk.

The 1990 FDA Total Diet Study found 53% of the cow's milk tested to contain DDT and dieldrin, chemicals banned 21 years ago.

In 1987, the NAS studied 28 pesticides approved by the EPA for use on food and concluded that exposure to them could result in 20,000 cases of cancer each year (Sonberg, 1992). Furthermore, the NRDC calculated that the actual risk of all pesticides in our food and drinking water could represent more than one million additional cases of cancer over the course of our lifetimes.

Children are more vulnerable to residue ingestion because their livers are unable to detoxify many of the chemicals. Probable carcinogens, like benomyl, permithrin, captan, dieldrin, and heptachlor, which are also neurotoxins, can cause damage to the developing nervous system. Studies have also linked pregnant women's exposure to pesticides to increased risk of miscarriage and premature labor (Heins, 1991).

The four major classes of insecticides present on produce are organochlorines (DDT, PCB's), organophosphates (malathion, parathion), carbamates (carbaryl, also known as Sevin), and pyrethroids (in some circles, botanicals). The pyrethroids resmethrin and allethrin are the active ingredients of "Raid."

Insecticides function to disrupt proper nerve transmission. Organochlorines (O.C.'s) and pyrethroids disrupt the flow of sodium ions into the nerve axon. Organo-phosphates (O.P.'s) and carbamates block the activity of acetycholine, a neurotransmitter which is responsible for carrying nerve signals between nerve cells.

When a pesticide has been approved for use on a crop, that doesn't mean the chemical was used or that the residue will be present at the time of harvest. For example, there are more than 100 pesticides approved for use on apples, yet according to the 1990 FDA Total Diet Study, only the residues carbaryl, captan, and endosulfan were ever found in 20 percent of the samples tested.

When a fruit or vegetable is contaminated with a known residue, the processed products from that produce will be even more contaminated. Therefore, a 12-ounce glass of apple juice will contain more residue than 12 ounces of apples. In addition, some pesticides become more toxic after being processed.

When alar (fungicide)-treated apples were processed into apple juice or applesauce, the carcinogen UDMH (unsymmetrical dimethylhydrazine) was formed, adding further to the product's contamination.

Residues found in meat, meat products, cow's milk, milk products, and eggs are a result of what the animal is fed. Just remember that most residues will accumulate in the skin and fat. The fat, skin, and dark meat of many products made from sea animals can contain PCB's, DDT, and dieldrin, with some species being laced with mercury, which can cause brain damage. Meat-eaters must also contend with meat containing antibiotics, hormones, sulfa drugs, and other toxic residues.

One could easily think that we are drowning in a sea of toxic waste. But there are ways to limit the ingestion of these toxic residues.

⇒ **Wash fruits and vegetables using a dilute soap solution and peel them completely to remove surface residues.** However, keep in mind this may remove some of the nutritional value and will not affect the residues that may have been introduced systemically into the produce.

⇒ **Buy certified organically grown fruits and vegetables.** If a local market doesn't carry organic food, see the produce manager and write a letter to corporate management declaring your concerns about residues and that you want the option of buying organic. Investigate mail-order organic foods and local farmers' markets where you can personally ask the grower which chemicals were used. Although domestically grown products usually have lower residues, some foreign items, for example, citrus fruit, have less. (See Table 1.)

⇒ **Select baby foods carefully.** Earth's Best is one company that provides baby food made with organically grown produce.

Heinz voluntarily excluded from its baby food 12 pesticides considered potentially hazardous by the EPA, and in 1991, Beech-Nut launched a new line of certified organically grown baby food.

⇒ **Peel waxed produce if possible.** Waxing can trap food pesticide residues, naturally occurring fungi, and benomyl, a fungicide that is often added to waxes to prevent spoilage during shipping.

⇒ **Try growing some of your own produce**. Weed the plots and remove the pests manually.

Try not to be too cynical about government agencies. For example, the FDA recently pulled all boxes of Lucky Charms and Cheerios, because the manufacturer used oats contaminated with a chemical not registered for use on oats, chlorpyrifos-methyl.

Consumers simultaneously demand high quality agricultural products and food that is free of toxic chemicals. Being Americans, we refuse to eat worm laden apples or corn that has little "wiggly" caterpillars sticking out of the kernels. Although entomologists are working hard to develop alternative forms of pest control, consumers may need to change their views on the aesthetics of their food and be willing to eat blemished fruits and vegetables.

REFERENCES

Food and Drug Administration. *Residues in Foods 1990*. J. of Assoc. of Official Analytical Chemists. Volume 74, 1991.

Heins, Henry C. *Your Healthy Pregnancy*. American Baby, March 1991.

Natural Resources Defense Council. *Intolerable Risk: Pesticides in Our Children's Food*. 1989 NRDC Report.

Sine, C. *Farm Chemicals Handbook*. Meister Publ. Co., Ohio, 1993.

Sonberg, Lynn. *A to Z Guide to Toxic Foods*. Simon and Schuster, N.Y., 1992.

TABLE 1

Percentages of pesticide residues found in some common domestic and imported fruits and vegetables. (Based on 1990 FDA Total Diet Studies)[1]

PRODUCT	% RESIDUE (Domestic)	% RESIDUE (Imported)
Apples	56	46
Apricots	38	56
Bananas	13	28
Barley	46	*
Blueberries	38	28
Broccoli	13	25
Cabbage	17	35
Cantaloupe	22	63
Carrots	49	47
Cauliflower	8	8
Corn	0	0
Grapefruit	70	23
Grapes	22	40
Green Beans	45	48
Lemon	76	61
Lettuce	55	51
Mushrooms	24	10
Oats	53	25
Onions	7	15
Oranges	77	22
Peaches	64	57
Pears	55	49
Peas	31	40
Pineapple	0	29
Plums	31	49
Potatoes	53	29
Rice	17	8
Soybeans	41	*
Spinach	50	63
Squash	14	37
Strawberries	75	78
Tomatoes	38	50
Wheat	64	*

[1]Percentages indicate the percent of the product tested that contained pesticide residues.

*Percentages either not known or not measured.

Dr. Craig D. Reid received his Ph.D. in entomology from the University of Illinois. He is an Integrated Pest Management specialist with training in toxicology, medical entomology, and chemical ecology.

Small-Space, Little-Work (Well, Almost)
Vegetable Gardening

By Judith Grabski Miner

Vegetarians feel a special relationship with plants. Peter Singer noted this when he wrote in Animal Liberation, "Without meat to deaden the palate we experience an extra delight in fresh vegetables taken straight from the ground." So this distinguished philosopher followed the example of many vegetarian friends and took up vegetable gardening.

You may be hearing the call back to Eden yourself. Life in the '90s, though, means that your back 40 is probably a forty-foot yard and that you will have to squeeze your agricultural chores into an already overbooked lifestyle. The solution to this dilemma? A well-planned, well-tended small garden patch that fits the space and time you have. Your mini-garden won't make you food self-sufficient, but it will put plenty of fresh organic vegetables on your table for much of the year.

If you want the nutritional and flavor advantages that just-picked food can provide, first select a sunny, well-drained, and fertile site for your garden. You can improve drainage and fertility, but only Nature can supply the abundant sunshine vegetables must have to thrive. You may be able to let the sunshine in by trimming shrubs or tree branches, but if something immovable (like a building) is casting shade, look for another garden spot. (By the way, dare to break the rules, if you must. Plants, like people, sometimes flourish despite adversity.)

Try to avoid putting a garden where puddles linger for hours after a rain. Plants don't like wet feet! The simplest way to improve drainage is to build raised beds for your plants, which is easier than it sounds. You can find directions in a good gardening book.

Your soil will become more fertile as you work in compost, other organic matter, and rock powders like lime and rock phosphate. Mulches from your lawn clippings or shredded leaves cost nothing and do wonders. Feed your soil and it will feed you, the old-timers say. They're right!

If you are turning a patch of lawn into a vegetable garden, be prepared for some hard work the first year. You need to break up the sod and try to remove roots of obnoxious perennial weeds. You may have trouble with destructive insects, like wireworms and white grubs, that live in grassy soil. Just remember that the first year is the worst, and your garden will get less weedy every year thereafter.

For sod-busting, rent or borrow a powerful rear-tine rototiller. You can also dig up the garden site with a spade or spading fork -- a back-breaking job, but great exercise for the physically fit. Again, check your gardening book for directions.

You should have an inexpensive, but essential, soil test done by your county Extension Service (probably in the phone book under United States Government -- Agriculture Department), or you can buy your own kit. The test will tell you how acid or alkaline your soil is and what to do about it, as well as levels of nitrogen, phosphorus, and potassium (NPK in gardening jargon). Plants resist pests and disease better when they are grown in well-balanced soil.

How big should you make your garden? Smaller than you think it should be, if you are a new gardener. Nothing turns new gardeners into ex-gardeners faster than watching the patch you planted in April turn into an impenetrable jungle of weeds and bugs in July. First see whether you can find time for and enjoy the work load of a tiny garden. If so, you can always make it bigger next year.

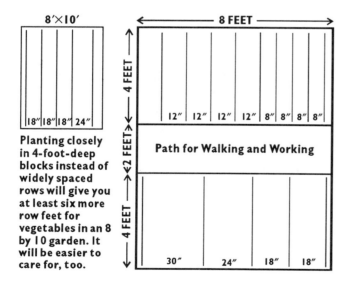

Planting closely in 4-foot-deep blocks instead of widely spaced rows will give you at least six more row feet for vegetables in an 8 by 10 garden. It will be easier to care for, too.

Besides, that little garden is going to yield more vegetables than you expect, if you plan it right and tend it faithfully. **The trick to producing a lot in a small space is to use every inch of soil for growing vegetables, not for walkways or unneeded between-row space.** You can comfortably reach across two feet for tending and harvesting. So, if you are running your vegetable garden along a fence, make it two feet deep. If your plot sits surrounded by lawn, make it four feet deep and work it from both sides.

Even a larger garden, say ten by ten feet or ten by twenty feet, can utilize this layout method. Put a two-foot-wide path down the middle, leaving four-foot-deep planting sections on each side. This wide dividing row will allow you to sit or kneel comfortably as you tend or pick the four-foot sections.

Don't waste space by planting everything in single rows one to two feet apart within the sections. Instead, think of the space a mature plant takes. That is what you need between plants. Space between rows should equal the top growth of the plant. For example, a leaf lettuce plant needs about eight inches between rows. As the lettuce plants grow, thin them out in the rows (eat the thinnings) until the plants are six inches apart. Beets need about three inches between plants in rows, and rows eight inches apart (to give room to the edible leafy top growth). Give broccoli plants about 18 inches and staked tomatoes 30 inches. Your goal is to space the rows so the top growth of the plants will touch and form a canopy. This will shade the soil around the plants and discourage weed growth. If you are using close spacing, remember to maintain soil fertility by adding plenty of organic matter.

As for what to plant, choose vegetables that 1) you like; 2) produce abundantly in a small space; and 3) taste much better when absolutely fresh. When every inch counts, those high-yielding turnip greens nobody will eat are just wasting valuable space.

Plants that produce the most in the least space include leafy greens (like lettuce, Swiss chard, and kale), root vegetables (carrots, beets, and rutabagas), zucchini, staked tomatoes, broccoli, and green beans. Put up a 36-inch-high trellis and you can raise quantities of crisp oriental snow peas. Cucumbers can also grow on a trellis. Each broccoli plant yields a large head and numerous side shoots after you cut the head. Just-picked green peas (that need shelling) and sweet corn taste scrumptious fresh, but yield poorly in relation to the room they require.

You can save space in your vegetable garden by growing bell peppers and eggplants as ornamentals among your flowers. Some tomato varieties, like Pixie, Presto, and Patio, can thrive in containers on (you guessed it) your patio.

To keep your garden productive all season, **plant small amounts at regular intervals.** A garden diagram and planting schedule will help you use your space well. As soon as the ground thaws and dries out enough to work, you can put in all the spinach you want for a spring crop. Other hardy vegetables for early planting include leaf lettuce (two to four row feet are enough), broccoli transplants (three plants will give you flowerets until winter), cabbage, radishes, tiny onion bulbs called sets (for green onions), snow peas, chard, and root crops. In two months, the spinach, radishes, and green onions will be gone. Replant their space with another crop. You should put in another two feet of lettuce every four weeks for a continuous supply (lettuce bolts to seed, but not so rapidly as spinach). You can replant onion sets continuously. One small planting of Swiss chard and kale will last until very cold weather. As you harvest leaves, the plants produce more.

Crops like green beans, cucumbers, zucchini, and transplants of peppers, eggplant, and tomatoes should go in after danger of frost. Two six-foot rows of beans planted three weeks apart will keep you in beans all season. If you pick all the beans off, the plants will reflower and bear another crop. One zucchini plant will supply all the zucchini you may care to eat.

Most hardy crops do well when planted again for a fall harvest. Determine your planting date by finding out the average date of your area's first frost and counting back how-

ever many days are required for maturity. For example, beets take sixty days. If your first frost usually comes around October 7th, plant your fall beets no later than August 7th. They will continue to grow until the weather becomes consistently cold. Kale, broccoli, and the cabbage family taste best after a few good frosts.

Swiss Chard

At the end of the gardening season, put your garden to bed by tilling or digging in all non-diseased plant residues, or add them to your compost pile. Cover the soil with shredded leaves or dry glass clippings. Take stock of your results. What did well? What didn't? (Often how plants do depends more on weather, rainfall, and pest outbreaks than on the quality of your care.) Did you have too much of something and too little of something else? Did you like the taste and size of a variety enough to plant it again, or should you try a different one next year?

Then, take a breather until the seed catalogs come in January. If you are like most gardeners, you will spend the winter impatiently anticipating another gardening season of good food, good exercise, and good, dirty fun.

Judy Miner has grown vegetables organically in Vermont for over twenty years.

WHOLESOME BABY FOODS FROM SCRATCH

By Karna S. Peterson, R.D., M.P.H.

Making your own baby food is simple, convenient, and can save you money. Nutritionally, it's hard to beat the wholesomeness of foods right from your kitchen. You can feed baby some of your family's regular foods knowing that they are free from the additives and fillers found in some store-bought baby foods.

Family foods, if prepared with salt, spices, sugar, or fat, are not suitable for infants. You will need to prepare foods separately, or remove the baby's portion before salt, sugar, or other seasonings are added.

Making your own baby food doesn't require a lot of expensive equipment. At a minimum, all you need to get started is a clean pot to cook in and equipment to get the foods to the right consistency.

EQUIPMENT FOR PURÉEING BABY FOODS

- Some foods, such as bananas and other ripe fruits, require only a **fork** for mashing. A **potato masher** also works well to purée cooked apples, winter squash, potatoes, or carrots. Be sure to remove lumps, pieces of skin, strings, or seeds before feeding to baby.

- A fine mesh **sieve** or **strainer** may be used to strain cooked foods.

- Most foods can be puréed with a **blender.** Be sure to remove tough peels and seeds from vegetables and fruits before blending or they will be ground into the food. Use a blender to grind a handful of uncooked brown rice, cook well until soft and smooth, and you have a nutritious, inexpensive cereal for baby. For a good source of protein, nut butters (like peanut butter) can be made in a blender from whole nuts. Thin with water or formula into a consistency suitable for older babies.

- Raw or cooked foods can handily be prepared in a small, hand-operated **baby food mill.** Peels and seeds are strained out of the food, and its small size is perfect for taking to the table or restaurant.

- Some foods are ready to serve baby right from the grocery store. Try canned pumpkin, unsweetened applesauce, instant mashed potatoes, Cream of Wheat or rice cereal for quick, ready-to-eat additions to meals.

PREVENT FOOD-BORNE ILLNESS

Cleanliness is a priority when making foods for baby. Bacteria can easily upset a baby's digestive system; so anything that touches the food -- your hands and all equipment -- must be absolutely clean. The same rule applies when storing, heating, and serving baby foods, too. Always wash your hands and equipment with hot, soapy water, rinse, and let air dry.

COOKING METHODS

Steaming is one of the best cooking methods to preserve vitamins and minerals in foods.

Place the food in a steam basket, sieve, or colander above boiling water and cook in the rising steam.

Microwave cooking is another way to prepare foods, especially vegetables, which cook quickly in very little water.

Boiling or simmering fruits and vegetables is an acceptable cooking method but will result in loss of some nutrients in the cooking water. Be sure to use only a small amount of water and save the cooking liquid to thin the puréed food to eating consistency.

Since babies do not have a preference for salty or sweet, you should not add salt or sugar to their food. It's a good idea to keep your child from developing an early taste for such additions. Studies suggest that feeding babies too much sodium may trigger high blood pressure later in life in those individuals who are likely to develop high blood pressure.[1]

SERVING AND STORING BABY FOODS

Puréed foods spoil more easily than other foods; so baby's food must be used immediately or frozen for future use. If you store food in the refrigerator, keep it in there only 2 to 3 days. If you don't use it by then, it should be discarded. Remember: refrigeration does not kill bacteria; it only slows down their growth.[2, 3]

Large batches of puréed foods can easily be frozen in ready-to-use serving sizes. One such method is to pour puréed food into plastic ice-cube trays, cover with waxed paper, and freeze. When frozen, transfer cubes to freezer bags. Another method is to "plop" drops of puréed food on a cookie sheet, freeze, and then transfer to freezer bags. These frozen portions will keep about one month.

Thaw cubes in the refrigerator, in a double boiler, in the microwave (at low setting), or in the plastic bag under cold water. Do not thaw at room temperature.

WHAT TO SERVE

- Fresh and frozen fruit juice, fruits and vegetables without added sugar or salt.
- Home-canned and frozen fruits and vegetables without sugar, salt, or seasonings.
- Whole-grain cereals such as rice, oats, barley, corn, and other grains. As with any new food, wait 5-7 days before adding another new food to see if any allergic reactions occur.

Honey Alert: Do not feed honey in any form to infants under 1 year of age. Serious food poisoning (infant botulism) may result.[4]

RECIPES

Here are some simple baby food recipes to get you started.

COOKED LEAFY GREENS
(Makes 10 food cubes)

Many of the most nutritious veggies, especially the green leafy ones, are not available in commercial baby foods. It's easy to make your own.

1 pound fresh greens (kale, collards, etc.)
1 Tablespoon water
3 Tablespoons fruit juice

Wash leaves thoroughly. Steam most greens 5-15 minutes, leaving the lid off for the first few minutes. Purée in blender with the water and juice.

TOTAL CALORIES PER CUBE: 11
TOTAL FAT AS % OF DAILY VALUE: <1%   FAT: <1 gm
PROTEIN: <1gm   CARBOHYDRATES: 3 gm
CALCIUM: 11 mg   IRON: <1 mg   SODIUM: 6 mg
DIETARY FIBER: <1 gm

BASIC VEGETABLE RECIPE
(Makes 8 food cubes)

Do not add salt, sugar, or fat.

1 cup cooked fresh or frozen vege-
    tables without salt (use potatoes,
    green beans, peas, carrots, yellow
    squash)
4-8 Tablespoons cooking liquid,
    formula, or water

Press vegetable chunks through a sieve or
baby food mill, thinning with cooking liquid
or formula to eating consistency. Or, purée
vegetables and liquid in blender until smooth.
Serve or freeze.
    Note: After trying single foods, good
combinations are potatoes and carrots or
carrots and peas.

NUTRITIONAL ANALYSIS PER SERVING: VARIES

FRESH FRUIT
(Makes 4 food cubes)

Try different varieties of fruit in this recipe.

3/4 cup ripe fruit (uncooked peaches,
    nectarines, bananas, pears, apri-
    cots, apples, etc.)
1 teaspoon unsweetened fruit juice
1 teaspoon lemon-flavored water (1
    teaspoon lemon juice to 1 cup
    water to prevent darkening)

Remove skin and seeds from fruit. Purée
ingredients in baby food mill or blender until
smooth. Serve or freeze.

NUTRITIONAL ANALYSIS PER SERVING: VARIES

KNÄCKBRÖD
(SWEDISH HARD BREAD)
(Makes 20)

*Unlike store-bought varieties, this homemade
version of "hard tack" crumbles and melts in
baby's mouth and is great for teething.*

1 cup all-purpose flour
1 cup graham flour
2 Tablespoons sugar or other
    sweetener
1/2 teaspoon baking soda
1/2 teaspoon baking powder
8 ounces commercial corn muffin
    mix, dry (check for animal fat)
3 Tablespoons soft margarine
3/4 cup soy milk

Mix dry ingredients. Cut in margarine. Add
soy milk. Mix well. Roll thin, cut into shapes
and bake 10-15 minutes at 350 degrees until
brown.

TOTAL CALORIES PER CRACKER: 114
TOTAL FAT AS % OF DAILY VALUE: 5%   FAT: 3 gm
PROTEIN: 2 gm   CARBOHYDRATES: 19 gm
CALCIUM: 20 mg   IRON: 1 mg   SODIUM: 194 mg
DIETARY FIBER: 1 gm

SOYBEAN PURÉE
(Makes 2-1/2 cups or 12 food cubes)

Serve this nutritious dish to your baby.

1 cup dry soybeans
3 cups water
3/4 cup unsalted tomato juice for
    thinning

Rinse and soak the soybeans overnight in the
refrigerator. Simmer beans in 3 cups water
for about 2 hours. Purée with any equipment, adding tomato juice to thin.

TOTAL CALORIES PER CUBE: 42
TOTAL FAT AS % OF DAILY VALUE: 3%   FAT: 2 gm
PROTEIN: 3 gm   CARBOHYDRATES: 4 gm
CALCIUM: 23 mg   IRON: 1 mg   SODIUM: 2 mg
DIETARY FIBER: <1 gm

FRESH ORANGE SHERBET
(Makes 1-2 cups)

Babies will love this dish.

1 sweet orange, peeled, sectioned, and seeds removed
1 cup fruit juice

In a blender, liquefy the fruit. Add the juice and blend. Pour into loaf pan, cover, and freeze until fairly firm, about 1 hour. Pour back into blender, and blend at low speed until smooth. Return to pan and freeze until firm.

TOTAL CALORIES PER 2 TABLESPOONS: 15
TOTAL FAT AS % OF DAILY VALUE: <1%   FAT: <1 gm
PROTEIN: <1 gm   CARBOHYDRATES: 4 gm
CALCIUM: 6 mg   IRON: <1 mg   SODIUM: 1 mg
DIETARY FIBER: <1 gm

HOMEMADE FRUITY GEL
(Serves 4)

This recipe uses fruit juice instead of sugar to add sweetness. Agar, the thickener, is derived from seaweed. It is available in natural food stores and food co-ops or may be ordered from the Community Mercantile, 901 Mississippi, Lawrence, KS 66044. Phone 913-843-8544. An ounce of agar costs $5-$6 but it goes a long way.

1/2 cup cool water
1 Tablespoon agar flakes
1-1/2 cups fruit juice
1 cup puréed fruit

Place water in small saucepan. Sprinkle in agar and stir to dissolve. Add juice and heat for 1 minute, stirring well. Pour into 4 small cups. Place in refrigerator. After 1/2 hour, stir in puréed fruit.

NUTRITIONAL ANALYSIS PER SERVING: VARIES

CARROT/APPLE MIX
(Serves 2)

This is a delicious dish.

1/2 medium apple, cored and peeled
1/2 carrot, washed and peeled
2 Tablespoons fruit juice
1 teaspoon lemon juice

Purée all ingredients in blender. Or, grate apples and carrot and mix with juice before serving.

TOTAL CALORIES PER SERVING: 34
TOTAL FAT AS % OF DAILY VALUE: <1%   FAT: <1 gm
PROTEIN: <1 gm   CARBOHYDRATES: 9 gm
CALCIUM: 7 mg   IRON: <1 mg   SODIUM: 8 mg
DIETARY FIBER: 1 gm

REFERENCES

[1] National Research Council (1989) *Diet And Health -- Implications for Reducing Chronic Disease Risk,* Washington, D.C.: National Academy Press.

[2] USDA (1992) *Food News for Consumer,* p. 9, Winter.

[3] Cooperative Extension Service, Kansas State University, Manhattan, Kansas: "Making Baby Food," L-524.

[4] S. S. Arnon et al. 1979, "Honey and other environmental risk factors for infant botulism," *Journal of Pediatrics* 94:331-336.

Karna Peterson is a Registered Dietitian in Kansas.

Healthy Fast Food for Pre-Schoolers

By Lisa Rivero

"Peanut-butter-and-jelly-sandwich-and-juice, peanut-butter-and-jelly-sandwich-and-juice."

The chant usually begins to come from my pre-schooler's bedroom at about 6:00 a.m. He wakes up early, and he wakes up hungry. For the rest of the day, our kitchen will be the busiest room in the house. If he's not eating a meal, he's eating a snack, or requesting a glass of juice or soy milk.

All parents of pre-schoolers know the challenge of providing nutritious, fast foods for our children. We are often tempted by the convenience of packaged "goodies," but we know our children are better served by wholesome meals and snacks.

Parents of vegan pre-schoolers face the additional challenge of finding healthful dairy-free and egg-free fast foods. And peanut butter and jelly goes only so far.

I've found that by serving several mini-meals throughout the day, I'm less likely to succumb to a lot of packaged snack foods. By following a few guidelines, I've been able to keep my son happily and healthfully fed, without spending hours over a stove.

PLAN TO HAVE LEFTOVERS

First, plan to have leftovers, especially leftover grains. When you're cooking pasta or rice for supper, make a little extra for tomorrow's lunch, then dress it up with a vegetable-based sauce. Introduce a variety of grains by occasionally making barley or millet instead of rice. The next time you're in the grocery store, look for pastas made of corn (kids love the bright yellow color), amaranth, spelt, artichoke, brown rice, and buckwheat flours. Children seem to like small pasta shapes such as spirals, shells, wagon wheels, elbow macaroni, and, of course, alphabet pasta. To make spaghetti more manageable for young children, snap it into two or three pieces before cooking.

Some children like cold foods, and will eat leftovers straight from the refrigerator. If you want to warm up leftover rice or vegetables, simply steam them for a minute or two, then fluff with a fork. Leftover pasta can be reheated for a few seconds in boiling water, then drained. Cooked vegetables and grains can also be puréed and used as sauces, spreads, or puddings.

BUILD ON FAMILIAR TASTES

Pre-schoolers often have a few select foods that they like to eat again and again. If your child is going through a nothing-but-green-peas phase, serve peas with brown basmati rice or whole wheat couscous, or even alone in a bowl drenched with a nutritious sauce. A little peanut butter mashed with cooked beans may be more acceptable to your pre-schooler than the beans alone. Adding a bit of fruit juice is another good way to lend familiar flavor to unfamiliar foods.

SATISFY YOUR CHILD'S SWEET TOOTH NATURALLY

Satisfy your child's sweet tooth naturally with ripe bananas, sweet potatoes, winter squash, and dried fruit. If your child is used to having sweet desserts, try offering a fruit ambrosia salad made with sliced bananas, cubed steamed sweet potatoes, and a sprinkling of chopped dates or dried apricots.

Ten Speedy Breakfasts
Beyond the Peanut Butter and Jelly Routine

Fast breakfasts for pre-schoolers can be almost any combination of grains and vegetables or fruits that your child enjoys. Here are some ideas to get you started.

1) Mash a ripe banana, add a spoonful or two of wheat germ, and moisten with soy milk. Sprinkle with raisins and cinnamon. Children learning to use a spoon love this cereal.
2) Mix leftover whole-wheat couscous with grated carrot and peas. Top with Orange-Raisin Sauce.
3) Scramble some soft tofu, stuff it in a whole-wheat mini pita, and drizzle with Quick Carrot Sauce.
4) Fill a whole-wheat mini pita with Simple Peanut Butter/Tahini Sauce and chopped dates.
5) Dip chunks of steamed sweet potato in Banana Pudding Sauce.
6) Mix mashed cooked butternut squash with cinnamon or nutmeg and a diced apple. Thicken with soft, fresh bread crumbs.
7) Make a breakfast smoothie with soft tofu, soy milk, and your child's favorite soft fruit.
8) Grind some low-fat granola in a blender (children sometimes have difficulty chewing whole nuts and seeds). Mix ground granola with unsweetened applesauce, or sprinkle it over Sweet Potato Fig Sauce.
9) Simmer a handful of bread cubes and some leftover rice with mashed soft tofu, some soy milk, dried currants, and a touch of cinnamon for a warm breakfast pudding.
10) We call this dish Tofu Albert: Toast one-half of an English muffin. Top it with a very thin slice of firm tofu, add some steamed broccoli or sliced bananas, and drench with Sweet Albert Sauce.

KEEP FOOD SIMPLE
Perhaps nothing is more frustrating than spending an hour making a complicated meal that your child refuses to touch. Children are often less suspicious of simple dishes, and by spending less time cooking, you can spend more time with your child.

LET YOUR CHILD HELP
Let your child help to fix the food whenever possible. Even a two-year-old can mash tofu or add dried fruit. While you're in the kitchen, talk to your child about the ingredients you're using, and give the child a choice when you can -- for example, "Should we put a banana or an apple in this cereal?"

EAT WITH YOUR CHILD
You'll not only be providing companionship, but if you eat the same food your child does, your example will be more influential than your pleading or reasoning.

If you pack a lunch or snack for your pre-schooler, consider sending pasta salads made of multi-colored pasta, broccoli trees, and a simple sauce. Or pack a fondue lunch with a thick dip, cubed vegetables and fruit, and bread sticks or whole-grain crackers. Small whole-wheat pita pockets can be filled with bean spreads or stuffed with shredded vegetables. Older children enjoy home-made trail mixes consisting of pieces of dried fruit, nuts, and sugar-free cereals.

Here are six fast sauces that you can make in a blender, no chopping or cooking required. If you always have on hand pre-cooked or canned legumes and some steamed sweet potatoes, you can make each of these sauces in five to ten minutes, just about the maximum waiting time of a hungry pre-schooler! If you've tried unsuccessfully to get your child to eat beans or tofu, these sauces may be your answer.

My son likes these sauces over pasta, but you can also use them to dress up rice, pancakes, fruit, or vegetables. Or you can reduce the amount of liquid, and serve them simply in a bowl with a spoon.

SIMPLE PEANUT BUTTER/ TAHINI SAUCE
(Serves 2 to 3 children, or 1 child and 1 adult)

Toss this comforting sauce with macaroni and peas, or use as a dip for carrot sticks and pita triangles.

2/3 cup cooked navy beans
2 to 3 Tablespoons peanut butter or toasted sesame tahini
1/4 to 1/3 cup water, orange juice, or apple juice

Blend all ingredients in a blender until smooth.

TOTAL CALORIES PER CHILD'S SERVING: 121
TOTAL FAT AS % OF DAILY VALUE: 9%   FAT: 6 gm
PROTEIN: 6 gm   CARBOHYDRATES: 12 gm
CALCIUM: 32 mg   IRON: 1 mg   SODIUM: 50 mg
DIETARY FIBER: 3 gm

SWEET ALBERT SAUCE
(Serves 2 to 3 children, or 1 child and 1 adult)

Drizzle this delicious sauce over a bowl of fruit chunks for a special breakfast or fast dessert.

Half a 10.5 ounce package soft silken tofu
1/4 cup brown rice syrup
1 to 2 Tablespoons almond butter, peanut butter, or tahini
1 teaspoon brown rice vinegar
2 to 4 Tablespoons water

Blend all ingredients in a blender until smooth.

TOTAL CALORIES PER CHILD'S SERVING: 140
TOTAL FAT AS % OF DAILY VALUE: 8%   FAT: 5 gm
PROTEIN: 3 gm   CARBOHYDRATES: 23 gm
CALCIUM: 40 mg   IRON: 2 mg   SODIUM: 24 mg
DIETARY FIBER: 1 gm

BANANA PUDDING SAUCE
(Serves 2 to 3 children, or 1 child and 1 adult)

Pour over pancakes or waffles, or mix with cooked rice and sprinkle with cinnamon and raisins for an instant rice pudding.

Half a 10.5 ounce package soft silken tofu
1 very ripe banana
1/4 to 1/3 cup plain soy milk or water

Blend all ingredients in a blender until smooth.

TOTAL CALORIES PER CHILD'S SERVING: 75
TOTAL FAT AS % OF DAILY VALUE: 3%   FAT: 2 gm
PROTEIN: 3 gm   CARBOHYDRATES: 13 gm
CALCIUM: 22 mg   IRON: 1 mg   SODIUM: 21 mg
DIETARY FIBER: 1 gm

QUICK CARROT SAUCE
(Serves 2 to 3 children, or 1 child and 1 adult)

Serve this Oriental-style sauce over rice and stir-fried bok choy or thinly shredded cabbage. It's a great source of vitamin A (beta-carotene).

1 cup grated raw carrot (1 medium-
    large carrot)
1/4 to 1/3 cup water
2 ounces soft tofu
1 teaspoon soy sauce
1 teaspoon toasted sesame oil
1/8 teaspoon dried ground ginger

Blend all ingredients in a blender until smooth.

TOTAL CALORIES PER CHILD'S SERVING: 44
TOTAL FAT AS % OF DAILY VALUE: 3%   FAT: 2 gm
PROTEIN: 2 gm   CARBOHYDRATES: 4 gm
CALCIUM: 43 mg   IRON: <1 mg   SODIUM: 128 mg
DIETARY FIBER: 1 gm

SWEET POTATO FIG SAUCE
(Serves 2 to 3 children, or 1 child and 1 adult)

My son likes to eat this sauce with nothing more than a spoon. It's another great Vitamin A source.

3/4 cup cooked, mashed sweet potato
1/3 to 1/2 cup water or plain soy
    milk
2 teaspoons toasted sesame tahini
Pinch of ground nutmeg
4 dried figs, chopped

Blend sweet potato, water or soy milk, tahini, and nutmeg in a blender until smooth. Stir in figs.

TOTAL CALORIES PER CHILD'S SERVING: 174
TOTAL FAT AS % OF DAILY VALUE: 3%   FAT: 2 gm
PROTEIN: 3 gm   CARBOHYDRATES: 38 gm
CALCIUM: 61 mg   IRON: 1 mg   SODIUM: 15 mg
DIETARY FIBER: 5 gm

ORANGE RAISIN SAUCE
(Serves 2 to 3 children, or 1 child and 1 adult)

Toss with wagon wheel pasta and steamed green beans, or serve over brown rice and peas.

3/4 cup cooked chickpeas
1/4 to 1/3 cup orange juice
1/2 teaspoon mild curry powder
1/4 cup raisins

Blend chickpeas, orange juice, and curry powder in a blender until smooth. Stir in raisins.

TOTAL CALORIES PER CHILD'S SERVING: 137
TOTAL FAT AS % OF DAILY VALUE: 2%   FAT: 1 gm
PROTEIN: 6 gm   CARBOHYDRATES: 27 gm
CALCIUM: 46 mg   IRON: 2 mg   SODIUM: 8 mg
DIETARY FIBER: 1 gm

Lisa Rivero is the proud mom of a vegan pre-schooler.

CHILDREN IN THE KITCHEN!!!

By Amy Shuman, R.D.

Does this visualization inspire you or depress you? While working with children in various settings throughout the years, I have found that if we are properly prepared for their energy and willingness to help, then we can provide for optimum learning and growth experiences (and the making of special memories) for all involved.

No matter what the age of the child, a good rule is "safety first!" These ideas may help to make sure that the kitchen is a safe haven for those little helping hands:

- Maintain close supervision around heat. Never let a child near hot oil or boiling syrups.

- Point all saucepan handles toward the back of the stove to avoid spills and burns.

- Use long-handled wooden spoons, which don't get hot.

- Use extra-big bowls to avoid spills and large messes.

- Use small oven mitts for older children. (You can shrink an adult-size mitt in your dryer.)

- Use aprons to protect clothing. (An adult's old shirt put on backwards for fun, or a cobbler's small apron or frock, can be used.)

- Cut fruit/vegetables in half; then place flat side down to cut. Use a cutting board on a flat surface for chopping.

- Teach children the proper way to use equipment. If you have hand-beaters or hand-graters, let the child experiment with these.

- When older children use an electric mixer, show them the slow and medium speeds. Use an extra-large bowl with a wet dish towel underneath to keep it steady.

- Allow young children to have their own cooking equipment drawer or cupboard to store their special things.

- Use a serrated plastic knife for young children. Older children can use regular knives to chop fruits and vegetables.

As you begin to think about a meal or snack, imagine what you will be doing and what the children in your life can do to help. Prepare some things ahead of time, if needed. When it's time to work together, make sure that the work space is at the child's level. For instance, place a sturdy chair with its back to the stove, sink, or counter for the child to hold onto for balance. Use stools of various heights to make the experience pleasant. Of course, cooking activities offer a great opportunity to teach cleanliness. Children need to learn always to wash their hands before preparing or eating any meals or snacks. Gentle reminding is often necessary, sometimes for years, in order for these ideas to become ingrained as habits.

While working with children in schools, clinics, and at home, I have found the following recipes always to be fun for them. Adapt as necessary to fit to the needs of your family.

SPARKLING FRUIT JUICE

Children enjoy "adding the bubbles," even when they are very young.

Put ice in a cup and then half fill with your favorite unsweetened juice, such as orange, pineapple, or apple. Add seltzer water to fill cup. You can also add a piece of fruit if desired.

APPLE SANDWICH

Use a serrated knife for safety. Help children find the "star" in the center of the apple.

Slice favorite apple crosswise into about 6 to 8 slices. Spread peanut butter on half the slices and top with another slice of apple to make sandwiches.

TRAIL MIX

Large quantities of this mix keep well if stored in a tightly covered container or jar. Use any mixture of cereals and fruits that your children like.

1/2 cup your favorite breakfast cereal
1/2 cup Wheat or Corn Chex or other cereal
1/2 cup Bite-Sized Shredded Wheat
1/2 cup small pretzel sticks or tiny pretzels
1/2 cup peanuts (omit for children under age 5)
1/2 cup raisins or other chopped dried fruit

Combine all the ingredients in an oversized bowl and mix gently with a wooden spoon.

PAPER PLATE DELIGHT

This activity is great for birthday parties or rainy days. Allow a lot of time to be creative and then to consume their treat.

Give each child a paper plate. Encourage them to arrange assorted pieces of fruit or vegetables, such as pears, apples, bananas, raisins, strawberries, grated carrots, or sprouts to make a face or entire body design such as a clown or monster. An example would be a peach half face with raisin eyes, banana-slice ears, a strawberry mouth, and grated carrot hair.

FUNNY SANDWICHES

Offer children a plate of all types of toppings and allow them a lot of time to be creative.

Spread whole wheat bread with any variety of nut butter. Decorate with fruit, vegetables, nuts, seeds, etc., to make faces. Grated carrot or cabbage or bean sprouts make fun hair.

From the time my nephew, Ben, was two, he helped my husband, John, make whole-grain oatmeal yeast bread. During those early years, the three of us huddled closely together, with me holding Ben on a high "bar-type" stool. Ben could then add flour into a bowl, one cup at a time, as Uncle John kneaded it. My mom lent me old-fashioned tiny loaf pans that she had collected through the years and "Ben's buddy bread" became "the thing" to do. He asked John to bake every day during his two-week vacations with us. As he grew, the jobs became more involved, until the time that he helped to knead the bread and would insist on putting a "nose print" in it, as it smelled so good. The idea here is to "match the child's age to the job." This list may help to identify what to expect from children.

AGE 2

- Spin lettuce and tear it into bite-sized pieces
- Mix bean or nut loaves with hands
- Help set table (maybe put out napkins)
- Put pre-measured dry ingredients into an over-sized bowl.
- Put in a pinch of salt.

AGE 3

- Gather ingredients
- Pour frozen vegetables into a pot to be steamed
- Count carrots for a vegetarian stew
- Squeeze a lemon or orange
- Mix dough for muffins/cookies
- Cut greens (with child-size blunt-edge scissors)
- Snap fresh beans

AGE 4

- Cut parsley or other herbs with blunt-edge scissors
- Shuck fresh corn
- Cut cucumbers/strawberries/bananas with a plastic knife
- Mix homemade salad dressing
- Mix cereal
- Wash grapes/apples
- Continue to learn more about setting a table

AGE 5

- Make sandwiches/peanut butter crackers
- Fill napkin holders
- Stir pudding
- Make cake/other desserts

AGE 6

- Mash potatoes
- Do simple recipes once child can read
- Learn to measure correctly

AGE 7 ON UP

- Progress as child learns more
- Make tofu French toast/pancakes (takes coordination)
- Peel/chop harder vegetables
- Put water on to boil

When I was a child, my mom decided that, because I was always underfoot in the kitchen, she would "give me" the drawer at my eye level underneath the oven. She tells me stories of how I would play for hours with the metal measuring cups and spoons, small pots and pans, etc., that she had designated as mine. She gave me a real gift -- my "own stuff" and the freedom to play as I liked in an area where she spent a lot of time.

Here are a few more ideas that might help you to assist your children in the kitchen:

1. Cooking boosts self-confidence and self-image. Children are artists. Let them create something that is pleasing to their eyes and stomachs.
2. Children don't eat "because it's good for them." They eat because it looks and tastes good.
3. Don't expect perfection. Let children be creative. Be sure to offer praise.
4. Children are more likely to eat something they helped prepare or grew in a garden.
5. Helping children learn to be self-sufficient combats their wanting all the convenience foods on television advertisements. Being "couch potatoes" decreases activity levels, and encourages eating foods which are high in fat, sugar, and salt.
6. If vegetables are disliked, wait awhile and give the child a chance for change. Then reintroduce the foods.
7. Serve small portions. As adults, we think children should be eating much more than they usually need. For the first few years, offer one tablespoon of each food for each year of the child's age.
8. Don't bargain by saying statements such as, "Eat everything and you get dessert." Children like a food even less when this is suggested. Give a taste of dessert and don't make it a big deal.
9. Allow children to experience hunger and how hungry they are. In America, we have forgotten what it is to be hungry. We generally eat three meals a day, regardless of our body's needs.
10. Adults can set healthy eating patterns for children. Be a good role model!
11. Smart parents learn that it's more fun at mealtime to serve colorful, nutritious foods that taste good, and have the kids happy and eating, than to face fights at each meal. Mealtime should be pleasant, not a battleground.
12. Create a party-like atmosphere. Have a picnic inside on the floor on a rainy day or create an Italian night with a red and white tablecloth and some special napkins. Your children will think mealtime is the greatest!
13. Parents can share more time with children when they involve them in mealtime. While learning, the children get attention and enjoy the fact that they are helping.

Our local WIC program features a video for parents and caretakers of children ages 2 through 5. Its title, *No Better Gift,* is well chosen. The narrator states at the end that, "there may be no better gift to give our children than the sense of good nutrition." My challenge to readers is this: Find a child, even if there are none in you life at this time, and plan some special food experiences to create positive memories for that little one. Making food fun helps us to be children again. Relive the fun and enjoy! At the same time you will be teaching vegetarianism to young children.

Amy Shuman, R.D., works for the Allegany County, Maryland Health Department. She designed and produced a video, with an accompanying cookbooklet called, Cooking with Ben and Aunt Amy, in which Amy's 10-year old nephew starred with her. Many of the ideas presented in this article are taken from that compilation of information. To obtain one of the cookbooklets, send a self-addressed stamped envelope with two first-class stamps to: Amy Shuman, R.D., PO Box 1745, Cumberland, MD 21501-1745.

EAT BETTER, PERFORM BETTER:
SPORTS NUTRITION GUIDELINES FOR THE VEGETARIAN

EATING TO EXERCISE AND COMPETE

Enette Larson, M.S., R.D.

Active individuals often wonder what, and even if, they should eat before a workout -- especially when hunger seems to strike just around workout time -- or when the race or tennis match begins too early to consider eating beforehand. Experienced athletes may remember eating the wrong food at the wrong time and wondering why they felt awful or performed poorly. Can the timing and choice of foods consumed close to and during a workout really make a difference in how you perform?

Following a good diet with adequate amounts of energy, carbohydrates, protein, vitamins, and minerals is critical for optimal performance. No one performs their best by starting a workout hungry or with low glycogen (carbohydrate) stores or after eating the wrong types of food too close to exercising. Also, failing to replace depleted carbohydrates, protein, and fluids after a workout can decrease performance in the days that follow. Because the recommendations for food and fluid intake before, during, and after exercise vary somewhat with different sports activities, this article will cover guidelines for all types and levels of vegetarian athletes.

FUELING UP BEFORE -- THE PRE-EVENT MEAL

The purpose of eating prior to a workout or competition is to provide the body with fuel and fluid. The idea is to choose foods which will prevent hunger, provide additional carbohydrate fuel, and minimize possible intestinal complications. Generally, the meal should be consumed far enough in advance to allow for stomach emptying and intestinal absorption. A good rule of thumb is to limit the pre-event meal to about 800 calories, and give yourself one hour before the workout for each 200 calories you eat. For example, 5 pancakes, syrup, a banana, and juice would be eaten about 4 hours before a workout. A smaller 200 calorie meal such as a bowl of cereal or a bagel and juice would be eaten between 1 and 2 hours before starting. Meal timing is especially important in activities such as running, aerobic dancing, and swimming, and less critical in sports such as cycling. Athletes who have a "nervous stomach" before competition may find liquid meals such as blenderized fruit shakes with tofu or soy yogurt easier to tolerate.

The pre-event meal should contain fluid and foods that are high in carbohydrates, and low in fat, protein, salt, simple sugars, and concentrated fiber. Cereal with sliced bananas and skim milk or juice, pancakes with fresh fruit topping, oatmeal with fruit, a baked potato topped with soy yogurt and vegetables, and tofu spread on bread with fruit are good examples. Too much protein, fiber, and fat in the pre-event meal can lead to heartburn, nausea, diarrhea, or constipation in certain individuals.

Adequate fluid intake is the single most important recommendation for all types of exercise.

SUPPLEMENTING -- INTAKE DURING THE EVENT

Replacing both fluid and carbohydrate during exercise is important. What and how much to replace depends on the type, duration, and intensity of the exercise. Adequate fluid intake is the single most important recommendation for all types of exercise. The general recommendation is to drink 1/2 to 1 cup of water every 10 to 20 minutes. In a hot environment, when perspiration is especially heavy, drinking up to 2 cups of water every 15 minutes may be necessary to replace fluid losses. Adequate hydration enables the active body to regulate its temperature effectively and allows for good circulation and muscle function.

Carbohydrate replacement is necessary in events lasting longer than 90 minutes and may even be beneficial during high intensity exercise of shorter duration. This applies to both continuous events like cycling, running, and hiking, and sports with intermittent activity like soccer and weight training. Under these conditions, consuming carbohydrates during exercise increases both the time and the intensity the athlete is able to exercise before becoming exhausted. Researchers believe that carbohydrate feedings delay fatigue by providing additional fuel for the working muscle and preventing blood sugar from dropping.[1] A carbohydrate intake of approximately 30 to 80 grams per hour[2] (1 to 3 large bananas or 15 to 60 ounces of a 6 to 7% fluid replacement beverage) are recommended for delaying fatigue during prolonged strenuous exercise.

REFUELING -- THE POST-EVENT MEAL

The meal following a workout is nutritionally the most important meal for aiding recovery from exercise and maintaining the ability to train the following days. Fluid, carbohydrate, and protein intake after exercise is critical, especially after heavy exercise. A high carbohydrate intake is required to replace depleted muscle glycogen stores. Delivery of a protein source may also aid in repairing and rebuilding damaged muscle tissue and replenishing the amino acid stores. Collective evidence indicates that exercise significantly alters protein metabolism, especially as the exercise becomes more prolonged and more strenuous.[3] Since the body begins to replace its depleted stores and repair any microscopic damage to muscle fibers almost immediately after exercise, provision of these depleted nutrients in the post-event meal may accelerate recovery.

Researchers investigating the role of carbohydrate in exercise performance suggest that consuming a carbohydrate source starting 15 to 30 minutes after exercise, followed by additional carbohydrate feedings, will optimize muscle glycogen replacement.[4] Delaying the ingestion of carbohydrates by several hours slows down the rate at which the body is able to store glycogen. For the casual exerciser, this means packing a piece of fruit, fruit juice, or a fluid replacement beverage for a post-workout snack, and then eating a mixed high carbohydrate and protein meal (such as pasta with lentil spaghetti sauce or tofu, vegetables, and rice) shortly thereafter. For the heavily training endurance athlete, a meal containing both a good source of protein and 100 grams of carbohydrate is recommended, followed by additional carbohydrate feedings every 2 to 4 hours.

Guidelines for Planning The Pre-event Meal

	Protein (Grams)	Carbohydrate (Grams)
200 CALORIES		
- 2 Starch Servings	6	30
- 1 Fruit Serving	0-4	6-15
	6-10	36-45
400 CALORIES		
- 3 Starch Servings	6	45
- 1 Fruit or Vegetable	0-2	5-15
- 1 cup Fruit Juice or 4 oz. Tofu	0-9	3-15
	6-17	53-75
600 CALORIES		
- 4 Starch Servings	8	60
- 2 Fruit or 6 Vegetable	0-12	30
- 1 cup Fruit Juice or 4 oz. Tofu	0-9	3-15
- 1 tsp. Preserves or Syrup	0	13
	8-29	106-118
800 CALORIES		
- 5 Starch Servings	10	75
- 3 Fruit or 6 Vegetable	0-12	30-45
- 1 cup Fruit Juice or 4 oz. Tofu	0-9	3-15
- 1 tsp. Preserves or Syrup	0	13
	10-31	121-148

ONE STARCH SERVING:
- 1/3 cup cooked rice, legumes, sweet potato
- 1/2 cup corn, potato, cooked cereal, pasta (cooked)
- 3/4 cup ready-to-eat cereal
- 3/4 cup winter squash
- 1 slice bread, 6-inch tortilla, 4-inch pancake
- 1/2 bagel, bun, English muffin, 6-inch pita bread

ONE FRUIT SERVING:
- 1 average piece fruit
- 1/2 banana or mango
- 1/2 cup fruit, canned fruit, or fruit juice
- 2 TB raisins, 3 prunes, 7 apricot halves

ONE VEGETABLE EXCHANGE:
- 1/2 cup non-starchy vegetable

Note: The fat content of the pre-competition meal can vary with food choices. Select foods that contain no more than 2 grams of fat per serving. Any more than this will increase both the calories and the fat composition of the pre-exercise meal greater than that recommended.

FASTING -- A DETRIMENT TO PERFORMANCE

Research shows that meal skipping and fasting can be detrimental to performance. An overnight fast depletes sugars stored in the liver (liver glycogen) and can contribute to light-headedness and the early onset of fatigue.[5] A high carbohydrate meal before exercise increases the carbohydrate available for the exercising muscle which provides benefit during both prolonged endurance exercise and high-intensity exercise. Starting any exercise session hungry or light-headed, however, keeps you from performing your best. If time or calories are a factor, eat a small high-carbohydrate snack (banana, bagel, cereal, vegan "energy bar") about an hour and a half before exercise or drink a glass of a fluid replacement beverage about 10 minutes prior to exercise.

FIBER -- A HELP OR A HINDRANCE?

Vegetarian diets are generally high in both soluble and insoluble fiber. A small amount of soluble fiber before or during exercise may be beneficial by preventing rapid highs and lows in blood sugar. However, some athletes are sensitive to fiber before exercise,[6] especially major competitions. If you experience stomach or intestinal cramps, or diarrhea before exercise, limiting high fiber foods such as legumes, whole grain products, bran products, and dried fruit in the meal preceding exercise may eliminate this distress. Sensitive athletes may need to reduce their fiber intake 24 to 36 hours before competition. Regular meal times and bowel habits also prevent exercise-induced intestinal complications.

It is also important to consider that adequate fiber intake is easily met and often exceeded by vegetarian athletes who have high calorie intakes. Sometimes, trying to eat a high calorie diet containing excess fiber can cause discomfort. Cyclists, for example, participating in a simulated Tour de France had difficulty maintaining adequate energy intake of 8,000 to 10,000 calories when whole grains and high fiber food were selected.[7] Those athletes with high calorie intakes should not be overly concerned about fiber and should select a variety of high carbohydrate foods that both contain fiber and are low in fiber (white bread, pasta, white rice, potatoes without skin, and fruit juice).

CONCLUSIONS AND PRACTICAL IMPLICATIONS

- Maintain an overall diet high in complex carbohydrates and low in fat. Eating a well-balanced diet containing adequate amounts of calories, protein, vitamins, and minerals is critical for optimal performance.

- Choose pre-exercise meals that work well for you, including complex carbohydrates and fluids. Limit fat, protein, salt, and simple sugar. Before major competitions, don't shock your body by introducing unfamiliar foods.

- Fasting or meal skipping before exercise can impair performance. Wait approximately 1 hour for every 200 calories you consume before exercise.

- Drink plenty of fluids during exercise. If exercise lasts longer than 90 minutes, eat or drink 30 to 80 grams of carbohydrate per hour to prolong performance time.

- To aid recovery from exercise, consume a high-carbohydrate snack within 30 minutes after exercise and follow with a mixed high carbohydrate and protein meal.

- If you experience stomach or intestinal complications during exercise, your pre-exercise meal may have been too high in fat or fiber.

SELECTED REFERENCES

[1] Coyle EF, Coggan AR, Hemmert MK and Ivy JL. Muscle glycogen utilization during prolonged strenuous exercise when fed carbohydrate. J Appl Physiol 61:165-172, 1986.

[2] Murray R, Paul GL, Seifert JG and Eddy DE. Responses to varying rates of carbohydrate ingestion during exercise. Med Sci Sports Exerc 23:713-718, 1991.

[3] Paul G. Dietary protein requirements of physically active individuals. Sports Medicine 8:154-157, 1989.

[4] Coyle EF. Carbohydrates and athletic performance. Gatorade Sport Science Exchange 1(7), 1988.

[5] Hultman E. Nutritional effects on work performance. Am J Clin Nutr 49:949-957, 1989.

[6] Rehrer NJ, vanKemenade MC, Meesler TA, Saris WHM and Brouns F. Nutrition in- to GI complaints among triathletes. Med Sci Sports Exerc 22:s107, 1990.

[7] Brouns F and Saris WHM. Diet manipulation and related metabolic changes in competitive cyclists. American College of Sports Medicine Annual Meeting, 1990.

VITAMINS, MINERALS AND EXERCISE PERFORMANCE

What's in a vitamin and mineral pill except all the vitamins and minerals your body needs to do those sit ups, run that extra lap or win tonight's game? Unfortunately, many of us are misled into thinking that vitamin and mineral pills are packed with "magic fat burners," "energy boosters" or "performance enhancers" -- or perhaps just take supplements for "nutritional security." While the concern about meeting our vitamin requirements when exercising regularly and following a vegetarian diet is certainly legitimate, neither the need to worry about or the need to supplement a balanced vegetarian diet is necessary. This article will address the vitamin and mineral needs of the beginner, casual exerciser, and serious vegetarian athlete and how these nutrients influence exercise performance.

VITAMIN AND MINERAL REQUIREMENTS FOR ACTIVE VEGETARIANS

Vitamins and minerals are required in the diet in small amounts primarily to regulate important body processes. With the exception of vitamin D, vitamins and minerals cannot be made by the body, and must be obtained from the diet. Certain vitamins can also be made by "helpful" bacteria living in the gut. Although the role of these nutrients is varied, their function during exercise is to help the body obtain energy from carbohydrate, fat, and protein and to help build and repair blood cells, muscle, and other tissues.

Regular exercise does not appear to increase the need for most of the vitamins and minerals despite the excess demands placed on the body during exercise. Exercise, however, has been found to increase the need for certain vitamins such as riboflavin and the loss of some trace minerals from the body. For most active individuals, the vitamin and mineral needs can be met by a vegetarian diet containing adequate calories from a variety of vegetables, fruit, and whole grain sources.

The B-Complex Vitamins. The B vitamins are often called the "Energy Vitamins." These vitamins do not actually serve as fuel themselves -- but as helpers in converting carbohydrates, fat and protein into energy. The requirements for three of these vitamins -- thiamin, niacin and riboflavin -- are increased with increasing calorie requirements and are therefore elevated in active individuals. Research has suggested that the riboflavin requirement is independently elevated in women at the start of an exercise program[1] but may be elevated only until certain stores are built-up. Generally, meeting the requirements for the B vitamins is easy if you get enough calories and are consuming legumes and whole or enriched grain products. For the beginning exerciser, good food sources of riboflavin include spinach, broccoli, and turnip greens.

Vitamins A, C, and E. One role of vitamin A, C, and E is to prevent the deterioration (or oxidation) of body tissues. Recent research suggests that these vitamins work as antioxidants to reduce a specific exercise-induced reaction known as free radical formation.[2] Free radicals may have damaging effects on muscle and other tissue. The antioxidant vitamins occur naturally in many fruits and vegetables including apricots, broccoli, Brussels sprouts, cabbage, carrots, kale, spinach, squash, sweet potatoes, and tomatoes.

Calcium. Calcium is an important component of muscle contraction, nerve function and bone maintenance. Exercise, however, does not increase the requirement for this mineral. Maintaining an adequate calcium intake, nevertheless, is very important. Studies suggest that low calcium intakes are linked to increased incidence of stress fractures,[3] especially among women who have abnormal menstrual cycles. Athletes, therefore, need to be aware of their calcium intake and include calcium-rich foods in their daily

diet. Good calcium sources include: tofu treated with calcium sulfate, collards, broccoli, mustard greens, turnip greens, oranges, dried figs, and legumes. Spinach, chard, beet greens, and rhubarb are not recommended as a sole source of calcium despite their high calcium content because they contain oxalates. Oxalates bind the mineral and reduce its absorption. Athletes should also recognize that excess protein intake, often as a result of consuming protein or amino acid supplements, appears to lead to increased calcium losses.[4]

Iron. Iron is a key nutrient in hemoglobin, the part of blood which carries oxygen from the lungs to the muscles, brain, and other parts of the body. Iron is present in all cells and helps the cells use oxygen. It is especially important that active individuals obtain enough iron in their diet to maintain normal levels of iron stores. Low iron levels in the blood can reduce your endurance ability during exercise[5] and can even make you feel "sluggish."

Published reports show that all athletes,[5] including vegetarian athletes[6] may be more susceptible to low iron stores than other individuals. Inadequate iron intake is the most likely culprit. Additionally, both runners and beginning exercisers often experience greater iron losses due to the destruction of red blood cells from the impact of exercise. Competitive long-distance runners also experience intestinal blood loss during competition.

To avoid low iron stores or iron-deficiency (anemia), vegetarians, particularly females, should: 1) include several iron-rich foods such as legumes, dark green vegetables, prunes, blackstrap molasses, and enriched breads and cereals in their diets each day; 2) eat high iron foods with a vitamin C source such as tomatoes, citrus fruit, cantaloupe, broccoli, or peppers to enhance iron absorption; and 3) avoid drinking tea with iron-rich foods because it contains tannin which inhibits iron absorption. Also, the use of cast-iron cook-ware to prepare foods with a long cooking time (such as baked beans) or acidic foods (such as spaghetti sauce) increases the absorbable iron content of the food. Iron supplements should be taken only if stores cannot be maintained by diet and a little planning. Iron tablets are known to cause constipation, diarrhea, and irritation of the stomach lining in some individuals.

Trace minerals. Exercise causes an increased loss of zinc and chromium in the urine.[7] Zinc and copper may also be lost in sweat. Losses of these minerals are especially a concern in warm climates. Whole grains are a good source of each of these minerals. Additionally wheat germ and legumes are high in zinc, and nuts and legumes are high in copper.

CAN VITAMINS AND MINERALS IMPROVE EXERCISE PERFORMANCE?

Since vitamins and minerals are so important in exercise, will excess improve performance? Over 40 years of research on different vita-mins and minerals suggests the same answer -- exercise performance is not enhanced by vitamin/mineral supplements unless the individual is deficient in the first place.[1,7] Athletes who are following low calorie diets for the purpose of weight loss or participation in a weight-control sport such as wrestling, judo, light-weight crew, or gymnastics, how-ever, should consider a vitamin and mineral supplement. Vitamins and minerals should not be supplemented in amounts greater than The Recommended Dietary Allowances (RDA) as recommended by the National Re-search Council unless prescribed by a physi-cian. The excess intake of many vitamins and minerals can have harmful effects.

CONCLUSIONS AND PRACTICAL IMPLICATIONS

- Meeting the body's vitamin and mineral needs is easily accomplished on a vege-tarian diet. Strive to obtain most of your calories from a variety of whole food sources including different grains, fruits, legumes, greens, and other vegetables. The need for certain vitamins and miner-als is increased by exercise. However, a varied vegetarian diet should meet these slightly elevated needs.

- Make it a practice to consume several calcium and iron rich foods each day. Both nutrients are critical to optimal physical performance. Two to three cups of dark green vegetables will provide generous amounts of iron and calcium; two to three cups of cooked dried beans can provide ample iron.

- Select whole grains and produce con-taining the antioxidant vitamins, vitamins A, C, and E, which may help to reduce exercise-induced muscle damage. Half a cup of carrots, sweet potatoes, or winter squash meets vitamin A needs. One citrus fruit or 1 cup of citrus juice or broccoli provides the daily requirement for vitamin C.

- After strenuous workouts, especially in warm environments, ensure that any zinc and copper lost in sweat are replaced by eating whole grains, wheat germ, nuts, and legumes. For example, by eating two to three cups of whole grains and legumes, a handful of nuts, and several servings of whole grain breads, trace mineral needs can be met.

- Consider taking a vitamin or mineral supplement if you are exercising and restricting caloric intake for any reason. Do not choose a supplement that provides quantities in excess of the Recommended Dietary Allowances because excess intakes can have harmful effects.

SELECTED REFERENCES

[1] Belko AZ. Vitamins and exercise -- an update. Med Sci Sports Exerc 19:S191-S196, 1987.

[2] Kanter MM and Eddy DE. Effects of eccentric exercise on skeletal muscle damage and serum antioxidant vitamin status (abstract). Med Sci Sports Exerc 23:S149, 1991.

[3] Myburgh KH, Hutchins J, Fataar AB, Hough SF and Noakes TD. Low bone density is an etiological factor for stress fractures in athletes. Ann Intern Med 113:754-759, 1990.

[4] Kerstetter JE and Allen LH. Dietary protein increases urinary calcium. J Nutr 120:134-136, 1990.

[5] Haymes EM. Nutritional concerns: need for iron. Med Sci Sports Exerc 19:S197-S200, 1987.

[6] Snyder AC, Dvorak LL and Roepke JB. Influence of dietary iron source on measures of iron status among female runners. Med Sci Sports Exerc 21:7-10, 1989.

[7] Clarkson PM. Trace mineral requirements for athletes: to supplement or not to supplement. Sports Science Exchange 4(33) July, 1991.

Enette Larson, M.S., R.D. is a doctoral student in nutrition at the University of Alabama in Birmingham.

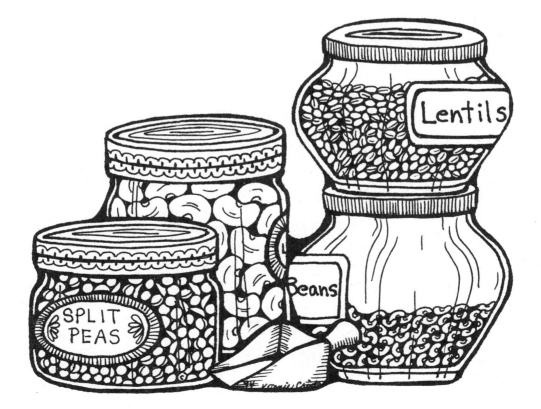

WHAT'S FOR BREAKFAST?

By Bobbie Hinman

Every morning, all across America, millions of children ask the same question and millions of parents respond. But, how many of these well-meaning parents give their children the same old boring, unhealthy breakfast day after day?

First, let's deal with the issue of nutrition. To put it very simply, carbohydrates are our bodies' main source of fuel. A nutritious breakfast that supplies us with these necessary carbohydrates would consist mainly of fruits, vegetables, grains, and nuts. So, we'll eat cereal and fruit. Right? Well, that's only partly right. Unfortunately, many of the best-selling breakfast cereals in our country are made from processed grains and added sugar.

Even well-meaning vegetarians often feed their children (and themselves) breakfasts that are very high in fat. The main culprits are cheese (including soy cheese), eggs, croissants, hashed-brown potatoes, cream cheese, butter, and even some cereals. The answer? Choose whole grain cereals that do not contain added sugar or fat. Read the labels on cereal boxes and look for ingredients such as whole wheat, whole oats, puffed rice, and puffed corn. Of course, another benefit of whole grains is that they add needed fiber to our diets.

Does all this make breakfast sound boring? Do you think that in order to give yourself or your family a healthy and hearty breakfast, you'll be doomed forever to eat puffed rice and bananas? Not so! To show you the way, I've compiled a list of some unusual and delicious breakfast ideas, followed by some tasty recipes from *Lean and Luscious, Lean and Luscious and Meatless*, and *Oat Cuisine*. I hope you and your children will find them "eye-opening."

BREAKFAST HINTS

- Mix left-over rice, or other grains, with soft tofu. Add cinnamon, vanilla, raisins, and a sweetener.

- Replace at least half of the flour in your favorite pancake recipe with whole wheat flour, corn meal or oat bran, and top your pancakes with fruit-only jams.

- Combine plain soy yogurt or soft tofu with your choice of fresh fruit. Sweeten to taste and add your favorite cereal.

- If you have a crock pot, before you go to bed, fill it with oats or rice. Add water, raisins, and cinnamon. You'll wake up to a delicious hot breakfast.

- Try a baked sweet potato topped with cinnamon, a sweetener, and sprinkled with wheat germ.

- Children of all ages will love to spread peanut butter on a sliced apple.

- Try a breakfast milkshake made from soy milk, fruit, and ice in a blender.

- Spread left-over hot cereal in a shallow pan and chill overnight. In the morning you can cut it into squares and cook it in a non-stick skillet with a small amount of soft margarine. Sprinkle with cinnamon and top with a little maple syrup for wonderful breakfast patties.

- Make a breakfast "banana split" by topping oatmeal with sliced bananas, nuts, and strawberry fruit-only jam.

BANANA TOAST
(Serves 2)

From Lean and Luscious, *this is an unbeliev- able eggless version of French toast. The whole family will love it.*

1 ripe medium banana
1/4 cup lite soy milk
1/2 teaspoon vanilla extract
2 teaspoons sweetener
2 slices whole wheat bread
2 teaspoons soft margarine
Ground cinnamon

In a blender container, combine banana, milk, vanilla, and sweetener. Blend until smooth
Place bread in a shallow pan. Pour banana mixture over bread and turn bread several times, until it has absorbed the banana mixture.
Melt margarine in a non-stick skillet over medium heat. Place bread carefully in skillet, using a spatula.
Drizzle any remaining banana mixture over bread. Brown toast carefully on both sides. Sprinkle with cinnamon.

TOTAL CALORIES PER SERVING: 175
TOTAL FAT AS % OF DAILY VALUE: 8%   FAT: 5 gm
PROTEIN: 4 gm   CARBOHYDRATES: 31 gm
CALCIUM: 37 mg   IRON: 1 mg   SODIUM: 216 mg
DIETARY FIBER: 4 gm

TOFU RICE PUDDING
(Serves 5)

From my book, Lean and Luscious and Meat- less, *this easy no-bake pudding is a favorite in our house.*

9 ounces soft tofu
1/4 cup confectioners sugar
2 teaspoons vanilla extract

1/2 teaspoon ground cinnamon
1-1/2 cups cooked brown rice
1/3 cup raisins

In a blender container, blend tofu until smooth. Spoon into a bowl and add remain- ing ingredients. Mix well.
Chill several hours to blend flavors. Serve cold.

TOTAL CALORIES PER SERVING: 151
TOTAL FAT AS % OF DAILY VALUE: 3%   FAT: 2 gm
PROTEIN: 6 gm   CARBOHYDRATES: 27 gm
CALCIUM: 100 mg   IRON: 1 mg   SODIUM: 5 mg
DIETARY FIBER: 1 gm

MUESLI
(Serves 6)

From Oat Cuisine, *this is our family's favorite version of the traditional Swiss breakfast cereal. Just mix and chill.*

1 cup rolled oats
3 Tablespoons oat bran
3 Tablespoons wheat germ
1/2 teaspoon ground cinnamon
1/8 teaspoon nutmeg
1 large, sweet apple, unpeeled,
    coarsely shredded
1/4 cup raisins
2 dried figs, chopped
1/4 cup slivered almonds
1/3 cup apple juice
1 cup lite soy milk
1/3 cup water
2 teaspoons vanilla extract
1 Tablespoon liquid sweetener

In a large bowl, combine dry ingredients. Add remaining ingredients, mixing well.
Cover and chill overnight. Serve cold. (Cereal will keep several days in the refrig- erator.)

TOTAL CALORIES PER SERVING: 179
TOTAL FAT AS % OF DAILY VALUE: 6%   FAT: 4 gm
PROTEIN: 6 gm   CARBOHYDRATES: 32 gm
CALCIUM: 56 mg   IRON: 2 mg   SODIUM: 24 mg
DIETARY FIBER: 3 gm

OVERNIGHT OATS
(Serves 6)

Steel-cut oats make a hearty stick-to-your-ribs breakfast. Put all the ingredients in the crock pot before you go to bed and enjoy a nutritious breakfast that's ready when you are.

1 cup steel-cut oats
1/3 cup raisins
1/3 cup chopped mixed dried fruit
1-1/2 teaspoons ground cinnamon
1/4 teaspoon ground allspice
1-1/2 teaspoons vanilla extract
1/4 teaspoon grated fresh lemon peel
3-1/2 cups water

Combine all ingredients except water in a large crock pot. Mix well. Add water, cover, and cook on low setting 6 to 8 hours, or overnight.

If a thinner cereal is desired, stir a little water or milk into the finished cereal. Sweeten to taste.

TOTAL CALORIES PER SERVING: 191
TOTAL FAT AS % OF DAILY VALUE: 3%   FAT: 2 gm
PROTEIN: 5 gm   CARBOHYDRATES: 41 gm
CALCIUM: 29 mg   IRON: 2 mg   SODIUM: 4 mg
DIETARY FIBER: 5 gm

SCRAMBLED TOFU SPANISH "OMELET"
(Serves 4)

Also from Lean and Luscious and Meatless, *here's a delicious, cholesterol-free substitute for a favorite egg dish. The use of turmeric, a delicately flavored spice, also adds a yellow color.*

2 teaspoons vegetable oil
1 cup chopped onions
1 cup chopped green peppers
1 pound medium or firm tofu, sliced, drained well
1/4 teaspoon garlic powder
1/4 teaspoon turmeric
1/8 teaspoon pepper
Salt to taste

Sauce:
1 eight-ounce can salt-free (or regular) tomato sauce
1/4 teaspoon dried basil
1/4 teaspoon dried oregano
1/8 teaspoon garlic powder

Heat oil in a large non-stick skillet over medium heat. Add onions and green pepper. Cook, stirring frequently, until onions are lightly browned, about 15 minutes.

While onions are browning, place tofu in a large bowl and mash with a fork. Add spices and mix well.

Combine all sauce ingredients in a small saucepan and heat until hot and bubbly.

Add tofu mixture to browned onions. Cook, stirring frequently, until heated through.

To serve, divide tofu mixture onto 4 serving plates. Top with sauce.

TOTAL CALORIES PER SERVING: 159
TOTAL FAT AS % OF DAILY VALUE: 12%   FAT: 8 gm
PROTEIN: 11 gm   CARBOHYDRATES: 14 gm
CALCIUM: 140 mg   IRON: 7 mg   SODIUM: 27 mg
DIETARY FIBER: 2 gm

NOT JUST FOR BREAKFAST:
LIGHT PANCAKES AND WAFFLES

By Nanette Blanchard

Most of the countries of the world serve some sort of pancake, from French crepes to Russian blini. Even waffles can either be Belgian or just plain American. Unfortunately, many waffle and pancake recipes are high in fat and really heavy. Is it possible to lighten up your morning pancakes? Yes, it is!

Sourdough starters, yeast, and other leaveners like baking soda and baking powder are used in dairy-free pancakes and waffles. All these batters will improve after standing; so don't be afraid to cover and refrigerate overnight before cooking. Leftover pancakes and waffles freeze quite well. I use the microwave to heat up frozen pancakes, and I pop frozen waffles into the toaster to regain their nice crispy texture.

Pancakes should be cooked on a hot griddle. One way to prepare pancakes for a large group of people at the same time is to use a large griddle or two or three non-stick skillets at once. I have a nice enameled cast iron griddle that fits over two range burners; so I can prepare about 8-10 pancakes at the same time. To keep pancakes warm until serving time, place on a platter covered with foil in a 200- degree oven. Waffles should be placed directly on your oven's racks at 200 degrees to keep warm.

All waffle irons are not created equal. I've tested several different models and found some are more non-stick than others. To prevent a sticky waffle disaster, pre-season your waffle iron each time you make a batch by brushing with vegetable oil or spraying with vegetable cooking spray. Repeat this process if you notice the waffles beginning to stick.

Whether you use your grandmother's heavy old four-waffle baker or one of the new fancy-shaped non-stick models, you really don't need to use a lot of oil to cook waffles. Some new waffle irons have a temperature setting which gives you more control over the waffle's doneness. (All the waffles in this article were tested in Vitantonio's Five-of-Hearts non-stick waffler.)

APPLE PANCAKES
(Makes 10 three-inch pancakes; serves 3)

These thick, cake-like pancakes are wonderful served with homemade applesauce.

1-1/2 cups whole wheat pastry flour
1/4 teaspoon salt
1 Tablespoon baking powder
2 Tablespoons apple juice concentrate, thawed
3/4 cup lowfat soy milk
2 green apples, cored and grated

Mix the flour, salt and baking powder together; mix the apple juice concentrate and soy milk separately. Add wet ingredients to the dry; add the grated apples and stir gently until well blended. Spray skillet with vegetable cooking spray and preheat until it is moderately hot. For each pancake, use about 3 Tablespoons of batter. Cook 3 minutes on each side or until golden brown.

TOTAL CALORIES PER SERVING: 301
TOTAL FAT AS % OF DAILY VALUE: 3%   FAT: 2 gm
PROTEIN:9 gm   CARBOHYDRATES: 68 gm
CALCIUM: 320 mg   IRON: 3 mg   SODIUM: 710 mg
DIETARY FIBER: 10 gm

SOURDOUGH STARTER

(Makes about 1 cup starter)

It is simple to make your own sourdough starter at home, and you can add prepared sourdough starter to any of your waffle or pancake batters.

1 cup warm water
1/2 cup whole wheat flour
1/8 teaspoon active dry yeast

Mix all ingredients well, cover, and let stand in a warm place for 24-48 hours until bubbly and sour-smelling.

SOURDOUGH WAFFLES

(Makes 6 large waffles; serves 3)

This recipe can be used for either sweet or savory waffles. For a delicious breakfast or dessert waffle, add either 1 cup fresh or frozen blueberries or 1 cup peeled, diced peaches, slightly crushed. You do have to prepare part of this recipe the night before for the starter to work.

1 cup Sourdough Starter (see
    previous recipe)
1 cup lowfat soy milk
1-1/2 cups whole wheat flour
1/2 teaspoon baking soda
1 teaspoon baking powder
1/2 teaspoon salt

Mix sourdough starter, soy milk, and 1/2 cup of the whole wheat flour. Cover and let stand at room temperature for 12-24 hours.

When ready to cook, add the remaining 1 cup whole wheat flour, baking soda, baking powder, and salt. Heat waffle iron, pour in the appropriate amount of batter for your specific model, and spread to the edges of the waffle iron. Close and cook until gently browned.

TOTAL CALORIES PER SERVING: 302
TOTAL FAT AS % OF DAILY VALUE: 3%   FAT: 2 gm
PROTEIN: 12 gm   CARBOHYDRATES: 64 gm
CALCIUM: 146 mg   IRON: 3 mg   SODIUM: 790 mg
DIETARY FIBER: 10 gm

ORANGE WAFFLES

(Makes about 6 waffles; serves 3)

This batter burns easily; so set your waffle iron on a low setting. If your waffle iron doesn't have a temperature setting, peek to see if the waffles are done when the waffle maker opens easily. Orange oil, made from the natural oils in orange rind, can be found at gourmet stores. One mail order source is the King Arthur Flour Baker's Catalogue at (800) 827-6836.

1 Tablespoon active dry yeast
1 cup freshly squeezed orange juice,
    warmed (about 120 degrees)
1/2 cup lowfat soy milk, at room
    temperature
1 Tablespoon oil
1 teaspoon vanilla extract
1/8 teaspoon orange oil or 1 Table-
    spoon grated orange rind
1/2 teaspoon salt
2-1/4 cups whole wheat pastry flour
1 teaspoon baking powder

Dissolve yeast in warm orange juice and let sit for 10 minutes. Add remaining ingredients and stir well for several minutes. Let batter rest, covered, in a warm spot for 30 minutes. Heat waffle iron, pour in the appropriate amount of batter for your specific model, and spread to the edges of the waffle iron. Close and cook until gently browned.

TOTAL CALORIES PER SERVING: 410
TOTAL FAT AS % OF DAILY VALUE: 11%   FAT: 7 gm
PROTEIN: 15 gm   CARBOHYDRATES: 78 gm
CALCIUM: 147 mg   IRON: 4 mg   SODIUM: 566 mg
DIETARY FIBER: 4 gm

SPICY CORN PANCAKES
(Makes 12 three-inch pancakes; serves 4)

These delicious pancakes make a terrific dinner when served with a bottled salsa for topping. I use chipotle chili peppers that are canned in adobo sauce, but you can also use dried chipotles. Let the dried peppers soak in warm water for several minutes before you dice them.

2 cups whole wheat flour
1 teaspoon salt
1 teaspoon baking powder
2 cups corn kernels, fresh or frozen
2 chipotle chili peppers, diced
2 cloves garlic, minced
4 scallions, diced
1 cup lowfat soy milk

Mix whole wheat flour with salt and baking powder. In a separate bowl, mix corn, chipotles, garlic, scallions, and soy milk. Gently blend wet ingredients with dry until well mixed. Spray skillet with vegetable cooking spray and preheat until it is moderately hot. For each pancake, use about 1/4 cup batter. Cook 3 minutes on each side or until brown.

TOTAL CALORIES PER SERVING: 315
TOTAL FAT AS % OF DAILY VALUE: 5%   FAT: 3 gm
PROTEIN: 13 gm   CARBOHYDRATES: 51 gm
CALCIUM: 119 mg   IRON: 3 mg   SODIUM: 725 mg
DIETARY FIBER: 10 gm

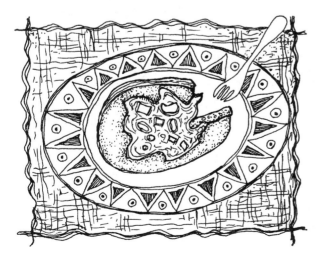

CORNMEAL WAFFLES WITH CHILI TOPPING
(Makes 4 large waffles; serves 4)

This chili topping is also good with the Spicy Corn Pancakes. The chili topping can be made in advance and reheated once the waffles are hot.

3/4 cup whole wheat flour
1/2 cup cornmeal
1 teaspoon salt
2 teaspoons baking powder
1 cup lowfat soy milk
1 Tablespoon oil

Chili Topping:
Vegetable cooking spray
1 large onion, chopped
1 green pepper, chopped
1 Tablespoon chili powder
2 cups cooked pinto or kidney beans

Mix flour, cornmeal, salt, and baking powder. Add soy milk and oil and stir gently until well blended. Heat waffle iron, pour in the appropriate amount of batter for your specific model, and spread to the edges of the waffle iron. Close and cook until gently browned. Serve immediately.

For Chili Topping: Spray non-stick skillet with vegetable cooking spray and sauté onion and pepper over medium heat for 3-4 minutes or until translucent. Add chili powder and beans and cook 5 minutes over medium heat. Pour chili topping over cornmeal waffles.

TOTAL CALORIES PER SERVING: 333
TOTAL FAT AS % OF DAILY VALUE: 9%   FAT: 6 gm
PROTEIN: 13 gm   CARBOHYDRATES: 61 gm
CALCIUM: 221 mg   IRON: 4 mg   SODIUM: 865 mg
DIETARY FIBER: 12 gm

Nanette Blanchard is author of a vegetarian Christmas cookbook for Fireside/Simon & Schuster.

CORNFLAKE CRUSADE

A BOOK BY GERALD CARSON, ARNO PRESS, 1976

Reviewed by Charles Stahler

Since we are a minority in society, vegetarians tend to be individualistic. I think if the rest of society would finally stop eating meat, some people would start eating meat just to be different. However, for most people this is not true. Their vegetarianism stems out of strong convictions of health, animal rights, religion, environmental concerns, and ethics.

Because there are so many reasons for being vegetarian, we may disassociate ourselves from others who are vegetarian for different reasons. This is probably especially true of people who are vegetarian for animal rights reasons, or people who are health vegetarians for scientific reasons and do not want to be thought of as trendy health people or "nuts among the berries." Yet, outsiders studying us probably tend to see all of us as one broad movement (just as Europeans would look at all Americans as the same, whether you are a cowboy from Lubbock, Texas, a coal miner from West Virginia, or a computer programmer from Manhattan, New York).

In order to understand ourselves better, and the direction of our movement, we need to look at our historical roots, even if it means seeing some of our ancestors as flakes (having off-the-wall ideas). The *Cornflake Crusade*, by Gerald Carson, is a fascinating book that talks about vegetarianism in the late 1800's and early 1900's, and the resulting changes in American society. We need to look closely at what happened to the past vegetarian movement, and analyze whether our work will result in a changed society which still eats meat, or a vegetarian nation.

Carson states that "Saints, backwoods visionists, inventors, and dreamers, creators of industries, are seldom well-adjusted people... In these pages, then, appear much singularity, a passionate attachment to truth and half-truth, many instances of vanity, high and low motives, the will to power, the urge to improve the erring brother even if it kills him. Many in the cast of characters were called cranks... The cause of *Right Living* is never lost, never won. Its advocates left a heritage of broad social significance, and some memories not without their entertaining aspects."

Though writing about a period over 100 years ago, Carson surely describes the vegetarian and animal rights movements today. Though we want to bring changes to the world for the better, being an individualist and ahead of your time often takes its toll. We may be seen as cranks and troublemakers. Like all people, we are not saints. We do things that we know are wrong, and we take actions we do not realize are wrong. Yet our passion for change, if not enough to create a utopia for today, we hope that passion will push the world in that direction when our wiser descendants will be able to continue the battle for a more just and healthier world.

WHERE DID THE AMERICAN VEGETARIANS COME FROM?

Towards the end of the eighteenth century, Reverend William Cowherd was in a dilemma "that was likely to cost him his living." In addition to studying science, after reading his bible closely, he decided to stop eating meat. He took seriously the sixth commandment that stated thou shalt not kill. (This is usually thought to mean thou shalt not murder, i.e., referring only to human beings.) After leaving the Church of England, Cowherd started a church of his own, with vegetarianism as its cornerstone. William Metcalfe, who also gave up meat for ethical reasons, became a follower of the new church, and in 1817 led a flock of Christians to America, where he became the first public advocate of vegetarianism in this country.

Metcalfe established his vegetarian church in Philadelphia, where he served without compensation, similar to the leaders of most vegetarian groups today. For his support, he opened a school, as well as treated patients with homeopathy. The church continued on for about 100 years, and the American Vegetarian Society even met there, and published a vegetarian magazine. One of their vegetarian feasts was attended by Susan B. Anthony and Horace Greeley, who presided.

Unfortunately, the group went out of business in a few years because of the inability to pay printing bills. The church struggled for about 100 years before expiring, but not before many years of singing this hymn in church:

No flocks that range the valley free
to slaughter we condemn.
Taught by the Power that pities us
We learn to pity them.

We often think that the vegetarian movement was always health based. However, it appears that historically, we always had strong underpinnings of health, ethics, and a spiritual belief.

After the demise of the American Vegetarian Society (the first vegetarian group), the Reverend Henry Stephen Clubb, a successor of Reverend Metcalfe, put together a new national society of vegetarians, and called the group the *Vegetarian Society of America*. Clubb was its president, and edited their official publication, called *Food, Home and Garden*. Clubb believed that the early Christian Church was vegetarian, and was later corrupted by Constantine.

Clubb was in contact with many vegetarians around the country. Though they had common ground, like today, there were many subgroups. Some vegetarians would not eat tubers, but only foods grown in the light of the sun. Some would eat only plants grown in virgin soil. Others put their faith in nuts and milk. One group ate only raw food. Fruitarians abstained from all food obtained by inflicting pain. Some people would not wear leather shoes, because they were made from skins of animals, and sent off for Dutch wooden shoes. Does this all sound familiar?

The poet Shelley wrote:

No longer now
He slays the lamb, who looks him in
the face,
And horribly devours its mangled
flesh
Which, still avenging Nature's
broken law
Kindled all putrid humors in his
frame

Other famous people who were involved with vegetarianism included Thomas Edison, Emerson, and Thoreau. However, Edison had a healthy diet only when his kidneys kicked up, but returned to his former habits when they calmed down. Many people, then, as today, had the same problem of consistency.

Another famous vegetarian, who lived from 1794 to 1851, was Reverend Sylvester Graham. As you might have guessed, he invented the forerunner of the graham cracker. He pushed whole wheat products, denounced white bread, and pointed to the unpleasant problems of excessive drinking and a high protein diet. Graham's ideas were discussed throughout the popular newspapers of the day.

Vegetarians, one hundred years ago, as today, worked closely with other groups, from the Society for the Prevention of Cruelty to Animals to theosophists, from those against vaccination to Indian mystics. "The vegetarian frame of reference included agitators and fighters in all the liberal causes which stirred the social conscience of idealistic men and women." Back in the 1860's, there was a group of "Alcott ladies" who would not use cotton because it was the product of slave labor, and stayed away from wool because it deprived sheep of their property. Even Clara Barton was involved with vegetarians.

Out of the early health and church movements grew the Seventh-day Adventist religion and its pro-vegetarian stance on diet. Carson gives a fascinating history of the rise of Ellen White, a Seventh-day Adventist prophet, and the eventual interplay between science, religion, and commercialism. In 1866, the Adventist Western Reform Health Institute opened for business in Battle Creek, Michigan, without the blessing of the American Medical Association. As the sanitarium floundered in the 1870's, Ellen White felt they needed a medical person to run the place. She was responsible for sending a young Seventh-day Adventist, John Harvey Kellogg, to college.

Thus began the medicalization of religious teachings. For example, *Laws of Life*, a Seventh-day Adventist magazine, was eventually taken over by Dr. John Kellogg. He changed the name of the magazine to *Good Health*, broadened the appeal, and played down the Old Testament hygiene in favor of reports on German bacteriological research, and world-wide developments in surgery, nutrition and chemistry. The Seventh-day Adventist sanitarium run by Kellogg, though still vegetarian, started to downplay natural cures, and rely more on men and women who had medical training. Kellogg started to experiment with new vegetarian foods such as nut meats, and granola, and even started a small mail order business.

According to Carson, Kellogg never tired of emphasizing the antisocial behavior of the meat eaters. While Kellogg was a skilled surgeon, administrator, and publicist, a follower of scientific truth, and in good repute with the American Medical Association, he still stuck closely to the Seventh-day Adven-tist -- Sylvestor Graham line of thinking. "The doctor's spiritual vegetarianism was a heritage which he could not slough off. It brought him into relation with a strange crew: anti-fur wearers, Rosicrucians, and Indian swamis, Buddhists and antivivisectors, alfalfa-tea men, nudists, raw fooders, assorted bird lovers and New Thoughters." (Today, 80 years later, it sounds like some vegetarian conferences a few of us have attended.)

Like vegetarians of today, Kellogg went to great lengths to justify some of his beliefs. He proved that a dog could be kept healthy on a cereal diet, and then tried to convert a wolf to a more progressive view of eating. On one Thanksgiving day, the sanitarium guests were served something which looked like roast turkey and tasted like roast turkey, but wasn't. In the dining room Dr. Kellogg had placed a live turkey on a stage with a legend that said, "A Thankful Turkey." According to spectators, the turkey ate his grain ration like all the other guests, flapped his wings and gobbled his appreciation.

However, according to Carson, Kellogg was also very practical. While he believed in his nut and cereal meats from a nutritional viewpoint, he realized it was a lot cheaper to serve patients vegetarian items than expensive meat. Creating appetizing foods that would keep patients at his sanitarium, yet keep costs down, brought Kellogg's to corn flakes.

As Dr. Kellogg developed his small empire, he wanted to downplay his religious connections with the Seventh-day Adventist Church. The church was upset because Kellogg taught young men "spurious scientific theories," i.e., evolution. Also involved was economics. The church depended on free will offerings, but the medics had a better source of revenue because their work was income producing. While Kellogg was set up by the Church, he had begun to keep his funds out of the reach of the Church.

The cooperation and rivalries between Kellogg and the Church, and other spiritual/ economic entrepreneurs; Kellogg's brother's founding the Kellogg's Company; and the evolution away from health food into the cereal empires of Kellogg's, Nabisco, and Post all add up to a story line rivaling that of the old television show, *Dallas*. Whether you like novels or history, the *Cornflake Crusade* is worth reading.

Charles Stahler is the co-founder and co-director of The Vegetarian Resource Group. He's been a vegetarian for over 20 years.

DR. JOHN HARVEY KELLOGG

By Amy South

The Physicians' Committee for Responsible Medicine has proposed that the familiar, "basic four" food groups that have been around since 1956 be changed to the four new food groups, which would be, "whole grains, vegetables, legumes, and fruit." Meat, dairy products, fats, and oils are to be optional.

Of course it does not surprise anyone here in Battle Creek, Michigan. One hundred years ago Dr. John Harvey Kellogg, a vegetarian and director of the Battle Creek Sanitarium, was saying some of the same things we're hearing today.

The Battle Creek Sanitarium was a nationally known health resort, popular for many years, especially prior to the Depression. It was founded by the Seventh-day Adventists in 1866 as the Western Health Reform Institute. As director, Dr. Kellogg changed the name to the Battle Creek Sanitarium -- a name he said meant, "a place where people learned to stay well." It was at this institution that ready-to-eat cereal was developed. W.K. Kellogg, founder of the Kellogg Company, was Dr. John Harvey Kellogg's brother.

Dr. Kellogg proposed "biologic living," which for the most part meant preventive medicine. His goal was to help people stay well rather than to recover from illness. To him, "biologic living" meant total abstinence from alcohol, tea, coffee, chocolate, and tobacco. He stressed a simple vegetarian diet as the most "natural." He also believed in proper rest, exercise, fresh air, and healthful dress, with proper diet being the most important.

Today, spokespersons from The Livestock Marketing Association, The National - American Wholesale Grocer Association, and the National Dairy Council are not so happy with The Physicians' Committee for Responsible Medicine's new proposal, and neither were those kinds of organizations thrilled with Kellogg when he proposed such things years ago.

According to Richard W. Schwarz, in his book, *John Harvey Kellogg, M.D.* (Southern Publishing Association, Nashville, Tennessee 1970), the meat packers arranged for the U.S. Department of Agriculture to prepare a large poster portraying meat as a highly desirable food. The posters were displayed in post offices around the country. Dr. Kellogg objected. He protested by having the same poster produced, at his expense, adding the words, "See other side." On the back of the poster he listed all the reasons why people should not eat meat.

The meat packers filed a complaint with the Federal Trade Commission in Washington, D.C., to prohibit Dr. Kellogg from circulating his revised posters. An attorney was sent to Battle Creek to investigate.

After spending time here with Dr. Kellogg, the counselor decided to drop the matter. He saw Kellogg some time later and said, "You know, Doctor, I haven't tasted meat since I saw you in Battle Creek!"

Regarding eating meat, Dr. Kellogg had an argument for everyone. For the religious he would quote from the Bible. For the Darwinists, who believed that we're descendants of monkeys, he told them that the great apes ate no meat. To the moralists he would point out that it was not right to kill animals.

He often remarked that it took huge amounts of grain to produce small amounts of beefsteak, grain that could just as well have been used as food, a point environmentalists are making today. He also said that the average American ate more protein than needed, something not only wasteful, but possibly harmful. He believed a low protein diet increased resistance to disease, encouraged longevity, and contributed to greater physical and mental endurance. Meat-eating he thought was responsible for cancer, diabetes, and other illnesses.

At one time, Dr. Kellogg, recommended against cheese, eggs, and milk. He did, however, later support clean fresh raw milk from healthy cows as being superior to pasteurized milk and especially recommended yogurt. He also believed that humans consumed too much salt. Humans' natural diet he maintained was a combination of grains, fruits, and nuts.

Dr. Kellogg promoted two seeds, sesame and psyllium, being the first to introduce psyllium into the United States. He was one of the first Americans to recognize the potential use of soybeans as a food.

He believed that Americans ate too much food in general. For everyone he recommended two or three meals a day, with the heaviest meal at noon, the lightest one in the evening, and no eating between meals.

Doctor Kellogg attributed his own longevity to the ideas which he proposed in "biologic living." At the age of 77 he founded and directed the Miami, Florida, branch of the Battle Creek Sanitarium. At 78 he took the Florida state medical licensing examination and passed the two-day test with a score higher than many younger examinees. In his eighties he was riding his bike, giving lectures, doctoring, and working every day. He performed 22,000 operations, the last when he was 88.

Although he believed in regular rest and relaxation, Dr. Kellogg didn't always follow his own advice. In his sixties he could work for weeks at a time on an average of only about 4 hours of sleep per night. By the age of 80 he cut his workday to 12 to 15 hours.

At the age of ninety, Dr. Kellogg went to Washington to negotiate for materials to renovate a building into a new location for the Battle Creek Sanitarium. Because of World War II, he was told to forget his idea and to close up the Sanitarium. He didn't give up and after going from office to office, he came home with orders for the necessary materials.

Doctor Kellogg based his theories on studies he had made of Asian people, and that is exactly what many studies are being based on today. It has taken a long time for the world to come around to the thinking of Dr. John Harvey Kellogg, but here in Battle Creek we're not surprised.

Amy South resides in Michigan.

WHAT BENJAMIN FRANKLIN
REALLY SAID ABOUT VEGETARIANISM

By Larry Kaiser

While it is becoming more common to see articles on vegetarian diets in general interest publications, references to the history of vegetarianism often don't appear in the media. Many articles treat vegetarianism as something new. In other cases, when early American vegetarians are mentioned, the account may not be very accurate or complete. Often the coverage fails to appreciate adequately the long tradition vegetarianism has in this country.

Few people know that Benjamin Franklin was vegetarian for part of his lifetime. How did vegetarianism actually appear to this famous man?

Background for an answer to this question can be gathered from his writings, from the written sources that influenced him, and from the words of other vegetarians Franklin knew and befriended. All this evidence shows that, whether or not he was able to live up to them himself, the reasons he saw for vegetarianism in the 1700's were ethical and practical.

His writings demonstrate that in addition to the moral aspects, Franklin also saw a pragmatic side to vegetarianism. As a young printer's apprentice in the 1720's, he came upon a book by Thomas Tryon. This was probably *Wisdom's Dictates* (1691), a digest of Tryon's lengthy *The Way to Health, Wealth, and Happiness.* Franklin recalls:

When about 16-years-of-age, I happen'd to meet with a book written by one Tryon, recommending a vegetable diet. I determined to go into it. My brother being yet unmarried, did not keep house, but boarded himself and his apprentices in another family. My refusing to eat flesh occasioned an inconveniency, and I was frequently chid for my singularity. I made myself acquainted with Tryon's manner of preparing some of his dishes, such as boiling potatoes or rice, making hasty pudding, and a few others, and then propos'd to my brother, that if he would give me weekly half the money he paid for by board, I would board myself. He instantly agreed to it, and I presently found that I could save half what he paid me. This was an additional fund for buying books: but I had another advantage in it. My brother and the rest going from the printing-house to their meals, I remain'd there alone, and dispatching presently my light repast (which often was no more than a biscuit or a slice of bread, a handful of raisins or a tart from the pastry cook's, and a glass of water) had the rest of the time till their return for study, in which I made the greater progress from that greater clearness of head and quicker apprehension which usually attend temperance in eating and drinking.[1]

So, along with the ethical dimension, a vegetarian diet meant savings in both money and time to the young apprentice. He had been desperate from a young age to acquire books and read them; now he had extra means of doing both. Franklin does not make any exaggerated claims for the health benefits of abstaining from meat, nor does he criticize meat-eating as unhealthy.

Exactly what did the young Franklin find in Tryon's work? *Wisdom's Dictates* is 150 pages of rules about health. These include commentary on diet, exercise, and cleanliness.

The concluding pages consist of "A Bill of Fare" which supplies 75 recipes; most likely these were the ones tested and adopted by Franklin.

Tryon defends the vegetarian diet as superior, both physically and spiritually. He bases this on his interpretation of Christianity. The moral emphasis of *Wisdom's Dictates* can be seen on the title page, which refers to the bill of fare as "Seventy-five Noble dishes of Excellent Food, far exceeding those made of fish or flesh, which banquet I present to the sons of wisdom, on such as shall decline that depraved custom of eating flesh and blood."

Tryon goes on to say in the opening pages:

Refrain at all times such foods as cannot be procured without violence and oppression. For know, that all the inferior creatures when hurt do cry and fend forth their complaints to their maker...Be not insensible that every creature doth bear the image of the great creator according to the nature of each, and that he is the vital power in all things. Therefore, let none take pleasure to offer violence to that life, lest he awaken the fierce wrath, and bring danger to his own soul. But let mercy and compassion dwell plentifully in your hearts, that you may be comprehended in the friendly principle of God's love and holy light. Be a friend to everything that's good, and then everything will be a friend to thee, and co-operate for thy good and welfare.

The author also warns his readers against "Hunting, hawking, shooting, and all violent oppressive exercises" due to their immoral nature.

When describing the recipes at his book's end, Tryon again stresses the ethical reasons for adopting the vegetarian diet. These dishes, he informs the reader, are "prepared without flesh and blood, or the dying groans of God's innocent and harmless creatures." He asks the reader to "consider also that thy life is near and dear to thee, the like is understood of all other creatures."[2]

Even if he had never read Tryon or become a vegetarian himself, Franklin still would have been acutely aware of the moral arguments for vegetarianism. This is because, based in Philadelphia, he was well-acquainted with Quakerism and those Quakers who espoused a vegetarian diet. Some of the best known Quaker proponents of the abolition of slavery were also vegetarian.

The first of these was Benjamin Lay. In 1731, he and his wife moved to Philadelphia from Barbados. There they had witnessed the horrors of the slave trade. This experience, along with his Quaker upbringing in England, deeply influenced his views. Lay was known among Philadelphians for his temperance and his refusal to harm animal life in order to obtain food or clothing. Lay fought against slavery in Pennsylvania and nearby colonies. This battle brought him into contact with Franklin, with whom he maintained a friendship until Lay died in 1759.

There is no doubt that Franklin knew of Lay's beliefs. Lay was far from reserved in expressing his views, whether it be about slavery or the abuse of animals. He once "kidnapped" his neighbors' six-year-old son, and when the worried parents came looking for him, Lay told them, "Your child is safe in my house and you may now conceive of the sorrow you afflict upon the parents of the Negro girl you hold in slavery, for she was torn from them by avarice." He once took a bladder filled with blood into the Yearly Meeting of the Quakers, and puncturing it with a sword, sprinkled blood on some of his companions, telling them, "Thus shall God shed the blood of those persons who enslave their fellow-creatures."[3] His efforts to promote abolition were rewarded, when shortly before his death, the Society of Friends called on all Quakers to release their slaves as a religious duty.

Another Quaker abolitionist and vegetarian known to Franklin was the itinerant preacher John Woolman. In his *Journal*, Woolman states that he was "early convinced in my mind that true religion consisted in an inward life, wherein the heart doth love and reverence God the Creator and learn to exercise true justice and goodness, not only toward all men, but also toward the brute creatures..."[4] Woolman, over the course of 30 years, traveled throughout the colonies, speaking against slavery and promoting his views on respect for life. His two-part work, *Considerations on the Keeping of Negroes,* was read in England as well as America and may have been more influential than any other document in turning the Society of Friends against the practice of slavery. Franklin printed the second part of Woolman's essay, as well as other anti-slavery publications.

Woolman also campaigned against the misuse of animals, particularly horses and oxen. He felt that the abuse of domestic animals for profit was a great evil, and urged relatives not to write when he was traveling due to the conditions endured by those horses used on the stage coaches which delivered the mail.

In Franklin's world, a vegetarian diet was primarily associated with moral choices, not claims of health benefits. Those who would dismiss vegetarianism as a passing fad must not be aware of this long history of ethical vegetarianism in America.

Franklin had his differences with Quakers, in particular over the refusal of some of them to participate in the defense of the colony. However, through his association with Quakers such as Lay and Woolman, he was exposed to arguments against flesh-eating and knew them to be based on ethical principles.

In Franklin's world, a vegetarian diet was primarily associated with moral choices, not claims of health benefits. Those who would dismiss vegetarianism as a passing fad must not be aware of this long history of ethical vegetarianism in America. This tradition continued into the nineteenth century and helped form the moral basis for the vegetarian movement of the 1830's. It was this later movement that first popularized the case for the health benefits of a vegetarian diet in America.

FOOTNOTES

[1] Benjamin Franklin, *Autobiography* (1790), (New York, W. W. Norton and Company, 1986), p. 28.

[2] Thomas Tryon, *Wisdom's Dictates* (London, 1691), pp. 1, 6-7, and 139.

[3] John Thomas Scharf, *History of Philadephia* (Philadelphia, L. H. Everts, 1884), p. 1249. Also, *American Reformers: H. W. Wilson Biograhical Dictionary* (New York, H. W. Wilson Company, 1985), pp. 514-5.

[4] John Woolman, *Journal*, (1772) (New York, Oxford University Press, 1971), p. 28.

Larry Kaiser is a freelance writer living in Dexter, Michigan.

AMOS BRONSON ALCOTT:
IDEALIST, TRANSCENDENTALIST, VEGETARIAN

By Donna Maurer

Amos Bronson Alcott (1799-1888) is not among the most popularly well-known vegetarians of the 19th century, but his contributions to the vegetarian ideal -- on both a philosophical and practical level -- should not be lost or ignored.

Bronson Alcott, perhaps best known as the writer Louisa May Alcott's father, made significant contributions to the world in two areas: education and diet. His philosophies on both of these subjects were based on the idea that humans are innately good. He believed, for example, that children are closest to perfection while adults tend to become more corrupt with age, especially under the influence of industrialization and competition. He proposed that the duty of each individual is to try to regain the original purity that people are closest to at birth.

Alcott saw vegetarianism as an important and necessary means of restoring this lost purity. Meat, in Alcott's view, corrupts both the body and the soul. Not only did he consider the slaughter of animals to be morally reprehensible, but Alcott also claimed that a pure soul could not possibly emanate from a body made impure through meat consumption.

Alcott considered raising animals for food to be an ecologically unsound practice.

In an 1843 letter, Alcott wrote:

It is calculated that if no animal food were consumed, one-fourth of the land now used would suffice for human sustenance. And the extensive tracts of the country now appropriated to grazing, mowing, and other modes of animal provision, could be cultivated by and for intelligent and affectionate human neighbors.[1]

Alcott started his transition to vegetarianism in 1835 after reading the works of Pythagoras and became a confirmed vegetarian a year later when he attended a series of Sylvester Graham's lectures on the "Science of Life." Graham, a well-known 19th century health reformer, lectured not only on vegetarianism, but on the benefits of cold baths, sexual restraint, and eating fibrous whole-

---

[1] From a letter by Alcott and Charles Lane published in the newspaper *Herald of Freedom*, September 8, 1843, and reprinted in *Transcendental Wild Oats and Excerpts from the Fruitlands Diary*, William Henry Harrison, ed. (Harvard, MA: The Harvard Common Press, 1981, p. 88).

wheat biscuits (ancestors of our 20th century graham crackers).

Soon after attending Graham's lectures, Alcott dreamed of creating a communal environment, which he called a consociate family, within which people could mature both intellectually and spiritually. In 1843, Alcott and English educational reformer Charles Lane purchased a property in Harvard, Massachusetts, where they established their short-lived experiment called Fruitlands.[2]

Although Fruitlands lasted only for about seven months, it was a significant contribution to vegetarian history as the first intentionally vegan communal arrangement.

Not only did the people at Fruitlands eschew meat, but they also did not allow the use of dairy products, wool, leather, cotton (as a product of slavery), or manure for fertilization (they called it "as filthy a practice as an idea").[3]

Although Alcott was a life-long friend of the famous transcendentalist Ralph Waldo Emerson and a contributor to the prestigious literary journal The Dial, Alcott was often

subject to ridicule because of his unusual beliefs, leading to such nicknames as the "Sage of Apple Slump" and "Consecrated Crank." Amos Bronson Alcott did not publish many works during his lifetime, and nothing specifically about vegetarianism; yet his contribution to the vegetarian ideal through his speech and actions is immeasurable.

ADDITIONAL REFERENCES

Francis, Richard, "Circumstances and Salvation: The Ideology of the Fruitlands Utopia," *American Quarterly*, 25 (May 1973), pp. 202-234.

Herrnstadt, Richard L., ed., *The Letters of A. Bronson Alcott* (Ames, Iowa: Iowa University Press, 1969).

Hoeltje, Hubert, *Sheltering Tree: A Story of the Friendship of Ralph Waldo Emerson and Amos Bronson Alcott* (Port Washington, New York: Kennikat, 1943)

Sanborn, F.B., *Bronson Alcott: At Alcott House, England, and Fruitlands, New England* (Cedar Rapids, Iowa: The Torch Press, 1908).

Shepard, Odell, ed., *The Journals of Bronson Alcott* (Boston, Massachusetts: Little, Brown, 1938).

Shepard, Odell, *Peddler's Progress: The Life of Bronson Alcott* (Boston, Massachusetts: Little, Brown, 1938).

---

[2] Detailed information on the Fruitlands experiment is fairly scarce. Of all the sources Clara Endicott Sears' *Bronson Alcott's Fruitlands* (Philadelphia: Porcupine Press, 1915, 1943, 1975) is the most thorough.

[3] Quoted in *Amos Bronson Alcott: An Intellectual Biography* by Frederick C. Dahlstrand (Fairleigh Dickinson University Press, 1982, p. 194).

Donna Maurer is a graduate student in sociology at Southern Illinois University in Carbondale.

Sylvester Graham

A Vegetarian Advocate of the Nineteenth Century

By Larry Kaiser

GRAHAM'S LIFE

Graham was born in 1794, the youngest of seventeen children. His elderly father died soon after. Because his mother was unable to care for him, he was put under the care of a succession of relatives. His early years contained little formal schooling as he worked on relatives' farms, clerked in stores, and labored in a paper mill. At the age of sixteen, he started to show signs of tuberculosis, which would trouble him on and off for the rest of his life.

Graham received tutoring in his late teens and worked for a time as a teacher until illness forced him to quit. At the age of twenty-nine, he enrolled at Amherst College. He studied conscientiously and made a reputation for his dramatic oratorical style. He soon fell ill again, however. Upon recovering, he married one of the women who had attended him in his sickness.

Not long after his marriage, Graham became a preacher in the Presbyterian Church. His attention was captured by the growing temperance movement and, in 1830, he moved to Philadelphia to be a full-time speaker for the Pennsylvania Temperance Society. His interests led him to study health more generally. While doing this, he came into contact with William Metcalfe of the vegetarian Bible Christian Church and read widely about diet.

Graham came to national attention in 1832. As the first great cholera epidemic slowly moved toward the United States, people's health fears were heightened. Graham lectured on the uses of proper diet as a preventive for disease and people came to hear him lecture by the hundreds. Throughout the 1830's Americans debated the teachings of Graham, and he was both acclaimed and scorned. Graham boarding houses, Graham restaurants, and Graham publications sprang up, all inspired by his views.

During the last decade of his life, Graham continued his writing while living in Northampton, Massachusetts. He died there at the age of fifty-seven in 1851.

THE GRAHAM SYSTEM

What Graham developed was a preventive health system with vegetarianism at its heart. In doing this, he was opposing the traditional medical wisdom of his day, which called for bleeding, purges, and other violent treatments for ailments. Americans of 1830 knew very little about how to maintain health. In his lectures, he noted that most Americans "regard diseases as substances or things which enter their bodies with so little connection with their own voluntary actions and habits that nothing which they can do can prevent disease."[1] It was that attitude he tried to change by convincing people to take more responsibility for their health. "If human existence is worth possessing, it is worth preserving," he exhorted his listeners.[2] Graham's ideas found an eager audience among Americans, many of whom were deeply distrustful of the doctors of their day.

Graham produced a variety of arguments for vegetarianism. He believed that God had outlined for mankind the ideal diet and proper healthful practices, and that scripture ordained a vegetarian diet in its description of foods provided for people in the Garden of Eden. He also argued from anatomy, saying that the human has the physiology of the herbivore. In addition, he took examples from the history of vegetarian cultures, discussed anecdotes about vegetarian societies from around the world, and opposed the cruelty involved in the raising and killing of animals for food. He called his most important book *Lectures on the Science of Human Life* and felt that science would vindicate his beliefs.

Meat, he believed, was an unnatural food. However, as with the use of tobacco or alcohol, meat-eating could become a habit or even an addiction. Graham taught that dairy products were also capable of causing problems.

Graham provided detailed rules for his lowfat, high-fiber diet. Special care was to be given to the preparation of bread at home. (Graham accused commercial bakeries of adulterating their products.) He also felt the times of eating were important, saying that meals should be no closer than six hours apart. Graham saw over-eating as the root of many health problems.

The Graham system extended beyond diet to other areas of health. He described the positive effects of getting enough sleep and the benefits of regular bathing. Exercise and proper ventilation were also promoted.

INFLUENCE OF GRAHAM'S WORK

The ideas of preventive health were not original to Graham. His uniqueness was to gather them together and present them to the public. Graham believed in teaching physiology to the public, an idea unheard of at the time, but one that has become part of a basic education today. He touted prevention over traditional treatments and helped make this idea part of popular culture. This concept caught on so strongly that mainstream doctors were forced to begin to come to terms with it. Graham and his followers were not the only

promoters of public health, but they were the first, the best organized, and the most energetic. One historian has noted that "their efforts' success has meant much to our people in terms of esthetic values, decreasing illness and even a lowered mortality rate."[3]

Graham's diet, with its emphasis on vegetarianism, high fiber, and low fat, is remarkably similar to the diets being promoted today to improve health. In a sense, science has spent much of this century proving Graham right. When vitamins were first discovered, an article in a 1914 issue of the *Scientific American* saw this as a vindication of the Graham system with its championing of fruits and vegetables. Countless studies since have confirmed the superiority of the vegetarian diet described by Graham.[4] Those groups of Americans who have followed diets similar to Graham's have shown significantly better health than the population as a whole.

Graham and his followers' stress on exercise is believed by some historians to have helped fuel the sports boom that began in the 1830's. His educational efforts regarding cleanliness and proper rest also had an impact on the popular mind.

Sylvester Graham would have liked to convince every American to adopt his system and become a vegetarian. This, obviously, did not happen. Nevertheless, he was a crucial influence on our modern concept of a healthy lifestyle.

FOOTNOTES

[1] Sylvester Graham, *Lectures on the Science of Human Life*, (London, William Horsell, 1854), p. 420.
[2] Graham, p. 530.
[3] Richard Harrison Shryock, *Medicine in America: Historical Essays*, (Baltimore, Johns Hopkins, 1966), p. 125.
[4] Percy G. Styles, "Vitamines", *Scientific American Supplement*, LXXII (June 27, 1914), p. 402.

Larry Kaiser is a freelance writer from Michigan.

SAVORY WINTER STEWS

By Jacqueline Dunnington

Tasty, aromatic vegetarian stews win high honors as satisfying one-dish meals, enjoyed the world over. This collection of savory stews is drawn from international and American kitchens and runs the gamut from exotic delights to those that are hearty farm-house simplicity at its best.

When most people think of stew, they think of a meat-based dish. Is the vegetarian deprived of the pleasure of a steaming bowl of stew that has been simmering in a pot until all the ingredients are perfectly blended? The answer is -- not at all!

POTATO, CARROT AND GREEN BEAN DISH
(Serves 4)

This is a chunky and hearty stew that is easy on the budget.

3 cups unpeeled and boiled pota-
    toes, cubed
1 cup unpeeled carrots, cut in thin
    rounds
2 cups water
1 Tablespoon oil
2 medium onions, coarsely chopped
Salt to taste
2 cups fresh green beans, slivered
1/4 cup fresh parsley, chopped
Pepper to taste

Place potatoes and carrots in deep stew pot. Cover with water and bring to a boil. Turn heat down to simmer. Cook until all vegetables are soft (about 30 minutes).

Meanwhile, heat oil in separate skillet. Add onions and salt. Brown onions lightly. Add onions to stew pot, along with beans. Simmer another 12 minutes. Stir in parsley and pepper. If at any time the stew seems too dry, add hot water sparingly. You can also add a dash of paprika for color. Serve with a tossed salad.

TOTAL CALORIES PER SERVING: 248
TOTAL FAT AS % OF DAILY VALUE: 6%   FAT: 4 gm
PROTEIN: 6 gm   CARBOHYDRATES: 50 gm
CALCIUM: 70 mg   IRON: 3 mg   SODIUM: 28 mg
DIETARY FIBER: 6 gm

CORN STEW

(Serves 6)

A steaming bowl of corn stew makes a hearty dish.

1 Tablespoon corn (or olive) oil
1 cup onions, finely chopped
1 large green pepper, finely chopped
1 large red pepper, finely chopped
2 cups low-sodium canned tomatoes
2 cups fresh (or canned) corn
    kernels
1 teaspoon pepper
2 teaspoons salt
1 cup nearly-cooked brown rice
    along with the cooking water
1/2 cup fresh parsley, chopped
Dash of hot pepper sauce to taste

Heat oil in deep stew pot and add onions and peppers slowly. Sauté until soft, stirring often. Add tomatoes, corn and seasonings. (Save parsley until end.) Cover pot, stew slowly for at least 20 minutes. Add rice and water. Cook until done to taste. Stir in parsley and hot pepper sauce. Serve with slices of avocado.

TOTAL CALORIES PER SERVING: 146
TOTAL FAT AS % OF DAILY VALUE: 6%   FAT: 4 gm
PROTEIN: 4 gm   CARBOHYDRATES: 16 gm
CALCIUM: 44 mg   IRON: 1 mg   SODIUM: 400 mg
DIETARY FIBER: 4 gm

RANCH STYLE CHILI

(Serves 4)

From the Southwest comes a great stew that can be prepared in less than half an hour.

1 cup onions, coarsely chopped
1 large clove garlic, crushed
1 Tablespoon olive oil
2 teaspoons chili powder
Salt to taste
1/2 cup fresh cilantro, chopped (or
    1/4 cup dried)
Pepper to taste
2 cups low-sodium tomato sauce
3 cups cooked pinto beans
1 cup (approx.) water mixed with
    bean liquid

In deep stew pot, sauté onions and garlic in heated oil until soft. Turn down heat, add all seasonings and tomato sauce. Stir in beans and liquid. Cook at least 20 minutes in partially covered pot. Serve bubbling hot with wheat crackers.

TOTAL CALORIES PER SERVING: 323
TOTAL FAT AS % OF DAILY VALUE: 8%   FAT: 5 gm
PROTEIN:13 gm   CARBOHYDRATES: 46 gm
CALCIUM: 98 mg   IRON: 5 mg   SODIUM: 51 mg
DIETARY FIBER: 12 gm

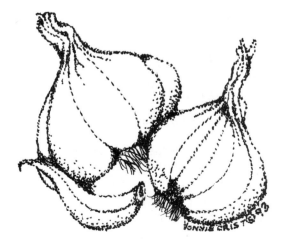

FRENCH MOCK "LAMB" STEW

(Serves 6)

This recipe is well worth the effort. Tofu replaces lamb in this version.

1 pound tofu, cut in 1-1/2-inch
    cubes
1/4 cup soy sauce
Pepper to taste
1 cup onions, chopped in long
    slivers
1 Tablespoon olive oil
1 cup carrots, cut in thin rounds
1 cup tomato wedges, drained
1 cup boiled potatoes, diced into
    small cubes
Salt and pepper to taste
1 packet of favorite herbs in a
    cheesecloth bag
1 cup vegetable broth
1/2 cup fresh (or frozen) green peas,
    shelled

Dip cubed tofu in soy sauce and dust all sides with pepper. Set on lightly-oiled baking sheet and bake at 350 degrees for 30 minutes. Turn once during the process so that all sides are browned evenly. Set aside.

In a deep-sided skillet, brown onions in heated oil. Lower heat and stir in carrots, tomato wedges, potatoes, salt, and pepper. Introduce herb packet while adding broth.

Cover and let stew simmer for at least 45 minutes. Stir several times. Uncover and add peas. Simmer until they are tender. Remove herb packet. Stir in tofu mixture and serve piping hot. Don't be afraid to add your own touches, as the French always do, such as parsley, a cooked turnip, or whatever pleases your fancy. The idea of stew is to be creative!

Note: This stew needs no side dish. However, oatmeal cookies and fruit can be ideal final touches.

TOTAL CALORIES PER SERVING: 163
TOTAL FAT AS % OF DAILY VALUE: 9%   FAT: 6 gm
PROTEIN: 10 gm   CARBOHYDRATES: 20 gm
CALCIUM: 104 mg   IRON: 5 mg   SODIUM: 735 mg
DIETARY FIBER: 3 gm

FRUIT HOT POT
(Serves 6)

This is an elegant, virtually fat-free stew for dessert. Serve this stew at parties.

2 cups fresh (or canned) pineapple
    chunks in natural juice
2 cups fresh (or canned) apricot
    halves in natural juice
2 cups fresh (or canned) figs in
    natural juice
1-1/2 cups mixed juices from above
1/2 cup raspberry jam
1 lemon studded with 6-8 cloves
1 stick cinnamon
1/2 cup seedless raisins or currants

Drain enough juice from each fruit to yield about 1-1/2 cups liquid. Place all the fruit (except raisins or currants) in deep oven-proof pot. Add juices, jam, lemon, and cinnamon. Blend well with wooden spoon and bake at 325 degrees or simmer over lowest heat for at least 30 minutes. Remove the lemon and cinnamon. Mix in raisins or currants and set aside (covered) until plumped by juices. Serve warm, topped with slivered almonds, if desired.

    If more tartness is desired, add a few drops of lemon juice.

    Note: Cooked prunes, peach halves, or pitted cherries can replace any of the fruits, as long as three different fruits are used.

TOTAL CALORIES PER SERVING: 281
TOTAL FAT AS % OF DAILY VALUE: <1%   FAT: <1 gm
PROTEIN: 2 gm   CARBOHYDRATES: 73 gm
CALCIUM: 61 mg   IRON: 1 mg   SODIUM: 11 mg
DIETARY FIBER: 4 gm

PROVENCAL VEGETABLE STEW
(Serves 6)

This is a flavor-packed adaptation of classic ratatouille.

1-1/2 cups onion, finely chopped
1 large clove garlic, crushed
2 Tablespoons olive oil
2 cups zucchini, diced
2 cups eggplant, peeled and cubed
2 cups green pepper, seeded and
    diced
2 cups canned or fresh tomatoes
1 Tablespoon dried basil, crumbled
1 small bay leaf, crumbled
    (optional)
Salt and pepper to taste
1/2 cup toasted wheat germ

In a deep stew pot, sauté onions and garlic in heated oil until soft. Add all other vegetables, except the tomatoes. Cook over medium-low heat, turning mixture often, until all the ingredients are tender. Add tomatoes and seasonings. Cover pot and simmer at least half an hour. Serve hot or cold and garnish with wheat germ.

    Note: Leftovers make an ideal pita pocket filling.

TOTAL CALORIES PER SERVING: 142
TOTAL FAT AS % OF DAILY VALUE: 9%   FAT: 6 gm
PROTEIN: 5 gm   CARBOHYDRATES: 20 gm
CALCIUM: 49 mg   IRON: 2 mg   SODIUM: 135 mg
DIETARY FIBER: 3 gm

Jacqueline Dunnington is a freelance writer from Santa Fe, New Mexico

MAIN DISHES

By Reed Mangels, Ph.D., R.D.

Seitan Quick Mix

Since my introduction to mock chicken with vegetables at a vegetarian Chinese restaurant, I have been fond of products containing gluten (also called seitan or wheat meat). Up until now I have been reluctant to make my own gluten, since a fair amount of time and work are involved. All that changed when I found Arrowhead Mills' Seitan Quick Mix. After less than 10 minutes of actual work and under an hour of cooking, I had well flavored, chewy textured gluten for use in stir fries, barbecue sandwiches, stews, and other dishes. The resulting product is low in fat, cholesterol free, and the recipe can be adapted to produce a low-sodium dish. Seitan Quick Mix is available at many natural foods stores. It is manufactured by Arrowhead Mills, Inc., P.O. Box 2059, Hereford, TX 79045-2059. I highly recommend it.

SEITAN STEW
(Serves 8)

Seitan Stew is perfect for a blustery day with hot biscuits and an apple salad.

Seitan prepared from Seitan Quick Mix, following directions on package for 14 ounces
4 carrots, cut in 1-1/2 inch chunks
4 medium potatoes, cut in chunks
1 large onion, diced
2 turnips, diced

Gravy:
1/2 cup whole wheat flour
1 small onion, chopped
1 teaspoon thyme
1 teaspoon sage
1 teaspoon dried parsley
1/2 teaspoon salt
1/4 teaspoon pepper
2 Tablespoons olive oil
2 cups broth from cooking seitan or vegetable broth

Prepare seitan as directed on package. Reserve cooking broth. Cut seitan into 1 or 1-1/2 inch chunks. Set aside. Cook vegetables in boiling water until just tender. Drain.

Meanwhile, toast flour in a dry skillet until light brown and aromatic, stirring frequently. Remove flour and sauté onion and spices in oil until onion is tender. Add flour, then the reserved broth. Bring to a boil, add cubed seitan, and cooked vegetables. Lower heat and cook for 5-10 minutes.

TOTAL CALORIES PER SERVING: 339
TOTAL FAT AS % OF DAILY VALUE: 8%   FAT: 5 gm
PROTEIN: 31 gm   CARBOHYDRATES: 43 gm
CALCIUM: 35 mg   IRON: 4 mg   SODIUM: 261 mg
DIETARY FIBER: 7 gm

EGGPLANT-RICE BURGERS
(Makes 10 patties)

Enjoy these delicious burgers!

1 large eggplant, peeled
1 large carrot
1 small onion
1/4 cup low-sodium tomato paste
1 teaspoon basil
1 teaspoon oregano
Dash of pepper
2 cups pre-cooked brown rice

Preheat oven to 375 degrees.

Grate eggplant, carrot, and onion (food processor makes this easy). Mix well.

Add remaining ingredients, mixing well. Shape into 10 patties, using about 1/2 cup mixture per patty, and place on lightly oiled or nonstick cookie sheet.

Bake 15 minutes at 375 degrees, then turn and bake for another 15 minutes.

TOTAL CALORIES PER BURGER: 80
TOTAL FAT AS % OF DAILY VALUE: 2%   FAT: 1 gm
PROTEIN: 2 gm   CARBOHYDRATES: 17 gm
CALCIUM: 17 mg   IRON: 1 mg   SODIUM: 10 mg
DIETARY FIBER: 1 gm

SOUTHERN BURGERS
(Makes 16 patties)

Try these unique burgers.

4-1/2 cups water
1 cup grits (not instant)
1 sweet potato, chopped
1 small onion, minced
1/2 teaspoon salt
1/2 teaspoon oregano
1/4 teaspoon sage
Dash of pepper
1/2 cup wheat germ
1 Tablespoon oil

Bring water to a boil. Add remaining ingredients, except wheat germ and oil. Cook, stirring occasionally, until thick. Stir in wheat germ. Cool until mixture can be handled. Form into 1/2-inch thick patties, and fry on both sides in oil over medium-high heat until done.

TOTAL CALORIES PER BURGER: 66
TOTAL FAT AS % OF DAILY VALUE: 2%   FAT: 1 gm
PROTEIN: 2 gm   CARBOHYDRATES: 12 gm
CALCIUM: 5 mg   IRON: 1 mg   SODIUM: 73 mg
DIETARY FIBER: <1 gm

Reed Mangels, Ph.D., R.D., is a nutrition advisor for The Vegetarian Resource Group and co-author of Simply Vegan.

North of the Border
Vegetarian Recipes from the Southwest

By Jacqueline Dunnington

Southwestern-style cooking originated in Mexico, which was the home of the Meso-Americans long before Cortez landed in 1519. The Spaniards brought with them new flavors and ingredients such as wheat flour, olive oil and spices from Iberia and the Middle East. These additions enhanced the already delicious native cuisine. The natural foods that the Spaniards found in the New World are still abundant: corn, chili pods, tomatoes, potatoes, avocados, and a wide variety of beans.

Incidentally, the Aztec word chilli gave birth to the standard Spanish word chile and the English word chili (plural - chilies); the plant belongs to the capiscum family. Chilies range in flavor from extra hot to mild; be careful to select according to taste. Cilantro, a leafy herb used in some of these recipes, is also called coriander or Chinese parsley.

When the conquistadors moved north in search of gold, they brought with them a spicy and unique blend of Mexican and European cuisine now called "Southwestern" or "Tex-Mex." All ingredients used in the following recipes are now widely available north of the border and offer exciting and healthful additions to the vegetarian diet.

MEXICALI CORN AND SQUASH BAKE
(Serves 4)

Try this tangy vegetable casserole.

4 cups yellow squash
1 large yellow onion, chopped
1/2 cup green pepper, finely chopped
1 Tablespoon corn oil
1-1/2 cups vegan cream-style corn
1/2 cup (or 4 oz. can) roasted and peeled green chilies, chopped
2 Tablespoons prepared pimientos
1 clove garlic, crushed
1/4 cup cilantro leaves, finely chopped
1/4 cup cornmeal
Salt and pepper to taste

Cut squash into thin rounds and steam until tender. Drain well, set aside, and reserve some liquid. Sauté onion and green pepper in oil until soft. Combine all seasonings and vegetables. Layer half of mix into lightly oiled casserole and sprinkle with half the cornmeal. Layer rest of mix and top with rest of cornmeal. Bake covered at 350 degrees for about 15 minutes and 5 minutes uncovered. Add squash liquid if needed.

TOTAL CALORIES PER SERVING: 176
TOTAL FAT AS % OF DAILY VALUE: 6%   FAT: 4 gm
PROTEIN: 5 gm   CARBOHYDRATES: 34 gm
CALCIUM: 38 mg   IRON: 2 mg   SODIUM: 481 mg
DIETARY FIBER: 4 gm

GOLDEN CHILI CHOWDER
(Serves 6)

A hearty chowder from Texas, potent with chilies. If you like spicy food, add more chilies of any variety. Serve with toasted tortilla chips.

4 cups diced, unpeeled, red potatoes
1 large yellow onion, finely chopped
1/2 cup young green onions, finely
    chopped
2 teaspoons oil
4 cups potato water* mixed with
    instant vegetable broth or 4 cups
    plain soy milk
Salt and pepper to taste
1 medium carrot, finely shredded
1/2 cup (or 4 oz. can) roasted and
    peeled green chilies, finely
    chopped
Dash of hot pepper sauce
1 to 2 teaspoons cornmeal (optional)
2 cups fresh or canned yellow corn
    kernels
Red or green pepper flakes (or both)
    for garnish

In a deep pot, boil potatoes uncovered until barely tender. *Drain, save cooking liquid.

In a wide skillet sauté yellow and green onions in oil over medium heat. Remove from heat and pour into large (at least 4-quart), deep pot with lid.

Add liquid, seasonings, cooked potatoes, and remaining ingredients, except the corn kernels. Simmer, covered, for 30 minutes until stew thickens. (If stew isn't thick enough, mix in some cornmeal.)

Add corn kernels, cook ten more minutes uncovered, stirring often. Garnish with pepper flakes.

TOTAL CALORIES PER SERVING: 239
TOTAL FAT AS % OF DAILY VALUE: 5%   FAT: 3 gm

PROTEIN: 6 gm   CARBOHYDRATES: 39 gm
CALCIUM: 25 mg   IRON: 2 mg   SODIUM: 293 mg
DIETARY FIBER: 5 gm

MEATLESS BAKED BLACK BEAN BURRITOS
(Serves 4 -- two burritos per person)

This recipe is from a private kitchen in Arizona. Serve with corn on the cob.

1 large yellow onion, finely grated
1 can (15 oz.) cooked black beans,
    drained
1/2 cup (or 4 oz. can) peeled, roasted
    green chilies, finely chopped
1 teaspoon red chili powder
2 Tablespoons fresh cilantro, finely
    chopped
2 cups pre-cooked brown rice
Salt and pepper to taste
8 tortillas made of whole wheat flour
    or cornmeal
1 cup finely chopped tomatoes

Preheat oven to 350 degrees. Grate onion into deep mixing bowl. Add beans previously mashed with fork. Stir in chilies and all seasonings.

Spread tortillas on a counter, place equal amounts of spiced bean mixture on each, followed by an equal measure of rice. Overlap all four sides of each tortilla to envelop contents.

Set each burrito, seam side down, in non-stick baking pan. Drizzle with fresh chopped tomatoes. Bake at 350 degrees for 15 to 20 minutes.

TOTAL CALORIES PER SERVING: 508
TOTAL FAT AS % OF DAILY VALUE: 11%   FAT: 7 gm
PROTEIN: 19 gm   CARBOHYDRATES: 93 gm
CALCIUM: 141 mg   IRON: 6 mg   SODIUM: 548 mg
DIETARY FIBER: 8 gm

CHILI-STUFFED BAKED POTATOES
(Serves 4)

A tangy Santa Fe favorite, easy to prepare and economical. Serve with steamed broccoli or asparagus. The recipe can readily be adapted for more servings. Freezes well.

4 large russet potatoes
1 cup non-dairy sour cream or plain soy yogurt
1/2 cup chopped chives
1/2 cup (or 4-oz. can) roasted and peeled green chilies, finely chopped
Pinch of red chili powder
Salt and pepper to taste

Pierce each raw potato with fork, bake for 1 hour at 375 to 400 degrees. Don't wrap in foil or grease skins.

Remove from oven, cut off a length of skin at top and scoop out interior pulp to form a deep bowl. Set potato shells aside.

Mix pulp with all ingredients and stuff shells very carefully, leaving a mound of mix above the top. Set on cookie sheet. Return to oven until potato tops are browned.

TOTAL CALORIES PER SERVING: 328
TOTAL FAT AS % OF DAILY VALUE: 3%   FAT: 2 gm
PROTEIN: 9gm   CARBOHYDRATES: 69 gm
CALCIUM: 45 mg   IRON: 4 mg   SODIUM: 236 mg
DIETARY FIBER: 7 gm

FIESTA SALAD
(Serves 4-6)

A colorful blend of southwestern foods. Serve with corn tortillas.

2 cups cooked black, pinto, and kidney beans, mixed if possible
1 cup mixed, raw red and green pepper, finely chopped
1 cup cooked brown rice
1 cup corn kernels
1/2 cup young green onions, finely chopped
3 large, ripe tomatoes, finely chopped
2 Tablespoons cilantro, finely chopped
Salt and pepper to taste
No-fat salad dressing of choice

Place all ingredients in a large salad bowl. Toss with dressing at last moment to maintain crunchiness.

TOTAL CALORIES PER SERVING: 326
TOTAL FAT AS % OF DAILY VALUE: 3%   FAT: 2 gm
PROTEIN: 12 gm   CARBOHYDRATES: 57 gm
CALCIUM: 50 mg   IRON: 3 mg   SODIUM: 496 mg
DIETARY FIBER: 9 gm

Jacqueline Dunnington is a freelance writer from New Mexico.

TAMING OF THE "WILD RICE"

By Enette Larson, M.S., R.D.
and Stephen Knutson

W hat is wild rice? Is it rice that stands up on end and dances away from the more tame and sedate rice on your plate....jumps off your fork when you try to eat it....scampers off to join the legendary wild rice packs who shun man's taming and domestication, to live lives of self-determination, "*wild and free*"?

No evidence has been found to refute such possibilities! What we have found, however, is that what is referred to as "wild rice" is an imposter. It is not a rice at all, but the seed of the wild grass (*Zizania aquatica*), belonging to an entirely different botanical family from rice and other grains. This wild grass grows in shallow, mud-bottom rivers and lakes in the northern United States and Canada, and most abundantly in the Upper Great Lakes Region. It requires the northern climes because the soil must be stirred so that the seeds get the oxygen and nutrients they need to sprout. The spring thaw and melting of ice and snow creates this stirring process.

A HARVEST TRIP THROUGH WILD RICE COUNTRY

Native Americans of the Upper Great Lakes Region have harvested and processed wild rice for cooking for many, many moons. Let's imagine ourselves at a shallow lake in northern Minnesota. It is late summer. Two of us go out in a canoe. One stands in the back with a long pole, like those used in river rafting, to dig into the bottom and push the craft through the shallow water, mud, and grass stalks. The other person sits in the middle of the canoe with two long wooden sticks (called "knockers"), bends the grass stalks over the canoe and knocks the grain off the stalks. When the canoe is full or the day is done, we steer the canoe toward land, where we put our grain into bags.

Next, we pour the grain into a large metal kettle for "parching": dry-heating over a wood fire, until it dries enough to separate the husks from the seeds. To keep the grain from burning, we stir it with a long wooden paddle. After parching, we pour the contents into wooden buckets and "jig" or dance on the grain (to our favorite rap song, Native American chant or Irish jig). The purpose of "jigging" is completely to grind away the husks from the seeds. We must use moccasins because hard-soled shoes will break the seeds.

Our contents are then poured into tray-like baskets for "winnowing." Winnowing involves tossing seeds and chaff (ground up husks) into the air, letting the wind blow the lighter chaff away, while the heavier seeds, one hopes, fall back into the basket. After winnowing, the seeds are ready for washing and cooking.

BEGINNING SEEDS OF OUR RICEFUL KNOWLEDGE

Webster indicates that we have written references to "water rice" and "water oats," as wild rice was also referenced, as early as the 1750's. The Oxford Dictionary gives this defining reference for the year 1814: "The seeds... are a good substitute for rice, and for this reason it is called wild rice in America." Wild rice has always been a staple in the diet of the region's Native Americans. However, it was not until after World War II that the Upper Great Lakes Region began to market "naturally grown" wild rice regionally and nationally. In the 1960's, scientists at the

University of Minnesota developed a new strain of wild rice which did not break easily when picked by machine. Today, most of our wild rice production comes from these commercial "rice paddies," as they are called in Minnesota, California, and Canada.

THE TAMING OF THE WILD RICE -- FROM PACKAGE TO PLATE

Although wild rice is becoming increasingly popular, it is still more expensive than regular rice and other grains. In larger metropolitan areas, commercial wild rice is available for around $2 to $3 per pound. Naturally grown, hand picked wild rice, however, may cost a little more. In smaller communities, wild rice may be available only at specialty grocery stores, or you may have to order it through the mail.

For the meatless-meal connoisseur, the nutty flavor and chewy texture of wild rice makes it worth the extra effort and price. Its hardiness allows it to be the center of focus at any meal. (We are told it may even satisfy those who feel meat is necessary at every meal.) Wild rice can be tossed into a green salad, stuffed into a pita with vegetables, thrown into your favorite soup, or mixed with other grains. The creative cook can replace wild rice for ground meat in many recipes. (That was what sparked the idea for our cabbage rolls and pizza.)

Nutritionally, wild rice is similar to brown rice. Both are great, low-fat sources of carbohydrate, fiber, and B vitamins. Wild rice, however, is slightly higher in protein than brown rice and is an excellent source of vitamin E. Interestingly, one cup of cooked wild rice provides approximately half the recommended dietary allowance of this antioxidant vitamin.

The preparation of wild rice is similar to that of other rice. Wild rice, however, should be rinsed before cooking. Add 1 cup wild rice to 4 cups water or vegetable broth (1 part rice to 4 parts liquid). Bring to a boil, reduce heat, cover and boil gently for 30 minutes. Turn off heat and let stand 15-30 minutes until the wild rice reaches desired texture -- a shorter time produces a chewier rice, while a longer time gives a softer rice. Drain, and if desired, save liquid for other use. **One cup of dry rice yields 3 to 4 cups cooked.** Cooked wild rice also freezes well. For quick meal preparation, we recommend preparing a large batch of wild rice and freezing recipe-sized portions. Try a few of our "wilder" recipes.

WILD RICE PANCAKES
(Makes ten 4-inch pancakes)

Try these delicious pancakes.

1-1/4 cups whole wheat flour
1/4 teaspoon salt
2 teaspoons baking powder
1/4 teaspoon hot paprika
2 Tablespoons brown sugar or other sweetener
2 Tablespoons vegetable oil
1-1/4 cups lite soy milk
1 teaspoon lemon juice
1/2 teaspoon vanilla
1-1/4 cups wild rice, cooked
1/3 cup finely chopped pecans
1/2 cup grated carrot

Combine dry ingredients in a large bowl and make a well in the center of the mixture. In a separate bowl, combine the remaining ingredients and beat until smooth; quickly pour into the well and combine with a few quick strokes. Meanwhile, heat a non-stick griddle over medium heat; spray with vegetable cooking spray. Pour batter from the tip of a large spoon onto hot griddle. Cook 2-3 minutes until top bubbles and becomes dry. Turn and cook until the second side is done. Serve warm with fresh berries or apple sauce and tofu sour cream or soy yogurt.

BAKED CABBAGE ROLLS WITH GARLIC AND WILD RICE STUFFING
(Makes 10 rolls)

Serve these with brown rice and green salad.

2-1/2 cups wild rice, cooked
1/4 cup finely chopped onion
1/2 cup finely chopped fresh parsley
2-4 cloves garlic, minced
1/2 teaspoon sage
1 medium head of cabbage
1/2 - 1 Tablespoon olive oil
3/4 cup tomato juice
1/2 cup soy yogurt or sour cream

Combine the first five ingredients; chill for several hours to develop flavors.

Preheat oven to 375 degrees. Cut the stem from the cabbage deep enough to start a separation of the very outer leaves from the core. Dip the head in boiling water. This will loosen several leaves. Dip again and continue to remove the loosened leaves. (1 head of cabbage should yield 10 leaves of usable size.) Blanch the leaves 2 minutes in the boiling water. Drain and plunge into cold water. Arrange 10 cabbage leaves on damp towel.

Fill with approximately 1/10 of the wild rice mixture per leaf. Fold in outer right and left edges and roll. Place in large baking dish. Dip fingers into oil and lightly coat the top of each cabbage roll. Cover the rolls with tomato juice. Bake covered at 375 degrees for about 50 minutes. Serve each roll with a spoonful of the baked tomato juice and a dab of tofu "sour cream" or soy yogurt.

WILD RICE, MUSHROOM AND PEPPER PIZZA
(Makes 8 slices)

Cheese makes a more traditional pizza but it is delicious with wild rice and vegetables alone.

1 cup pizza sauce
10 ounces homemade pizza dough
1-1/2 cups cooked wild rice
8 ounces fresh mushrooms, sliced
1/2 medium onion, thinly sliced
1 red pepper, sliced in thin strips

Preheat oven to 450 degrees. Spread pizza sauce evenly over pizza dough. Sprinkle wild rice over pizza sauce and top with the remaining ingredients. Bake according to the directions of the pizza dough recipe you choose.

WILD RICE, CILANTRO AND GARLIC PIZZA
(Makes 8 slices)

Here's another creative pizza.

3/4 cup pizza sauce
10 ounces homemade pizza dough
2 cups cooked wild rice
1 cup packed fresh cilantro
4 cloves garlic, minced

1/2 medium onion, thinly sliced
2 large or 3 small fresh tomatoes

Preheat oven to 450 degrees. Spread pizza sauce evenly over pizza dough. Sprinkle wild rice over pizza sauce. Finely chop fresh cilantro, mix with minced garlic, and sprinkle over wild rice. Top with onions and tomatoes. Bake according to the directions of the pizza dough recipe. Turn oven to broil, and broil 1-2 minutes to brown onions and tomatoes lightly.

TOTAL CALORIES PER SLICE: 158
TOTAL FAT AS % OF DAILY VALUE: 2%   FAT: 1 gm
PROTEIN: 6 gm   CARBOHYDRATES: 30 gm
CALCIUM: 19 mg   IRON: 2 mg   SODIUM: 237 mg
DIETARY FIBER: 1 gm

WILD RICE PICNIC SALAD
(Makes six 3/4-cup servings)

Here's a unique salad.

2-1/2 cups cooked wild rice
2 cups sliced red grapes
8-ounce can water chestnuts, drained
    and chopped
1/4 -1/3 cup soft tofu or plain soy
    yogurt
2 Tablespoons eggless mayonnaise
1 Tablespoon dill weed
1/4 cup slivered almonds

In a large bowl combine wild rice, grapes, and water chestnuts. In a separate bowl, beat tofu or yogurt with a fork until smooth. (If the tofu does not beat to the consistency of mayonnaise, add a few drops of water.) Add mayonnaise and dill weed, and stir well. Pour over wild rice mixture and mix thoroughly. Chill for several hours. Toss in almonds before serving.

TOTAL CALORIES PER SERVING: 147
TOTAL FAT AS % OF DAILY VALUE: 6%   FAT: 4 gm
PROTEIN: 5 gm   CARBOHYDRATES: 24 gm
CALCIUM: 39 mg   IRON: 1 mg   SODIUM: 40 mg
DIETARY FIBER: 2 gm

SHERRIED WILD RICE AND MUSHROOM CASSEROLE
(Serves 4)

Delicious served with fresh asparagus, whole wheat bread, orange slices, and white wine.

8 ounces fresh mushrooms, sliced
1 Tablespoon olive oil
6 Tablespoons dry sherry
2 Tablespoons flour
1/4 teaspoon black pepper
1 cup lite soy milk
2-1/2 cups cooked wild rice

Preheat oven to 350 degrees. Sauté mushrooms over low heat in olive oil and 4 Tablespoons of sherry. Add flour and stir until liquid and flour make a smooth paste. Add black pepper and soy milk; cook over medium heat until sauce thickens. Stir in remaining sherry and wild rice. Bake in covered dish at 350 degrees for 40 minutes.

TOTAL CALORIES PER SERVING: 243
TOTAL FAT AS % OF DAILY VALUE: 6%   FAT: 4 gm
PROTEIN: 7 gm   CARBOHYDRATES: 35 gm
CALCIUM: 30 mg   IRON: 2 mg   SODIUM: 8 mg
DIETARY FIBER: 2 gm

Enette Larson is currently a Ph.D. student in nutrition sciences at the University of Alabama at Birmingham. Stephen Knutson has a B.A. in theater from the University of Minnesota and is presently on the trail of the wild rice packs in the Arizona desert.

A BIT O' IRISH COOKIN' -- VEGETARIAN STYLE

By Enette Larson, M.S., R.D.

"If yer're lookin' to catch a leprechaun this Saint Patrick's Day, surin' ye know leprechauns are tricky! Ye'd be better off relaxin' and sharin' in another pot of gold -- the discoverin' of a bit of Irish Cookin -- and the learnin' of a bit about the traditional Irish Diet."

Everyone is Irish on Saint Patrick's Day! Even the most Irish of the Irish vegetarians, however, are out of luck when it comes to celebrating with Corned Beef and Cabbage, Irish Stew or Limerick Ham. Ah, out of luck at New World celebrations, perhaps, but not out of luck according to history or tradition -- and there are plenty of Ol' Irish vegetarian favorites to prove it.

Through the centuries, it is clear that the Irish diet had very little meat in it. In fact, although even the poorest family owned at least one cow or goat, the animals were considered of great value and were rarely killed. The Irish feasted instead on whole grains, vegetables, and fruit which included oats, wheat, barley, root vegetables, mushrooms, leeks, leafy greens, grapes, pears, apples, and berries, along with an array of herbs for flavor.

How corned beef and cabbage can be recognized as Ireland's national dish is a reflection of the change in the Irish diet that happened after the "Great Potato Famine" and World War II. History records that most Irish people had not even tasted corned beef -- a method of preserving meat with salt, brown sugar, and saltpeter -- until they set sail on the famine boats to the New World.[1]

A BIT O' IRISH HISTORY

The food of Ireland, as of most countries, is part of its history and civilization. According to archaeologists, the first evidence of settlement in early Ireland was around 600 BC. These early settlers cleared the forests, planted wheat and barley, and herded cattle, sheep, and goats. About 400 years later, the

Celts (Gaels) arrived from Europe, settled in Ireland and developed the basis of the Irish language (Gaelic), beliefs, and civilization. Of course, it was in the third century that Saint Patrick was recognized for spreading Christianity throughout Ireland.

In 1580, an Irishman named Walter Raleigh planted the first potato -- a vegetable that considerably changed the Irish diet and directed the course of Irish history. By 1680, the potato had become the mainstay in the Irish diet -- potatoes grew well in the moist, mild climate and a small patch could feed a whole family. Although there were many small agricultural and political "potato famines," the big four-year famine that began in 1845 was so devastating to the Irish people that it caused starvation, death, and emigration. It was at this time that many Irish immigrants were first introduced to corned beef.

Back in Ireland, the potato, now associated with poverty and famine, was no longer the center of the Irish diet. By the mid 1900s, the Irish had pushed it to the side of their plates and later almost right out of their diet. Unfortunately, meat was being eaten more and more, and after World War II it became fashionable to have it at every meal.

A BIT ABOUT HEALTH

The change in the Irish diet after the mid 19th century created "recipes for disease." It seems the Irish were much healthier when the mainstay of their diet consisted of potatoes. However, as important as the potato was both economically and nutritionally (the potato is rich in many nutrients including complex carbohydrates, protein, vitamin C, thiamin, niacin, riboflavin, and iron), the potato alone cannot be credited for keeping the Irish healthy. According to a report issued from the Human Nutrition Unit at Trinity College in Dublin, Ireland[3], along with the potato, the variety of vegetables, fruits, and whole grains was similarly pushed to the sides of plates to make room for meat, cream dishes, and refined carbohydrates. This change from a primarily ovo-lacto vegetarian diet that was rich in carbohydrates, vitamins and minerals to one that is high in protein and fat[2] has been linked with a decline in health status in Ireland[3], including the increased incidence of heart disease, cancer, and other ailments.

FINDIN' THE POT OF GOLD

It is clear that the pot of gold has been around for centuries! Before sharin' in the gold, however, there is one more question needin' an answer. What, if not corned beef and cabbage (and no arguments here) deserves recognition as Ireland's true national dish? Not surprisingly, according to the Folklore Council of Ireland, a vegetarian dish called Colcannon (also known locally as poundy or cally) deserves this honor.[4] Colcannon is a festival dish traditionally served on All Hallows' Day (Hallowe'en), but represents the harvest. It is made from new potatoes, kale and leeks to which milk, wild garlic and butter are added. Nutritionally speaking, Colcannon and the other recipes included in this pot are rich in complex carbohydrates, protein, vitamins, mineral and fiber. They can be prepared traditionally using milk products or with a modern milk alternative coincidentally made from the historical mainstay of the Irish diet - the potato.

SELECTED REFERENCES

[1]McCormick M. *Malachi McCormick's Irish Country Cooking.* New York: Crown Publishers, Inc, 1988.

[2]Robertson JA and Kevany JJ. Trends in the availability of foods for human consumption in Ireland. *Ir Journal Med Sci* 1982; 151:272.

[3]Whitehead, RG. Dietary goals: their scientific justification. *Royal Soc Health J* 1979; 5:181.

[4]MacNeill M. *The Festival of Lughnasa.* Ireland: The Folklore Council of Ireland, 1982.

COLCANNON
(Serves 4)

Besides being a traditional favorite, this dish contains two of the top foods with cancer-preventive properties (cabbage and parsnips).

1 pound potatoes, sliced
2 medium parsnips, peeled and sliced
2 medium leeks
1 cup potato or soy milk (Vegelicious, a potato milk, is found in some natural food stores, along with several different types of soy milks.)
1 pound kale or cabbage
1/2 teaspoon mace (optional)
2 cloves of garlic, minced
Salt and Pepper to taste
2 Tablespoons soft soy margarine
Parsley

Cook the potatoes and parsnips in water until tender. While these are cooking, chop leeks (greens as well as whites) and simmer in the milk until soft. Next, cook the kale or cabbage and have warm and well chopped. Drain the potatoes, season with mace, garlic, salt and pepper, and beat well. Add the cooked leeks and milk (being careful not to break down the leeks too much). Finally, blend in the kale or cabbage and margarine. The texture should be that of a smooth, buttery potato with well distributed pieces of leek and kale. Garnish with parsley.

Note: Colcannon is also made by cooking layered vegetables, starting with potatoes, in a slow cooker during the day. Drain vegetables, blend with milk and margarine as above and garnish with parsley.

TOTAL CALORIES PER SERVING: 288
TOTAL FAT AS % OF DAILY VALUE: 11% FAT: 7 gm PROTEIN: 6 gm
CARBOHYDRATES: 54 gm
CALCIUM: 213 mg   IRON: 4 mg
SODIUM: 145 mg
DIETARY FIBER: 9 gm

CARROT AND PARSNIPS
(Serves 8)

Carrots are also at the top of the list of foods with cancer-preventive properties.

1 pound (7-8) small carrots, peeled and sliced
1 pound (2-3) new parsnips, peeled and sliced
1 Tablespoon soft soy margarine
1/2 teaspoon cloves (optional)
Parsley

Simmer vegetables in about 2 inches of water until tender (about 10 minutes). Remove from heat, drain, and mash with margarine and cloves. Serve hot garnished with parsley.

TOTAL CALORIES PER SERVING: 82
TOTAL FAT AS % OF DAILY VALUE: 3% FAT: 2 gm PROTEIN: 1 gm
CARBOHYDRATES: 17 gm
CALCIUM: 37 mg   IRON: 1 mg
SODIUM: 42 mg
DIETARY FIBER: 4 gm

COLD SPINACH SOUP
(Serves 8)

Garnished with lemon slices before serving.

4 cups cooked fresh spinach (save liquid)
2 cups spinach stock or water
1 vegetable broth cube
1 cup soy sour cream alternative or plain soy yogurt
1 Tablespoon lemon juice
Lemon slices

Dissolve vegetable broth cube in spinach stock. Mix all ingredients in a blender until smooth. Serve cold.

TOTAL CALORIES PER SERVING: 46
TOTAL FAT AS % OF DAILY VALUE: 2% FAT: 1 gm PROTEIN: 4 gm
CARBOHYDRATES: 6 gm
CALCIUM: 130 mg   IRON: 3 mg
SODIUM: 99 mg
DIETARY FIBER: 2 gm

GUINESS BREAD

(Makes 1 loaf--16 slices)

Enjoy this unique bread!

2 packages dry yeast
1/2 cup warm water
1 Tablespoon sugar or
    other sweetener
1/2 bottle of Guiness
    Stout (6 ounces)
2 Tablespoons liquid
    sweetener
1 Tablespoon margarine
1-1/2 cups all purpose
    flour
1 teaspoon caraway
    seeds (optional)
1 teaspoon salt
1 teaspoon ginger
2-1/2 cups whole wheat
    flour

Dissolve yeast and sugar in water and set aside. Heat stout, liquid sweetener, and margarine until warm. Add stout mix to the dissolved yeast and stir in the all purpose flour. Beat until smooth and elastic. Stir in the caraway seeds, salt, ginger, and enough whole wheat flour to make a soft dough. Turn onto a floured board and knead until smooth (about 3 minutes). Shape into a round loaf and put into an 8-inch greased round pan. Cover with a tea towel and let rise in a warm place for 1 hour. Bake at 375 for 30 minutes or until bread makes

a hollow sound when tapped. Brush top lightly with melted soy margarine.

TOTAL CALORIES PER SLICE: 146
TOTAL FAT AS % OF DAILY VALUE:
3%   FAT: 2 gm PROTEIN: 5 gm
CARBOHYDRATES: 30 gm
CALCIUM: 152 mg   IRON: 2 mg
SODIUM: 255 mg
DIETARY FIBER: 4 gm

SCANNELS' SODA BREAD

(Makes 1 loaf -- 8 slices)

This is a modification of my great grandmother Scannel's recipe. Use 2 cups of flour and no oat bran for the traditional version.

1-1/2 cups whole wheat
    pastry flour
1 cup oat bran
1-1/2 teaspoons baking
    powder
1/4 teaspoon baking
    soda
1/4 teaspoon salt
1 Tablespoon sugar
    or other sweet-
    ener
2 Tablespoons caraway
    seeds
1/4 cup currants or
    raisins
1 cup potato or soy
    milk plus 1 Table-
    spoon lemon juice

Mix dry ingredients well, then blend in caraway seeds and currants. Add milk stirring to make a soft dough. Turn onto a lightly floured board and knead for 1 minute. Shape into a round loaf and put into an 8-inch greased round pan. With a floured knife, cut a cross into the top. Bake at 350 for 40 minutes or until lightly browned. Cut into slices crosswise when cool.

TOTAL CALORIES PER SLICE: 146
TOTAL FAT AS % OF DAILY VALUE:
3%   FAT: 2 gm PROTEIN: 5 gm
CARBOHYDRATES: 30 gm
CALCIUM: 152 mg   IRON: 2 mg
SODIUM: 255 mg
DIETARY FIBER: 4 gm

IRISH BREAKFAST SCONES

(Makes 16 small scones)

Less rich and much simpler than English Tea Scones

1-1/2 cups whole wheat pastry flour
1/3 cup whole meal flour
3/4 cup wheat bran
1 teaspoon baking powder
2 Tablespoons soft soy margarine
2 Tablespoons corn or rice syrup
1 cup potato or soy milk

Mix dry ingredients. Add margarine and mix well. Add the syrup and enough milk to mix to a loose dough. Turn onto a floured board and knead until smooth. Roll out into a square with a thickness of about 3/4 inch. Cut dough in half, then into quarters and then in eighths. Bake on a lightly floured baking sheet at 400 degrees for approximately 20 minutes. Cool on a wire rack. Split and serve with whole fruit preserves.

TOTAL CALORIES PER SCONE: 84
TOTAL FAT AS % OF DAILY VALUE:
3%   FAT: 2 gm PROTEIN: 2 gm
CARBOHYDRATES: 16 gm
CALCIUM: 63 mg   IRON: 1 mg
SODIUM: 65 mg
DIETARY FIBER: 2 gm

LEPRECHAUNS' SPICE CAKE

(Makes 1 cake -- 24 slices)

A delicious rich treat that's high in carbohydrate.

2 cups brown sugar
1 cup hot water (2 cups if Guiness is not used)
1 cup warm Guiness (optional)
2 Tablespoons soft soy margarine
15 ounces raisins
1 teaspoon salt
1/2 teaspoon cloves
1 teaspoon cinnamon
1/2 teaspoon nutmeg
3 cups whole wheat pastry flour
1 teaspoon baking soda
1 teaspoon baking powder

Bring sugar, water, Guiness, margarine, raisins, salt, and spices to boil in a heavy saucepan; simmer for 5 minutes. Allow to cool. Sift dry ingredients together. Mix into cooled mixture. Bake in a lined (with 2 layers of wax paper) large loaf tin at 350 degrees for 1-1/2 hours.

TOTAL CALORIES PER SERVING:
168
TOTAL FAT AS % OF DAILY VALUE:
2%   FAT: 1 gm PROTEIN: 3 gm
CARBOHYDRATES: 39 gm
CALCIUM: 39 mg   IRON: 1 mg
SODIUM: 186 mg
DIETARY FIBER: 3 gm

POTATO CAKES

(Makes 8 to 10 cakes)

Once baked, split the potato cakes and serve piping hot.

4 Tablespoons soft soy margarine
2 cups whole meal flour
1 Tablespoon baking powder
1-1/2 cups cold mashed potatoes
1/4 cup potato or soy milk

In a bowl, mix the margarine into the flour and baking powder with your hands. Using a wooden spoon, blend in the potato and the milk. Turn onto a floured board and knead several times to form a soft ball. Roll out to a thickness of about 1-1/4 inches. Cut out the cakes using a 3-inch biscuit cutter or drinking glass. Bake on a greased cookie sheet at 450 for 20-25 minutes, until golden brown.

TOTAL CALORIES PER CAKE: 180
TOTAL FAT AS % OF DAILY VALUE:
9%   FAT: 6 gm PROTEIN: 5 gm
CARBOHYDRATES: 39 gm
CALCIUM: 124 mg   IRON: 1 mg
SODIUM: 254 mg
DIETARY FIBER: 4 gm

Enette Larson is a dietitian working on her Ph.D. in nutrition in Birmingham, Alabama. She enjoys keeping track of her Irish heritage.

SPANISH
VEGETARIAN COOKING MADE SIMPLE

By Habeeb Salloum

Not many culinary experts are aware that Spanish cuisine is primarily based on the dishes developed by the Moors in the Iberian Peninsula and, later, enhanced by Native American foods brought back from the Western Hemisphere after Columbus' voyage. Without these contributions to the kitchens of that land, the victuals of Spain would be poor indeed.

Traces of Phoenician, Greek, Roman, and Jewish food can be found in Spanish cuisine, but it was the Arabs who left the most profound and lasting legacy. During their 800 years in the Iberian Peninsula, they greatly popularized native edibles such as hazelnuts and olive oil, and brought in innumerable new fruits and vegetables. Today, a good number still carry their Arabic names. From among these, eggplants, in Spanish, berenjena, from the Arabic [badhinjan]; lemon - limon [laymun]; orange - naranja [naranj]; rice - arroz [al-ruzz]; saffron - azafran [al-za faran]; spinach - espinaca [isbanakh]; and sugar - azucar [sukkar], all essential in Spanish cooking, are leftovers from the Moorish kitchen.

To many, the Andalusian fields and gardens diffusing the smell of lemon, orange, and pomegranate flowers bring to mind the romantic days of the caliphs in Cordova; to others, the Moors live in the taste of almonds, cinnamon, and lemon, the mainstays of Spanish desserts. Culinary historians believe that a great many Spanish dishes, such as the famous gazpacho and paella, are concoctions inherited from the Arabs.

The second most significant development in the Spanish kitchen happened after Columbus' voyage. The available food ingredients in the cuisine of Spain more than doubled, and this revolutionized not only the diet of the people of the Iberian Peninsula, but that of the whole world. All types of peppers and beans (except broad beans), corn, chocolate, peanuts, potatoes, tomatoes, vanilla, and every species of squash, are some of the foods brought by the Conquistadors from the New World. Many of these, like potatoes and tomatoes, became staples in the Spanish diet, and the others greatly enriched the tried and true dishes of the Peninsula.

Today, all these past influences have been instrumental in the development of modern Spanish cuisine. There are a number of things common to that country's kitchen. Garlic and olive oil, which impart an authentic and unique flavor to Spanish food, form the base of most cooking. Vegetables are usually slowly sautéed until tender, fast-fried, or combined in casseroles and slowly cooked. Four herbs: bay leaves, oregano, rosemary, and thyme, preferably fresh, are often employed in seasoning. Saffron is generally utilized in rice dishes. Breads are commonly used as binders, especially in soups and stuffing, and chocolate is an important ingredient in numerous sweets. Pulverized nuts are often utilized to flavor sauces, and dried legumes such as chickpeas, lentils, and numerous types of beans are favored in many dishes.

In Spain's larder there is a host of vegetarian dishes. When a number are combined to make a meal, they produce a world of gourmet ecstasy.

EGGPLANT CAVIAR
Caviar de Berenjena
(Serves 6)

Serve as an appetizer or side dish.

1 eggplant (about 1 pound)
2 cloves garlic, minced
4 Tablespoons onion, finely chopped
1 Tablespoon olive oil
2 Tablespoons tomato paste, unsalted
1 Tablespoon vinegar
1/2 teaspoon salt
1/4 teaspoon pepper
1/8 teaspoon cayenne

Roast eggplant in a 375 degree oven until the skin darkens and becomes crisp, then remove and cool.

Peel eggplant, then mash in a mixing bowl. Add remaining ingredients and thoroughly mix. Place on a platter and chill.

TOTAL CALORIES PER SERVING: 49
TOTAL FAT AS % OF DAILY VALUE: 3%   FAT: 2 gm
PROTEIN: 1 gm
CARBOHYDRATES: 7 gm
CALCIUM: 12 mg   IRON: <1 mg
SODIUM: 197 mg
DIETARY FIBER: <1 gm

LIMA BEAN APPETIZER
Judias Alinadas
(Serves 8)

Cooked chickpeas or lentils can be substituted for the lima beans in this recipe.

4 cups cooked green lima beans
1 medium sweet pepper, finely chopped
4 Tablespoons parsley, finely chopped
4 Tablespoons green onions, finely chopped
2 Tablespoons olive oil
4 Tablespoons lemon juice
1 clove garlic, minced
1 teaspoon salt
1 teaspoon thyme
1/2 teaspoon pepper

Combine beans, sweet pepper, parsley and green onions in a salad bowl and set aside.

Mix remaining ingredients, then pour over vegetables. Toss and serve immediately.

TOTAL CALORIES PER SERVING: 140
TOTAL FAT AS % OF DAILY VALUE: 6%   FAT: 4 gm
PROTEIN: 6 gm
CARBOHYDRATES: 22 gm
CALCIUM: 35 mg   IRON: 2 mg
SODIUM: 304 mg
DIETARY FIBER: 6 gm

WHITE GARLIC SOUP
Sopa de Ajo Blanco
(Serves 6)

This soup should be eaten in moderation since it is not lowfat.

1/4 pound bread, crust removed
4 cups water
3/4 cup pulverized blanched almonds
6 cloves garlic, minced
1 Tablespoon olive oil
3 Tablespoons vinegar
1/2 teaspoon salt
1/2 pound seedless white grapes

Place bread and water in a bowl and allow to soak for 2 minutes. Transfer bowl contents to a food processor, then add remaining ingredients, except grapes. Process for a few moments, then transfer to a serving bowl. Chill and serve garnished with the grapes.

TOTAL CALORIES PER SERVING: 183
TOTAL FAT AS % OF DAILY VALUE: 17%   FAT: 11 gm
PROTEIN: 6 gm
CARBOHYDRATES: 20 gm
CALCIUM: 89 mg   IRON: 2 mg
SODIUM: 292 mg
DIETARY FIBER: 2 gm

PICKLED EGGPLANT
Berenjena En Escabeche
(Serves 8)

Refrigerate this dish for three days before serving.

1 pound very small
   eggplants
1/2 cup vinegar
4 cloves garlic, minced
2 Tablespoons olive
   oil
1-1/2 teaspoons salt
1 teaspoon cumin
1/2 teaspoon pepper
1/4 teaspoon chili
   powder
1/2 cup water

Place eggplants in a pot and cover with water. Bring to boil and cover. Cook over medium heat for 10 minutes. Drain and place in a glass or Pyrex utensil, then allow to cool.

Combine remaining ingredients and pour over eggplants. Add water to cover eggplants, if needed.

TOTAL CALORIES PER SERVING:
47
TOTAL FAT AS % OF DAILY
VALUE: 5%   FAT: 3 gm
PROTEIN: 1 gm
CARBOHYDRATES: 5 gm
CALCIUM: 11 mg   IRON: <1 mg
SODIUM: 432 mg
DIETARY FIBER: <1 gm

ESCAROLE SALAD
Ensalada a la Almoraina
(Serves 6)

Try this unique salad.

1 large head escarole,
   washed and
   chopped
1-2/3 cups stewed
   tomatoes
2 Tablespoons olive
   oil
3 Tablespoons vinegar
2 cloves garlic, minced
1 teaspoon cumin
1 teaspoon paprika
1/2 teaspoon thyme
1/2 teaspoon salt
1/4 teaspoon pepper
Pitted olives (optional)

Place escarole in a salad bowl and set aside.

Combine remaining ingredients, except olives, and pour over the escarole. Mix before serving and decorate with olives.

TOTAL CALORIES PER SERVING:
72
TOTAL FAT AS % OF DAILY
VALUE: 8%   FAT: 5 gm
PROTEIN: 2 gm
CARBOHYDRATES: 7 gm
CALCIUM: 64 mg   IRON: 1 mg
SODIUM: 379 mg
DIETARY FIBER: 3 gm

TOMATO RICE
Arroz de Tomate
(Serves 6)

Serve this as a side dish.

1 Tablespoon olive oil
1 medium onion,
   finely chopped
2 cloves garlic, minced
1 cup white rice
2 cups stewed toma-
   toes
1 cup water
1 small sweet pepper,
   finely chopped
1 teaspoon basil
1/2 teaspoon salt
1/4 teaspoon pepper
1/8 teaspoon cayenne

Heat oil in frying pan, then sauté onions and garlic over medium heat for 12 minutes. Add rice and stir-fry for another 2 minutes. Stir in remaining ingredients and bring to boil. Cover and cook over medium heat for 25 minutes. Turn heat off and allow to cook in own steam for another 30 minutes. Serve hot.

TOTAL CALORIES PER SERVING:
171
TOTAL FAT AS % OF DAILY
VALUE: 5%   FAT: 3 gm
PROTEIN: 3 gm
CARBOHYDRATES: 33 gm
CALCIUM: 41 mg   IRON: 2 mg
SODIUM: 400 mg
DIETARY FIBER: 2 gm

VEGETARIAN PAELLA
Paella Vegetariana
(Serves 8)

This recipe can be served as a main dish.

1 Tablespoon oil
2 medium onions, finely chopped
2 cloves garlic, minced
1-1/2 cups white rice
3-1/2 cups water
1 cup fresh or frozen peas
1/2 cup chopped green olives
1 medium sweet pepper, finely chopped
1 teaspoon oregano
1 teaspoon salt
1/2 teaspoon pepper
A few threads or pinch of pure saffron
1 cup lightly fried sliced mushrooms
1 cup asparagus, chopped
1/2 cup toasted blanched almonds

Pre-heat oven to 400 degrees. Heat oil in a frying pan, then sauté onions and garlic over medium heat for 12 minutes. Add rice and stir-fry for another 2 minutes. Transfer frying pan contents to a 9- x 13-inch Pyrex dish. Stir in water, peas, olives, sweet pepper, oregano, salt, pepper, and saffron, then cover. Bake in oven for 30 minutes.

Combine mushrooms, asparagus and almonds, then spread evenly over top. Re-cover and bake for a further 25 minute or until rice is well-cooked. Serve hot from pan.

TOTAL CALORIES PER SERVING: 236
TOTAL FAT AS % OF DAILY VALUE: 11%   FAT: 7 gm
PROTEIN: 7 gm
CARBOHYDRATES: 39 gm
CALCIUM: 54 mg   IRON: 3 mg
SODIUM: 407 mg
DIETARY FIBER: 3 gm

CHICKPEAS AND BROAD BEAN STEW
Garbanzo y Habas a la Andaluza
(Serves 6)

This dish can be served hot or cold.

1 Tablespoon olive oil
2 medium onions, chopped
2 cloves garlic, minced
1/2 small hot pepper, finely chopped
2 Tablespoons fresh coriander leaves, finely chopped
4 medium tomatoes, finely chopped
2 cups cooked chick-peas
2 cups fresh or frozen broad beans
1 teaspoon salt
1/2 teaspoon pepper
1/2 teaspoon cumin
A few threads or pinch of pure saffron
2 cups water

Heat oil in a saucepan, then sauté onions, garlic and hot pepper over medium heat for 12 minutes. Add coriander and tomatoes, then stir-fry for another 8 minutes. Stir in remaining ingredients and bring to boil. Cover and cook over medium heat for 40 minutes, checking once in a while and adding more water if necessary.

TOTAL CALORIES PER SERVING: 243
TOTAL FAT AS % OF DAILY VALUE: 6%   FAT: 4 gm
PROTEIN: 12 gm
CARBOHYDRATES: 40 gm
CALCIUM: 97 mg   IRON: 4 mg
SODIUM: 439 mg
DIETARY FIBER: 3 gm

Habeeb Salloum is a free-lance writer and cookbook author from Ontario, Canada.

SATISFYING VEGETARIAN FOODS FROM MIDDLE EASTERN LANDS

By Habeeb Salloum

No one walking through the streets of Damascus -- the oldest continuously inhabited city in the world -- engulfed in the smoke of barbecuing kabobs will dream that behind these aromas there is a world of vegetarian delights. Yet, in the historic Fertile Crescent lands, non-meat dishes have been the food of the masses since time immemorial. For millennia the peasants and laborers in that part of the world have been nourished on these simple, but tasty, victuals. Rich, wholesome, economical, and full of flavor, they have stood the test of centuries.

Broad beans (also known as fava beans or horse beans), bulgur, chickpeas, lentils, rice, yogurt, and all types of cultivated and wild greens -- flavored by just the right amount of condiments -- produce hearty, scrumptious appetizers, salads, soups, stews, and vegetable patties. The seasonings permeating the vegetables and grains give the food a mouthwatering and delightful quality. Condiments are only employed in moderation, just enough to give taste and enticement. The hot spicy dishes of the mysterious Orient are not to be found in the lands of the Middle East.

Stuffed vegetables, mainly a number of greens such as cabbage, kohlrabi, Swiss chard, and vine leaves make excellent main courses for both ordinary meals and classy banquets. Herbs and spices enhance the taste of almost every type of stuffing, soaking, and blending with the vegetables. Allspice is especially effective and used most often. For lovers of vegetarian foods, stuffed leaves are, perhaps, the most toothsome of the meatless dishes.

From the simple appetizer to stuffed vegetables, all dishes are prepared to perfection and presented to family and guests with pride. With a half dozen of these vegetarian foods, amazing gourmet meals can be prepared. The never-ending storehouse of Middle Eastern non-meat dishes, as these few recipes will no doubt testify, is a world of nutritious and satisfying foods.

YOGURT SALAD -- SALATAT LABAN
(Serves 6)

This tasty and simple-to-prepare salad is an excellent summer dish.

2 cups plain soy yogurt
1 medium cucumber, peeled and cut into small pieces
1 Tablespoon fresh mint, finely chopped
1 Tablespoon fresh coriander leaves, finely chopped
2 cloves garlic, minced
1/4 teaspoon salt
1/4 teaspoon pepper

Place all the ingredients in a salad bowl, and toss well. Chill and serve.

TOTAL CALORIES PER SERVING: 68
TOTAL FAT AS % OF DAILY VALUE: 3%   FAT: 2 gm
PROTEIN: 4 gm   CARBOHYDRATES: 8 gm
CALCIUM: 24 mg   IRON: 1 mg   SODIUM: 120 mg
DIETARY FIBER: 2 gm

EGGPLANT PURÉE --
BABA GHANOUJ
(Serves 8)

This is a very tasty dish -- colorful and pleasing to the eye. Baba Ghanouj, a traditional delight of the Middle East, is to be found in every North American Middle Eastern Restaurant. It is excellent as an appetizer, dip, or side dish.

1 large eggplant (1-1/2 pounds)
1 medium Spanish onion, chopped
4 Tablespoons lemon juice
3 Tablespoons tahini (sesame butter)
1 Tablespoon olive oil
1 Tablespoon water
1 clove garlic, minced
1/2 teaspoon each salt and pepper
1/8 teaspoon cayenne
1 small tomato, finely chopped
2 Tablespoons parsley, finely
   chopped

Grill eggplant over open fire or bake in an oven, turning over a few times until skin turns crisp. Allow to cool.

Peel eggplant and place in a food processor along with the remaining ingredients (except tomato and parsley). Process into a paste.

Place mixture on a flat serving platter. Garnish with tomato and parsley.

TOTAL CALORIES PER SERVING: 81
TOTAL FAT AS % OF DAILY VALUE: 8%   FAT: 5 gm
PROTEIN: 2 gm   CARBOHYDRATES: 9 gm
CALCIUM: 21 mg   IRON: 1 mg   SODIUM: 149 mg
DIETARY FIBER: 1 gm

LENTIL SOUP --
SHAWRBAT 'ADAS
(Serves 6)

Lentils, cooked in untold ways, stand at the top of Middle Eastern vegetarian foods.

2 Tablespoons olive oil
2 large onions, chopped
4 cloves garlic, minced
1 cup split lentils
1/2 teaspoon salt
3/4 teaspoon pepper
3/4 teaspoon coriander powder
1/2 teaspoon cumin
7 cups water
4 Tablespoons rice
6 Tablespoons lemon juice

Heat oil in a saucepan. Sauté onions and garlic over medium heat for 10 minutes. Add lentils, salt, pepper, coriander, cumin, and water. Bring to a boil and cover. Cook over medium heat for 30 minutes. Add rice, and cook for 25 minutes longer or until lentils and rice are thoroughly cooked.

Place mixture in batches in a blender and purée. Return to the saucepan and reheat. Stir in lemon juice. Serve hot.

TOTAL CALORIES PER SERVING: 168
TOTAL FAT AS % OF DAILY VALUE: 8%   FAT: 5 gm
PROTEIN: 7 gm   CARBOHYDRATES: 25 gm
CALCIUM: 30 mg   IRON: 3 mg   SODIUM: 193 mg
DIETARY FIBER: 4 gm

RICE WITH VERMICELLI --
RIZZ BISH-SHI 'ARIYYA
(Serves 6)

Brown rice can be substituted for vermicelli.

2 Tablespoons soft margarine
1/4 cup thin vermicelli, broken into
    small pieces
1 cup rice
2 cups boiling water
1/2 teaspoon salt
1/4 teaspoon pepper

Melt soft margarine in a frying pan. Add
vermicelli and stir-fry until light brown. Add
rice and stir-fry for an additional 3 minutes.
Stir in remaining ingredients and bring to a
boil. Cover and cook over medium-low heat
for 25 minutes. Turn off heat and allow rice
to cook in its own steam for 20 minutes.
Serve hot.
    Note: If brown rice is utilized, increase
the water by a 1/4 and double the cooking
time.

TOTAL CALORIES PER SERVING: 160
TOTAL FAT AS % OF DAILY VALUE: 6%   FAT: 4 gm
PROTEIN: 2 gm   CARBOHYDRATES: 28 gm
CALCIUM: 6 mg   IRON: 2 mg   SODIUM: 236 mg
DIETARY FIBER: <1 gm

CABBAGE ROLLS IN OIL --
MIHSHEE MALFOUF BI ZAYT
(Serves 10)

*Swiss chard and other vegetable leaves or vine
leaves may be substituted for the cabbage.*

1 large head of cabbage
Water
2 cups cooked chickpeas
1 cup brown rice
1 small bunch green onions, finely
    chopped
2 large tomatoes, finely chopped
1 medium onion, finely chopped
1/2 cup fresh mint, finely chopped
4 Tablespoons fresh coriander leaves,
    finely chopped
1/4 cup olive oil
1/4 cup vegetable broth
1 teaspoon pepper
1/2 teaspoon allspice
1/4 teaspoon cayenne pepper
3/4 teaspoon salt
8 cloves garlic, chopped into large
    pieces
1/2 cup lemon juice

Place cabbage in a pot of boiling water and
cook for a few minutes to soften leaves.
Loosen leaves from bottom and trim down
thick ribs. If leaves are still not tender, boil
again. Set aside.
    Combine remaining ingredients (except
1/2 teaspoon salt, garlic, and lemon juice) to
make a filling.
    Place some filling, depending on size of
cabbage leaf, on wide end and roll, tucking in
ends to complete the process. Continue until
all leaves are stuffed.
    Cover the bottom of a saucepan with
pieces of cabbage ribs and extra leaves.
Arrange rolls side by side in alternating layers,
placing garlic pieces between layers. Sprinkle
remaining salt on top and add lemon juice.
Place an inverted plate over rolls. Barely cover
plate with water.
    Bring to boil. Cover saucepan, and cook
over medium heat for 30 minutes. Turn heat
to low and simmer for another 30 minutes.
Serve hot or cold as a main course or as a
snack.

TOTAL CALORIES PER SERVING: 258
TOTAL FAT AS % OF DAILY VALUE: 11%   FAT: 7 gm
PROTEIN: 9 gm   CARBOHYDRATES: 42 gm
CALCIUM: 151 mg   IRON: 3 mg   SODIUM: 244 mg
DIETARY FIBER: 4 gm

CHICKPEAS AND GREEN BEANS
-- HUMMUS MA' LOUBYA
(Serves 6)

Goes well with a side dish of cooked rice.

3 Tablespoons olive oil
4 medium onions, chopped
2 cups cooked chickpeas
1 pound green beans, washed and cut
    into 1/2-inch pieces
4 large tomatoes, finely chopped
1/2 teaspoon salt
1/2 teaspoon pepper
1/2 teaspoon allspice
1/8 teaspoon cayenne pepper
Water

Heat oil in a saucepan. Sauté onions over medium heat for 12 minutes. Add chickpeas and green beans. Stir-fry for 3 minutes. Add tomatoes and stir-fry for an additional 5 minutes. Add remaining ingredients, and barely cover with water. Bring to a boil and cover saucepan. Cook over medium heat for 40 minutes or until beans are well cooked. Serve hot or cold.

TOTAL CALORIES PER SERVING: 255
TOTAL FAT AS % OF DAILY VALUE: 15%   FAT: 10 gm
PROTEIN: 10 gm   CARBOHYDRATES: 35 gm
CALCIUM: 105 mg   IRON: 4 mg   SODIUM: 218 mg
DIETARY FIBER: 4 gm

BROAD BEANS IN OIL --
FOOLIYYA
(Serves 6)

Lima beans may be substituted for broad beans.

2 Tablespoons olive oil
1 large onion, chopped
2 cloves garlic, minced
2 Tablespoons, fresh coriander
    leaves, finely chopped
1/2 small hot pepper, finely chopped
1/2 teaspoon salt
1/4 teaspoon pepper
1/4 teaspoon allspice
3 cups shelled, fresh or thawed frozen
    broad beans
Water
3 Tablespoons lemon juice

Heat oil in a saucepan. Sauté onion, garlic, coriander leaves, and hot pepper over medium heat for 12 minutes. Add salt, pepper, allspice, and broad beans. Barely cover with water and bring to a boil. Cook over medium heat for 30 minutes or until broad beans are tender. Stir in lemon juice. Serve hot or cold.

TOTAL CALORIES PER SERVING: 146
TOTAL FAT AS % OF DAILY VALUE: 8%   FAT: 5 gm
PROTEIN: 7 gm   CARBOHYDRATES: 20 gm
CALCIUM: 43 mg   IRON: 2 mg   SODIUM: 195 mg
DIETARY FIBER: 1 gm

BEAN AND LENTIL POTTAGE -- MUJADDARA
(Serves 8)

For a delightful vegetarian meal, serve this dish hot with taboula.

1/2 cup dried kidney beans, soaked overnight in 3 cups water
3/4 cup lentils, rinsed
2 cups water
2 Tablespoons soft margarine
2 medium onions, chopped
2 cloves garlic, minced
2 Tablespoons fresh coriander leaves, finely chopped
1/2 cup rice
3/4 teaspoon salt
1/2 teaspoon pepper
1/4 teaspoon cumin
1/8 teaspoon cayenne
2 cups water

Place soaked beans with their water in a saucepan, and bring to a boil. Cover and cook over medium heat until beans turn tender. Stir in lentils. Add 2 cups water. Bring to a boil, and cover. Cook over medium heat for 25 minutes.

In the meantime, melt soft margarine in a frying pan, and sauté onions, garlic, and coriander leaves over medium heat for 12 minutes. Add rice and stir-fry for an additional 3 minutes. Add the frying pan contents and remaining ingredients into the bean and lentil mixture. Add 2 more cups of water and bring to a boil. Cook over medium heat for 20 minutes longer or until rice is done.

TOTAL CALORIES PER SERVING: 157
TOTAL FAT AS % OF DAILY VALUE: 5%   FAT: 3 gm
PROTEIN: 7 gm   CARBOHYDRATES: 26 gm
CALCIUM: 25 mg   IRON: 3 mg   SODIUM: 251 mg
DIETARY FIBER: 4 gm

BULGUR AND PARSLEY SALAD -- TABOULA
(Serves 10)

Taboula (The epitome of Middle Eastern salads) is found in many health food outlets.

1/2 cup bulgur (cracked wheat)
1 cup warm water
2 large bunches parsley, stems removed and finely chopped
1 small bunch scallions (green onions), finely chopped
3 medium tomatoes, diced into 1/4-inch cubes
4 Tablespoons fresh mint, finely chopped
4 Tablespoons olive oil
4 Tablespoons lemon juice
1 clove garlic, minced
1/2 teaspoon salt
1/2 teaspoon pepper
About 12 romaine lettuce leaves, washed

Soak bulgur in warm water for 15 minutes. Transfer to a strainer, and squeeze out excess water by hand. Place bulgur in a mixing bowl. Stir in remaining ingredients (except lettuce). Arrange lettuce to cover bottom and edges of a salad bowl (stem ends down). Place taboula over lettuce leaves and serve immediately.

TOTAL CALORIES PER SERVING: 91
TOTAL FAT AS % OF DAILY VALUE: 9%   FAT: 6 gm
PROTEIN: 2 gm   CARBOHYDRATES: 9 gm
CALCIUM: 41 mg   IRON: 2 mg   SODIUM: 129 mg
DIETARY FIBER: 2 gm

Habeeb Salloum is a freelance writer from Ontario, Canada.

THE WHOLESOME VEGETARIAN DISHES OF NORTH AFRICA

By Habeeb Salloum

No tourist who has enjoyed couscous, the national dish of North Africa, in all its non-vegetarian varieties, will dream that in the homes of the laborers and peasants this gourmet dish is prepared solely from home-grown garden vegetables and handmade semolina. In that part of the world, the poor people who rarely can afford meat, prepare not only couscous, but almost all their dishes from grains and vegetables. By using the right amount of traditional herbs and spices, they create incredibly tasty and wholesome meals. It is a simple and healthy kitchen, little known in the western world.

During my many travels to the lands bordering the southern edge of the Mediterranean, I have often sampled the delectable delights of traditional vegetarian fare. Roaming through the villages on the edge of the Sahara desert or exploring the ancient North African coastal cities, I have never been disappointed when dining in the people's eating places or the homes of the ordinary inhabitants. With limited means, the people of North Africa have created a savory and nourishing cuisine, consisting of a large repertoire of exotic and delightful dishes.

Usually visitors have little chance to sample these vegetarian meals. If one is fortunate enough to be invited to a North African home, meat is usually on the menu even if the host or hostess has to borrow money. Tradition has it that a guest must be fed meat.

On the other hand, one can find, hidden in the souks (open air markets) of the older part of the cities, exquisite tiny restaurants and food stalls which cater to the workers. In these eating places, unknown to most tourists, some of the finest North African dishes can be found. Visitors who have been fortunate enough to stumble on to such food outlets will remember with deep nostalgia the vegetarian victuals of these lands.

Yet, this need only be an initiation. When visitors return to their homes, they can continue on their journey into the culinary delights of North African peasant cooking. Besides the common vegetarian couscous, one can try many other non-meat foods like these few simple vegetarian dishes.

CHICKPEA SOUP ~ *LEBLABI*
(Serves 8)

Leblabi is served for breakfast in Tunisia.

1-1/2 cups chickpeas, soaked over-
    night in 10 cups water mixed with
    1/2 teaspoon baking soda
4 cloves garlic, crushed
1 hot pepper, finely chopped
4 Tablespoons finely chopped fresh
    coriander leaves
1/2 teaspoon salt
1 teaspoon ground caraway seeds
1 teaspoon oregano
3/4 teaspoon pepper
2 Tablespoons lemon juice
1 Tablespoon olive oil
2 cups or more crumbled toasted
    bread

Place chickpeas with their water in a saucepan and bring to boil. Cover and cook over medium heat for 1-1/2 hours or until chickpeas are tender. Stir in remaining ingredients, except lemon juice, olive oil, and bread. Re-cover and cook for 30 minutes longer or until chickpeas are well-cooked. Remove from heat and stir in lemon juice and olive oil. Serve, with each person adding bread to taste.

TOTAL CALORIES PER SERVING: 238
TOTAL FAT AS % OF DAILY VALUE: 8%   FAT: 5 gm
PROTEIN: 10 gm   CARBOHYDRATES: 39 gm
CALCIUM: 108 mg   IRON: 4 mg   SODIUM: 433 mg
DIETARY FIBER: 2 gm

BEAN AND ALMOND SOUP ~ *ASEEDA*
(Serves 6)

Morocco has a whole repertoire of vegetarian soups which, like this one, are very tasty and nourishing.

1/2 cup navy or similar beans, soaked
    overnight in 7 cups water
1 cup pulverized almonds
2 medium onions, chopped
4 cloves garlic, crushed
4 Tablespoons finely chopped fresh
    coriander leaves
1 small hot pepper, finely chopped
1 teaspoon cumin
1/2 teaspoon salt
1/2 teaspoon pepper
4 Tablespoons lemon juice

Place the beans with their water in a saucepan and bring to a boil. Cook over medium heat for 1 hour, then add remaining ingredients, except lemon juice, and bring to boil. Cook for 30 minutes or until beans are well-cooked. Purée in a blender. Reheat, then stir in lemon juice and serve immediately.

TOTAL CALORIES PER SERVING: 190
TOTAL FAT AS % OF DAILY VALUE: 15%   FAT: 10 gm
PROTEIN: 9 gm   CARBOHYDRATES: 19 gm
CALCIUM: 130 mg   IRON: 3 mg   SODIUM: 251 mg
DIETARY FIBER: 6 gm

ALGERIAN VEGETABLE STEW ~ *IJVAZ*
(Serves 6 to 8)

Serve this unique stew with cooked rice or mashed potatoes.

2 Tablespoons olive oil
2 medium zucchini (about 1 pound), cut into large pieces
1 large eggplant (about 1 pound), peeled and chopped into large pieces
2 large sweet peppers, seeded and chopped into small pieces
2 medium carrots (about 1/2 pound), peeled and chopped into small pieces
3 medium onions, chopped
1 head garlic, crushed
4 Tablespoons finely chopped fresh coriander
1/2 cup water
1/2 teaspoon salt
3/4 teaspoon pepper
2 cups stewed tomatoes
1 teaspoon dried basil

Heat oil in a saucepan, then add remaining ingredients, except tomatoes and basil.

Cover and cook over medium heat for 45 minutes. Stir in tomatoes and cook for 15 minutes longer. Stir in basil and serve.

TOTAL CALORIES PER SERVING: 140
TOTAL FAT AS % OF DAILY VALUE: 8%   FAT: 5 gm
PROTEIN: 3 gm   CARBOHYDRATES: 23 gm
CALCIUM: 81 mg   IRON: 2 mg   SODIUM: 415 mg
DIETARY FIBER: 5 gm

CHICKPEA AND TOMATO STEW
(Serves 8)

Enjoy this hearty stew!

2 cups chickpeas, soaked overnight in 8 cups water in which has been dissolved 1/2 teaspoon baking soda
1 Tablespoon olive oil
2 medium sweet red peppers, chopped into small pieces
2 medium onions, chopped
1 small hot pepper, finely chopped
4 cloves garlic, crushed
2 cups stewed tomatoes
4 Tablespoons finely chopped parsley
1/2 teaspoon salt
3/4 teaspoon pepper
1 teaspoon basil

Place chickpeas with their water in a pot and bring to boil. Cover and cook over medium heat for 1-1/2 hours or until chickpeas are tender. Set aside.

In the meantime, heat oil in a saucepan and sauté red pepper, onions, hot pepper, and garlic for 12 minutes. Stir in remaining ingredients, including chickpeas with their water, and bring to boil. Cover, then turn heat to low and simmer for 30 minutes.

TOTAL CALORIES PER SERVING: 248
TOTAL FAT AS % OF DAILY VALUE: 6%   FAT: 4 gm
PROTEIN: 12 gm   CARBOHYDRATES: 42 gm
CALCIUM: 127 mg   IRON: 5 mg   SODIUM: 435 mg
DIETARY FIBER: 3 gm

MINT AND CARAWAY SOUP ~ HAREERA KARAWIYA
(Serves 6)

This is a simple Moroccan dish which is great in the cold winter months.

6 cups water
4 Tablespoons flour, dissolved in 1/2
    cup water
2 cups finely chopped mint leaves
1 Tablespoon ground caraway seeds
1 Tablespoon olive oil
1/2 teaspoon salt
1/2 teaspoon pepper
1/8 teaspoon cayenne
1/3 cup lemon juice

Place water in a saucepan and heat. Just before it comes to a boil, stir in flour. Add remaining ingredients, except lemon juice, then stirring constantly bring to boil. Remove from heat and stir in lemon juice, then serve immediately. If not served at once, the taste will deteriorate.

TOTAL CALORIES PER SERVING: 53
TOTAL FAT AS % OF DAILY VALUE: 5%   FAT: 3 gm
PROTEIN: 1 gm   CARBOHYDRATES: 6 gm
CALCIUM: 56 mg   IRON: 1 mg   SODIUM: 196 mg
DIETARY FIBER: <1 gm

HOT SAUCE ~ HREESA
(Makes about 3/4 cup)

The Tunisian and Libyan kitchens are noted for their spicy hotness. In Tunisia, this sauce accompanies almost every meal. Diners use it according to their individual tastes.

1/2 cup olive oil
1/2 cup cayenne
4 Tablespoons cumin
2 Tablespoons salt
2 Tablespoons ground caraway seeds
5 cloves garlic, crushed

Thoroughly combine ingredients, then pour into a jar with a tight-fitting lid. Cover, then store in a cool place and use sparingly for flavor.

TOTAL CALORIES PER TEASPOON SERVING: 32
TOTAL FAT AS % OF DAILY VALUE: 5%   FAT: 3 gm
PROTEIN: <1 gm   CARBOHYDRATES: 1 gm
CALCIUM: 8 mg   IRON: <1 mg   SODIUM: 382 mg
DIETARY FIBER: <1 gm

Habeeb Salloum is a freelance writer from Ontario, Canada.

POEMS ☆ POEMS ☆ POEMS ☆ POEMS

Dedicated to Jason, who at a very young age, in farm country and never having heard of vegetarianism, refused to ever eat meat again when he was told where it came from after losing his treasured calf to the slaughterhouse. Any of these poems may be reprinted at any time by anyone, without permission.

THE HIGH PRICE OF EGGS

I was a pre-vet student, you see,
It was desirable to have experience with all
    types of animals;
When I saw the help-wanted ad put out by
    the Lone Pine Mink and Poultry Farm,
I jumped at the chance,
Never stopping to think
What the mink and poultry might be for.

I drove over in the full lushness of early
    summer,
Green hill pastures and endless woods,
Deserted back roads meandering through
    gentle mountains.
I thought how lucky I was
To be living in such beauty
After growing up in New York City.

Cresting a rise,
I spotted a high pine standing by itself,
Made one-sided by winter winds;
And I knew I was there.
The owner met me in the driveway
And pointed out his mink operation --
It was only an open-sided shed.
I'd pictured mink running all over fields and
    woods,
A sort of wildlife sanctuary;
But when I saw the tiny wire-mesh cages,
Each with a single inmate making non-stop
    circles
From floor to wall to ceiling and back again,
I realized that this was no wildlife refuge.

"There's only one opening left here," the
    owner informed me,
"Someone to help with the killing --
Don't think you'd be interested in that."
I looked at his face --
He wasn't making fun of me;
He took me to the poultry building
Where his wife was in need of an egg
    collector.

In an already dazed state,
I entered the tunnel they called a barn,
    and was hit by a wall of sound --
Thousands of chickens all shrieking at once in
    the heavy air,
The wife yelling above it all
As though nothing were wrong.
She took me on tour
Down a narrow walkway
Between high walls of vertical and horizontal
    rows of cages,
With no seeming embarrassment
That the hens were crammed so many to a
    cage,
Some had to be on top of others.
With traces of pride,
She explained the mechanized feeders and
    waterers,
And how the eggs dropped through wire-
    mesh floors
For their protection and easy collection;
Couldn't she see that her charges were
    pecked raw and bleeding?

She gave me a cart full of empty cartons,
And left me with the advice
Not to think about the end of the row;
That's when I noticed that no end could be
    seen,
Not because the lights were dim, which they
    were,
But because it was so far away.

Alone in the noise,
I began collecting the eggs
Like a mechanized feeder
That doesn't know what else to do.
I was supposed to pack the eggs big-side up;
What was wrong with me
That I couldn't tell which end was big?

I tried to concentrate --
"Speed is essential,"
But my eyes wouldn't stay on the eggs
Where they belonged.
I began to see worse things than I'd first
    noticed --
Wings caught in the wire bars,
Dislocated and broken by the movements of
    cage-mates;
I tried to free them,
Cringing at the way
Parts of living feeling beings snapped in my
    fingers.

At mid-morning the boss-lady returned,
She was concerned for me --
She'd pay minimum wage for three training
    days,
But after that,
Payment would be by the carton,
And I'd be on my own.
She cautioned that I'd have to develop four
    times my present speed
Just to earn the minimum.

But why were we talking about money?
We were in a concentration camp for birds,
And was the weight of our pocketbooks
All we could feel?

Yet, As hundreds of chalky eggs passed
    through my fingers,
Somewhere below awareness,
I came to the illogical conclusion
That if this was the system accepted
    everywhere,
It must be me that's crazy.

I worked mechanically,
Closing my eyes to all but the whiteness of
    eggs;
Though I could betray myself this way,
I couldn't do it efficiently --
I'd only finished one row and started the next
When the man and his wife arrived to say the
    day was over --
They'd have to finish the remaining five rows
    themselves.
I hoped they'd fire me,
But they weren't half bad where humans were
    concerned.

I bludgeoned myself into returning in the
    morning,
But I hadn't been working two hours
When I saw something
That even my cold steely eyes couldn't ignore.
A chicken had stuck her head out between
    two bars of her cage and back in between
    two other bars,
Wedged fast in that position for who knows
    how long.
I told myself to go on with my work,
That I'd only break her neck,
But how could I leave her like that?
I fumbled,
Precious time passing,
Time which became less precious
The longer I held suffering
Between my shaking fingers.
I couldn't get her loose and I couldn't go on,
I couldn't even see for the tears,
"God, take my clumsy hands,"
And suddenly she was free.

Numb at last
To my false sense of work responsibility,
I searched the rows in a haze,
Found my boss candling eggs in perfect
    oblivion,
And told her I quit.

She tried to pay me minimum wage,
But I took only what I'd earned by the carton
Four dollars and some change for ten hours
    work,
And still it weighed like thirty pieces of silver
In my pocket.

I stepped from screaming hell
Into the peace of a country morning,
Passed under a row of shady maples,
Sunlight beckoning beyond.
Why should I be allowed to walk away
When their only release would be death?

I didn't know then
That I would never be able
To shake off the noise and images of that
    place,
That I would carry their pain inside,
To be rekindled at the turn of a phrase by
    Vivaldi,
Or the stretched-out reds of an evening sky;
That I would lie awake in the night,
    and remember.

HE HONORS HIS FATHER

Remember our times under the aging apple,
    Pop,
When you were out cutting hay
And Ma would send me up with your lunch?
How all the cows would lie with us under
    that dying tree
Whose fewer leaves each year provided less
    and less shade
But all the comforts of familiarity?
I remember the year you decided that Straw-
    berry

Wasn't earning her keep anymore;
How, when the truck came to take her,
You had to pry me from her neck,
How she called to us as they drove away.

You explained to me then about slaughter-
    houses and profits,
And how the fact that Strawberry had spent
    her whole life giving us all the milk she
    could
Had no bearing in the ledger book;
How slaughterhouses were never meant to be
    cruel
But only turned out that way
Because making a profit requires expediency.

You thought you had to be rock hard, Pop,
To help me face the world;
You made me stand like a man
And accept reality.

I just didn't want it to be so violent;
If Strawberry had to die,
I wanted her to lie down one day
Under the old apple,
To lay her head on the grass beside us
And not wake up.
But you told me to accept the world as it was.

A lot of years later,
In a hospital after your heart attack,
A doctor told me you were feeling well
    enough
To have a little ice cream,
And I thought to myself
That you were in another kind of slaughter
    house;
But I accepted the world as it was.

You hadn't been home long
When your heart attacked you again,
Ma woke us all and we gathered around your
    bed.
I wanted to sit with you quietly,
But the ambulance crew pushed through and
    took you,

Laid you on the floor in a circle of machines
    and men in blue on their knees,
Pounding you hard on the chest.

If you had to die, Pop,
I didn't want it to be so violent
Or so soon.
You never got to meet my friend Angie
Or hear her ideas about veganism;
Would you have wanted to hear?

I stood like a man
When the undertaker came to take you,
And I accepted your reality.
But later Angie and I planted a young apple
    over your fresh grave,
and vowed that for the family we were
    planning,
We'd create a new reality.

WHERE UNFAIR REPUTATIONS HAVE NO JURISDICTION

Eastern kids on a college field course out west
Dropped by two's in barren sagebrush
    country.
August heat and the ugliness of isolated oil
    derricks sap my strength
Until we've walked to where no outward signs
    of man's intrusions are.

Our assignment is to map the geologic beds
    exposed in rock outcroppings.
We find a fine wall of endless layers,
But I can't tell which kind of rock is which,
And grouping them by ancient time periods
    seems an impossible task.
So I spend the afternoon half-heartedly
    drawing what I see for later interpretation.

Discouraged by not knowing what I'm doing,
Gritty with dusty sweat,
Longing for shelter from unrelenting sun,
I finally reach the top of a cliff.

Having decided that what I've drawn will
    have to do,
I shed the false scientific skin encumbrancing
    me,
And rest free on bluff's edge
To absorb what's real about the place.

As I breathe in things that restore my sanity,
I notice that I'm sitting near a rattler
Sunning himself on diamondbacked rock.
My heart jumps inside me --
I'd had two hopes for this trip --
To hear coyotes calling
And to meet a rattlesnake.

I want to share the moment,
And stand hollering into heavy heat
For a partner I haven't seen in hours.
After some time he appears,
Face fresh from geologic work he understands;
He pronounces the snake not a rattler because
    it isn't rattling.

My pocket guide to snakes is not in my
    pocket,
But I know there's one sure proof --
With a stick I nudge our sleepy subject,
"Won't you rattle for us, please?"
He only rearranges himself tolerantly
Like an uncle wolf under attack by ear-
    chewing cubs --
No amount of repeated botherings will make
    him angry or afraid.
At last he slithers a few feet to the dubious
    protection of a nearby scrawny sagebrush--
Two or three scraggly branches, not enough
    to make a shadow,
And surely not sufficient to foil my pesterings.

One can almost hear a tired "Oh, all right" in
    the rattle when it finally sounds,
Devoid as it is of aggression or fear --
Not even our whooping dance of exuberant
    joy
Disturbs our indulgent snake friend.

Elation vented,
We sit with him (or her) a long silent while,
Savoring the acquaintance of a being whose
    possession of deadly power does not pre-
    determine his use of it,
Our minds empty of thoughts,
The whole of us full of an unconscious
    knowing
That rock and snake and sky and we
Are one.

SILENT VOICES CAN NEVER BE STILLED

I stare at tree-covered mountain across the
    way,
Shuddering at repeated volleys.

In those woods walks beauty
That can't be destroyed or dragged out by
    hunters.
They've cheated themselves --
The corpses on car hoods are devoid of the
    Presence
Still in the woods,
Shadows walking quietly with those who
    come in peace.

4-H BOY

4-H Boy, you look so all-American,
Come to the fair with your cow;
Why is there no joy in your eyes, 4-H Boy?
She's a sure bet for a ribbon, your cow,
So obviously well cared for.
I can see hours of brushing in the sheen of her
    coat,
Hours of laughter in the way she butts your
    backside,
Lifetimes of love in the way she looks at you.
Why do you cry, 4-H Boy, when no one's
    around?

You're the pride of the family as you lead
    your beauty into the ring,
Uncles and grandfathers and strangers
    guffawing with pleasure at the small boy
    and his big cow;
Why is there no pleasure in it for you?
Why does your limp hand let the blue ribbon
    drag in the sawdust?

Friday night,
and the same ring transformed into auction
    floor.
Gone is the patient slow pace allotted for
    children.
Frenzy is everywhere:
In the auctioneer's babble,
In the voices of animals newly separated from
    their 4-H friends,
In the rough treatment shown them by
    auction-house crew,
In the eyes of eager money-changers;
In minutes they change months of mutual
    devotion into dollars and cents.
Why do you sit so unnoticed in the bleachers
    now, 4-H Boy,
Shrunken against your father's knee?
Why does your gentle cow look so wild-eyed
    and bewildered as she's prodded up the
    ramp to slaughterhouse-bound truck?
Where have you gone, 4-H Boy, while your
    father collects your money.

The stall is empty now where boy and cow lay
    exhausted, napping side by side in the
    heat.
Why do you go back there, 4-H Boy?
Why do you finger the straw where she last
    lay,
Alone in the dark, with only her scent left
    behind?

*The author was a pre-vet student, but
dropped out of school the week before having
to watch the upperclassmen practice on living
animals. Most of her poems are auto-
biographical.*

THE LIFE OF PETE

- OR -

THE MALE BOVINE IS NOT WELCOME ANYWHERE

By Israel Mossman

Pete didn't really object to being separated from his bovine lady friends. He could admire them from a short distance away, and when one of them was in a receptive mood, he had full confidence that a visit would be arranged. But when Pete discovered that a brash young adolescent bull, Junior Johnson by name, was living on HIS farm, a potential rival for HIS harem, it was a little too much.

Late one summer evening, he let his displeasure be known. There he was, 1,700 pounds of Holstein bull looking into our bedroom window. Bellowing and snorting, he was wreaking havoc in my mother-in-law's garden. The unearthed carrots were flying, dislodged by furious front hoofs. He was glaring at us, and rightfully so. How dare we bring in this intruder?

How do you coax a massive male bovine to go back to his pen when he is so upset? Very calmly, and with a lot of patience. It took most of the night. Junior Johnson had to go.

Being new in this business of farming, I was not aware of the sad future of the rambunctious young Junior Johnson. Later I learned that he would suffer several hours of excruciating pain in the process of changing from a bull to a steer. Eventually, he would grace the table of his new owners, but not as a guest.

The crisis solved to his satisfaction, Pete settled down to his quiet life in his small pen, always happy to entertain a lady friend when the occasion arose. One day, out of sheer boredom, he began to rub his huge head, supported by rather powerful neck and shoulder muscles, against the wooden rails of his pen. Then he made an amazing discovery -- he could move them! And move them he did -- to the ground. Quickly, I picked up a large hammer, some long glue-coated nails, and several 4' x 8' boards, which were almost too large to lift.

After completing the repair, I smiled my victorious smile at Pete, and said "GOTCHA." Pete didn't say a word, but proceeded to remove the huge boards, which were nailed to discarded railroad ties used as posts. We were now playing a game, and Pete was winning.

Not to be outsmarted by a Holstein bull, I jumped into my usually reliable '52 Dodge pick-up, and tore down the road to the nearest farm supply store, some miles away. There I purchased an electric transformer, a hundred feet of galvanized wire, and some insulators with double headed nails. Pete watched me carefully as I made the installation from outside his pen.

"Let's see if friend Pete will mess with an electrified fence." He did. With his horn stump, this male Bovine journeyman electrician-carpenter slowly and deliberately pushed several insulators from the fence posts, dropping the hot wire to the ground, shorting out the electric fence, making it useless. We had resumed playing the game, and Pete was winning again.

As we could not control Pete anymore, we could not keep him. An unconfined bull is dangerous. Although my mother-in-law's farm was well known for its high milk production and healthy cows, with some thanks to Pete, we could not sell him as a breeding bull. All the dairy farmers in our area were changing to artificial insemination, just as we were doing. It was safer than handling a bull and it raised milk production by better breeding. There was no choice but to sell Pete at the livestock auction. He would become beef, but he could not know that.

When the truck came to pick him up, Pete would not go. He would not leave his home and his many wives. And he did not trust this strange contraption called a truck. Pete had torn out his nose ring earlier in life (it is extremely painful) and we could not lead him up the ramp into the truck. A rope around his neck would choke him to death. Finally, we tied a rope around his horn stumps, and pulled him onto the truck. It took all afternoon. Poor Pete, he was visibly shaken.

I have never seen a more frightened or disoriented animal than Pete, when he was being sold in the auction ring. Pete did not see me. I could not have stood the guilt if he had seen me. Today, thirty years later, I still have not forgiven myself for selling Pete. He had never shown aggression toward me, only ANGER.

Israel Mossman is a retired Eastern Shore of Maryland businessman and associate editor of *The Jewish Vegetarians Newsletter.* **He spent several years on his mother-in-law's dairy farm in North Carolina during his younger days.**

MILK ALTERNATIVES:

What do vegetarians who don't use dairy products put on their breakfast cereal? Popular choices include a variety of soy milks, nut milks, rice or potato milks, and juices. Some may choose to make their own beverages at home. Many of us, however, find the convenience of commercial non-dairy milks quite attractive. Today, soy milk and other non-dairy beverages can be found in natural foods stores and in supermarkets. They are packaged in aseptic shelf-stable cartons, in glass or plastic jugs, and in powdered form. Until recently, vegans could not rely on non-dairy milks as particularly good sources of calcium. Now, several companies add calcium to their products, so that these beverages have a calcium content which is closer to cow's milk. Several companies are also adding vitamin B12 to their product.

Here's a sample list of non-dairy beverages available today: Amazake Original (made from cultured brown rice); Edensoy Original and Extra Original (made from soybeans); Ener-G Foods Nut Quick (made from almond meal) and Soy Quick (made from soy flour); Imagine Foods Rice Dream (made from brown rice); Solait (made from soybeans); Vitasoy Original and Light Original (made from soybeans); Westsoy Lite Plain and Plus Plain (made from soybeans); and White Almond Beverage (made from almonds).

THE SON OF BIG SUE

By Israel Mossman

Editor's note: In this brief essay, Israel Mossman shares aspects of dairy farming invisible to most consumers: the removal of calves from their mothers, the role of dairy farming in the "production" of veal calves, and the anguish of animals. Israel notes that calves are removed from their mothers at once before more bonding takes place. Four out of five calves end up now in veal crates, as only one in five is needed as a replacement. The cows must be impregnated once a year to remain in milk "production." Veal calves are the by-product of the dairy industry.

B ig Sue was due to "come fresh" any day now. When she did not return with the herd from night pasture, it could only mean that she had given birth and probably was in the woods, hiding from dairy farmers and other predators who might harm her newly arrived offspring. I jumped on my temperamental steed, an old cantankerous, International Farmall "C" tractor. From that elevated, mobile observation platform, I could quickly check the fences adjoining the pasture to see where she had broken through. Finding the break, I jumped off the tractor and entered the woods, hoping not to encounter any unfriendly, woodsy creatures such as snakes, ticks, or poison oak.

There she was, in the woods, nervously guarding her newborn bull calf. There is no way to transport a calf on a tractor, so I knelt on one knee, placing my right arm under his hindquarters and my left arm under his chest, and slowly lifted the noisy, squirming, 90-pound bundle of joy. Then I carried him the half mile back to the barn area, with the new mommy following close behind.

Big Sue was upset beyond belief. She bellowed loudly enough to be heard in the next county. She was afraid that I would take

her baby from her, and her fears were well-founded. But I knew that she would not attack me, at least not now. She was too intent on following her son. But she cried in her own bovine way with all the anguish that a human mother would have if her baby were taken from her.

It was necessary to separate cow and calf at once, before permanent bonding could take place. Big Sue, heartbroken and howling, was ushered into the milking barn. Her son was carried into the calf stable. There, he would learn to drink from a galvanized bucket by having liquid splashed into his face by a hand that he could suck. He no longer had a mother to nuzzle against.

Big Sue went to her usual stall to be relieved of her colostrum, the predecessor of her milk that nature intended her newborn calf to have. But when a pulsing, throbbing, milking machine was applied to her teats instead of her rambunctious calf suckling her, she kicked at me but missed -- hitting the milking machine instead. She knocked the heavy contraption 25 feet, and it broke apart at its seams. If she had connected with me below the rib cage with that much force, it would have ruptured my aorta and my wife would have become my widow. Dairy farming is indeed more dangerous than coal mining.

It was necessary to separate cow and calf at once, before permanent bonding could take place.

Trying to calm both myself and the rightfully angry cow, I said in my most soothing voice that it was illegal to repair a stainless steel milker (bacteria might hide in the mended seams) and, besides that, it was expensive to do so. Fortunately, my mechanic had mastered the delicate technique of brazing stainless steel with silver at low heat. Big Sue was still angry, unimpressed by my comforting monologue. The only remaining alternative was to restrain her by looping a rope forward of her pelvis and udder, and drawing it tight. The resulting

There is no need for a young bull on a dairy farm.

pressure on her sciatic nerve would temporarily weaken her rear legs so she could not kick. But I tightened the rope too much, and she began to fall slowly on me. Not wanting to be buried by more than one-half ton of cow, I loosened the rope just enough so she could stand again but not kick. She was now subdued but not very happy. The milking process then continued without further incident.

There is no need for a young bull on a dairy farm. Since Thursday's livestock auction was a few days away, he would be lucky enough to be nourished by his mother's colostrum for a short time. Then he would live on "milk replacer" -- heavily laced with antibiotics but short on nutrients. In a few months he would become veal to satisfy the appetites of his new owner's family.

Since Big Sue became her old sassy self again in a few days, she must have forgotten all about her young son. But I never did, and it has been over 30 years now.

Note: The writer asked the dairy farm owner, his mother-in-law, to sell the farm. She did and the farm did not remain a dairy farm after it was sold.

WATER USE AND DISPOSAL IN POULTRY PROCESSING

By Mark Rifkin

The animal rights and vegetarian movements have enjoyed rising popularity and publicity in recent years. One of the many reasons may be the increasingly common use of arguments based upon the environmental destruction directly attributable to a meat-based diet. Of particular concern is water usage by the livestock industries, including poultry.

A 1981 article in *Newsweek* stated that "drought, waste and pollution threaten a water shortage whose impact may rival the energy crisis" [of the 1970s.] One result of our wasteful water usage is the condition of the Ogallala Aquifer, which is the major groundwater formation in the plains states. According to the *Newsweek* article, 21 billion more gallons of water are removed each day from the Ogallala (much of it for livestock production) than flow in. At this rate, the Ogallala has a maximum life of about another 30 years. Some experts say that certain parts of the United States may suffer permanent loss of their groundwater supplies for agriculture. [1]

As the consumption of chickens increases in this country, research into water use and disposal in poultry processing would certainly be appropriate. As we shall see, in terms of water usage, **the poultry processing industry is one of the worst polluters in the United States.** I will attempt, where possible, to minimize details of the actual slaughter, but some references to the process will be necessary.

While the Ogallala Aquifer underlies the plains states, the poultry industry is centralized in the South and Southeast, so that the problems of the Ogallala are not substantially worsened by the poultry industry. However, damage is potentially and actually done to our environment through the consumption of animal products.

It is well-known that most chickens are raised in warehouse-type structures with populations reaching up to 100,000 birds per house. After hatching, about one gallon of water per day is required for every 100 birds. [2] As they get older, their water needs increase. By the time chickens are seven weeks old, which is about the age when they are sent to slaughter, the birds will require about six gallons of water per day for every 100 birds. [3] Therefore, a chicken house with 100,000 birds will require up to 6,000 gallons of water per day.

Other types of birds, such as laying hens, require about nine gallons of water per day for every 100 birds. Turkeys require fifteen to twenty-five gallons of water per day for every 100 birds. [3] All these water requirements can be affected by temperature and humidity, various dietary factors, drug intake, and genetics. Water is also used as a convenient medium to deliver various vaccines, vitamins, minerals, and antibiotics to the birds. Fortunately, water does not seem to be used as a common means to remove the birds' waste material, for that would introduce a whole new world of problems.

There are over 400 poultry processing plants (slaughterhouses) in the United States, most of which are in the South and Southeast states. [4] The poultry industry has seen tremendous growth in recent years, as many plants are processing more than twice as many birds as they were twenty-five years ago -- with the same equipment.[5] **In 1986, more than 5 billion chickens and turkeys were killed for food[6] with many, if not most, plants processing between 60,000 and 250,000 birds per day.[7]** With numbers like these, water usage is of great concern, and according to a United States Department of Agriculture (USDA) official, "poultry processors...[are] among the most water-intensive users in the food industry."[8] Most chicken plants use between three and ten gallons of water to process each bird[9]; therefore, **it's no wonder that many plants use between 500,000 and 2 million gallons of water per day.[7]**

According to a United States Department of Agriculture (USDA) official, "poultry processors...[are] among the most water-intensive users in the food industry."

One study done in 1982 cited data from eight plants in Maryland, Delaware, Virginia, and North Carolina. Some of these plants had familiar names such as Perdue and Holly Farms. At one of these plants 360,000 birds were killed per day. Average production among the eight plants was 178,000 birds per day, and average water usage at each plant was 1.06 million gallons per day. In addition, each plants generates 5,000 pounds of grease to be disposed of each day.[10]

Turkey plants are no better, as they use 11 to 23 gallons of water per bird[11], which is double the rate of chicken plants. Even with the lower number of turkeys killed, they can use extremely large quantities of water as well.

Annual use for the entire poultry industry is 20 to 75 billion gallons of water.[6]

Wastewater is produced either directly or indirectly at each step in poultry processing. In order, these steps are reception, slaughter, scalding and defeathering, evisceration, chilling, grading, and packing. Water has always been considered a convenient medium for almost any process.[12]

Poultry processing also produces vast quantities of highly-polluting substances in the wastewater, including such items as grease, fat, blood, various suspended solids including chicken parts, and pathogenic microorganisms (bacteria that can cause disease).

The government was not seriously concerned about water usage until 1977, when the United States Department of Agriculture established guidelines to improve sanitation and disposal of wastewater, as well as to reduce the amounts of water consumed. Water use and disposal costs have become increasingly expensive, so that it may be no surprise that the poultry producers themselves have begun to rethink and improve some of their practices and systems.[13]

The USDA now encourages several methods of water conservation, including recycling or re-use of the water at some points in poultry processing (mostly the scalding and chilling stages). Even though the untreated process water is usually laden with various pollutants and contaminants, most of these are easily removed with proper treatment for recycling.[13] There may be some concern for the environment here, but it is mostly a cost-saving measure.

One method of recycling deserves a special mention. According to publications from England, some food and agriculture experts are calling for the recovery of various types of food and agricultural waste for human food use, either directly or indirectly through feeding animals.[14] These and other similar ideas have recently become reality, as the livestock industries seek to maximize profits by lowering costs.

Eventually, disposal of the high-strength wastewater must be considered. Generally, disposal is either to a municipal sewer system or to an on-site treatment system, with final disposal to a water body or on land. Whichever method is chosen, preliminary treatment to remove grease, fats, and various solids is required, and the resulting sludge is then transported to landfills or lagoons, or spread on farmland. Sometimes the raw, effluent is spread directly on the land without any treatment at all.[12]

Secondary treatment can be chosen after preliminary treatment, and this entails using bacteria to convert the finer biodegradable materials into simple, common substances. After secondary treatment, the liquid may be discharged into a water body, and the sludge disposed of in a method similar to that from primary treatment. The liquid and sludge may also be spread together on farmland.[12] Unfortunately, land spreading may also entail clearing of natural vegetation specifically for the purpose of spreading slaughterhouse wastes.[5]

Whenever some discharge to land, water or a municipal sewer system is called for, permission to discharge is still needed, along with the appropriate monitoring of actual discharges. Up to now, neither the opponents of the livestock industries nor the environmental movement has performed any substantial investigation into whether the discharge regulations are being complied with.

Activists should contact the municipal sewer authority and/or the state environmental agency to get information on discharges from poultry and meat processing plants. Anyone can obtain copies of their discharge permits and monitoring reports by using the Freedom of Information Act. Although some may not care about blatant animal cruelty and exploitation, they may care about environmental pollution.

In summary, the poultry industry is one of the major polluters among the livestock industries, as it consumes enormous quantities of water with the possibility of causing severe water supply depletion. Even with recycling, the industry also has a large potential to introduce polluted wastewater into our environment. This is just one more reason why poultry should not be consumed.

FOOTNOTES

[1] Adler, Jerry, et al. "The Browning of America," *Newsweek*, February 23, 1981, pp. 26-37.

[2] Nesheim, Malden C., et al. *Poultry Production*, 12th edition, Philadelphia: Lea & Febiger, 1979.

[3] Amato, S. V., and Minear, L. R. "Water Consumption of Broiler Breeders Under Commercial Conditions," *Poultry Science*, 64 (May 1985), pp. 803-808.

Bennett, C. D. and Leeson, S. "Water Usage of Broiler Breeders," *Poultry Science* 68 (May 1989), pp. 617-621.

American Association for Vocational Instructional Materials, "Planning for an Individual Water System," 1982, 4th edition.

Water System Council, "Water Systems Handbook," 1979.

Midwest Plan Service, "Private Water Systems Handbook," 1979.

Ernst & Young (accountants), "What to Consider When Selecting Your Water Supply," *Water Well Journal*, June 1990, pp. 55-63.

[4] Ritter, William F. "Land Disposal of High Grease Content Poultry Processing Sludge," *in Agricultural Waste Utilization and Management: Proceedings of the Fifth International Symposium on Agricultural Wastes, December 1985*, Chicago, Il., American Society of Agricultural Engineers, pp. 560-568.

[5] Starkey, John E. "Case Histories of Nitrogen Removal Upgrade, Mechanical Dewatering Systems, and Overland Flow" in *Proceedings of the National Poultry Waste Management Symposium, April 1988*, Columbus, Oh., by USDA and Ohio State University, pp. 81-87. (This volume will hereinafter be cited as "USDA Symposium".)

[6] Chang, Y. H., and Sheldon B. W. "Effects of Chilling Broiler Carcasses with Reconditioned Poultry Prechiller Water," *Poultry Science* 68 (May 1989), pp. 656-662.

[7] Davis, J. A. "Grease/Fat Waste Utilized as Fuel," Final Report, US Department of Energy (September 1982). National Technical Information Service, Springfield, Va. (microfiche).

Simon, Donald F. "Potential Savings to the Processor from Water Conservation and Reuse," *Poultry Science* 64 (March 1985), pp. 485-486.

[8] Houston, D. L. "An Overview of US Department of Agriculture Requirements." *Poultry Science* 64 (March 1985), pp. 481- 484.

[9] Davis, J. A., "Grease/Fat Waste Utilized as Fuel."

Nesheim, Malden C., et al. *Poultry Production*.

Nielsen, V. C. "Treatment and Disposal of Processing Wastes" in *Processing of Poultry*, pp. 361-411. Edited by G. C. Mead. Essex, England: Elsevier Applied Sciences, 1989.

[10] Davis, J. A. "Grease/Fat Waste Utilized as Fuel."

[11] Simon, Donald F. "Potential Savings to the Processor from Water Conservation and Reuse."

[12] Nielsen, V. C. "Treatment and Disposal of Processing Wastes."

[13] Andelman, Julian. "A Review of Wastewater Recycling Research Performed at the Sterling Processing Company, Oakland, Maryland," *Poultry Science* 64 (March 1985) pp. 479-480.

Chang, Y. H. and Sheldon B. W. "Effects of Chilling Broiler Carcasses with Reconditioned Poultry Prechiller Water."

Houston, D. L. "An Overview of US Department of Agriculture Requirements."

Merka, William. "Water Quality Criteria for Recycling in Poultry Processing Plants," *USDA Symposium*, pp. 152-155.

Simon, Donald F. "Potential Savings to the Processor from Water Conservation and Reuse."

Wesley, R. L. "Symposium: Water Reuse and Conservation in Poultry Processing," *Poultry Science* 64 (March 1985), pp. 476-478.

[14] El Boushy, A. R., et al. "A Preliminary Study of the Suitability of Dehydrated Poultry Slaughterhouse Wastewater as a Constituent of Broiler Feeds," *Agricultural Wastes* 10 (1984), pp. 313-318.

Ledward, D. A., et al. *Upgrading Wastes for Feeds and Food*, Kent, England: Butterworth's, 1983.

Mark Rifkin is employed as a sanitarian with the Howard Country Health Department in Maryland. He inspects wells and septic systems. Mark is also an animal rights activist.

A Shopper's Guide To Leather Alternatives

By Michael Keevican

On many occasions, after turning down a hamburger or hot-dog at a summer barbecue and explaining that I'm vegetarian, the next question I'm asked (if I'm wearing my leather-like Birkentstocks) is, "Then why are you wearing leather?" I tell them that the sandals are made from synthetic materials that look like leather, and this usually pacifies them. They do ask a valid question though, if you are choosing a vegetarian diet for ethical reasons, "How can you stop eating animals, but continue to wear them?" There are many different answers to this question, but if your answer is, "I can't," then what do you do? Like a vegetarian diet, people often choose to "quit leather" at different stages.

According to Webster's Dictionary leather is, "a material consisting of animal skin prepared for use by removing the hair and tanning." Since cow hide is the most common animal hide used, links to the meat industry are undeniable. According to the Leather Industries of America, the leather industry's trade association, very few animals are raised specifically for their hides. But cows are just one of the animals whose skins are used for shoes, wallets, coats, belts, accessories, and clothing. Critters like pigs, deer, horses, and sheep are also used for their skins. Some shoes and accessories are even made from "exotic" animal skins ranging from alligator and lizard to sealskin and snakeskin.

You may ask, "Well what should I do with all the leather I have?" Again, just as some people go vegetarian overnight and others do it slowly, taking weeks or months, the same goes for leather. Some people choose to gradually replace worn out leather items with non-leather alternatives. Others donate their leather goods to charities. Many throw the stuff away, and although you might prefer that no one wear animal hides (besides the animals), most leather is not biodegradable due to the tanning process, so a charity might be the best bet.

That brings up the question of which causes less damage to the environment -- petroleum-based synthetic leathers or leather treated with multiple chemicals? While petroleum-based products often cause pollution from manufacturing and its waste, leather manufacturers are still dealing with problems that the chemicals used for tanning cause. Either alternative leads to some environmental damage, but while your supporting the exploitation of animals by purchasing leather, choosing leather alternatives will at least help alleviate some cruelty to animals.

Fortunately, many of the new mail order companies that are selling or making strictly non-leather shoes, are employing manufacturing techniques that are Earth-friendly. *Ecotrek* makes backpacks from recycled soda bottles, milk bottles, shipping waste, and foam scrap; *Ex-tredz, Just in Case,* and *Used Rubber USA* all make bags, wallets, and other accessories from recycled rubber products; and *Deja Shoe* makes a full line of leather-free shoes for men and women from recycled products and sustainably harvested materials from the rain forest that are assembled with non-toxic, water-based adhesives. While some of these companies do charge more for the environmental alternatives to petroleum-based synthetic leathers, if you'd like to continue buying ecologically sound, non-leather alternatives, it's best to support them.

Whether you are finally giving up leather for a kinder alternative, or you've already done that and are looking for a greater selection, you will find an array of non-leather goods from vegan hiking boots to a James Dean-style un-leather jacket listed below. To make your selection as effortless as possible the companies listed are separated into several categories. The *Vegan Mail Order* section indexes companies that sell only totally animal-free products. The *Catalogs, Companies, and Stores* section, lists companies that sell or manufacture not only leather-free, but also leather goods, so check these carefully to make sure what you're buying is non-leather. The remaining sections list specific styles of shoes (athletic, dress, etc.) and the companies who make them or the stores/catalogs that carry them. We've aimed to be complete and accurate in doing this listing, but if you know of any changes or additions we should make please send them to The Vegetarian Resource Group, Box 1463, Baltimore, MD 21203.

VEGAN MAIL ORDER

The following companies sell only animal-free, cruelty-free products in their catalogs.

Aesop Inc.
PO Box 315, N. Cambridge, MA 02140; (617) 628-8030
Aesop aims to "help promote a more peaceful world," by offering products that are "good to the earth and kind to animals." Their catalog includes footwear, belts, wallets, and other non-leather items.

The Compassionate Shopper
175 W. 12th St., #16G, NY, NY 10011-8275
This newsletter, published three times a year by Beauty Without Cruelty, lists companies that sell non-leather footwear, as well as other cruelty free products. Send $15 for a year's subscription.

Creatureless Comforts
702 Page St., Stroughton, MA 02072; (617) 344-7496

They carry a line of synthetic leather purses for women, with men's and women's synthetic leather belts to be included soon.

Ecotrek
PO Box 9638, Amherst, MA 01059-9638; (800) 858-1383
Several styles of backpacks made of totally recycled and vegan materials. These backpacks are made from "recycled soda bottles, milk bottles, shipping waste, foam scrap -- and a ton of imagination." Although the current brochure states that recycled wool is used, this has been discontinued. Backpack styles range from daypacks to technical packs for serious hikers and trekkers.

Ethical Wares
84 Clyde Way, Rise Park, Romford, Essex RM1 4UT, UNITED KINGDOM; Telephone: 01708 739293
This ethically based company sells leather-alternative shoes and belts, all of which carry the Vegan Society trademark. Besides being animal-free, Ethical Wares states that they do not trade with countries that have "repressive regimes or exploitative working practices." Shoe styles include trekking and hiking boots, dress boots, steel-toe safety boots, and dressy shoes for men and women.

Ex-tredz
Ontario, Canada; (605) 795-9205
Although this company doesn't sell directly to the public, call this number to find a store in your area that sells their products. They make vests, coats, etc. from recycled rubber.

Heartland Products, Ltd.
PO Box 218, Dakota City, IA 50529; (800) 441-4692
Everything in the Heartland catalog is non-leather, from western-style boots and baseball gloves to clogs and bomber jackets!

Just In Case
2718 Main St., Santa Monica, CA 90405;

(800) 326-4036
This mail-order catalog offers cruelty-free bags and gifts. Several leather-like "professional" briefcases, knapsacks, travel kits, bags, diaper bags, organizers, checkbook and credit card holders, and wallets.

Pangea
7829 Woodmont Ave., Bethesda, MD;
(301) 652-3181
This mail-order company and store carries all cruelty-free, vegan products, including leather alternative shoes, clothing, and bags.

People for the Ethical Treatment of Animals (PETA)
PO Box 42516, Washington, DC 20015;
(301) 770-7382
Besides vegan flats for women and vegan dress shoes for men, made from linen, the PETA catalog also offers faux fur parkas, hats, and coats.

Vegetarian Shoes
12 Gardner St., Brighton BN1 1UP,
UNITED KINGDOM;
Telephone: 0273 691913
Over 50 styles of synthetic leather and synthetic suede shoes including genuine Doc Marten boots and shoes, Birkenstocks, dress shoes, hiking boots, work boots, "leather" jackets, and belts.

CATALOGS, COMPANIES, AND STORES WITH LEATHER ALTERNATIVES
The following catalogs, mail order companies, and stores carry some non-leather products, but they are not totally animal-free. Just like reading food labels, carefully check the merchandise to make sure it is leather-free -- if you're not sure ask customer service or a sales clerk, they can usually answer your questions! Of course, this is only a partial listing of the thousands of catalogs and stores with synthetic options.

Active Souls, 20 Wapping Rd., Kingston, MA 02364; (800) 881-4322
They distribute several styles of New Balance shoes, made from synthetic materials, for men and women.

American Hemp Mercantile, Inc.,
506 2nd Ave., Ste. 1323, Seattle, WA 98104; (800) 469-4367
For retail orders check out the World Wide Web sight at http://www.betterworld.com/ahm where you can purchase Kender Gear Bags which are vegan bags and wallets made from hemp (kender is the Hungarian word for hemp).

Birkenstock Footwear, 486 First St., Solvang, CA 93463; (800) 824-1228
The Birki Too, Birki's, and Birki Kids lines of Birkenstocks are made of Birko-Flor synthetic uppers. For a totally animal-free shoe ask for Birkolon synthetic footbed liners. Birki-Clogs are made with all polyurethane and a removable washable footbed.

Deja Shoe
15806 SW Upper Boones Ferry Rd., Lake Oswego, OR 97035; (503) 598-9171
Although this company doesn't sell directly to the public, call this number to find a store in your area that sells their products. They make a full line of leather-free shoes for men and women made from recycled products and sustainably harvested materials from the rain forest. They are assembled with non-toxic, water-based adhesives. Styles include oxfords, sandals, and clogs. Vegan styles include the Eco-sneak and Envirolite (other style's insoles made from recycled wool blankets and clothing).

Ecolution, PO Box 2279, Merrifield, VA 22116; (800) 769-HEMP
The briefcase, mini backpack, campus style backpack, and two-pocket fanny pack are made from 100% hemp.

Forestry Suppliers, Inc., PO Box 8397, Jackson, MS 39284; (800) 647-5368
Several styles of all-rubber boots available.

J. Crew, One Ivy Crescent, Lynchburg, VA 24506; (800) 782-8244
Canvas deck shoes and basketball sneakers, nylon sneakers, flannel deck sneakers, and rubber thongs.

Lane Bryant, PO Box 8301, Indianapolis, IN 46283; (800) 477-7070
Man-made casual shoes, pumps, and sandals in a variety of styles.

L.L. Bean, Freeport, ME 04033; (800) 221-4221
Merrel and Teva sports sandals, Birkis by Birkenstock with synthetic uppers and polyurethane footbed, canvas athletic shoes, NB Walking Shoes with synthetic suede uppers, canvas Pathfinder boots, Nordic fleece boots, and north col primaloft booties. L.L. Bean also has non-leather handbags, watch bands, and coats.

Masseys, 601 Twelfth St., Lynchburg, VA 24504; (800) 462-7739
Masseys carries several canvas and synthetic slip-ons, plus a wide variety of leather-like flats, pumps, and other styles. They carry name brands such as Auditions, Esprit, Keds, New Balance, and Tretorn.

Nike, Inc., One Bowerman Dr., Beaverton, OR 97005; (800) 352-6453
Call the 800 number to receive a men's or women's sourcebook that lists all Nike shoes and which are made with synthetic uppers. They also have synthetic children's and baby's shoes.

The Ohio Hempery Catalog, 7002 State Route 329, Guysville, OH 45735; (800) BUY-HEMP
Hemp sandal, oxford, and slide by Deja.

Payless Shoe Source
This store has one of the widest selections of synthetic leather shoes available in men's, women's, and children's styles. The Richard Simmons line of shoes for women is all synthetic, as is the Rugged Outback line which includes styles for the whole family. Call (800) 444-7463 for a store in your area.

Premier Sports, 938 S. Andreasen, Ste. G, Escondido, CA 92029; (800) 822-7788
Women's running shoes from Saucony, Adidas, Brooks, New Balance, and Avia.

REI, 1700 45th St., E. Sumner, WA 98390; (800) 426-4840
Adidas Adventure Sandals, Teva sports sandals, Merrell sports sandals, and Nike sports sandals. They also offer non-leather belts and watch bands.

Road Runner Sports, PO Box 910129, San Diego, CA 92191; (800) 551-5558
Carry several non-leather running shoes from Brooks, Asics, New Balance, Saucony, Reebok, Adidas, Etonic, and Aviva. Watches with non-leather bands also available.

Roaman's, PO Box 8360, Indianapolis, IN 46283; (800) 274-7130
Several leather-like and canvas casual and dress shoes.

Used Rubber USA, 597 Haight St., San Francisco, CA 94117; (415) 626-7855
Recycled rubber inner tubes and tires are used to make wallets, organizers, and bags in a variety of sizes.

Unlisted by Kenneth Cole; (800) UNLISTED
This company offers a line of leather-like shoes, belts, and handbags for women. Carried in department stores like Macy's and Nordstrom. Call the 800 number for locations near you.

ATHLETIC SHOES

There are now leather alternatives in almost every style of athletic shoe. While some companies offer "classic" styles that remain leather-free, like Tretorn and Converse All-Stars; other styles, especially running shoes, change their look (and materials) frequently. For each company below there may be more non-leather styles than included (or the style listed may be made in the future with leather) so always check to make sure that the shoe you are looking for is still animal-free. Besides some of the mail-order catalogs and stores listed above, national chain stores that carry athletic shoes include **The Athletes Foot** and **Foot Locker**.

Women

Adidas: Synthetic sports shoes in a variety of styles. At retail stores the side of the box lists what each part of the shoe is made from -- look for the word synthetic. If you're interested in a specific style, but don't know what it's made of call (800) 448-1796 for information.

Asics: GT-2010

Avia: Stability Trainer

Converse: Chuck Taylor All-Stars, high-top and low-top, come in many styles, colors, and fabrics; and canvas One Stars.

Etonic: Stableair

Keds: Canvas oxfords and slip ons in a variety of colors and patterns

New Balance: All styles of running shoes, and the 590 walking shoe are made with leather alternatives and/or suede alternatives.

Nike: Leather-free running, basketball, volleyball, golf, cross training, and cheerleading styles available. Call (800) 352-6453 to receive a sourcebook that lists all animal-free Nike shoes.

Payless Shoe Source: The Richard Simmons line of shoes for women include several athletic styles made with synthetic materials.

Saucony: G.R.I.D. Sensation II

Tretorn: Canvas tennis-style shoes.

Vans: Styles include canvas, linen, and flannel oxfords; mules; and Mary Janes. Call (800) 750-VANS for stores in your area that carry Vans.

Men

Adidas: Synthetic sports shoes in a variety of styles. At retail stores the side of the box lists what each part of the shoe is made from -- look for the word synthetic. If you're interested in a specific style, but don't know what it's made of call (800) 448-1796 for information.

Asics: GT-2010

Avia: Stability Trainer and Defender styles.

Brooks: Vanguard

Converse: Chuck Taylor All-Stars, high-top and low-top, come in many styles, colors, and fabrics; and canvas One Stars.

Etonic: Stableair

K-Swiss: Canvas sneakers

New Balance: Most of the running shoes have all-synthetic uppers. Some of the walking shoes are synthetic. Write to 61 N. Beacon St., Boston, MA 02134, for a current catalog that lists which shoes are non-leather.

Nike: Non-leather/suede shoes include running, basketball, tennis, cross training, cycling, and golf styles. Call (800) 352-6453 to receive a sourcebook that lists all animal-free Nike shoes.

Saucony: G.R.I.D. Sensation II

Vans: Styles include canvas, linen, and flannel oxfords. Call (800) 750-VANS for stores in your area that carry Vans.

Children

Kids Footlocker: This store sells all major brands of athletic shoes for children.

Nike: Athletic shoes in several styles for children and babies. Call (800) 352-6453 to receive a sourcebook that lists all animal-free Nike shoes.

Payless Shoe Source: Always a great place to find leather-free shoes for children, athletic styles often feature popular cartoon characters.

DRESS SHOES

Women are probably going to have an easier time than men in finding decent alternatives to leather dress shoes, although men are getting more options. Make sure that the entire shoe is made from synthetic material -- that the lining or sole, in addition to the upper, are leather-free. Value shoe stores like **Payless Shoe Source**, as well as discount stores like **K-Mart** and **Walmart** often offer a wealth of styles for men, women, and children.

Women

Auditions: This brand of shoe comes in leather-like flats and pumps in a variety of colors.

Beacon Shoe Company: Several different styles available.

Daniel Green: Dressy leather-like slipper sandals and flats.

Hush Puppies: Pumps.

Lane Bryant: Man-made pumps in a variety of styles.

Life Stride: Pumps.

Masseys: This mail-order catalog carries leather-like flats, pumps, and other styles. They carry name brands such as Auditions.

Naturalizer: Wedge pumps.

Payless Shoe Source: One of the best places to find non-leather dress shoes, including the Richard Simmons line.

Roaman's: Several leather-like dress shoes.

Unlisted by Kenneth Cole, 1-800-UNLISTED. This company offers a line of synthetic leather shoes, belts, and handbags for women. Carried in department stores like Macy's and Nordstrom. Call the 1-800 number for locations near you.

Men

The best places for men to find leather alternative dress shoes are **Aesop, Inc.; Deja Shoes; Heartland Products, Ltd.;** and **Vegetarian Shoes** which are all listed in the Vegan Mail Order section of this article. If you're not interested in mail order the next best place would be discount shoe stores like **Payless Shoe Source**.

Beacon Shoe Company: This company has several different styles available.

Lyle Richards International: Dress shoes found at large retailers.

Payless Shoe Source: You should have no trouble finding a stylish dress shoes here.

Children

Payless Shoe Source: Wow, this store just keeps popping up, but you should have no trouble finding a few styles here -- and at reasonable prices!

HIKING BOOTS

For light hiking there are several boots available that will probably meet your needs, even some of the athletic shoe companies are making rugged shoes for day hikes. Canvas shoes with lug soles will perform well under ordinary hiking conditions. The serious hiker, e.g., mountain climbers and trekkers, have fewer choices, but there are some boots that look like they could take on McKinley or The Himalayas. The **Vegan Hiking Boot**, **Veggie Trekker,** and **Ranger** appear to offer the most ankle support and are made with leather alternatives that appear similar in durability.

Aesop: The Merrill Ridge Runner is a low-top shoe for all terrain hiking. It's also suitable for biking and some running. The Vegan Hiking Boot is similar in appearance to the typical hiking boot with all-leather uppers.

Ethical Wares: Weald, Ranger, Woodland, and Trekking styles.

Heartland Products, Ltd.: The Aviva Defender is geared toward off-road activities like mountain biking, hiking, and climbing.

Vegetarian Shoes: Offers the Veggie Trekker which is similar in appearance to the typical hiking boot with all-leather uppers.

WORK BOOTS

Work boots don't have to be leather to keep your foot protected. The following boots should all do the job -- some even have steel-toe protection.

Ethical Wares: Safety Boot with a steel-toe.
Forestry Suppliers, Inc.: Listed in the catalog section.
Heartland Products carries three leather-like working boots: a steel-toe safety shoe, a work boot without a steel-toe, and logger boot. See vegan mail order section.
LaCrosse Boots: Several styles of rubber boots: insulated, non-insulated, and steel toe. Available from large retailers.
Lyle Richards International: Found at large retailers.

COATS AND JACKETS

Heartland Products, Ltd.: Bomber jackets, parkas, riding vests, and touring jackets.
L.L. Bean: Several styles of winter coats made from synthetic fibers, some with synthetic fur ruffs.
PETA: Faux fur coats for women in swing coat and parka styles.
Vegetarian Shoes: Leather-like jackets in classic styles.

BELTS AND BAGS

Belts
Aesop: Several styles of leather-like and military-style belts for men and women.
Ethical Wares: Stylish unisex belts.
Heartland Products, Ltd.: Black, tan, and navy belts for men and women.
Vegetarian Shoes: Dressy non-leather belts.

Bags
Aesop: Wallets, purses, portfolios, and briefcases for men and women.
American Hemp Mercantile, Inc.: Vegan bags and wallets made from hemp.

Creatureless Comforts: Several styles of synthetic leather purses for women.
Ecolution: The briefcase, mini backpack, campus style backpack, and two-pocket fanny pack are made from 100% hemp.
Ecotrek: Daypacks to technical backpacks made totally of recycled and vegan materials.
Heartland Products, Ltd.: Vinyl attaches and non-leather "overnighter briefcase."
Just In Case: Leather-like "professional" briefcases, knapsacks, travel kits, bags, diaper bags, organizers, checkbook and credit card holders, and wallets.
Used Rubber USA: Recycled rubber inner tubes and tires are used to make wallets, organizers, and bags in a variety of sizes.

WHERE DO I FIND...

Ballet Shoes
Capezio: Call (800) 533-1887 for information on where to purchase.

Baseball Gloves
Heartland Products, Ltd.: Adults and children's sizes.

Western-Style Boots
Heartland Products, Ltd.: Styles for women, men, and boys.

Ice Skates
L.L. Bean: Bauer hockey skates made with nylon and synthetic leather uppers.

Snow Boots
L.L. Bean: Nordic Fleece and North Col Primaloft boots. Styles for children also available.
Masseys: Leather-like waterproof boots by Naturalizer.

Michael Keevican researched and wrote this article while as an employee of The Vegetarian Resource Group.

HALLOWEEN HORRORS
For Children Only

By Mary Clifford, R.D.

Raising vegetarian children can be tough on you and on them. Being "different" from classmates and friends can be a strain on youngsters who just want to fit in.

One of the best ways to help your child's peers accept a vegetarian lifestyle is through birthday or holiday parties, either at home or at school. A chance for kids to sample vegetarian food in a fun, relaxed atmosphere can help take the mystery out of your child's eating habits.

A Halloween party, with games and diversions, is a particularly good time to start the ball rolling. It's not as "weird" as Thanksgiving without turkey, Christmas without ham, or the Fourth of July without hot dogs. Halloween has the virtue of not being associated with any particular meat, making it fairly easy to have a vegetarian party without the feeling that something is missing.

LET YOUR KIDS HELP

These recipes are meant to look messy, so let children help as much as possible. Even very small children can do all the stirring. (They'll have more fun if they can use their [clean] hands instead of a spoon.) Young children can also peel bananas and dish out the dessert. Older children can measure and help serve. And be sure to ask children for advice on the menu -- they can help you mix and match from the following combinations of eccentric eats.

MENU

Main Dishes:
Swampy Spuds
Crazy Corn Dogs
Sloppy Pockets

Side Dishes:
Crunchy Crud
French Frights
Nefarious Nachos

Desserts:
Slime
Putrid Pudding
Muffin Mash

SWAMPY SPUDS
(Serves 8)

"Cheese"- and green vegetable-stuffed baked potatoes are filling enough to make a meal on their own. As a plus, all of these ingredients can be prepared ahead of time, then assembled and reheated at the last minute.

8 large baking potatoes, scrubbed
   and pierced

"Cheese" Sauce:
1 cup nutritional yeast *
1/4 cup whole wheat flour
1 Tablespoon minced onion

1/2 teaspoon turmeric
1/4 teaspoon white pepper
2 cups water
2 Tablespoons soft margarine
1 Tablespoon Dijon-style prepared
   mustard

<u>Vegetables:</u>
1/2 cup cooked peas
1/2 cup chopped, cooked broccoli
1/2 cup lima beans
1/2 cup chopped, steamed zucchini
2 Tablespoons chopped chives for
   garnish (optional)

Heat oven to 375 degrees. Bake potatoes until tender, about 1 hour. (To ensure the driest baked potato possible, use baking potatoes, not all-purpose potatoes. Also, avoid wrapping potatoes in foil before baking -- this will cause them to steam, leading to a moister product.)

Meanwhile, prepare sauce: Combine all sauce ingredients in a medium-size saucepan. Heat to boiling over medium heat, whisking constantly until thickened and bubbly.

To serve, split each potato and carefully scoop insides into mixing bowl. Stir in cooked vegetables. Divide mixture back into potato shells and top with sauce mixture. Sprinkle with chives, if desired.

TOTAL CALORIES PER SERVING: 365
TOTAL FAT AS % OF DAILY VALUE: 5%   FAT: 3 gm
PROTEIN: 13 gm   CARBOHYDRATES: 75 gm
CALCIUM: 46 mg   IRON: 4 mg   SODIUM: 131 mg
DIETARY FIBER: 8 gm

(*Nutritional yeast is also known as good-tasting yeast and has a cheesy taste. It is <u>not</u> Brewer's Yeast. Nutritional yeast is sold in many natural foods stores. It can also be ordered from Walnut Acres, Penns Creek, PA 17862.)

CRAZY CORN DOGS
(Serve 8)

Traditional corn dogs are not only bad for the pig's health, but ours, too. They're hot dogs that have been batter-dipped, then deep-fat fried. This version uses a cornmeal biscuit to approximate a cross between corn dogs and that other artery-clogging favorite, pigs-in-a-blanket.

1 cup yellow cornmeal
3/4 cup unsifted whole-wheat flour
1 Tablespoon baking powder
1/8 teaspoon salt
1/4 cup soft margarine
1/2 cup water
8 non-fat vegan hot dogs
Relish, sauerkraut, mustard, ketchup,
   onions (optional)

Heat oven to 350 degrees. Lightly oil a baking sheet.

In a medium-size bowl, stir together dry ingredients. With pastry cutter or two knives, cut in margarine until mixture resembles coarse crumbs. With wooden spoon, stir in water until mixture pulls away from side of bowl.

Turn dough out onto lightly floured board; gently press out to between 1/4-inch and 1/2-inch thickness. With biscuit cutter or drinking glass, cut 8 circles from dough, rerolling and cutting scraps until all dough is used. Slightly flatten each circle of dough. Wrap one circle around each "hot dog," leaving ends uncovered. Pinch dough to seal.

Bake corn "dogs" on oiled baking sheet about 20 minutes, or until dough is very lightly browned. Serve immediately with toppings as desired.

TOTAL CALORIES PER SERVING: 196
TOTAL FAT AS % OF DAILY VALUE: 9%   FAT: 6 gm
PROTEIN: 12 gm   CARBOHYDRATES: 23 gm
CALCIUM: 128 mg   IRON: 4 mg   SODIUM: 453 mg
DIETARY FIBER: 2 gm

SLOPPY POCKETS
(Serves 8)

A vegetarian version of curried chicken salad stuffed into pita bread and full of crunchy veggies. Make this up ahead of time to allow the flavors to blend.

2 pounds extra firm tofu, well
    drained
2 to 3 teaspoons curry powder
1/4 teaspoon pepper
1/8 teaspoon salt
1/2 cup eggless mayonnaise
3 large carrots, sliced
1 stalk celery, sliced
3/4 cup peas
2 sliced green onions
8 pita pockets
Shredded lettuce, chopped tomato
    (optional)

In a large bowl, crumble or cube tofu. Stir in remaining ingredients except pita pockets and optional garnishes.

To serve, divide into pita pockets. Garnish with lettuce and tomatoes, if desired.

TOTAL CALORIES PER SERVING: 327
TOTAL FAT AS % OF DAILY VALUE: 14%   FAT: 9 gm
PROTEIN: 18 gm   CARBOHYDRATES: 42 gm
CALCIUM: 255 mg   IRON: 3 mg   SODIUM: 504 mg
DIETARY FIBER: 2 gm

CRUNCHY CRUD
(Serves 8)

It may look like coleslaw, it may taste like coleslaw, but isn't it more fun to eat when you call it something goofy like this?

Dressing:
1/3 cup eggless mayonnaise
3 tablespoons apple cider vinegar
4 teaspoons maple syrup
1 Tablespoon prepared spicy brown
    mustard
1 Tablespoon minced onion
1 clove garlic, minced
1/8 teaspoon pepper
1/8 teaspoon salt

Salad:
1/2 pound green cabbage, shredded
1/2 pound red cabbage, shredded
2 large carrots, thinly sliced
2 stalks celery, sliced
1 Tablespoon sunflower seeds

In a small bowl, stir together dressing ingredients until well combined.

In a large bowl, toss salad ingredients (except sunflower seeds). Pour in dressing, and toss until vegetables are coated. Sprinkle with sunflower seeds before serving.

TOTAL CALORIES PER SERVING: 66
TOTAL FAT AS % OF DAILY VALUE: 5%   FAT: 3 gm
PROTEIN: 1 gm   CARBOHYDRATES: 9 gm
CALCIUM: 46 mg   IRON: 1 mg   SODIUM: 155 mg
DIETARY FIBER: 2 gm

FRENCH FRIGHTS
(Serves 8)

These fiendishly colorful oven-baked potato wedges are the perfect size for tiny hands to hold.

3 pounds medium-size all-purpose
   potatoes
2 Tablespoons vegetable oil
1 teaspoon chili powder
1 teaspoon turmeric
1/8 teaspoon salt and pepper

Heat oven to 425 degrees. Coat a large, rimmed baking pan with vegetable cooking spray. Cut each potato in half, then cut each half into quarters lengthwise.

In a large bowl, toss together potatoes and remaining ingredients until well coated.

Spread potatoes on oiled pan. Bake about 20 minutes or until browned.

TOTAL CALORIES PER SERVING: 156
TOTAL FAT AS % OF DAILY VALUE: 6%   FAT: 4 gm
PROTEIN: 4 gm   CARBOHYDRATES: 28 gm
CALCIUM: 23 mg   IRON: 2 mg   SODIUM: 50 mg
DIETARY FIBER: 3 gm

NEFARIOUS NACHOS
(Serves 8)

The "cheese" sauce for Swampy Spuds is the perfect topping for this vegan version of every kid's favorite snack.

1 recipe "Cheese" Sauce (see
   "Swampy Spuds")
7-ounce bag no-oil tortilla chips
1/2 cup sliced black olives
2 Tablespoons mild chopped green
   chilies
2 Tablespoons sliced green onions
1/4 cup finely chopped sweet red
   pepper

Spread tortilla chips on serving platter. Top with "cheese," then sprinkle with remaining ingredients. Serve immediately.

TOTAL CALORIES PER SERVING: 188
TOTAL FAT AS % OF DAILY VALUE: 11%   FAT: 7 gm
PROTEIN: 8 gm   CARBOHYDRATES: 27 gm
CALCIUM: 77 mg   IRON: 1 mg   SODIUM: 379 mg
DIETARY FIBER: 3 gm

SLIME
(Serves 8)

A simple fruit purée, yet its pale green tint makes this perfect for a special occasion like Halloween. Make this close to serving time, since the bananas will discolor if it sits too long. And, be sure to start with well-chilled fruit. (You can refrigerate unpeeled bananas -- the skin will blacken, but the flesh inside will be fine.)

3 kiwi fruit, peeled
1/2 teaspoon vanilla extract
2 pounds (about 6) ripe medium-size
   bananas, peeled
10.5 ounce package silken tofu
Cinnamon, fruit-juice sweetened
   cookie crumbs for garnish
   (optional)

In blender or food processor, purée kiwi fruit. Set aside about 1/3 of mixture and stir in vanilla extract. Add bananas and tofu to remaining kiwi fruit. Process until smooth.

To serve, divide fruit mixture into dessert dishes. Sprinkle with cinnamon and cookie crumbs, if desired. Stir some of remaining puréed kiwi fruit into each serving, swirling slightly to keep a darker green streak visible.

TOTAL CALORIES PER SERVING: 147
TOTAL FAT AS % OF DAILY VALUE: 3%   FAT: 2 gm
PROTEIN: 5 gm   CARBOHYDRATES: 32 gm
CALCIUM: 23 mg   IRON: 1 mg   SODIUM: 28 mg
DIETARY FIBER: 3 gm

PUTRID PUDDING
(Serves 8)

Served chilled or warm, rice pudding takes on a sweet new twist when studded with dried fruit.

2 cups cooked rice
2 cups unsweetened applesauce
1-1/2 cups soy milk
1 cup chopped, mixed dried fruit
    (such as apricots and raisins)
2 Tablespoons tahini
2 Tablespoons vanilla extract
2 Tablespoons chopped nuts for
    garnish (optional)
Apple wedges for garnish (optional;
    red-skinned apples are prettiest)

In a heavy 3-quart saucepan, combine all ingredients except vanilla and optional garnishes. Heat to boiling over medium heat.

Reduce heat to low, cover and simmer, stirring occasionally, until rice is very tender (this will depend on how tender it was cooked originally; it may take up to 30 minutes).

Remove from heat, and stir in vanilla. Let cool slightly to serve warm (can also be refrigerated several hours or overnight to serve chilled). Sprinkle with chopped nuts and garnish with apple wedges, if desired.

TOTAL CALORIES PER SERVING: 192
TOTAL FAT AS % OF DAILY VALUE: 5%   FAT: 3 gm
PROTEIN: 4 gm   CARBOHYDRATES: 39 gm
CALCIUM: 34 mg   IRON: 1 mg   SODIUM: 44 mg
DIETARY FIBER: 3 gm

MUFFIN MASH
(Makes about 1-1/2 dozen regular or 3 dozen mini-muffins, approximately 2-1/2-inch or 1-inch diameter)

Forget what the recipe books say about filling muffin tins only 1/2 or 2/3 full -- spoon the batter in right to the top for this recipe, so you get larger muffins. Just make sure to oil the top of the tins as well, to make cleanup easier.

2 cups whole wheat flour
1 teaspoon baking soda
1 teaspoon baking powder
1/8 teaspoon salt
3/4 cup golden raisins
1 cup orange juice
1 cup soy milk
2 Tablespoons vegetable oil
1 teaspoon vanilla extract
2 ripe bananas, well mashed

Heat oven to 350 degrees. Lightly oil muffin tins.

In a large bowl, stir together dry ingredients and raisins.

In a medium-size bowl, stir together remaining ingredients. Quickly stir wet ingredients into flour mixture. Do not overmix -- batter should be slightly lumpy.

Spoon batter into oiled muffin tins. Bake 20 to 25 minutes, or until golden. Serve immediately, or let cool on wire rack and refrigerate until ready to serve. (If left at room temperature, they will get soggy because of the high moisture content). If desired, split and toast before serving.

TOTAL CALORIES PER REGULAR MUFFIN: 107
TOTAL FAT AS % OF DAILY VALUE: 3%   FAT: 2 gm
PROTEIN: 3 gm   CARBOHYDRATES: 22 gm
CALCIUM: 29 mg   IRON: 1 mg   SODIUM: 110 mg
DIETARY FIBER: 2 gm

Mary Clifford is a Registered Dietitian living in Roanoke, Virginia.

A VEGETARIAN THANKSGIVING

By Susan Stafursky

CRANBERRY/ORANGE/NUT RELISH
(Serves 8-12)

If you don't own a food processor, you can use a food grinder to prepare this recipe.

1 orange (unpeeled)
1 bag cranberries, washed
1/2 cup pecans
2/3 cup sugar or other sweetener

Cut orange in eighths and remove seeds. Process half the berries with nuts and half the orange in food processor, pulsing so as not to over-process. Repeat with remainder. Combine with sweetener to taste in a bowl. Cover and refrigerate over night.

TOTAL CALORIES PER SERVING: 137
TOTAL FAT AS % OF DAILY VALUE: 8%   FAT: 5 gm
PROTEIN: 1 gm   CARBOHYDRATES: 26 gm
CALCIUM: 17 mg   IRON: <1 mg   SODIUM: 1 mg
DIETARY FIBER: 3 gm

CHICKPEAS WITH VEGETABLES
(Serves 4)

Enjoy this delicious dish!

1 small onion, chopped
1/2 large red bell pepper, chopped
1 stalk celery, sliced
1 Tablespoon olive oil
19-ounce can chickpeas, drained
Tamari or soy sauce to taste

Sauté vegetables in oil in non-stick pan until tender. Add chickpeas, mashing them gently just to flatten the beans. Add tamari to taste. Continue to fry over medium heat until mixture begins to brown, carefully turning mixture to prevent browning. Add pepper and/or hot sauce to taste.

TOTAL CALORIES PER SERVING: 173
TOTAL FAT AS % OF DAILY VALUE: 9%   FAT: 6 gm
PROTEIN: 7 gm   CARBOHYDRATES: 25 gm
CALCIUM:61 mg   IRON: 4 mg   SODIUM: 545 mg
DIETARY FIBER: 7 gm

SQUASH/APPLE CASSEROLE
(Serves 4)

Serve this dish hot.

1 small butternut squash, baked, sliced
1 small onion, chopped
1 teaspoon olive oil
1 Granny Smith apple, cored and sliced
Tamari or soy sauce to taste
2 Tablespoons raisins
1 Tablespoon brown sugar or other sweetener

In small casserole dish (lightly oiled), arrange slices of squash on bottom. Sauté onion in oil until soft. Spread over squash. Sprinkle lightly with tamari. Arrange apple slices over top and sprinkle with raisins, sugar, and more tamari. Microwave or bake at 350 degrees until apples are soft.

TOTAL CALORIES PER SERVING: 104
TOTAL FAT AS % OF DAILY VALUE: 2%   FAT: 1 gm
PROTEIN: 1 gm   CARBOHYDRATES: 24 gm
CALCIUM: 51 mg   IRON: 1 mg   SODIUM: 6 mg
DIETARY FIBER: 3 gm

VEGAN MASHED POTATOES
(Serves 4-6)

It's best to serve this dish immediately.

4 medium red skinned potatoes
2 Tablespoons soft margarine
Salt and pepper to taste

Peel and chop potatoes. Cook in boiling water until very tender. Drain and return to pan. Shake pan over flame to remove more moisture. Mash with a potato masher until smooth. Add margarine, salt and pepper to taste.

TOTAL CALORIES PER SERVING: 165
TOTAL FAT AS % OF DAILY VALUE: 9%   FAT: 6 gm
PROTEIN: 2 gm   CARBOHYDRATES: 27 gm
CALCIUM: 12 mg   IRON: <1 mg   SODIUM: 72 mg
DIETARY FIBER: 3 gm

BRUSSELS SPROUTS WITH CHESTNUTS
(Serves 4)

Correct seasoning before serving hot.

1 Tablespoon oil
16 fresh Brussels sprouts, washed, trimmed, and halved lengthwise
2 Tablespoons water
Tamari or soy sauce to taste
1/2 cup roasted chestnuts, halved
1/2 lemon, squeezed

Heat oil in non-stick skillet. When hot, carefully lay sprouts, cut sides down in skillet. Cook over medium heat until they begin to brown. Add water, cover skillet, and reduce heat. Simmer 5 minutes. Sprinkle with tamari and top with chestnuts. Add a little more water if necessary. Cover and continue cooking over low heat until sprouts are tender. Squeeze lemon juice over mixture.

TOTAL CALORIES PER SERVING: 109
TOTAL FAT AS % OF DAILY VALUE: 6%   FAT: 4 gm
PROTEIN: 4 gm   CARBOHYDRATES: 17 gm
CALCIUM: 46 mg   IRON: 2 mg   SODIUM: 27 mg
DIETARY FIBER: 5 gm

VEGETARIAN "STUFFING"
(Serves 8-10)

For variety, you can add raisins, substitute nuts for chestnuts, or use different vegetables.

1 onion, chopped
2 stalks celery, sliced
1/2 pound mushrooms, sliced
1/4 cup vegetable broth
2 cups water
1 pound bag *Pepperidge Farm Herb Stuffing* or equivalent stuffing
1/2 pound of *Pepperidge Farm Corn Bread Stuffing*
1 cup cooked brown rice
1 cup roasted chestnuts, chopped

Sauté onion, celery, and mushrooms in broth until tender. Add water and bring to a boil. Turn off heat.

Preheat oven to 400 degrees. In a large bowl combine *Pepperidge Farm Herb Stuffing*, *Pepperidge Farm Corn Bread Stuffing*, cooked brown rice, and roasted chestnuts.

Combine both mixtures. Spread into a large shallow, lightly oiled baking dish. Bake at 400 degrees for 35 minutes until top and bottom are browned. Serve hot.

TOTAL CALORIES PER SERVING: 404
TOTAL FAT AS % OF DAILY VALUE: 6%   FAT: 4 gm
PROTEIN: 11 gm   CARBOHYDRATES: 82 gm
CALCIUM: 113 mg   IRON: 5 mg   SODIUM: 1096 mg
DIETARY FIBER: 4 gm

Susan Stafursky is a member of The Vegetarian Resource Group and owner of The Savannah Inn, a vegetarian Bed and Breakfast located in Lewes, Delaware.

MEATING OF THE MINDS
Vegetarian Meals Even Carnivores Can Enjoy

By Mary Clifford, R.D.

You're hosting a formal family dinner, but your spouse's relatives are the founders of Billy Boy's Pig Heaven Pork Pit Restaurant. Your boss wants to invite a few clients to your house to close an important deal, and cautions you not to even think about serving bean sprouts. Or you've finally gotten a date with your gorgeous new downstairs neighbor, who loves home cooking.

What's a vegetarian to do? (Pretend, just for a moment, that leaving the country is out of the question.)

Above all, don't panic. With a little advance planning, even inexperienced cooks can pull off a lovely evening that both omnivores and herbivores will enjoy.

First, consider the atmosphere. Even if you don't ordinarily set the table for dinner, be sure to do so for any special occasion. A tablecloth, cloth napkins, and a centerpiece go a long way towards elevating any food to "elegant" status. Don't worry if you don't have matching gold-plated dinnerware handed down from the Queen Mother. The idea is to show that you've put some thought and care into the meal, so if mismatched thrift-shop dishes are what you've got, use them proudly. Fresh flowers, fruit baskets, and candles are simple, yet classic, centerpieces.

Second, keep color in mind when planning your menu. Maybe baked potatoes, sautéed mushrooms, and tempeh with gravy is your favorite meal, but a plate full of brown food is simply not going to win any points in the creativity department.

Likewise for texture: A meal of mashed potatoes, scrambled tofu, and applesauce has all the appeal of a root canal. A variety of textures and colors will excite the taste buds and keep even the most skeptical meat-eater from complaining too much.

Third, you may want to avoid any "way-out" foods if this is your guests' first foray into vegetarian fare. Hold the Sea Vegetable Stew and Agar-Agar Pudding until the fourth gathering, when your guests have become more comfortable with meatless meals.

Finally, don't forget dessert. There are enough wonderful desserts on the market, even for vegans, that special recipes aren't included here. For a simple dessert, offer a selection of cookies and an assortment of herbal teas. A fresh fruit platter, frozen desserts, or cake are other easy ideas.

The following recipes really are easy (don't let lengthy ingredient lists scare you; lots of spices make the recipes longer, but also add plenty of familiar flavor), and many of the dishes can be made ahead of time. As a bonus, you won't need any special equipment (not even a food processor); so novice entertainers should be able to handle these dishes with ease.

MENU

APPETIZERS
Black and Gold Salad
Antipasto Platter

ENTREES
Multi-Grain Croquettes with Sage-Onion Gravy
Rosemary-Scented Polenta

SIDE DISHES
Ginger-Roasted Vegetables
Puffed Sweet Potatoes
Green Beans with Toasted Walnuts

BLACK AND GOLD SALAD
(Serves 4)

For more intense color, contrast the black and gold by serving it on red leaf or radicchio lettuce.

2 cups cooked black beans
1 cup whole kernel corn
1/2 cup chopped, seeded tomato
1/4 cup chopped fresh cilantro
2 Tablespoons lime juice
2 Tablespoons olive oil
1 teaspoon maple syrup
1 green onion, sliced
1/2 teaspoon ground cumin
Pinch of chili powder
Salt and pepper to taste
Radicchio or red leaf lettuce
　(garnish)

In a large bowl, combine all ingredients except lettuce. Let sit several hours or overnight.

To serve, let salad come to room temperature. Arrange in lettuce cups or on beds of shredded lettuce.

TOTAL CALORIES PER SERVING: 226
TOTAL FAT AS % OF DAILY VALUE: 12%　FAT: 8 gm
PROTEIN: 9 gm　CARBOHYDRATES: 24 gm
CALCIUM: 33 mg　IRON: 2 mg　SODIUM: 9 mg
DIETARY FIBER: 5 gm

ANTIPASTO PLATTER
(Serves 4)

Serve this pungent, marinated platter in place of the usual crudite. Any vegetables will do here -- cauliflower, broccoli, sweet pepper strips, carrots, cherry tomatoes, and zucchini are some examples. Olives will also add a pretty shape and color.

3/4 pound raw or blanched vegetables
3 Tablespoons cider, red wine, or balsamic vinegar
4 teaspoons olive oil
1/2 teaspoon basil
1/2 teaspoon oregano
1/4 teaspoon garlic powder
Salt and pepper to taste

Toss vegetables with marinade ingredients. Let sit at least 3 hours or overnight. To serve, drain and arrange on platter. May be served chilled or at room temperature.

Note: Whenever marinating vegetables, do not add broccoli until just before serving or it will discolor and turn an unsightly olive green.

TOTAL CALORIES PER SERVING: 63
TOTAL FAT AS % OF DAILY VALUE: 8%　FAT: 5 gm
PROTEIN: 2 gm　CARBOHYDRATES: 5 gm
CALCIUM: 30 mg　IRON: 1 mg　SODIUM: 24 mg
DIETARY FIBER: 1 gm

MULTI-GRAIN CROQUETTES
(Serves 4)

TOTAL CALORIES PER SERVING: 255
TOTAL FAT AS % OF DAILY VALUE: 10%   FAT: 7 gm
PROTEIN: 10 gm   CARBOHYDRATES: 41 gm
CALCIUM: 52 mg   IRON: 2 mg   SODIUM: 170 mg
DIETARY FIBER: 3 gm

These savory croquettes can easily be made ahead of time and reheated before serving, but be sure to form them into thick patties so that they remain moist and aromatic when reheated.

1 Tablespoon oil
1/4 cup onion, finely chopped
1/4 cup carrot, finely chopped
1/4 cup celery, finely chopped
2 cups well-cooked brown rice
1 cup old-fashioned rolled oats, raw
1/2 teaspoon garlic powder
1/2 teaspoon cumin powder
1 cup vegetable broth
1 Tablespoon vegetarian Worcester-
    shire sauce
10.5 ounces firm lite tofu, crumbled

In a large, non-stick skillet, heat oil over medium heat. Sauté onion, carrot, and celery until vegetables are well browned.

Stir in remaining ingredients, except tofu. Simmer over low heat until broth is absorbed but mixture is still moist. Remove to large mixing bowl and let cool. Do not wash skillet.

With potato masher or clean hands, add tofu to cooled grain mixture. Mash until well combined. Form into 8 patties.

Coat skillet with vegetable cooking spray, or brush lightly with pastry brush dipped in oil to help prevent sticking. Fry croquettes, turning once, until lightly browned. Repeat until all are fried, adding additional coats of oil or spray to prevent sticking. Serve immediately.

Note: These may also be baked, but will not get as crispy or brown outside. To bake, place on greased pan in 400 degree oven 20 to 25 minutes, turning once.

SAGE-ONION GRAVY
(Serves 4)

A healthy dose of caramelized onions adds a great deal of substance to this condiment, making it a cross between a relish and a gravy. It's best made just before serving, although you can sauté the onions the day before and start from step two when you're ready to serve.

2 teaspoons oil
1/2 pound onions, sliced thinly into
    rings
1 bay leaf
1/8 teaspoon sage
1-1/3 cups chilled vegetable broth
1 Tablespoon red wine vinegar
1 teaspoon soy sauce
3 Tablespoons flour

In a large, non stick skillet, heat oil over medium-high heat. Add onions, bay leaf, and sage. Sauté, stirring occasionally, until very well browned.

In a cup or small bowl, whisk together broth, vinegar, soy sauce, and flour. Be sure broth is cooled to prevent flour from lumping.

Stir broth mixture into onions and heat to boiling, stirring constantly until mixture is thickened and bubbly. Remove bay leaf and serve immediately.

TOTAL CALORIES PER SERVING: 72
TOTAL FAT AS % OF DAILY VALUE: 5%   FAT: 3 gm
PROTEIN: 1 gm   CARBOHYDRATES: 11 gm
CALCIUM: 13 mg   IRON: <1 mg   SODIUM: 157 mg
DIETARY FIBER: 1 gm

ROSEMARY-SCENTED POLENTA
(Serves 4)

Fried cornmeal mush hardly sounds appetizing, but that's exactly what trendy restaurants are serving when you see "polenta" on the menu. This simple, colorful, dish is filling and flavorful, making it one of the best "company" dishes there is. Be sure to serve it with a fragrant tomato sauce and plenty of garlic bread.

3 cups water
3 cups vegetable broth
1/2 teaspoon rosemary, crumbled
1/4 teaspoon salt
2 cups yellow cornmeal
1 cup chopped black olives
1/2 cup chopped sweet red pepper
1 teaspoon margarine, melted
Homemade or prepared tomato sauce

Pre-heat oven to 400 degrees. Coat a 9- x 13-inch rimmed baking pan with vegetable cooking spray. Set aside.

In a large saucepan, combine water, broth, and spices. Heat to boiling. Slowly whisk in cornmeal and cook over low heat, stirring constantly, until thickened and bubbly. Stir in olives and red pepper.

Pour mixture into greased baking pan. Let cool several hours or overnight.

Cut cooled polenta into 8 pieces. Brush with half of melted margarine. Bake 25 to 30 minutes, turning once and brushing with remaining margarine, until golden. Serve with tomato sauce.

TOTAL CALORIES PER SERVING (without sauce): 308
TOTAL FAT AS % OF DAILY VALUE: 9%   FAT: 6 gm
PROTEIN: 7 gm   CARBOHYDRATES: 58 gm
CALCIUM: 22 mg   IRON: 3 mg   SODIUM: 414 mg
DIETARY FIBER: 5 gm

GINGER-ROASTED VEGETABLES
(Serves 4)

The vegetables used here are merely a suggestion. Use your favorites, but keep in mind that heartier vegetables, such as eggplant, carrots, or winter squash, will hold up better under intense heat. Tomatoes will get mushy, but add lovely color and flavor. Mushrooms will shrivel and look perfectly awful, but add a marvelous, rich flavor, especially if you use an exotic species like shiitake or cremini. Cut the pieces rather large so they hold their shape and won't overcook.

2 teaspoons maple syrup
1 teaspoon sesame oil
1/2 teaspoon freshly grated ginger root
Dash hot red pepper sauce
1/2 pound eggplant, cut into slices or chunks
1 medium onion, quartered
1 medium tomato, quartered
1/4 pound mushrooms
1 large carrot, cut into thick diagonal slices

Heat oven to 400 degrees. In a large bowl, stir together maple syrup, sesame oil, ginger root, and red pepper sauce.

Toss vegetables with ginger mixture, making sure to coat evenly. Arrange ginger vegetables on greased baking pan, pouring any remaining marinade over vegetables.

Bake vegetables in oven 15 to 20 minutes, or until browned and tender. You may wish to briefly sear them under the broiler to intensify their color. Serve immediately.

TOTAL CALORIES PER SERVING: 66
TOTAL FAT AS % OF DAILY VALUE: 3%   FAT: 2 gm
PROTEIN: 2 gm   CARBOHYDRATES: 13 gm
CALCIUM: 21 mg   IRON: mg   SODIUM: 14 mg
DIETARY FIBER: 2 gm

PUFFED SWEET POTATOES
(Serves 4)

Scrumptious sweet potatoes are mashed and baked until they form a golden crust outside, while staying smooth and creamy inside. Maybe you should make extras.

1 pound sweet potatoes, peeled and
    cut into chunks
2 Tablespoons margarine
1/2 cup lite soy milk
Pinch of nutmeg
Salt and pepper to taste

Pre-heat oven to 400 degrees. In a large saucepan, cover sweet potatoes with water. Heat to boiling over high heat, then reduce heat to low and simmer until sweet potatoes are very tender. Drain well.

    With potato masher or wooden spoon, combine remaining ingredients with sweet potatoes. Mash until smooth and well mixed.

    Grease a 1-quart baking dish. Place potatoes in baking dish and bake in oven 25 to 30 minutes, or until golden. Serve immediately.

TOTAL CALORIES PER SERVING: 177
TOTAL FAT AS % OF DAILY VALUE: 9%   FAT: 6 gm
PROTEIN: 3 gm   CARBOHYDRATES: 30 gm
CALCIUM: 44 mg   IRON: 1 mg   SODIUM: 88 mg
DIETARY FIBER: 3 gm

GREEN BEANS WITH TOASTED WALNUTS
(Serves 4)

A very easy way to make plain old green beans special.

1 teaspoon margarine
1/4 cup chopped walnuts
1 pound green beans, trimmed and
    blanched
Pinch of marjoram
Salt and pepper to taste

In large, non-stick skillet, melt margarine over medium heat. Add walnuts and cook, stirring, about 2 minutes or until walnuts are lightly browned.

    Add green beans and spices to mixture in skillet. Stir until well coated. Serve immediately.

TOTAL CALORIES PER SERVING: 82
TOTAL FAT AS % OF DAILY VALUE: 8%   FAT: 5 gm
PROTEIN: 3 gm   CARBOHYDRATES: 7 gm
CALCIUM: 55 mg   IRON: 2 mg   SODIUM: 26 mg
DIETARY FIBER: 2 gm

Mary Clifford is a Registered Dietitian living in Roanoke, Virginia.

HOLIDAY GIFTS FROM YOUR KITCHEN

By Nanette Blanchard

Homemade gifts of food are my favorite holiday offerings. Anyone can go to a store to pick up a gift, but it takes someone special, someone who cares about you, to give homemade gifts. Be creative when you plan Christmas and Chanukah offerings for family and friends. Don't forget to give a little something to those other people in your life: your mail carrier, the paper deliverer, your secretary, your baby-sitter, your child's favorite teacher, and your plumber. Just a few baked goods wrapped in colored cellophane or recycled giftwrap, or a basket of homemade condiments, can go a long way in promoting good will at this time of year.

Homemade gifts of food are the perfect holiday offering.

Every year in December my neighbors have an annual tradition. We all swap holiday pies. It is a fun way to try new flavors and a really nice way to improve community relations. Holiday gifts of food don't have to be anything fancy -- try fixing some homemade herb seasoning mix tied up with a bow. I also try to make some edible gifts for my husband's co-workers, the UPS driver, the local used bookstore manager, and my friendly veterinarian. And don't forget to make an extra batch of goodies to drop off at the nearest nursing home or children's ward at a local hospital.

By giving smaller gifts and not buying any expensive items, I can afford to recognize most everyone who has been important in my life. Dressing up baskets is the really fun part of doing holiday gifts. Sometimes it's nice to use a practical container such as a big Pyrex measuring cup, a colorful colander, or a cute teapot to wrap up homemade goodies. A children's toy such as a large fire engine or lunch box is a nice container to give to the younger ones on your list.

Save old bottles, jars, and other containers for packaging your homemade gifts. They can easily be decorated with ribbons, stickers, small ornaments, and gift wrap. I buy fabrics for covering gift jar lids. A nice way to present trail mixes is to cover a cardboard tube from a roll of paper towels with wrapping paper and tie at both ends with ribbon.

SPICY GARBANZO NUTS
(Makes 2 cups -- Serves 4)

An unexpected bonus of making this recipe is the wonderful aroma that will fill your kitchen as the garbanzo beans bake. Don't drain the garbanzo beans too well or the spices won't stick to the beans. Fill a half-pint mason jar with Spicy Garbanzo Nuts for gifts.

2 cups pre-cooked, drained garbanzo beans
1/2 teaspoon garlic powder
2 teaspoons chili powder

Mix ingredients well on ungreased non-stick baking sheet. Bake at 350 degrees for 45 minutes. Remove from baking sheet to let cool.

TOTAL CALORIES PER SERVING: 184
TOTAL FAT AS % OF DAILY VALUE: 5%   FAT: 3 gm
PROTEIN: 10 gm   CARBOHYDRATES: 31 gm
CALCIUM: 78 mg   IRON: 4 mg   SODIUM: 26 mg
DIETARY FIBER: 6 gm

MOCK MINCEMEAT
(Makes about 4 cups -- Serves 8)

Put Mock Mincemeat in a pretty jar or crock. It can be heated and served plain or can be used as a topping for frozen desserts. To make Mock Mincemeat Pie, pre-bake a pie shell until light golden brown and fill with one recipe Mock Mincemeat. Then bake an additional 30 minutes at 350 degrees.

3 large Red Delicious apples, cored and diced
1/2 cup chopped dried figs
1/2 cup chopped dates
2 Tablespoons sunflower seeds
1/4 cup chopped walnuts
1/4 cup apple juice concentrate
1 teaspoon cinnamon
1/4 teaspoon ground cloves
1/2 teaspoon ground nutmeg
1/2 teaspoon ground ginger

In a heavy saucepan, simmer all ingredients over medium heat for 15 minutes, stirring occasionally.

TOTAL CALORIES PER SERVING: 154
TOTAL FAT AS % OF DAILY VALUE: 6%   FAT: 4 gm
PROTEIN: 2 gm   CARBOHYDRATES: 31 gm
CALCIUM: 32 mg   IRON: 1 mg   SODIUM: 5 mg
DIETARY FIBER: 4 gm

HERB AND SPICE VINEGAR
(Makes 2 cups -- Serves 16)

This flavorful vinegar is a delightful seasoning for steamed vegetables. Kitchenware stores now stock a wonderful selection of colored and sculptured bottles that are perfect containers for flavored vinegars.

2 cups red wine vinegar
3 dried small chili peppers
3 sliced garlic cloves
Two (3-inch) sprigs Italian parsley
1 teaspoon black peppercorns
1 teaspoon dill seed
1 teaspoon mustard seed

Bottle all ingredients together and let sit for 2 weeks in a dark, cool place. Strain and use.

TOTAL CALORIES PER SERVING: 14
TOTAL FAT AS % OF DAILY VALUE: <1%   FAT: <1 gm
PROTEIN: <1 gm   CARBOHYDRATES: 5 gm
CALCIUM: 16 mg   IRON: 1 mg   SODIUM: 54 mg
DIETARY FIBER: 2 gm

HERB SEASONING MIX

(Makes 2 Tablespoons Mix -- Serves 12)

This no-salt recipe is fun to make if you have a mortar and pestle. If you have any old spice bottles, fill them with this mixture and include some serving instructions. Herb Seasoning Mix is tasty over baked potatoes, in bean soup, over brown rice, and with sweet potatoes.

1 teaspoon tarragon
1 teaspoon oregano
2 teaspoons thyme
1/2 teaspoon celery seed
1/4 teaspoon black pepper
1/2 teaspoon paprika
1/2 teaspoon dry mustard
1/2 teaspoon garlic powder
1/2 teaspoon onion powder
1/4 teaspoon nutmeg

Crush all herbs and spices together well in a mortar and pestle or in a blender.

TOTAL CALORIES PER SERVING: 3
TOTAL FAT AS % OF DAILY VALUE: <1%   FAT: <1 gm
PROTEIN: <1 gm   CARBOHYDRATES: 1 gm
CALCIUM: 9 mg   IRON: <1 mg   SODIUM: <1 mg
DIETARY FIBER: <1 gm

CROCKPOT APPLE BUTTER

(Makes about 7-1/2 cups -- Serves 60)

This recipe for Crockpot Apple Butter makes enough for several gifts and the long, slow cooking guarantees a smooth, delicious butter. It keeps several weeks in the refrigerator and can also be frozen.

12 cups sliced and cored tart green
    apples
2 cups apple cider
1-1/2 cups apple juice concentrate or
    to taste

1 teaspoon cinnamon
1/2 teaspoon allspice

Cook apples and cider in a crockpot, covered, 12 hours over a low heat. Drain off any excess juice. Purée in batches in food processor until smooth. Add apple juice concentrate to taste and cinnamon and allspice. Return mixture to crockpot, cover, and simmer for 1-2 hours.

TOTAL CALORIES PER SERVING: 29
TOTAL FAT AS % OF DAILY VALUE: <1%   FAT: <1 gm
PROTEIN: <1 gm   CARBOHYDRATES: 7 gm
CALCIUM: 4 mg   IRON: <1 mg   SODIUM: 2 mg
DIETARY FIBER: <1 gm

CRANBERRY ORANGE SAUCE

(Makes 2-1/2 cups -- Serves 5)

This simple sauce is a wonderful change from bottled or canned cranberry sauces. Serve Cranberry Orange Sauce as a filling for baked acorn squash or as an unusual dessert topping.

1 cup freshly squeezed orange juice
1/2 cup water
3/4 cup apple juice concentrate
12-ounce bag cranberries, fresh or
    frozen
2 teaspoons minced orange peel

Bring all ingredients to boil in a heavy saucepan and continue cooking over medium heat until cranberries pop and mixture becomes foamy. Cool, pour into serving dish, and cover. Refrigerate until serving time.

TOTAL CALORIES PER SERVING: 64
TOTAL FAT AS % OF DAILY VALUE: <1%   FAT: <1 gm
PROTEIN: 1 gm   CARBOHYDRATES: 16 gm
CALCIUM: 11 mg   IRON: <1 mg   SODIUM: 2 mg
DIETARY FIBER: 3 gm

Nanette Blanchard is a freelance writer from Durango, Colorado.

CHOOSING AND USING A DIETITIAN

By Virginia Messina, M.P.H., R.D.

I am the first to admit that there are pros and cons to using a registered dietitian when you need a nutrition counselor, especially if you are a vegetarian. Conservative attitudes towards vegetarian diets still prevail in many dietetic programs. Many conventional dietitians cling to the "variety and moderation" approach to nutrition. For some, lowfat vegetarian diets, and especially lowfat vegan diets, tend to defy those two parameters.

On the other hand, dietitians have at least rudimentary knowledge about nutrition science. Dietitians need to take a variety of physiology, chemistry, and biochemistry courses, all of which are necessary to understand fully the science of nutrition and to separate erroneous nutrition information from facts. Registered dietitians need to take a national exam to make sure they are well versed in at least the basics.

In many states, anyone can call him- or herself a nutritionist and can set up a dietary counseling practice. There is a variety of certification programs that allow people to earn nutrition "degrees" with minimal training. So if you choose a nutrition counselor who is not a registered dietitian, you may not have any way of evaluating that person's nutrition knowledge.

Another thing that sets dietitians apart is that they know both nutrition and food. In addition to science courses, a dietitian's training includes course work in food science and food preparation. While every dietitian isn't necessarily a gourmet chef, it is important to know your way around a kitchen and a grocery store when giving clients practical information about how to change their diet. Other health care professionals who have an extensive science background and who have read up on nutrition may not have much knowledge about food products and preparation. In one clinic where I worked, I remember a physician who kept telling all his patients to stop using salad dressing on their salads and to just sprinkle vinegar on top instead, ignoring the fact that there are plenty of non-fat alternatives that you can whip up in your kitchen or buy in the grocery store. Another health care practitioner once told all his patients to replace all the margarine in their diet with olive oil. I had visions of my clients pouring olive oil over their toast in the morning, instead of reducing the margarine!

I'm not saying *only* registered dietitians are knowledgeable about nutrition and food. There are plenty of people with hard-earned degrees in nutrition who have chosen not to go the registered dietitian route. And there are well-trained people in other fields who are extremely knowledgeable about diets.

Finding a Dietitian

If you decide to use a dietitian as a nutrition counselor, will you be able to find one who is knowledgeable about and supportive of your vegetarian diet? Well, there is a good chance that you will, but you'll have to hone your sleuthing skills a bit first. That's especially true if you want advice about a vegan diet.

The first step is to generate a list of registered dietitians in your area. There are a number of ways to locate a dietitian. You can check the Yellow Pages under nutrition, dietitian, or weight loss. (Even if you don't want to lose weight, this is a good place to look for a nutrition counselor.) Depending on where you live, there may be a lengthy list or no one listed at all. Another good resource is the American Dietetic Association's (ADA) referral service (1-800-877-1600). Tell them that you want a dietitian who specializes in vegetarian nutrition. The ADA has a specialty group of dietitians with an interest in vegetarianism. This Vegetarian Nutrition Dietetic Practice Group has 1,500 members. While that sounds like a lot of dietitians, bear in mind that all of them don't offer nutrition counseling and members have different reasons for joining the group. You can also contact The Vegetarian Resource Group (410-366-VEGE) to see if one of our dietitian members lives in your area.

Once you have a list of prospective counselors, you will want to call and interview them. Nutrition counseling can be expensive, and it pays to know ahead of time that this is a person who can help you and with whom you will feel comfortable. A 10-minute phone interview should be enough to help you determine whether this is the counselor for you.

What to Ask

One way to assess the dietitian's experience with vegetarianism is to ask how many vegetarians she has counseled or how frequently she sees vegetarian clients. While this is a good piece of information to have, don't let it make or break your decision to work with a particular dietitian. I consider myself to have expertise in vegetarianism, but because I live in a rural community, I actually don't counsel very many vegetarians; there just aren't that many around.

Do be up front about your needs. You can quiz your prospective counselor endlessly and still not find what you need to know. But if you say, "I eat a strictly vegan diet and need to know that you are knowledgeable about that type of diet and that you are comfortable with this dietary choice," you should get the answer you need.

You might want to quiz your prospective counselor a bit regarding her knowledge about particular foods. If you use a lot of Asian vegetables, or build every meal around whole grains like quinoa and kamut, it helps if your nutrition counselor has at least heard of these foods and knows something about their preparation and nutrient content.

You will also want to know how the dietitian works. Does she take a personal approach? Look for someone who will work with your food likes and dislikes and your lifestyle to work out a menu pattern that is appropriate for you; you don't want to pay someone who is just going to hand you a standard vegetarian diet.

Finally, what is your gut feeling? When all is said and done, you have to like this person and feel comfortable with her. After all, this is the person to whom you're going to confess your deepest, darkest dietary secrets.

Most people go to dietitians because they feel that their diet is bad -- and they often feel embarrassed about it. It can make it hard for them to be completely honest about those habits sometimes. Your dietitian needs to be shock-proof and completely non-judgmental, but at the same time she needs to help you identify problem areas in your diet. It's a hard act to balance, and it might be hard for you to judge, over the phone, the dietitian's ability to do this -- but you may be able to get a feeling for how comfortable you are talking to this person.

What to Expect
Your First Session

Actually, the work starts before your first session. The first thing your dietitian will ask you to do is to keep a log of your food intake. Those of us who live for logs, lists, and diaries love this sort of thing. Others find it to be incredibly tedious. But I insist on it with all my clients and most other dietitians do, too. I'll settle for 3 days, but I really like to see at least a week's worth of food intake. Without a food diary, it is just too difficult to reconstruct food habits. You don't have to weigh and measure everything you eat but do estimate portion sizes as best you can. And write it *all* down.

In behavior modification programs, you would also be expected to note the time that you ate, the activity you were engaged in, whom you were with, and how you were feeling. Though most dietitians don't insist on that, there is some real benefit in logging this information. Many people who see dietitians need more than information about what is wrong with their diet. They often need to solve problems in eating behavior. Getting all the facts down about that behavior can really help to identify problems.

Regardless of how much information you choose to log, chances are good that you'll learn something from your food diary. Some of the surprises might be pleasant ones -- like

you eat much more fiber than you realized. But you also might find that some of the vegetarian convenience items you are eating are pushing your fat intake sky high, that you eat fewer vegetables than you thought, or that you snack out of boredom.

Some people find that keeping a food diary is more than a fact-finding mission. It can actually help you to change your diet. Writing foods down forces you to think about what you are eating. You might find that this alone causes you to make better food choices.

The goals of a first 1 to 1-1/2 hour counseling session should be for the dietitian to have a clear understanding of why you are there and to get a good picture of your eating habits, to help you to identify areas of strength in your current eating pattern and areas for improvement, and to set up a specific plan for making necessary changes.

Your dietitian will most likely start by taking a brief medical history and will ask you to articulate the dietary problem. She may or may not weigh you and/or take your measurements so that you can measure your progress if weight loss is a goal. Personally, I'm categorically opposed to weighing and measuring but would rather measure success in terms of diet and exercise behavior changes.

Next, the dietitian will review your log, asking you to clarify some of the details. Then she will draw up a list of dietary strengths -- this is partly for some positive reinforcement, but also is part of your diet education. After all, if you are doing some good things, you want to know what they are so that you can keep doing them.

She also will identify the areas for improvement. Then it is time to brainstorm. Your dietitian can provide the basic information you need to know to correct the situation, but she will need your input to develop a strategy. For example, one problem might be that the only quick, easy lunch you can come up with every day is a fatty grilled cheese sandwich from the cafeteria at work. Your dietitian will be able to come up with a number of potential solutions to that problem -- but obviously you are the only person who can decide which of those solutions will work for you. If your vegan diet looks a little short on vitamin B12, your dietitian can come up with a list of vegan alternatives, including fortified foods and supplements -- but you need to decide which of those ideas you like and then work with the dietitian to develop strategies for getting those foods into your diet.

Once you've identified problems and solutions, your dietitian can help you to put the information together in a couple of different ways. She might work with you to put it all together in a menu plan; and indeed, many clients prefer to go home with something very structured and reassuring like that. Others are overwhelmed by the enormous difference between how they have been eating and how they are expected to eat.

For people who have lots of changes to make *and* who are not in immediate danger, I prefer to prioritize changes, beginning with the easiest one. I suggest making one or two changes at a time. I also encourage clients to concentrate first on what is missing from their diet, rather than what needs to be deleted. That is, focus on getting 8 or 9 servings of whole grains, 5 or 6 servings of fruits and vegetables, and 2 or 3 servings of legumes in their diet every day. Once people learn to enjoy great-tasting, healthy foods, it becomes easier to work on reducing the fatty stuff.

Do You Need to Go Back?

Whether you need to go back and see your dietitian again depends a lot on your nutrition problem and on you. People with serious conditions who need to make considerable dietary changes and make them fast are going to need some support and follow-up. I do recommend at least biweekly visits. Some people who don't have serious problems still need the support. That assistance might come from a monthly visit. If a client lives far away or if money is a problem, I usually present another option whereby a client can mail in a food record every few weeks and I will give feedback either through the mail or over the phone. If you want some follow-up, you might ask your dietitian if you can make a similar arrangement.

For some, nutrition counseling can be a one-time experience. You may just need some basic pointers about your diet. Once in the right direction, you're you may be ready to take off on your own.

Virginia Messina is a Registered Dietitian in Washington and co-author of several vegetarian books including The Vegetarian No-Cholesterol Barbecue Cookbook.

Dietary Exchange Lists for Meal Planning

By Virginia Messina, M.P.H., R.D.

There are two schools of thought about Dietary Exchange Lists. Many nutritionists and their clients find the exchange lists to be just too rigid and cumbersome for long-term use. Poring over lists of food groups, counting exchanges, and measuring food is definitely not for everyone.

On the other hand, some people prefer a little structure to their meal planning. For these people, the *Dietary Exchange Lists for Meal Planning* can be useful. They allow you to feel confident that you are planning a well-balanced, healthy diet but provide plenty of food choices to keep that diet interesting. As structured a planning tool as they are, they actually allow for a great deal of flexibility.

I used a number of different sources for compiling the information in this article, including data from the United States Department of Agriculture and data on food packages. I also rounded some serving sizes off to make the information more user friendly.

Even those who like a more casual approach to menu planning may find that the Exchange Lists can help to set them on the right track. Using the Exchange Lists for a couple of weeks allows you to develop a feel for what a lowfat diet at a particular calorie level looks like. Once you are confident about serving sizes and number of servings, you'll probably find that you have to refer to the lists less and less often. And for those for whom more rigid calorie control is important -- especially diabetics who take insulin -- the exchange lists can be a reassuring guide to avoiding problems with blood sugar levels.

In fact, the Exchange Lists sometimes are referred to as the Diabetic Exchange Lists because they are used most frequently in planning meals for diabetics. But they can be used by anyone as a meal planning tool since they were designed to be a simple way to control the amounts of calories, fat, protein, and carbohydrate consumed and to assure a diet that meets the Recommended Daily Allowance for other nutrients.

Using the Exchange Lists is simple once you get the hang of it. Diet planning is based on six groups of foods: fruits, vegetables, starches, milk, protein, and fats. All foods are assigned to one of those groups based on the carbohydrate, protein, and fat content of that food. That means that within the vegetable group, for example, all the foods are roughly similar to each other in their carbohydrate, protein, and fat content. If your diet specifies that you should eat three servings --or "exchanges" -- of vegetables a day, you can choose from any of the vegetables on the list. But you can't "exchange" a vegetable for a fruit, because fruits and vegetables have different nutrient makeups.

Sometimes a food will span groups, and will count as exchanges from more than one group.

The one problem with the exchange lists is that they were not designed with the average vegetarian (or vegan) in mind. Though the lists have grown more extensive over the years, you still won't find tempeh, quinoa, or Rice Dream on many versions of these lists. While the protein group includes some vegetarian choices, the traditional milk group doesn't include vegan choices.

I've offered a vegan diet plan at three calorie levels. which don't include choices in the "milk" group. Note that the starred (*) foods are good sources of calcium. Vegans should also consume a reliable source of vitamin B12 such as a fortified breakfast cereals or soy milk.

Since, for weight loss, the number of calories in the diet is less important than the amount of fat, I haven't offered a plan for fewer than 1,500 calories, but I have kept all of the plans very low in fat.

Vegan Menu Plans

1,500 calories
3 vegetables
3 fruits
11 starches
5 proteins
3-1/2 fats

1,800 calories
3 vegetables
3 fruits
14 starches
6 proteins
4-1/2 fats

2,000 calories
3 vegetables
3 fruits
16 starches
6-1/2 proteins
4 fats

EXCHANGE LISTS FOR MEAL PLANNING

VEGETABLES

An exchange is 1/2 cup cooked vegetables or 1 cup raw vegetables. These foods provide approximately 5 grams of carbohydrate, 2 grams of protein, no fat, and 25 calories.

Alfalfa sprouts
Artichoke
Asparagus
Bamboo shoots
Beans (green, wax, Italian, etc.)
Beets
Bok choy*
Broccoli*
Brussels sprouts
Cabbage
Carrots
Cauliflower
Eggplant
Greens (kale*, collards*, mustard*, turnip*, beet, Swiss chard)
Jicama
Kohlrabi
Leeks
Mushrooms
Okra*
Onions
Pea pods
Pepper
Raddichio
Rutabaga
Sauerkraut
Sea vegetables
Spinach
Summer squash and zucchini
Tomatoes
Tomato or vegetable juice
Turnips
Water chestnuts

FRUITS: One exchange of fruit provides approximately 15 grams of carbohydrate, no protein or fat, and about 60 calories.

1 apple
1/2 cup applesauce (unsweetened)
4 fresh apricots
1/2 banana
3/4 cup blackberries
3/4 cup blueberries
1 cup cantaloupe chunks, or 1/3 melon
12 cherries
1/2 grapefruit
15 grapes
1/8 honeydew melon or 1 cup cubes
1 kiwifruit
1/2 mango
1 nectarine
1 orange
1 cup papaya or 1/2 of a whole papaya
1 peach
1 pear
3/4 cup pineapple
2 plums
1 cup raspberries
1-1/4 cups strawberries
2 tangerines
1-1/4 cups watermelon chunks

Dried Fruit
7 apricot halves
2-1/2 dates
1-1/2 figs*
3 prunes
2 Tablespoons raisins

Juices
1/2 cup apple juice or cider
1/3 cup cranberry juice cocktail
1/3 cup grape juice
1/2 cup grapefruit juice
1/2 cup orange juice
1/2 cup pineapple juice
1/3 cup prune juice
For mixed fruit juices, generally 1/2 cup
    equals an exchange.

STARCHY FOODS: Each serving provides approximately 15 grams of carbohydrate, 3 grams of protein, a trace of fat, and 80 calories.

Breads
1/2 bagel
1/2 burger bun
1/2 English muffin
1/2 six-inch pita
1 dinner roll
1 slice whole grain bread
1 six-inch corn or flour tortilla

Cereals/Grains
1/3 cup bran cereal
1/2 cup bran, corn, or other flakes
1/2 cup shredded wheat
1 shredded wheat biscuit
3 Tablespoons Grape-Nuts
1-1/2 cups puffed rice or wheat cereal
1/2 cup cooked cereal: oatmeal, 7-grain, oat
    bran, bear mush, farina, Wheatena, etc.
1/2 cup cooked grits
1/3 cup cooked rice, white, or brown
1/2 cup cooked bulgur
1/3 cup cooked couscous
1/3 cup cooked millet
1/3 cup cooked quinoa
1/2 cup cooked pasta
1/3 cup polenta
1/3 cup cooked wheat berries
3 cups air-popped popcorn
3 Tablespoons wheat germ
5 Tablespoons bran

Starchy Vegetables
1/2 cup corn or 1 six-inch corn on the cob
1/2 cup lima beans
2/3 cups parsnips
1/2 cup green peas
1/2 cup plantain
1 three-ounce potato
1/2 cup mashed potatoes
1 cup winter squash
1/3 cup sweet potatoes or yams

Dried beans
(These count as 1 exchange of starch *and* 1 exchange of protein)

1/2 cup vegetarian baked beans
1/2 cup cooked beans, peas, or lentils

Other
4 Rye Crisps
3 graham crackers
5 oblong melba toasts
2 rice cakes
3/4 ounces matzo
8 animal crackers
2 thin breadsticks
2 Fig Newtons
3 ginger snaps
2 oatmeal cookies
6 vanilla wafers

Starchy Foods with Added Fat
(These count as 1 starch exchange and 1 fat exchange)

1/4 cup bread dressing
1 two and a half-inch biscuit
1 two-inch square corn bread
1/4 cup granola
2 four-inch pancakes
2 four-inch crisp taco shells

PROTEIN FOODS: The foods in this group are especially high in protein and tend to be low in carbohydrate. They are also higher in fat. An exchange provides about 7 grams of protein, 3 grams of fat, and 55 calories. (Foods in the starch, milk alternatives, and vegetable groups also provide considerable amounts of protein.)

1/2 cup tofu (if processed with calcium sulfate, higher in calcium)*
1 tofu hot dog*
1/4 cup tempeh*
1/2 cup cooked dried beans (counts as 1 protein exchange and 1 starch exchange)

1 ounce wheat gluten (seitan)
1/4 cup roasted soynuts
1/4 cup prepared (hydrated) TVP

Count as 1 protein and 1 fat exchange:
1 ounce vegan soy cheese*
1 veggie burger

Count as 1 protein and 2 fat exchanges
2 Tablespoons peanut butter, tahini*, or other nut or seed butters
2 Tablespoons nuts
1 Tablespoon seeds

MILK ALTERNATIVES: One exchange of milk alternatives provides approximately 12 grams of carbohydrate, 8 grams protein, trace of fat, and about 90 calories. (Note: Some soy milks are now fortified with calcium and/or vitamin B12)

1 cup "lite" soy milk
1 cup Vegelicious
1 cup Rice Dream
1 cup regular soy milk (counts as 1 milk exchange and 1 fat exchange)

FATS: One exchange of fats provides approximately 5 grams fat and about 45 calories.

1/8 avocado
1 teaspoon vegetable oil
10 small or 5 large olives
2 Tablespoons lowfat salad dressing
1 teaspoon margarine
1 Tablespoon reduced-calorie margarine
2 Tablespoons shredded coconut
1-1/2 Tablespoons tofu mayonnaise

Virginia Messina is a Registered Dietitian and resides in Washington. She is co-author of The Vegetarian No-Cholesterol Family-Style Cookbook.

HUMANS ARE OMNIVORES

(Adapted from a talk by John McArdle, Ph.D.)

There are a number of popular myths about vegetarianism that have no scientific basis in fact. One of these myths is that man is naturally a vegetarian because our bodies resemble plant eaters, not carnivores. In fact we are omnivores, capable of either eating meat or plant foods. The following addresses the unscientific theory of man being only a plant eater.

Much of the misinformation on the issue of man's being a natural vegetarian arises from confusion between taxonomic (in biology the procedure of classifying organisms in established categories) and dietary characteristics.

Members of the mammalian Order Carnivora may or may not be exclusive meat eaters. Those which eat only meat are carnivores. Dietary adaptations are not limited by a simple dichotomy between herbivores (strict vegetarians) and carnivores (strict meat-eaters), but include frugivores (predominantly fruit), gramnivores (nuts, seeds, etc.), folivores (leaves), insectivores (carnivore-insects and small vertebrates), etc. It is also important to remember that the relationship between form (anatomy/physiology) and function (behavior) is not always one to one. Individual anatomical structures can serve one or more functions and similar functions can be served by several different forms.

There are a number of popular myths about vegetarianism that have no scientific basis in fact. One of these myths is that a human is naturally a vegetarian because our bodies resemble plant eaters, not carnivores.

The key category in the discussion of human diet is omnivores, which are defined as generalized feeders, with neither carnivore nor herbivore specializations for acquiring or processing food, and who are capable of consuming and do consume both animal protein and vegetation. They are basically *opportunistic* feeders (survive by eating what is available) with more generalized anatomical and physiological traits, especially the dentition (teeth). All the available evidence indicates that the natural human diet is omnivorous and would include meat. We are not, however, required to consume animal protein. We have a choice.

There are very few frugivores amongst the mammals in general, and primates in particular. The only apes that are predominantly fruit eaters (gibbons and siamangs) are atypical for apes in many behavioral and ecological respects and eat substantial amounts of vegetation. Orangutans are similar, with no observations in the wild of meat eating.

Gorillas are more typically vegetarian, with less emphasis on fruit. Several years ago a very elegant study was done on the relationship between body size and diet in primates (and some other mammal groups). The only primates on the list with pure diets were the very small species (which are entirely insectivorous) and the largest (which specialize in vegetarian diet). However, the spectrum of dietary preferences reflect the daily food intake needs of each body size and the relative availability of food resources in a tropical forest. Our closest relatives among the apes are the chimpanzees (i.e., anatomically, behaviorally, genetically, and evolutionarily), who frequently kill and eat other mammals (including other primates).

Humans are classic examples of omnivores in all relevant anatomical traits.

EVIDENCE OF HUMANS AS OMNIVORES

ARCHAEOLOGICAL RECORD: As far back as it can be traced, clearly the archaeological record indicates an omnivorous diet for humans that included meat. Our ancestry is among the hunter/gatherers from the beginning. Once domestication of food sources began, it included both animals and plants.

CELL TYPES: Relative number and distribution of cell types, as well as structural specializations, are more important than overall length of the intestine to determining a typical diet. Dogs are typical carnivores, but their intestinal characteristics have more in common with omnivores. Wolves eat quite a lot of plant material.

FERMENTING VATS: Nearly all plant eaters have fermenting vats (enlarged chambers where foods sits and microbes attack it). Ruminants like cattle and deer have forward sacs derived from remodeled esophagus and stomach. Horses, rhinos, and colobine monkeys have posterior, hindgut sacs. Humans have no such specializations.

JAWS: Although evidence on the structure and function of human hands and jaws, behavior, and evolutionary history also either support an omnivorous diet or fail to support strict vegetarianism, the best evidence comes from our teeth.

The short canines in humans are a functional consequence of the enlarged cranium and associated reduction of the size of the jaws. In primates, canines function as both defense weapons and visual threat devices. Interestingly, the primates with the largest canines (gorillas and gelada baboons) both have basically vegetarian diets. In archaeological sites, broken human molars are most often confused with broken premolars and molars of pigs, a classic omnivore. On the other hand, some herbivores have well-developed incisors that are often mistaken for those of human teeth when found in archaeological excavations.

SALIVARY GLANDS: These indicate we could be omnivores. Saliva and urine data vary, depending on diet, not taxonomic group.

INTESTINE: Intestinal absorption is a surface area, not linear problem. Dogs (who are carnivores) have intestinal specializations more characteristic of omnivores than carnivores such as cats. The relative number of crypts and cell types is a better indication of diet than simple length. We are intermediate between the two groups.

Humans are classic examples of omnivores in all relevant anatomical traits. There is no basis in anatomy or physiology for the assumption that humans are pre-adapted to the vegetarian diet. For that reason, the best arguments in support of a meat-free diet remain ecological, ethical, and health concerns.

Dr. McArdle is a vegetarian and currently Scientific Advisor to The American Anti-Vivisection Society. He is an anatomist and a primatologist.

A SENIOR'S GUIDE TO GOOD NUTRITION

By Suzanne Havala, M.S., R.D.

Currently, one out of nine people in the United States is age 65 or older, and that number is expected to double within the next 30 years. Worldwide, a similar trend is unfolding, and yet relatively little is known about how the nutritional needs of older people differ from those who are younger. Although many people enjoy a generally healthy and vital old age, age-related health problems increase with advancing years and often have an effect on eating habits.

The science of gerontology, or the study of normal aging, is new. We have much to learn about the aspects of aging that are typically accepted as "normal." While there is a similar pattern of changes that takes place among all humans as they age, these changes can occur at a different rate in each individual. We do not know how much of this difference is due to genetic make-up, and how much is due to lifestyle factors such as diet.

There is abundant evidence to show that an optimum level of nutrition can extend the lifespan and also affect the quality of life. Findings from human experiments and population studies show a positive effect of diet on longevity and health. A large body of research examining the health of vegetarians, who typically consume a diet that is lower in calories, fat, and protein than nonvegetarians, shows that vegetarians suffer from less heart disease, obesity, high blood pressure, diabetes, and some forms of cancer. Vegetarians also tend to live longer than nonvegetarians.

Good eating habits throughout life can help to promote physical and mental well-being. For older people, eating right can help to minimize the symptoms of age-related changes that, for some, can cause discomfort or inconvenience. Although the aging process affects some people differently from others, everyone can benefit from eating a well-planned vegetarian diet.

DO SENIORS HAVE SPECIAL NUTRITIONAL NEEDS?

Very little is known about how the aging process affects the body's ability to digest, absorb, and retain nutrients such as protein, vitamins, and minerals. Therefore, little is known about how the nutritional needs of older people differ from those of younger adults. Recommended nutrient intakes for seniors are currently extrapolated from those of younger adults.

One point that is generally agreed upon, however, is that older people tend to take in less energy, or calories, than younger people. This may be due, in part, to a natural decline in the rate of metabolism as people age. It may also reflect a decrease in physical activity. If the total intake of food decreases, it follows that intakes of protein, carbohydrate, fat, vitamins, and minerals also decrease. If calorie intake is too low, then intakes of necessary nutrients may also be low.

Many other factors can affect the nutritional needs of older people and how successfully they meet those needs, including their access to food. For instance, some of the changes that take place as people age can affect the kinds of foods they can tolerate, and some can affect their ability to shop for or prepare food. As people age, problems such as high blood pressure or diabetes become more common, necessitating certain dietary modifications. Digestive system problems become more common, and some people may have trouble chewing or swallowing.

Generally, current dietary recommendations for adults also apply to older people. These are summarized in the following chart:

1. Limit:

sweets	regular coffee and tea
greasy or fatty foods	alcohol
oil, margarine, and other added fats	"junk" foods
	salt

2. Eat plenty of:

fruits	whole grain breads and cereals
vegetables	

3. Drink plenty of fluids, especially water

WHO SHOULD BE CONCERNED ABOUT THEIR DIET?

Older people need not be more concerned about their diets than younger people. Everyone benefits from eating well and understanding some nutrition basics. Diets should also be flexible enough to allow for treats to be enjoyed occasionally, as well as other favorite foods that may not be as "healthy" as other choices. Finding the right balance is the key.

Keeping some nutrition basics in mind will help make eating right an easier goal to achieve. For starters, since food intake usually declines with age, it may be increasingly important for older people to make sure that what they do eat is nutritious. There may be less room in the diet for sweets and other "empty calorie" foods, which provide little in the way of nutrition in exchange for the calories they contribute to the diet. Examples of foods that should be limited include: soft drinks, candy, snack chips, and alcohol.

While commercial cakes, cookies, pastries, and pies are often empty calorie foods, they can be made more nutritious at home from scratch with high-quality ingredients and some recipe modifications.

A sensible program of exercise, such as walking, may also be wise. People who are physically active have an easier time controlling their weight while still taking in more calories than those who are sedentary. The higher the calorie intake, the more likely a person is to obtain all the nutrients he or she needs.

A simple way to assess your own diet is to keep a written log or diary of everything that is eaten over a period of a few days to two weeks. Include some details about how foods were prepared, and be sure to make a note about portion sizes. Then compare the results to the general guidelines above. Write down ideas for improvement in areas that need some attention.

SHOULD I TAKE SUPPLEMENTS?

Vitamin and mineral supplements are rarely necessary for people who eat a reasonably varied diet and who eat enough food to meet their energy needs. In fact, taking large doses of some vitamins and minerals may cause imbalances in body stores of others, and some are toxic at high levels. Your best bet is to get the nutrients you need from whole foods, without the use of a supplement, unless otherwise directed by your dietitian or physician.

HOW CAN MY DIET HELP ME?

Digestive system problems are the most frequent source of discomfort for older people. Sometimes these problems cause people to avoid foods that would otherwise be a healthy addition to the diet. For instance, flatulence or intestinal gas may prompt some individuals to forgo certain vegetables such as cabbage or beans, which are good sources of vitamins, minerals, and fiber. In other cases, adding more of certain types of foods can reduce the severity of some problems. Let's take a look at how a well-planned diet can help with a variety of common complaints.

Constipation

Constipation can result from not drinking enough fluids and by eating a diet that is too low in fiber or bulk. Certain medications, including antacids made with aluminum hydroxide or calcium carbonate, can also cause this problem, and it can be made worse by the habitual use of laxatives.

There are several things that people can do to prevent constipation from occurring. Including a liberal amount of whole grain breads and cereals in the diet, as well as plenty of vegetables and fruits, is a start. Eating dried fruits such as prunes or figs, or drinking prune juice, may also help, since they have a natural laxative effect for many people. Drinking plenty of fluids is very important, and water is the best choice. Most people should drink six to eight glasses of water or other fluids each day. Foods that are high in fat, such as many sweets, meats and high fat dairy products, oils and margarine, or fried foods should be limited. These foods are very calorie dense and may displace foods that would otherwise provide needed fiber in the diet. Decreasing the consumption of fatty foods may also lessen the need for antacids. Don't forget, too, that a regular routine of exercise is effective in promoting good muscle tone and preventing constipation.

Gas and Heartburn

Many people experience general abdominal discomfort after eating, which may include belching, intestinal gas or flatulence, bloating, or burning sensations. These complaints have many causes, including overeating, eating too many high-fat foods, alcohol, or carbonated beverages, swallowing too much air when eating, lying down to rest immediately after eating, and taking some drugs or aspirin. Switching to a diet that is high in fiber may also cause some flatulence at the start, although it usually lessens as the body adapts to the increased fiber intake.

One way to help relieve problems such as these is to eat smaller, more frequent meals over the course of the day instead of eating one or two larger meals. Avoiding fatty foods, alcohol, and carbonated beverages is a good idea, too. It may also be helpful to eat slowly and to chew food thoroughly before swallowing. If heartburn is a problem, avoid reclining immediately after meals, or if you do so, keep the back elevated to at least 30 degrees so that you are not lying flat on your back. Regular exercise can also help to minimize trouble with intestinal gas.

Chewing and Swallowing Problems

These may occur for a variety of reasons. For people who have trouble chewing foods, it may be helpful to cut food into small pieces and to allow extra time to chew food at a comfortable, unhurried pace. Cooking some fruits and vegetables may also be helpful and necessary for some. Poorly fitting dentures should be checked by a dentist and possibly replaced.

Drinking plenty of fluids can alleviate some swallowing problems if the throat or mouth is dry, which may be caused by certain medications or may simply be related to commonly-occurring changes that accompany the aging process. Lozenges or hard candies may be helpful in keeping the mouth moist. It may be necessary to ask your physician about whether or not a particular medication may be contributing to the problem.

WHAT IF I HAVE TO FOLLOW A SPECIAL DIET?

The older people get, the more likely it is that they will develop medical problems that require a special, or therapeutic, diet. People who develop diabetes, high blood pressure, and heart disease, for instance, may have special considerations in meal planning. Most conditions, however, benefit from a diet that is high in fiber from whole grains, fruits, and vegetables, and low in animal products. Well-planned vegetarian diets can help to control blood sugar levels. By limiting fat, salt, and sugar, vegetarian diets can also be useful in controlling high blood pressure, heart disease, and other conditions. However, since individuals vary in their needs, those who must follow a special diet should consult a registered dietitian for more detailed recommendations and help with meal planning.

Many people also wonder if diet can aid in treating conditions such as arthritis and osteoporosis, which frequently afflict older people. At present, no conclusive evidence exists to recommend one kind of diet regimen over another for the treatment of arthritis. However, a lowfat vegetarian diet may be helpful if it allows an individual to maintain a normal weight, which in turn may help reduce or prevent some symptoms of arthritis.

Osteoporosis is considered to be influenced by many factors, including diet. Diets that are excessively high in protein can cause the accelerated loss of calcium from bones. On the other hand, increasing the calcium content of the diet has not been shown to increase bone mass or to offset the loss of calcium caused by a diet that is too high in protein. The moderate diet of most vegetarians is associated with a decreased incidence of osteoporosis, even when calcium intakes are below levels currently recommended in the U.S. Therefore, the use of calcium supplements may not be of any benefit, particularly for those who already limit their protein intake by following a prudent diet. Including plenty of greens and other vegetables in the diet will help to ensure an adequate intake of calcium.

One of the most common surgical procedures for older people is cataract surgery, and there is a considerable amount of research being conducted presently on the relationships between diet and the incidence of cataracts and macular degeneration.

WHAT IF I HAVE NO APPETITE?

Depression because of changes in living conditions, loss of companions, certain medications, and complications in preparing meals can all result in a loss of interest in food. Sometimes eating smaller, more frequent "mini-meals" can help. It may also be a good idea to seek out meals in a social context. For instance, local vegetarian societies may have regular organized potluck dinners or restaurant outings that provide an opportunity to make new friends and enjoy a meal in the company of others.

Some common nutrition-related problems that older people encounter, and suggestions for dealing with them, are summarized in the chart appearing on the next page.

Common Problems and Suggested Solutions

Flatulence or gas Burning sensation, heartburn

Eat smaller, more frequent meals.

Belching or bloating

Avoid alcohol, carbonated beverages, and high fat foods such as some sweets, meats, oils and margarine, and high-fat dairy foods. Eat slowly and chew foods well. Avoid lying down after meals. If you do, keep head and back elevated at a 30-degree angle.

Consider reducing aspirin intake. Ask physician to check medications.

Difficulty chewing

See dentist if problem is poorly fitting dentures.

Cut food into small pieces and chew food at a comfortable, unhurried pace.

Cook some vegetables and fruits to soften.

Difficulty swallowing

Ask physician to check medications.

Drink plenty of water.

Use lozenges or hard candies to keep throat moist.

Constipation

Eat liberal amounts of whole grains as well as vegetables and fruits. Try dried fruits such as prunes or figs, or drink prune juice. Drink 6 to 8 glasses of fluid, especially water, each day.

Limit greasy or fatty foods such as high-fat dairy foods, oils and margarine, fried foods, high fat sweets and meats.

Limit use of antacids.

Get into a regular routine of exercise, such as walking.

High blood sugar

Limit sweets and alcohol.

See a registered dietitian for help with planning a high-fiber, high carbohydrate diet.

High blood pressure

Limit salty foods.

See a registered dietitian for help in planning a heart-healthy diet.

Heart disease

See a registered dietitian for help in planning a lowfat, healthy diet.

Loss of appetite

Eat small, frequent meals or snacks.

See "Handy Hints for Quick Meals."

HOW CAN I MAKE PREPARING MEALS A LITTLE EASIER?

Some older people may find meal planning is more burdensome if shopping or preparing meals is difficult. Arthritis, for instance, or impaired hearing or poor eyesight may make it hard to drive to the grocery store, to read food labels or package instructions, or to open bottles and handle cooking utensils. It may also be difficult to maintain the motivation to cook for only one or two people.

For all these reasons, it may be necessary for meals to be simple, quick, and convenient to prepare. Ready-to-eat, whole grain breakfast cereals are a nutritious meal or snack anytime, as are quick-cooking hot cereals like oatmeal, which can be cooked in a microwave oven. Fresh fruit is also convenient, but canned fruits, packed in their own juice or water, will keep for months in the cupboard and can also make a simple snack. Whole grain breads, bagels, and lowfat muffins can be kept in the freezer and individual servings taken out as needed. Other good freezer and cupboard staples include bags of mixed, plain frozen vegetables, whole grain crackers, peanut butter, canned beans such as pinto beans or black-eyed peas, and jars of vegetable salads such as three-bean or beet salad.

It also makes sense, for those who are able to do more extensive cooking, to fix enough of a recipe so that some can be frozen in small batches to be reheated at a later date. For example, bean chili, vegetable lasagna, some casseroles, whole grain cookies, lowfat muffins, or pancakes all freeze well and can be stored in small containers that can be reheated in a conventional or microwave oven.

A summary of some handy hints for quick meals follows:

Handy Hints for Quick Meals

Cupboard staples

Ready-to-eat, whole grain breakfast cereals; quick-cooking whole grain cereals such as oatmeal; canned fruit packed in own juice; whole-grain crackers; nut butters; canned beans such as pintos or black-eyed peas; jars of vegetable salads such as beets or three-bean; low-sodium vegetarian soups; aseptically-packaged (long-life) containers of soy milk; popcorn; dried fruit.

Freezer staples

Frozen fruit pieces such as strawberries or raspberries; whole grain breads or lowfat muffins (to take out as needed); bags or boxes of plain, mixed frozen vegetables; fruit juice concentrate.

Make-aheads (to be frozen in small batches and reheated at a later date)

Bean chili; vegetable lasagna; vegetable and bean soups; whole grain-and-vegetable casseroles; whole grain cookies, lowfat muffins, or pancakes.

Also keep on hand

Flour tortillas; salsa and chutneys; fresh fruit.

Shopping tips

Split bags of fresh vegetables, such as carrots, celery, and onions, or heads of lettuce, with a friend to reduce the amount of spoiled food that has to be thrown away. Shop with a list, and keep a list on going at home.

DOES EATING WELL HAVE TO BE EXPENSIVE?

For many elderly people, a limited income or limited access to transportation to a grocery store can complicate meal planning. So, good planning can not only be efficient, it can also be economically helpful as well. Foods prepared from scratch at home are usually less expensive than packaged mixes and frozen entrees, for example, and the cook has more control over what ingredients are used, also. For example, salt or fat in a recipe can be reduced when food is prepared at home, or whole wheat flour can be substituted for refined white flour.

Wise food choices can help save money. Buying in bulk, whether an item is on special or not, can be cheaper than buying small containers of food, although storage space must be available. If a person has access to food outlet stores, substantial savings can be had on things such as baked goods or breads. If freezer space is available, trips to an outlet can be less frequent. Coupon clipping, especially for brands that are usually purchased anyway, can save as much as 10% off food bills. Many stores offer double or triple the face value of the coupon. On the other hand, store brands of certain items can be much cheaper than name brands, even after coupon discounts, and often with little detectable difference in quality. Paper goods, canned goods, jams and jellies, and breakfast cereals are just a few examples of items which may have store brand or generic options.

There are certain food items that tend to be relatively costly and also should be limited for health reasons for most people. Sweets, especially prepared desserts such as cakes, pies, and cookies, and junk foods such as chips and other fried snacks, snack cakes, and some candies can be fairly expensive. High-fat dairy foods such as cheese and ice cream are relatively expensive, and for nonvegetarians, meat is typically the costliest item on the grocery list.

Desserts can be prepared at home, with alterations in the recipe to make them more nutritious, and money can be saved. Junk food snacks can be replaced with less expensive snacks such as air-popped plain popcorn, mixtures of dry cereals, bagels, whole grain muffins, or seasonal fresh fruit. If cheese is eaten, buy small quantities and use it sparingly. Add a sprinkling of grated cheese to salads or on top of a casserole or sandwich, rather than using it as a more prominent ingredient. Meatless meals, incorporating mixtures of vegetables, whole grains, and legumes such as canned or rehydrated beans and lentils, are economical and healthful, not to mention delicious.

WHAT FOOD ASSISTANCE PROGRAMS ARE AVAILABLE?

Food assistance programs, such as food stamps, can increase buying power for people who are eligible. Food delivery programs, such as Meals-on-Wheels, are also available for people who are housebound or have difficulty getting around or preparing meals. Congregate meal programs are available in some areas, where older people can meet in a central location to enjoy a meal in the company of others, and transportation is frequently provided to the meal site.

It is usually necessary to ask if vegetarian meal options can be made available, and the ability of food service personnel to accommodate the vegetarian's needs may vary from site to site or city to city. If there is difficulty in obtaining vegetarian meal options, contact the local vegetarian society. They may be able to refer the problem to a local dietitian-member for assistance. Find out if others are interested in lowfat vegetarian meal options. Quantity recipes are available from the Vegetarian Resource Group and other organizations, and these can be provided to food service directors or dietitians who may be able to incorporate them into menus.

Meal delivery programs may be organized by community nonprofit organizations or health and social service agencies such as hospitals, churches, nursing homes, and visiting nurses associations. To determine who is eligible, call these organizations directly. Otherwise, people can be referred by another family member, a physician, a visiting nurse, or a social worker.

Grocery delivery service is also available at stores in some communities. For people who have trouble finding transportation to the grocery store, or for those with physical limitations, a list can be phoned in to a local grocery store and someone will deliver the purchases to the home.

SUMMING IT ALL UP

A well-planned vegetarian diet is health-supporting for all ages. While age-related changes affect different people in different ways, a good diet can help to overcome or reduce symptoms of certain problems that may become more common with age.

SAMPLE MEAL PLAN

Breakfast	6 oz. orange juice 1 cup cooked oatmeal with 1/4 cup chopped raisins and dates 6 oz. soymilk
Snack	1 banana 1 slice whole grain toast with 2 teaspoons peanut butter
Lunch	1 cup vegetarian chili * (* see recipe source below) 1/2 fresh green pepper, sliced 1 lowfat corn muffin * water
Snack	2 bagel halves with apple butter 6 oz. soymilk
Dinner	1-1/2 cups spinach salad with onions, mushrooms, and cherry tomatoes 2 tablespoons no-oil dressing 1 cup cooked spaghetti topped with 1/2 cup tomato-basil sauce Chunk of Italian bread 2 chilled, canned peach halves water
Snack	3 cups air-popped popcorn 6 oz. apple juice

14% fat	14% protein	72% carbohydrate	30 grams of fiber

Recipe Suggestions (from Simply Vegan, $13 available from The Vegetarian Resource Group, PO Box 1463, Baltimore, MD 21203):

Blended Delight (p. 18); Apple Raisin Spice Muffins (p. 20)*
Banana Muffins (p. 21)*; Corn Bread (p. 21)*
Oatmeal Medley (p. 22); Cindy's Light and Fluffy Pancakes (p. 23)*
Garbanzo Spread (p. 28); Peanut Butter and Fruit (p. 29)
Popcorn Treat (p. 34); Mini Pizzas (p. 34)
Apple Celery Salad (p. 41); Easy Pasta Salad (p. 44)
Quick Pea Soup (p. 47)*; Creamy Lentil Soup (p. 49)*
Tomato/Zucchini Stir-Fry (p. 57); Vegetable Medley (p. 58)

Mexican-Style Chickpeas (p. 73); Bean Tacos (p. 83)
Pumpkin Casserole (p. 83)*; Hearty Macaroni Dinner (p. 87)
Broccoli Pasta Dish (p. 88); Ginger Cookies (p. 109)*
Chocolate Pudding (p. 108); Karen's Creamy Rice Pudding (p. 115)

Suzanne Havala is a nutrition advisor for The Vegetarian Resource Group.

NUTRITION AND THE EYE

By Jay Lavine, M.D.

Which one of your five senses would you least like to lose? For most people, it is their vision. Our sight is so precious and we depend upon it so much that we can't imagine what life would be like if we could no longer see. Even when we eat delicious vegetarian food, we "eat" with our eyes: our first impression of the food comes from its appearance, and a bad first impression is hard to overcome no matter how good the food tastes. Not surprisingly, the eye, the delicate and complex end-organ of sight, is influenced by our nutritional status. Let's look at some common eye problems and see how they relate to our diets.

Glaucoma refers to a group of diseases characterized by a progressive loss of the nerve fibers which make up our optic nerves. Glaucoma can result from other eye problems, but we will limit the discussion here to chronic open-angle glaucoma, the most common type. The main risk factor for glaucoma is an elevated intraocular pressure (IOP), the fluid pressure inside the eye, which is different from blood pressure. Some feel that the blood circulation to the optic nerve also plays a role. Nevertheless, the only treatment we have for glaucoma is to lower the IOP. Normally, this is accomplished by drugs in the form of eye drops or pills, and laser or conventional surgery can be performed as a last resort. But drugs, even in eye drop form, have side effects. Therefore, let's explore non-drug, non-surgical alternatives for the lowering of IOP.

A potentially effective therapy is exercise training. One study showed that regular aerobic exercise on an exercise bike lowered the average IOP in patients suspected of having glaucoma by 4-1/2 mm, or about 20%, a significant amount.[1] Jogging, however, might raise IOP in people who have a less common form of glaucoma called pigmentary glaucoma.

Both eating and drinking can affect IOP. Drinking a large amount of liquid all at once can raise IOP and should be avoided. Dr. Carlo Pissarello published studies in 1915[2] which showed that the IOP falls right after eating and tends to be highest just before the next meal. This may explain why, in the daily variation of IOP, it tends to be highest early in the morning, since we have been fasting overnight. An interesting question would be whether a "grazing" type of diet, which seems to help lower cholesterol and facilitate weight loss, would help keep IOP down. When a

---

[1] Passo MS, Goldberg L, Elliot DL, Van Buskirk EM. Exercise training reduces intraocular pressure among subjects suspected of having glaucoma. Arch Ophthalmol 1991;109: 1096-8.

[2] Pissarello C. La curva giornaliera della tensione nell'occio normale e nell'occhio glaucomatoso e influenza di fattori diversi (miotici, iridetomia, iridosclerectomia, derivativi, pasti) determinata con il Tono-metro di Schiotz. Ann Ottalmol 1915;44: 544-636.

glaucoma patient goes to the ophthalmologist to have a pressure check, it might be a good idea occasionally to do it at a time when the IOP is likely to be at its zenith -- early in the morning before eating breakfast or else just before supper or lunch.

Can any particular diet lower IOP? The answer appears to be yes. In the late 1940's, Dr. Frederick Stocker and associates studied what they called the "rice diet." This diet had previously proved very effective in lowering blood pressure. The diet was limited to rice, sugar, fruit, and fruit juices, supplemented by vitamins and iron. It contained about 2,000 Calories with 20 gm of protein, 5 gm of fat, 460 gm of carbohydrate, 0.2 gm of sodium, and 0.15 gm of chloride. They found that "reductions [of IOP] of 5 or 7 mm, persisting over long periods, were not uncommon."[3] A reduction of this magnitude is considered quite significant for a glaucoma patient and is about the amount that one would expect to result from a successful laser treatment. The researchers were not sure why the diet was effective but speculated that the very low sodium and chloride content somehow influenced fluid secretion into the eye. I was able to speak with the third author, Dr. James Clower, who was a resident at Duke at the time, and who is still practicing ophthalmology in Florida. He said that no follow-up studies had been done, but he laughingly commented that perhaps Seventh-day Adventists would have the best pressures! [Note from the editors: Many Seventh-day Adventists follow a vegetarian diet. Perhaps Dr. Clower felt this diet would be lower in protein and sodium; although this is not necessarily true.]

A more recent study out of Israel followed people who were placed on intravenous feedings because of intestinal problems.[4] When the intravenous fluids were fat-free, IOP's were significantly lower than when fat was included. Since certain fat-derived blood chemicals called prostaglandins were greatly reduced in the fat-free phase, and since prostaglandins are known to influence IOP, they theorized that this was the reason for the effect they were observing. Therefore, it may have been the ultra-low fat content of the "rice diet" which was responsible for the lowering of IOP. Certainly, further studies on lowfat diets would be welcome. (Caution: the rice diet as described is nutritionally inadequate and should not be attempted on your own.)

Age-related macular degeneration (AMD) is the leading cause of loss of vision in people over the age of 55. The degeneration involves the central part of the retina where the best vision is, sparing peripheral vision. In a small minority of people with this condition, abnormal blood vessels can grow behind the retina where they can leak and bleed. If this is detected before the blood vessels reach the exact center of the retina, the vessels can sometimes be obliterated with laser.

Nutritional therapy is now all the rage in AMD. Zinc is the most abundant trace mineral in the eye, and a study published in 1988 showed that oral zinc sulfate, 100 mg twice a day, might slow the progression of AMD.[5] A plethora of zinc/antioxidant supplements has since appeared on the market. The products, promoted by drug companies and often sold by ophthalmologists, are now heavily used.

In examining whether high-dose zinc supplementation is justified, we encounter some problems and uncertainties. First, only

3 Stocker FW, Holt LB, Clower JW. Clinical experiments with new ways of influencing intraocular tension. I. Effect of rice diet. Arch Ophthalmol 1948; 40:46-55.

4 Naveh-Floman N, Belkin M. Prostaglandin metabolism and intraocular pressure. Br J Ophthalmol 1987; 71:254-6.
5 Newsome DA, Swartz M, Leone NC, Elston RC, Miller E. Oral zinc in macular degeneration. Arch Ophthalmol 1988; 106:192-8.

this one study has been published in a peer-reviewed journal. Generally, a study, no matter how well done, should be confirmed by additional studies. Second, only one dosage of zinc was studied. Perhaps a much smaller dose would also be effective. Third, large amounts of zinc can impair the immune system by affecting white blood cell function.[6] This was studied using 150 mg of elemental zinc twice a day. Whether the amount of zinc currently being prescribed for AMD can impair immune function remains to be determined. Our immune systems protect our bodies against cancer and infections. Fourth, zinc in high doses can interfere with the absorption of other minerals, such as copper and iron.

A copper deficiency anemia can occur,[7] and copper deficiency has also been theorized to be a cause of atherosclerosis (hardening of the arteries), which results in heart disease.[8] To lessen that risk, the supplements generally contain some copper. We cannot be sure, though, that they contain enough copper to prevent copper deficiency. On the other hand, some have speculated that perhaps it is not the zinc which is helping the AMD but a copper deficiency induced by the high zinc dose. (Subjects in the AMD study did not take copper along with the zinc.) If that is the case, then taking copper with the zinc may nullify the beneficial effect initially observed.

As you can see, there are no clear cut answers at present. We eagerly await further studies.

Oxidation of the polyunsaturated fatty acids found in the membranes of the rods and cones of the retina has been proposed as a possible cause of AMD. This is the rationale for the use of antioxidant vitamins, such as beta-carotene and other carotenoids, vitamin C, and vitamin E. One recent study did show, in fact, a reduced risk of visual loss from the bleeding from AMD in people with high blood levels of these antioxidants.[9] Another study showed that higher blood cholesterol levels seemed to reduce the risk of the dry, or non-bleeding, form of AMD.[10] The authors did not have a good explanation for this phenomenon. My theory is that since beta-carotene and vitamin E travel in the blood with cholesterol, people who are genetically predisposed to lower cholesterol levels carry a lesser amount of these antioxidants to their tissues. Vegetarians, however, have a higher antioxidant/cholesterol ratio than non-vegetarians,[11,12] and so they probably would not share the higher risk associated with low cholesterol levels. Again, studies are needed.

A small, controlled French study found that ginkgo biloba extract (50:1) had a beneficial effect on the vision of patients with AMD.[13] Ginkgo is a most interesting herb with many potential applications. It contains unique compounds called ginkgolides which are potent inhibitors of platelet-activating factor (PAF), a body chemical involved in inflammatory processes. PAF inhibitors have

6 Chandra RK. Excessive intake of zinc impairs immune responses. JAMA 1984; 252:1443-6.

7 Patterson WP, Winklemann M, Perry MC. Zinc-induced copper deficiency: megamineral sideroblastic anemia. Ann Intern Med 1985; 103:385-6.

8 Klevay LM. The homocysteine theory of arteriosclerosis [letter]. Nutr Rev 1992; 50:155.

9 Eye Disease Case-Control Study Group. Antioxidant status and neovascular age-related macular degeneration. Arch Ophthalmol 1993;111:104-9.

10 Klein R, Klein BEK, Franke T. The relationship of cardiovascular disease and its risk factors to age-related maculopathy: the Beaver Dam eye study. Ophthalmology 1993;100:406-14.

11 Pronczuk A, Kipervarg Y, Hayes KC. Vegetarians have higher plasma alpha-tocopherol relative to cholesterol than do nonvegetarians. J AM Coll Nutr 1992; 11:50-5.

12 Malter M, Schriever G, Eilber U. Natural killer cells, vitamins, and other blood components of vegetarian and omnivorous men. Nutr Cancer 1989;12:271-8.

13 Lebuisson DA, Leroy L, Rigal G. Traitement des degen-erescences "Maculaires seniles" par l'extrait de Ginkgo biloba. Presse Med 1986;15:1556-8.

been shown to combat inflammation and to increase blood flow to areas with reduced circulation. The ginkgo extract also has antioxidant properties. Whether it was one component or a synergistic effect among several components of this extract which had the beneficial effect is not certain. In any case, a much larger study needs to be done. Ginkgo should not be used by anyone who takes Coumadin or who has a bleeding tendency. Also, PAF inhibitors may impair natural killer cell (a type of white blood cell) function somewhat. Herbs, like any drug, should be used only with the consent of your physician.

Cataract refers to a cloudiness of the eye's lens. It is caused by changes in the protein which composes the lens. Since the lens and the fluid surrounding it are high in antioxidants, it is thought that the antioxidants may help the lens maintain its clarity. People with higher than average intakes of beta-carotene, vitamin C, and vitamin E appear to have a reduced risk of cataract. More definitive studies are now being conducted.

Diabetes increases the risk of cataract, but it can also cause more severe visual loss by affecting the blood vessels in the retina, a condition called retinopathy. The walls of the blood vessels are weakened, causing them to leak, which blurs vision. Abnormal, fragile blood vessels may also grow in. They can bleed into the eye, causing severe problems. Type II diabetes, the milder adult-onset form, is virtually absent in populations consuming high fiber diets.[14] Thus, a lowfat, high fiber vegetarian diet may be the best way to prevent or reverse this illness. Type I diabetes, the juvenile insulin-dependent form, may be triggered by a reaction to a cow's milk protein.[15] A high fiber, vegetarian-type diet can

lower insulin requirements and improve control, which may retard the progression of retinopathy. (Caution: diabetics should not change their diets without the consent of their physicians.)

Both types of diabetes can cause retinopathy. One study showed that diabetics without retinopathy had significantly higher carbohydrate and fiber intakes than did diabetics with retinopathy.[16] Furthermore, dietary or other treatment which aggressively lowers blood cholesterol levels can sometimes clear up the fat-rich leakage called hard exudates which many diabetics develop in their retinas.[17] This could conceivably eliminate the need for laser treatments in some individuals. In a small pilot study, an extract of the herb ginkgo biloba (see above) showed some promise in improving vision in patients with very mild retinopathy.[18]

To summarize, the ideal nutritional approach to maintain the health of the eye would appear to be a high fiber, high carbohydrate, high antioxidant, lowfat, low protein type of diet, typified by -- you guessed it -- a vegetarian diet.

Jay Lavine, M.D., is an ophthalmologist and resides in Phoenix, Arizona. He often speaks on vegetarian subjects.

14 Trowell HC. Dietary-fiber hypothesis of the etiology of diabetes mellitus. Diabetes 1975;24:762-5.
15 Karjalainen J, Martin JM, Knip M, et al. A bovine albumin peptide as a possible trigger of insulin-dependent diabetes mellitus. N Engl J Med 1992; 327: 302-7.

16 Roy MS, Stables G, Collier B, Roy A, Bou E. Nutritional factors in diabetics with and without retinopathy. Am J Clin Nutr 1989;50:728-30.
17 Gordon B, Chang S, Kavanagh M, et al. The effects of lipid lowering on diabetic retinopathy. Am J Ophthalmol 1991;112: 385-91.
18 Lanthony P, Cosson JP. Evolution de la vision des couleurs dans la retinopathie diabetique debutante traitee par extrait de Ginkgo biloba. J Fr Ophtalmol 1988;11: 671-4.

Are You Getting Enough Iron, Or Perhaps, Too Much?

By Eve Shatto Walton, R.D., L.D.N.

Recent evidence shows that heart attacks may be more likely in men with higher levels of stored iron. Should Americans be concerned about getting too much iron? Interest in this question was sparked about a decade ago when researchers noticed that women have a low incidence of heart disease prior to menopause. Heart disease increases dramatically after menopause when menstrual periods stop. This was always thought to be due to a drop in hormone levels, which is associated with a decrease in the level of good HDL cholesterol. Not surprisingly, iron deficiency is less common after menopause, since iron is no longer lost in menstrual blood each month. Some researchers say that the increase in iron stores during postmenopause may lead to an increased risk for heart disease. This may be because iron can work to make the bad LDL cholesterol worse by making it even more likely to clog arteries.

Since the jury is still out on the iron/heart disease relationship, it is still too early to make recommendations about changing iron in the diet to protect against heart disease. This is especially true since iron deficiency is a common problem in this country. The best advice to prevent heart disease is still to make changes that reduce known risk factors, like limiting fat and cholesterol in the diet, exercising, and not smoking.

Hemochromatosis, an iron overload syndrome, afflicts about one in every 200 to 500 Americans. This is a genetic disorder that causes the body to absorb large amounts of iron that it does not need. Excess iron gets stored in the liver, heart, and pancreas, where it often goes undetected until mid-life when iron levels reach 5 to 50 times normal amounts. The initial symptoms, fatigue, achy joints, and weakness, are sometimes misinterpreted as iron deficiency. Severe health problems like liver disease can result. Early identification and treatment are the way to go. Some doctors believe almost everyone should be tested for this disorder. Most recommend getting tested if you have a family history of the disease or have any symptoms which have not been successfully explained and treated. Blood tests called serum ferritin and transferrin saturation, which together cost about $75 to $100, help identify whether you are storing too much iron. Treatment is relatively simple. It involves getting rid of excess iron by drawing blood, and avoiding iron supplements and foods highly fortified with iron.

Iron deficiency is the most prevalent nutrient deficiency in this country. It is estimated to affect about ten percent of the population. Pregnant women, women of childbearing age, teenage girls, and infants are at highest risk of not getting enough iron. It can lead to anemia, fatigue, irritability, headaches, and lack of energy.

To prevent iron deficiency, every effort should be made to maximize iron from food sources. A good diet will safely help decrease the risk of inadequate iron and at the same time cause the least potential damage to those at risk for iron excess. A well planned vegetarian diet provides adequate iron.

How do you know if you are getting enough iron? The Recommended Dietary Allowance for iron is 10 mg daily for men and postmenopausal women and 15 mg for women of childbearing age. Women need more iron daily to replace the iron lost each month during menstruation. Eating a varied diet with emphasis on iron-rich foods is a good start to getting enough iron. Dried beans, dark green leafy vegetables, blackstrap molasses, bulgur, and prune juice are good vegetarian sources of iron. The body absorbs only about two to twenty percent of the iron available in vegetarian sources. To increase this figure, eat a vitamin C-rich fruit or vegetable at each meal. (See chart below.) Citrus fruit, leafy vegetables, tomatoes, and strawberries are good sources of vitamin C.

Another way to promote iron absorption is to eliminate coffee and tea with meals, especially those containing significant amounts of iron. Coffee has been shown to decrease iron absorption by as much as 39 percent and tea by 64 percent. This is thought to be due to tannins and other substances which bind with the iron and make it less absorbable. This effect has been shown to occur even when coffee was consumed one hour after the meal. Adding milk to coffee further decreases iron absorption. You can partially counteract this effect with vitamin C rich foods, but why not enjoy a glass of orange juice with your breakfast instead of a cup of coffee. If you must have your coffee, drink it at least one hour before mealtime to prevent interference with iron absorption.

Cooking with iron pots can significantly increase the iron content of food. This is especially true when cooking acidic foods like tomatoes. If you are still not sure you are getting adequate iron, have your diet evaluated by a registered dietitian.

Iron supplements can do more harm than good, especially in men who are more likely to have a problem with iron overload than with iron deficiency. Iron supplements should be taken only with the advice of a physician in cases where iron deficiency or an increased need for iron has been diagnosed. During pregnancy low-dose iron supplements are commonly recommended because it is difficult to meet iron needs through diet alone. Some researchers believe all supplements or products containing iron and vitamin C should come with a warning label for people at risk of iron overload. This includes multiple vitamin/mineral preparations. Iron supplements can also cause imbalance of other essential nutrients like copper and zinc.

BEST SOURCES OF VITAMIN C

Vegetables	Fruits
Broccoli	Cantaloupe
Brussels Sprouts	Cranberry Juice
Cabbage	Grapefruit
Cauliflower	Guava
Dark Leafy Greens	Honeydew Melon
Kohlrabi	Mango
Potato (white or sweet)	Orange
Sweet Pepper	Papaya
Tomato	Strawberries
	Tangerine
	Watermelon

The golden rule, still, is that it is best to get the nutrients your body needs, including iron, from the food you eat. A well planned vegetarian diet can provide adequate iron, minimizing the risk of iron deficiency. (See chart below.) This provides the least potential harm to those at risk for iron overload. It is still too early to tell whether limiting iron in the diet will protect against heart disease.

VEGETARIAN SOURCES OF IRON

Food	Portion Size	Iron (mg)
Beet Greens, cooked	1/2 cup	1.4
Bulgur, cooked	1 cup	1.8
Blackstrap Molasses	1 Tablespoon	3.5
Figs, dried	5	2.1
Kidney Beans, cooked	1 cup	5.2
Lentils, cooked	1 cup	6.6
Lima Beans, cooked	1 cup	4.5
Prune Juice	8 ounces	3.0
Spinach, cooked	1/2 cup	3.2
Swiss Chard, cooked	1/2 cup	2.0

References on Iron

Bothwell T. The importance of assessing iron status. In: Herbert V. *Diagnosis and Treatment of Iron Disorders. Hospital Practice.* 1991; 26[suppl 3]: 11-16.

Dwyer JT. Health aspects of vegetarian diets. *American Journal of Clinical Nutrition.* 1988; 48: 712-738.

Edwards CQ, Griffen LM, Kushner JP. Disorders of excess iron. In: Herbert V. *Diagnosis and Treatment of Iron Disorders. Hospital Practice.* 1991; 26[suppl 3]: 30-36.

Expert Scientific Working Group. Summary of a report on assessment of the iron nutritional status of the United States population. *American Journal of Clinical Nutrition.* 1985; 42: 1318-1330.

Fairbanks V. Laboratory testing for iron status. In: Herbert V. *Diagnosis and Treatment of Iron Disorders. Hospital Practice.* 1991; 26[suppl 3]: 17-24.

Food and Nutrition Board. *Recommended Dietary Allowances.* Washington, D.C.: National Academy Press; 1989.

Gambino R. Routine screening for iron status. In: Herbert V. *Diagnosis and Treatment of Iron Disorders. Hospital Practice.* 1991; 26[suppl 3]: 41-44.

Green R. Disorders of inadequate iron. In: Herbert V. *Diagnosis and Treatment of Iron Disorders. Hospital Practice.* 1991; 26[suppl 3]: 25-29.

Herbert V. Should everyone be tested for iron disorders? *Journal of The American Dietetic Association.* 1993; 93: 1502-1509.

Monsen, ER. Iron nutrition and absorption: Dietary factors which impact iron bioavailability. *Journal of The American Dietetic Association.* 1988; 88: 786-790.

Morck TA, Lynch SR, Cook JD. Inhibition of food iron absorption by coffee. *American Journal of Clinical Nutrition.* 1983; 37: 416-420.

Mutch PB. Food guide for the vegetarian. *American Journal of Clinical Nutrition.* 1988; 48: 913-919.

Pennington JAT. *Bowes and Church's Food Values of Portions Commonly Used.* New York: Harper & Row; 1989.

Position of The American Dietetic Association: Vegetarian diets. *Journal of The American Dietetic Association.* 1993; 93: 1317-1319.

Salonen JT, Nyyssonen K, Korpela H, Tuomilehtl J, Seppanen R, Salonen R. High stored iron levels are associated with excess risk of myocardial infarction in eastern Finnish men. *Circulation.* 1992; 86: 803-811.

Eve Shatto Walton is in private practice as a Registered Dietitian in Boca Raton, Florida.

Soyfoods As a Source of Iron in Diets Devoid of Meat

By Virginia Messina, M.P.H., R.D.
and Mark Messina, Ph.D.

Your diet, whether or not it contains meat, is abundant in iron. But how much of that iron actually gets into your bloodstream? That question has interested nutritionists for decades and with good reason.

For one thing, iron deficiency is a significant problem world-wide. And it doesn't occur just in developing countries. Inadequate iron intake is common in the United States, although the incidence of actual deficiency is rather low.[1] Since iron is critical to our ability to use oxygen, the effects of iron deficiency are serious.

The actual biological need for iron is pretty small -- about 1 to 1-1/2 milligrams a day seems to be enough to support all iron-dependent functions.[2] But in order to meet biological needs, people need to consume as much as 10 to 15 milligrams of iron each day. The reason that the recommended intake is so much higher than the actual requirement is because so little of the iron in foods is actually absorbed by the body.

A general rule of thumb is that we absorb about 10 to 15 percent of the total amount of iron in our diet.[2] The amount of iron we absorb depends on many different factors, though, so the amount of iron we actually need to consume becomes a pretty complex issue. For example, people whose diets are low in iron absorb far greater amounts of this nutrient.[3] Also, in times of need, iron absorption can increase ten fold.[3]

The *type* of iron found in a food affects its absorption, too. Plant foods contain *non-heme* iron, which is not well absorbed. Meat contains both non-heme iron and *heme* iron; heme iron is very well-absorbed. The whole dietary picture makes a difference, too. Vitamin C enhances the absorption of non-heme iron, although it has no effect on heme iron.[4] Vegetarians who rely solely on non-heme iron in their diet can boost the absorption of that iron by including a food high in vitamin C at every meal.

Most iron studies involving soy don't duplicate the eating patterns of vegetarians.

Other dietary components can interfere with iron absorption. Tannins, which are chemicals found in tea, greatly reduce the absorption of iron.[5] Frequent consumption of tea in developing countries is probably one reason for rampant iron deficiency in those areas of the world.[6]

These factors tend to complicate the iron picture quite a bit. Foods that are rich in iron may not necessarily be the best sources of iron. One food that has been the subject of much study is soybeans.

Soybeans, and the foods made from them, are high in non-heme iron. But traditional nutritional wisdom, which seems to be borne out by most studies, is that iron from soyfoods is poorly absorbed.[7] Soy protein also inhibits overall absorption of iron from meat.[8] But most iron studies involving soy don't duplicate the eating patterns of vegetarians.

In addition to combining soy with meat, (which of course vegetarians don't eat), these studies primarily use soy protein products, such as soy isolates and soy flour. Vegetarians are more likely to eat tofu and drink soy milk than to consume soy isolates. Even so, the results of these studies are worth noting.

In one USDA study, more than 200 adults and children consumed one or two meals a day that contained either an all-beef product, or a beef product that contained 20 percent soy protein.[9] The soy protein was in the form of soy isolate, soy concentrate or soy flour. In this study, the addition of soy did not adversely affect iron status. In fact, there was some indication that iron status actually improved. This may have been, in part, because researchers have found that while soy reduces the absorption of the non-heme iron in meat, it actually *increases* the absorption of heme iron.[4]

In another study, six male subjects consumed a diet that contained soy protein concentrate as the sole source of iron for 82 days.[10] Iron levels did go down slightly, but the researchers attributed it primarily to the fact that the students gave so many blood samples during the course of the study. In this study, it was estimated that about 16% of the iron was absorbed. Iron is absorbed better from soybeans than from many other plant foods, such as corn, rice, and other legumes,[11, 12] but that 16% figure is probably too

high when one considers a wider range of research. One very important study, which used traditional soy foods, found that on average, iron absorption from products such as tofu and miso, ranged from 5 to 10 percent.[13]

If one uses an average figure of 7.5% absorption, then one serving of tofu, which contains about 6.5 milligrams of iron, would provide about 1/2 milligram of iron, or about 1/2 the amount needed by an adult male.[14] That's impressive, when considering that one serving of ground beef provides 50% more iron, (using an absorption figure of 35%) but also supplies twice as many calories and many times more saturated fat.[14]

What Does It Mean?

Nutritionists are in agreement that iron from meat is better absorbed than iron from plants. But they also agree that the bottom line -- how much iron an individual actually absorbs -- is dependent on a lot more than whether or not a person eats meat. Studies show that vegetarians are, in fact, no more likely to be iron deficient than meat-eaters, although iron stores may be somewhat lower.[15, 16]

It may be that vegetarians eat copious amounts of iron-rich foods, so that even a low absorption rate won't keep them from getting enough iron. Vegetarians may also consume more vitamin C-rich foods with their meals. But remember that iron deficiency is common among all population groups. People need to pay particular attention to getting enough of this nutrient no matter what type of diet they eat. At the same time, it is worth noting that recent studies show that too much iron may be as great a public health problem as too little.[17, 18] High levels of iron in the body have been linked to increased risk of both heart disease and cancer. Plant-based diets may have the real advantage in that they provide adequate iron, but may have built in mechanisms that protect us from iron overload.

References

[1] Dallman PR, Yip R, Johnson C. Prevalence and causes of anemia in the United States, 1976-1980. *Am J Clin Nutr* 39: 437-445, 1984.

[2] National Research Council. *Recommended Dietary Allowances.* National Academy Press, Washington DC, 1989.

[3] Cook JD. Adaptation in iron metabolism. *Am J Clin Nutr* 51:301-308, 1990.

[4] Lynch SR, Dassenko SA, Morck TA, Beard JL, Cook JD. Soy protein products and heme iron absorption in humans. *Am J Clin Nutr* 41:13-20, 1985.

[5] Gillooly M, Bothwell TH, Torrance JD, Macphail AP, Derman DP, Bezwoda WR, Mills W, Chariton RW. The effects of organic acids, phytates and polyphenols on the absorption of iron from vegetables. *Br J Nutr* 49:331-342, 1983.

[6] Disler PB, Lynch SR, Charlton RW, Torrance JD, Bothwell TH, Walker RB, Mayet F. The effect of tea on iron absorption. *Gut* 16:193-200, 1975.

[7] Morck TA, Lynch SR, Cook JD. Reduction of the soy-induced inhibition of nonheme iron absorption. *Am J Clin Nutr* 36:219-228, 1982.

[8] Bodwell CE. Effects of soy protein on iron and zinc. *Cereal Foods World* 28: 342-348, 1983.

[9] Bodwell CE, Miles CW, Morris E, Prather ES, Mertz W, Canary JJ. Long-term consumption of beef extended with soy protein by men, women, and children: II. Effects on iron status. *Plant Fds Hum Nutr* 37:361-376, 1987.

[10] Istfan N, Murray E, Janghorbani M, Evan WJ, Young VR. The nutritional value of a soy protein concentrate (stapro-3200) for long-term protein nutritional maintenance in young men. *J Nutr* 113: 2524-2534, 1983.

[11] Layrisse M, Cook JD, Martinez C, Roche M, Kuhn IN, Walker RB, Finch CA. Food iron absorption: a comparison of vegetable and animal foods. *Blood* 33: 430-443, 1969.

[12] Lynch SR, Beard JL, Dassenko SA, Cook JD. Iron absorption from legumes in humans. *Am J Clin Nutr* 40:42-47, 1984.

[13] Macfarlane BJ, van der Riet WB, Bothwell TH, Baynes RD, Siegenberg D, Schmidt U, Tal A, Taylor JRN, Mayet F. Effect of traditional oriental soy products on iron absorption. *Am J Clin Nutr* 51: 873-880, 1990.

[14] Pennington JAT, Church HN. *Food values of portions commonly used.* Harper and Row, 1989.

[15] Anderson BM, Gibson RS, Sabry JH. The iron and zinc status of long-term vegetarian women. *Am J Clin Nutr* 34: 1042-1048, 1981.

[16] Worthington-Roberts BS, Breskin MW, Monsen ER. Iron status of premenopausal women in a university community and its relationship to habitual dietary sources of protein. *Am J Clin Nutr* 47:275-279, 1988.

[17] Weinberg ED. Roles of iron in neoplasia. *Biol Trace Element Res* 34:123-140, 1992.

[18] Salonen JT, Kyyssonen K, Korpela H, Tuomilehto J, Seppanen R, Salonen R. High stored iron levels are associated with excess risk of myocardial infarction in eastern Finnish men. *Circulation* (in press)

Virginia and Mark Messina are freelance writers from Washington. They devote a lot of their time to researching the role of soy foods in a healthy diet.

DIET AND BREAST CANCER

By Mary Franz, M.S., R.D.

Breast cancer is a disease characterized by fear: fear of pain, disfigurement, and death itself. It is fear grounded in alarming statistics. In 1991, 175,000 new cases of breast cancer were expected to be diagnosed in the United States, and nearly 45,000 American women died of the disease.[1]

Better screening techniques, such as mammography, have resulted in earlier detection and treatment for many women. But can a woman actually reduce her chance of getting breast cancer?

Some researchers now believe that by making some simple dietary and lifestyle changes, women can decrease their risk of breast cancer. This article will look at some of the suspected risk factors for the disease, and outline some of the specific dietary guidelines (especially those relevant to vegetarians) which have been developed to help women reduce their risk of breast cancer.

CAUSES OF BREAST CANCER

The causes of breast cancer are complex. The disease is known to begin as the mutation of a single cell, as a result of exposure to an agent that can cause cancer.[2] After a cell has mutated, it is likely that many "risk factors" act together to cause the growth of cancer.[2]

Established Risk Factors: Established risk factors are those known to increase risk for the development of the disease. The established risk factors for breast cancer are age, reproductive history, and family history.[2]

Age: As a woman ages, her risk of breast cancer rises steadily[3,4], with the highest rates seen after menopause.[4]

Reproductive History: Childbearing appears to be protective against breast cancer. Women who never bear children have higher rates of breast cancer than women who bear at least one child. Breastfeeding also appears to reduce risk for the disease.[5]

Family History: Women whose mothers or sisters have had breast cancer are at higher risk themselves.[2]

Suspected Risk Factors: Suspected risk factors are agents or influences which may play a role in the development of the disease, but which require further study. The suspected risk factors for breast cancer include oral contraceptive use, obesity, and diet.

Oral Contraceptives: Some studies have shown an increased risk of breast cancer among women who took oral contraceptives; others have shown no effect at all.[6]

Obesity: Higher rates of breast cancer have been seen in obese women.[7]

Diet: During the past ten years, great attention has been given to the role of dietary factors such as fat, fiber, and protein intake, in the development of breast cancer. Many studies have looked at both the independent and combined effects of these nutrients in promoting the development of breast cancer.

FAT INTAKE

Many researchers believe that a high-fat diet is most strongly linked with an increased risk of breast cancer. According to the National Research Council Committee on Diet, Nutrition, and Cancer, "Of all the dietary components, the combined evidence is most suggestive of a relationship between fat intake and the occurrence of cancer."[8]

Evidence pointing toward the role of a high-fat diet in the development of breast cancer comes from several sources. First, studies have shown that countries with the highest fat intakes have the highest rates of breast cancer. For example, countries having average fat intakes of 40-50 percent of total calories (such as the Netherlands and Denmark) have death rates from breast cancer that are 2-3 times higher than countries where the average fat intake is 10-30 percent of total calories (such as Japan, Chile, and Egypt)[9] The United States, with an average fat intake of about 35-40 percent, also has rates of breast cancer exceeding those of many other countries where fat intake is low.[9]

Breast cancer rates within specific populations are also affected by dietary factors. Between 1955 and 1975, deaths from breast cancer in Japan doubled in women aged forty-five to fifty-nine.[10] Researchers found that those women who ate a high-fat diet (defined as daily meat consumption) during this period had death rates from breast cancer two times higher than women eating an apparently low-fat diet.[10] In addition, first generation Japanese women who migrate to the United States have rates of breast cancer three times higher than those of Japanese women living in Japan, suggesting the powerful influence of environmental factors such as diet.[11]

Studies of groups of women with breast cancer have also shed light on the role dietary fat may play in promoting breast cancer. Rates of breast cancer appear to be 2-3 times higher among women who eat a diet rich in fat (defined as frequent or daily consumption of meat and/or whole milk), compared to women who abstain from these foods, or eat them less frequently.[8, 10, 12, 13]

The role of dietary fat in development of breast cancer has recently been questioned. A very large study of American nurses failed to find any link between fat intake and risk of breast cancer.[14] The women who participated in this study consumed an average of 30 percent of their calories from fat. Perhaps to reduce breast cancer significantly, fat consumption needs to be below 30 percent of total calories. This would mean that American women, who consume 35 to 40 percent of their calories from fat, would need to make some major dietary changes (i.e., reduce their total fat intake to well below 30 percent of total calories) to decrease their cancer risk. (See Appendix for Guidelines for Fat Reduction.)

Although a link has been seen in some studies between a high-fat diet and increased risk of breast cancer, less is known about the link between specific types of fat and breast cancer. Is saturated or unsaturated fat the culprit, or is the amount of total fat the most important factor? A recent combined analysis of breast cancer studies examined rates of the disease among 10,522 women in eight countries. Researchers determined that the risk of breast cancer was greatest in older women who reported eating the largest amount of saturated fat; the risk of cancer also rose as the level of total fat in the diet rose.[15] This study supports limiting both saturated and total fat.

OTHER DIETARY FACTORS

The link between protein intake and risk of breast cancer is much weaker than the relationship between fat intake and breast cancer.[8] The greater risk of breast cancer among meat eaters seems to be due mainly to fat intake, and not protein consumption.[8, 10]

The risk of breast cancer appears to be lower when a diet rich in dark green and deep yellow vegetables (particularly carrots) is eaten.[8, 12, 16] In addition, the consumption of fiber-rich foods and of food high in vitamin A appears to lower the risk of breast cancer.[8]

An increased risk of breast cancer has been seen among women who use moderate amounts of alcohol (1 to 3 drinks per day).[17, 18, 19] However, caffeine consumption has not been found to increase the risk of breast cancer.[20]

VEGETARIAN DIETS

Very few studies have looked at breast cancer incidence among vegetarians, and results of existing studies have been inconclusive. For example, British researchers found no difference in the rates of breast cancer between nuns eating a vegetarian diet, and single non-vegetarian British women.[21] Furthermore, Seventh-day Adventists, consuming minimal amounts of meat, did not have significantly lower rates of breast cancer.[22] However, the average total fat intake (36 percent) of Seventh-day Adventists in this study was similar to that of the general population in the United States, suggesting that the amount of fat in the diet is at least as important as the type of fat (animal vs. plant fat).[22]

These inconclusive findings do not mean that a vegetarian diet is not protective against breast cancer. Dietary modifications to reduce fat and increase fiber intake appear to reduce the risk of breast cancer. For some, these modifications may be easier to achieve on a vegetarian diet.

CONCLUSIONS AND RECOMMENDATIONS

The preceding suggests that a diet high in fat and low in fiber may be a risk factor for breast cancer. In addition, a diet rich in beta-carotene and/or vitamin A may offer protection against the disease.

What specific steps can a woman take to reduce her risk of breast cancer?

The following dietary guidelines, consistent with the recommendations offered by the Committee on Diet and Health of the National Research Council, may be helpful in reducing the risk of breast cancer[8]:

1. Reduce total fat intake to less than 30 percent of total calories.

2. Reduce saturated fat to less than 10 percent of total calories.

3. Increase intake of foods rich in beta-carotene.

4. Increase intake of fiber-rich foods.

5. Maintain ideal body weight.

6. Limit intake of alcohol to no more than 1 ounce of pure alcohol daily (1 ounce pure alcohol = two 12-ounce beers, 8 ounces of wine, or 2 "mixed drinks").

With a little planning, a vegetarian can easily meet these guidelines. Meat, whole-milk dairy products, butter, and traditional "fast foods" are major sources of total and saturated fat in the American diet. By avoiding these foods, using lowfat cooking methods (steaming or baking), and seasoning foods with herbs, lemon juice, soy sauce, and/or vinegars instead of margarine or oils, vegetarians can markedly reduce their intake of fat and saturated fat.

Choose a variety of fruits and vegetables, including those that are good sources of beta carotene (carrots, broccoli, spinach, winter squash, sweet potatoes, cantaloupe, etc.), and those that are good sources of fiber (apples, corn, peas, cabbage, etc.). The Committee on Diet and Health suggests eating at least five

1/2-cup servings of fruit and vegetables each day, concentrating on the deep green and yellow vegetables, and the citrus fruits.[8]

In planning a high-fiber lowfat diet, one of the most beneficial foods to include is legumes. Lentils, peas, and beans provide delicious, inexpensive sources of protein, with virtually no fat. These foods are also good sources of vitamins, iron, and zinc.

SAMPLE MENU

The following menu is based on the dietary guidelines suggested above. It provides about 2000 calories, and is approximately 62 percent carbohydrate, 14 percent protein, 24 percent total fat, and 5 percent saturated fat. Those who are watching their weight, or have smaller appetites, can reduce their intake to about 1500 calories by cutting the amounts of oil and salad dressing in half, and by skipping the rice at lunch and the dessert at dinner.

BREAKFAST
1/2 cup oatmeal with 1/2 cup soy milk
1 cup cantaloupe
1 cup orange juice

LUNCH
1 medium bean burrito (no cheese)
1/2 cup Spanish rice
lemonade

SNACK
1/2 cup fresh pineapple
1 cup fortified soy milk

DINNER
1 cup tofu stir-fried in 1 Tablespoon oil with
1-1/2 cups broccoli, zucchini, and scallions
1 medium baked potato with 1 teaspoon
   tahini
Tossed salad with 2 Tablespoons oil and
   vinegar dressing
Baked apple with cinnamon
Cranberry juice

HOW TO KEEP FAT INTAKE BELOW 30 PERCENT

The American diet is about 37 percent fat. To reduce risk of cancer and heart disease, it is recommended that fat intake be kept below 30 percent of total calories. The "typical" American man eats about 2000 calories per day, while the "typical" American woman eats about 1600 calories daily. Based on these estimates, a man eating 2000 calories should consume no more than about 67 grams of fat per day, while a woman eating 1600 calories should take in no more than 53 grams of fat per day.

The following guidelines may be helpful in reducing fat intake to less than 30 percent.

1. Eat more whole grains, legumes, and fresh fruits and vegetables.

2. Choose lowfat cooking methods such as baking, steaming, and broiling, and limit or eliminate fat added during food preparation.

3. Eat fewer convenience, processed, and traditional "fast foods" -- they are often loaded with fat.

4. Choose lowfat snacks like plain popcorn, pretzels, fresh fruit, vegetables, and ices.

5. Eat sauces and salad dressings in limited amounts; order them "on the side."

6. Use no more than 4-6 teaspoons of added fat (soft margarine, cooking oil, salad dressing, etc.) per day.

7. Choose high-fiber, lowfat cereals, crackers, and breads to provide a sense of satiety.

8. Carefully read labels of all foods to determine fat content.

FOOTNOTES

[1] *Cancer Facts and Figures - 1991.* American Cancer Society, 1991.

[2] Petrakis NL, Ernster VL, King MC. "Breast Cancer." In: Schottenfeld D, Fraumeni JF, eds. *Cancer Epidemiology and Prevention.* Philadelphia: W. B. Saunders, 1982: 855-70.

[3] Devitt JE. "The influence of age on the behavior of carcinoma of the breast." *Can Med Assoc J* 1970; 103:923-931.

[4] Pfeiffer CH, Mulliken JB. *Caring for the Patient with Breast Cancer: An Interdisciplinary and Multi-disciplinary Approach.* Reston, Virginia: Reston Publishing Co., Inc., 1984: 2-5.

[5] Macmahon B, Purde M, Cramar D, Hunt E. "Association of breast cancer risk with age at first and subsequent births -- a study in the population of the Estonian republic." *JNCI* 1982; 69: 1035-38.

[6] Baum M. *Breast Cancer: The Facts.* New York: Oxford University Press, 1981; 1-4.

[7] Verreault R, Brisson J, et al. "Body weight and prognostic indicators in breast cancer." *Am J Epidemiol* 1989; 129: 260-68.

[8] *Diet and Health: Implications for Reducing Chronic Disease Risk.* Committee on Diet and Health, National Research Council, National Academy of Sciences, Washington, D.C., 1989; 12-17 and 205-208.

[9] *Diet, Nutrition, and Prevention of Chronic Diseases: Report of a WHO Study Group.* World Health Organization, Geneva, 1970; 65-68.

[10] Hirayama T. "Epidemiology of breast cancer with special reference to the role of diet." *Prev Med* 1978; 7: 173-95.

[11] *The Breast Cancer Digest.* A guide to medical care, emotional support, educational programs, and resources. Office of Cancer Communications, National Cancer Institute, Maryland, 1979; 3-8.

[12] LaVecchia C, Decarli A, Franchesi S, et al. "Dietary factors and the risk of breast cancer." *Nutr Cancer* 1987; 10: 205- 14.

[13] Le MG, Moulton LH, Hill C, et al. "Consumption of dairy products and alcohol in a case-control study of breast cancer." *JNCI* 1986; 77: 633-36.

[14] Willett WC, Stampfer G, Colditz B, Rosner CH, Hennekens CH, Speizer FE. "Dietary fat and risk of breast cancer." *N Engl J Med* 1987; 316: 22-28.

[15] Howe GR, Hirohata T, Hislop TG, et al. "Dietary factors and risk of breast cancer: combined analysis of 12 case-control studies." *JNCI* 1990; 82: 561-69.

[16] Katsouyanni K, Trichopolous D, Boyle P, et al. "Diet and breast cancer: a case-control study in Greece." *Int J Cancer* 1986; 38: 815-20.

[17] Schatzkin A, Jones Y, Hoover RN, et al. "Alcohol consumption and breast cancer in the Epidemiologic Follow-up Study of the First National Health and Nutrition Examination Survey." *N Engl J Med* 1987; 316: 1169-73.

[18] Hiatt RA, Klatsky AL, Armstrong MA. "Alcohol consumption and the risk of breast cancer in a prepaid health plan." *Cancer Res* 1988; 48: 2284-87.

[19] Willett WC, Stampher MJ, Colditz GA, et al. "Moderate alcohol consumption and the risk of breast cancer." *N Engl J Med* 1987; 316: 1174-80.

[20] Skegg DC. "Alcohol, coffee, fat, and breast cancer." *Br Med J* 1987; 295: 1011-12.

[21] Kinlen LJ. "Meat and fat consumption and cancer mortality: a study of strict religious orders in Britain." *Lancet* 1982; 1: 946-49.

[22] Phillips RL, Garfinkel L, Kuzma JW, et al. "Mortality among California Seventh-day Adventists for selected cancer sites." *JNCI* 1980; 65: 1097-1107.

Mary Franz did her master's thesis on breast cancer. She is in private practice in Boston and is a consultant for the Framingham study of diet and heart disease.

Soybeans and Cancer Prevention

By Virginia Messina, M.P.H., R.D.
and Mark Messina, Ph.D.

Nutrition experts have long been interested in the eating patterns of Asian populations -- primarily because people in those countries enjoy much lower rates of the diseases that plague Westerners. The lower fat intake and higher intake of fiber have taken some credit for the low rates of heart disease and of colon and breast cancer in China, Japan, and Korea. But new research has inspired interest in another aspect of Asian cuisine that may play an important role in disease prevention. Some of the most intriguing scientific research taking place today involves the relationship of soybeans to cancer prevention. Several studies have shown that, in Asian countries, people who eat soyfoods regularly have less cancer than those who don't.

Nutrition experts have long been interested in the eating patterns of Asian populations -- primarily because people in those countries enjoy much lower rates of the diseases that plague Westerners. The lower fat intake and higher intake of fiber have taken some credit for the low rates of heart disease and of colon and breast cancer in China, Japan, and Korea. But new research has inspired interest in another aspect of Asian cuisine that may play an important role in disease prevention. Some of the most intriguing scientific research taking place today involves the relationship of soybeans to cancer prevention. Several studies have shown that, in Asian countries, people who eat soyfoods regularly have less cancer than those who don't.

Studies in China, Japan, and even the United States have found that consuming soyfoods such as tofu, soy milk and soy sprouts, cuts the risk of colon and rectal cancer in half.[1,2] In one Japanese study, subjects who consumed whole soybeans and tofu had an 80 percent lower risk of rectal cancer.[3] In Singapore, women who rarely ate soyfoods were twice as likely to develop breast cancer as those who consumed them regularly.[4] Other studies suggest that soyfoods may lower risk for lung, stomach and prostate cancer.[5,6] A study of 8,000 Japanese Hawaiians found that tofu consumption lowered the risk of prostate cancer more than any other dietary factor studied.[7]

These kinds of observations are not proof that soyfoods lower cancer risk. For one thing, not all studies of this type show a protective effect of soy; some show no effect. But the weight of evidence favoring soybeans has been impressive enough to inspire nutrition scientists to take a closer look at soy.

Soybeans and Isoflavones

Like all plant foods, soybeans contain a variety of compounds which scientists have dubbed *phytochemicals* -- or literally, "plant chemicals." These phytochemicals are not nutrients and therefore are not essential for life. However, they may actually perform some significant functions that make them important for optimal health.

Soybeans boast a variety of phytochemicals including several with anti-cancer activity. One of these is a group of chemicals called *isoflavones*. Isoflavones best explain the soybean's hypothesized anti-cancer activity.

Isoflavones have a chemical structure that is similar to the female hormone estrogen -- a hormone that is thought to raise risk for breast cancer and other hormonal cancers. How then, can isoflavones be protective against breast cancer? The answer is that the isoflavones are just different enough from natural estrogen to be considered *weak estrogens*.

They have only about 1/100,000th the activity of natural estrogen.[8] But because they look like estrogen, they have the ability to block the activity of the natural hormone.

To have any effect on breast tissue, estrogen must first attach to receptor sites on breast cells. Since isoflavones look so similar to estrogen, they attach to the same sites and block the more powerful, cancer-enhancing natural estrogen from exerting its effects. And because the isoflavones have such weak activity themselves, they don't exert those same cancer-causing effects. It is as though you have put the wrong key into a lock. The key may look the same and it may fit into the lock, but it won't turn the lock and open the door.

Isoflavones actually act in a way that is very similar to one of the most widely used drugs for treating breast cancer, called Tamoxifin.[9,10,11] Tamoxifin is also an anti-estrogen. Researchers are now studying Tamoxifin to see if it can also *prevent* breast cancer.

But this anti-estrogen activity of isoflavones is only a part of their anti-cancer powers. Isoflavones exhibit a variety of characteristics that are independent of their estrogen effects and that may help to combat cancer. Scientists have observed that many cancer cells require a special enzyme called protein tyrosine kinase for their activity. Interfering with the activity of this enzyme is thought to be one way to inhibit the cancer process. Isoflavones have been shown to inhibit this enzyme. As a result, isoflavones inhibit growth of a variety of cancer cells but have no effect on normal, non-cancerous cells.[12] Isoflavones also cause cancer cells to differentiate.[13] A unique -- and deadly -- feature of cancer cells is that they all begin to look the same, becoming more embryonic in a sense. Some drugs used to treat cancer act by inducing the cancer cells to become different from one another. Isoflavones have this same effect.

Finally, isoflavones are also antioxidants. Like vitamin C and beta-carotene they protect cells from damage by oxygen. Oxidation causes changes that can lead to cancer and other diseases.[14]

Because isoflavones work against cancer in a variety of ways, they help to protect against a variety of cancers. These include the estrogen-dependent cancers such as breast and endometrial cancer as well as those that are not hormone-related such as colon, lung, and stomach cancer.

As we noted earlier, soybeans contain a number of anti-cancer substances in addition to isoflavones. A variety of compounds may contribute to the soybean's anti-cancer profile. However, most of these are not unique to soybeans but are found in a variety of plant foods.

Isoflavones, on the other hand, *are* unique to soybeans. Soybeans are the only commonly consumed food that provide isoflavones in the diet.

Soy in the Diet

The variety of soy products on the market makes it easy to work some soy into your diet. A word of caution is in order, however. Not all products made from soy contain isoflavones. In some soyfoods isoflavones are found in lower amounts due to processing.

The whole soybean, soy flour, tofu, texturized vegetable protein (TVP), miso, and tempeh are all rich in isoflavones. Soy milk has lower, but still significant, amounts of isoflavones.[15] Based on studies of soy consumption and cancer risk in Asian countries, it seems that as little as one serving a day of these foods may help to protect against cancer.

The amount of isoflavones in other products made from soy will vary depending on the actual amount of soy used to make them and the ways in which the food is processed. That means that you can't necessarily depend on soy cheese and meat analogs (imitation meat products made from soy) to provide significant amounts of isoflavones.

Including a serving of soy in your diet can be pretty simple even if you don't have much time for cooking and don't have an extensive repertoire of soy recipes. Try one of the following ideas:

- Pour a half cup of soy milk over hot or cold cereal in the morning.

- Make a batch of muffins to have on hand for snacks or breakfast and replace one-quarter of the flour with soy flour. (If you bake your own bread, use a lighter hand with the soy flour. Since it does not contain gluten, you will end up with a bread that is a bit heavier and denser).

- Sauté some crumbled tofu or tempeh or TVP with a chopped onion and a packet of taco seasoning to make a quick taco stuffer.

- Blend soft tofu or soy milk with a banana and other fruits (try dates for an especially nice flavor) to make a quick breakfast shake.

- Try roasted soy nuts instead of peanuts or chips for a crunchy snack.

Don't forget about whole soybeans. Many people shy away from them because soybeans take longer to cook than other legumes and have a stronger flavor. Try cooking them to a pleasant softness in a pressure cooker and then baking in a sauce with a stand-up flavor of its own -- like a barbecue sauce. Black soybeans, available in some natural foods groceries, cook more quickly and have a mild taste.

Finally, if you can get your hands on them, try fresh, immature, green soybeans. These are the same as the yellow soybeans you see in the store, only they are harvested earlier. This delectable treat is a popular snack carried to school in paper sacks by Chinese school-children. You'll see why once you taste them. Unfortunately, they are hard to find; an Asian grocery store is your best bet. If you garden, you can grow your own to freeze and always have on hand.

Keeping the Whole Diet in Mind

Will a glass of soy milk a day keep disease away? Not if you use it to wash down your Big Mac. The research on soybeans and cancer prevention is turning up some truly exciting findings. Based on what we know, including a serving of soy in your diet each day is probably a good step towards reducing your risk of cancer. But it isn't enough. Soy products should be viewed as just one part of a healthy diet.

There is no quick fix or magic bullet for disease prevention. It is the whole diet that matters. A cancer preventative diet is one that is low in fat -- probably no more than 20 percent of calories from fat -- and high in fiber.[16] Base your diet on whole grains -- which have been shown to reduce risk of colon cancer[17] -- and eat generous amounts of fruits and vegetables. Over 120 studies have shown that people who eat fruits and vegetables regularly have lower risk of a variety of cancers.[18] Based on current findings, moderate amounts of soyfoods may be an important part of the cancer preventative diet, too.

References

[1] Hu J, Liu Y, et al. Diet and cancer of the colon and rectum: a case-control study in China. *Inter J Epidemiol* 20:362-367, 1991.

[2] Poole C. A case-control study of diet and colon cancer. Boston Mass: Harvard School of Public Health; 1989. Dissertation.

[3] Watanabe Y, Tada M, et al. A case-control study of cancer of the rectum and the colon. *Nippon Shoka-kibyo Gakkai Azsshi* 81:185-93, 1984.

[4] Lee HP, Gourley L, Duffy SW, et al. Dietary effects on breast cancer risk in Singapore. *Lancet* 337:1197-1200, 1991.

[5] Swanson CA, Mao BL, et al. Dietary determinants of lung cancer risk: results from a case-control study in Yunnan province, China. *Int J Cancer* 50:876-880, 1992.

[6] Yingman Y, Songlin Y. A study of the etiological factors in gastric cancer in Fuzhou city. *Chinese J of Epidemiology* 7:48-50, 1986.

[7] Severson RK, Nomura AMY, et al. A prospective study of demographics, diet, and prostate cancer among men of Japan-ese ancestry in Hawaii. *Cancer Res* 49: 1857-1860, 1989.

[8] Martin PM, Horwitz KB, et al. Phytoestrogen interaction with estrogen receptors in human breast cancer cells. *Endocrinol* 103:1860-1867, 1978.

[9] Willis KJ, London DR, et al. Recurrent breast cancer treated with the anti-estrogen tamoxifin: correlation between hormonal changes and clinical course. *Br Med J* 1:425-428, 1977.

[10] Jordon VC, Fritz NF, Tormey DC. Endocrine effects of adjuvant chemotherapy and long-term tamoxifen administration of node-positive patients with breast cancer. *Cancer Res* 47:624-630, 1987.

[11] Golder MP, Phillips EA et al. Plasma hormones in patients with advanced breast cancer treated with tamoxifen. *Eur J Cancer* 12:719-723, 1976.

[12] Akiyama T, Ogawara H. Use and specificity of genistein as inhibitor of protein-tyrosine kinases. *Meth Enzymol* 201:362-370, 1991.

[13] Sit K-H, Wong K-P, Bay B-H. Effects of geni-stein on ATP induced DNA synthesis and intracellular alkalinization in Chang liver cells. *Japan J Pharmacol* 57:1109-1111, 1991.

[14] Ibid.

[15] Murphy PA. Phytoestrogen content of processed soybean products. *Food Tech* (Jan):60-64, 1982.

[16] Butrum R, Clifford C, Lanza E. NCI dietary guidelines: rationale. *Am J Clin Nutr* 48:888-95, 1988.

[17] Greenwald P, Lanza E, Eddy G. Dietary fiber in the reduction of colon cancer risk. *J Am Diet Assoc* 87: 1178-88, 1987.

[18] Steinmetz DA, Potter JD. Vegetables, fruit, and cancer: I Epidemiology. *Cancer Causes Control* 2:325-57, 1991.

Virginia Messina is a Registered Dietitian. Mark Messina is a former program director in the Diet and Cancer Branch of the National Cancer Institute. They are authors of The Simple Soybean and Your Health.

EASY FRUIT DESSERTS

By Nanette Blanchard

Fresh fruit is one of the greatest joys of summer. Filling up the kitchen with the wonderful perfumed aromas of fruit is terrific, but what do you do with all that fruit? Many fruits are perishable, so it is essential that you have a selection of easy recipes on hand. These recipes are festive enough for a last-minute dinner party but simple enough for a leisurely weekend breakfast. Most of the recipes can be made in advance and refrigerated before serving.

ELEGANT FRUIT BOWL
(Serves 4)

This is a pretty dish that I like to serve in large goblets. For a more attractive look, use a melon baller to scoop out the cantaloupe. This dish is also a nice selection for a buffet.

1 cantaloupe, seeded, rind removed
    and cubed (about 4 cups)
1 cup blueberries
1 cup pitted cherries or raspberries
3/4 cup sparkling apple cider

Mix all ingredients together in serving bowl. Cover and let marinate in refrigerator for 2 hours or overnight. Serve chilled.

TOTAL CALORIES PER SERVING: 168
TOTAL FAT AS % OF DAILY VALUE: 2%   FAT: 1 gm
PROTEIN: 3 gm   CARBOHYDRATES: 42 gm
CALCIUM: 50 mg   IRON: 1 mg   SODIUM: 66 mg
DIETARY FIBER: 5 gm

STUFFED PEACHES
(Serves 6)

The new fruit-sweetened spreads available make stuffing other fruits quite easy. If you have trouble peeling the peaches, blanch them in boiling water for 1 minute using tongs, and the peel will slip off easily.

3 large peaches, peeled and pitted
2 Tablespoons blackberry fruit
    spread (fruit juice sweetened)
3 Tablespoons slivered almonds

Fill each peach half with one teaspoon of blackberry fruit spread and sprinkle almonds over all. This dish can be prepared several hours before serving if covered tightly.

TOTAL CALORIES PER SERVING: 61
TOTAL FAT AS % OF DAILY VALUE: 3%   FAT: 2 gm
PROTEIN: 1 gm   CARBOHYDRATES: 11 gm
CALCIUM: 15 mg   IRON: <1 mg   SODIUM: 1 mg
DIETARY FIBER: 1 gm

BROILED PLUM KABOBS
(Serves 4)

This is a wonderful dessert for both children and adults. The recipe calls for broiling the plums, but if you're grilling the rest of the meal, the plums can be cooked on the grill until they are soft.

5 plums, pitted and quartered
1/4 cup apple juice concentrate
Juice from 1 lime
2 Tablespoons grated fresh ginger
**   root**

In a small bowl, stir together the apple juice concentrate, the lime juice, and the ginger root. Add the plums and mix thoroughly. (You can also let the plums marinate in this mixture for several hours before broiling.)

Skewer the plums and broil 3 to 4 inches from the source of heat for 3 to 5 minutes, brushing with additional marinade at least once during broiling. If you have any marinade left over, serve it with the plum kabobs.

TOTAL CALORIES PER SERVING: 80
TOTAL FAT AS % OF DAILY VALUE: 2%   FAT: 1 gm
PROTEIN: 1 gm   CARBOHYDRATES: 19 gm
CALCIUM: 8 mg   IRON: <1 mg   SODIUM: 5 mg
DIETARY FIBER: 2 gm

RASPBERRY SHRUB
(Serves 4)

This is a simplified version of a traditional American drink that is very refreshing after a meal. Use a mild type of mint such as spearmint.

1-1/2 cups raspberries
1/4 cup mild apple cider vinegar
1/4 cup apple juice concentrate
2 Tablespoons chopped fresh mint
2 cups sparkling water or seltzer
Ice cubes

In a small dish, mix raspberries with apple cider vinegar, and let stand for several hours or overnight. Purée mixture in blender or food processor. Add apple juice concentrate and mint, and taste for sweetness. If too tart, add more apple juice concentrate. (This mixture can be made in advance and refrigerated before serving.) Mix 1/4 cup of raspberry mixture into 1/2 cup of sparkling water, seltzer or club soda for each serving, and serve over ice.

TOTAL CALORIES PER SERVING: 52
TOTAL FAT AS % OF DAILY VALUE: <1%   FAT: <1 gm
PROTEIN: 1 gm   CARBOHYDRATES: 14 gm
CALCIUM: 17 mg   IRON: 1 mg   SODIUM: 6 mg
DIETARY FIBER: 2 gm

Nanette Blanchard is a freelance food writer from Durango, Colorado.

BEYOND FRUIT SALAD

By Mary Clifford R.D.

While fresh fruit is great, it can sometimes be boring. To jazz up dinner parties or simply satisfy your own taste for something sweet after a meal, start experimenting. The following recipes lend themselves to your interpretation; so use your favorite fruits, or take the opportunity to try something you don't often eat.

If your vision of fruit consists of an occasional apple, a banana in your cereal every morning, or juice, you're missing out on one of life's sweetest treats.

Since the fruit family is so diverse, it's nearly impossible to give general advice on purchasing and storage. Some fruits ripen on the tree, bush, or vine on which they grow; others must be picked first. Some should be firm when purchased, while others should be soft. (The first time I purchased a persimmon, I chose a nice, ripe specimen; after biting into it, I realized I did something wrong -- most varieties should be almost mushy before they're ready to eat!)

If your supermarket doesn't have literature on how to purchase a particular fruit, ask the produce manager. They are often more than willing to discuss the intricacies of their craft with anyone who wants to listen.

SAVORY FRUIT AND LIMAS
(Serves 4)

A sophisticated dish that will dress up everyday meals or grace an elegant dinner.

1-1/2 teaspoons soft margarine
1 small onion, chopped
2 cups coarsely chopped fruit (try apples, apricots, pears, pineapple, or a combination)
2 tablespoons juice (pineapple, orange, or apple)
2 cups frozen and thawed or canned lima beans, drained

In non-stick saucepan, melt margarine over medium heat. Add onion and sauté until well browned.

Add fruit and juice; cook, stirring, until fruit is tender. Add lima beans and cook, stirring, until hot throughout.

TOTAL CALORIES PER SERVING: 168
TOTAL FAT AS % OF DAILY VALUE: 3%   FAT: 2 gm
PROTEIN: 7 gm   CARBOHYDRATES: 33 gm
CALCIUM: 40 mg   IRON: 2 mg   SODIUM: 43 mg
DIETARY FIBER: 9 gm

FRESH FIGS WITH STRAWBERRY CREAM
(Serves 4)

Figs and whipped cream are a classic combination. Here we've substituted silken tofu for a lovely, sweet and creamy topping. You can also use the topping for other fruits, if figs are not available. Peaches, strawberries, or other berries work nicely.

One 10.5-ounce package lite silken tofu
1/3 cup natural no-sugar-added strawberry jam
1 teaspoon vanilla extract
8 fresh ripe figs

In blender or food processor, combine tofu, jam, and vanilla until smooth. Refrigerate 1 hour.

When ready to serve, split figs and place on dessert dishes. Top with chilled cream.

TOTAL CALORIES PER SERVING: 135
TOTAL FAT AS % OF DAILY VALUE: 2%   FAT: 1 gm
PROTEIN: 5 gm   CARBOHYDRATES: 27 gm
CALCIUM: 58 mg   IRON: 1 mg   SODIUM:86 mg
DIETARY FIBER: 7 gm

TROPICAL SHERBET
(Serves 4)

This is certainly a great treat for a hot summer day!

3 cups ripe strawberries
1 cup unsweetened pineapple juice
1/2 cup chopped dates
1/4 cup shredded coconut
1 teaspoon vanilla extract

In food processor, combine all ingredients until strawberries are well chopped; mixture should be chunky.

Freeze mixture in ice cream maker according to manufacturer's directions. Or, pour into shallow pan and place in freezer, stirring every half hour or so, until mixture is frozen.

TOTAL CALORIES PER SERVING: 156
TOTAL FAT AS % OF DAILY VALUE: 5%   FAT: 3 gm
PROTEIN: 2 gm   CARBOHYDRATES: 35 gm
CALCIUM: 31 mg   IRON: 1 mg   SODIUM: 18 mg
DIETARY FIBER: 4 gm

SPARKLING MELON SOUP
(Serves 4)

In Europe, fruit soups are often served as dessert. You can serve this as an appetizer or dessert, or to refresh your palate between courses.

1 ripe cantaloupe, rind and seeds removed, cut into chunks
2 teaspoons lemon juice
1/2 cup thawed apple juice concentrate
1/2 cup champagne or sparkling cider
Mint leaves (garnish; optional)

In blender or food processor, combine cantaloupe, lemon juice, and apple juice concentrate until smooth.

Just before serving, stir in champagne or cider. Garnish with mint leaves, if desired.

TOTAL CALORIES PER SERVING: 177
TOTAL FAT AS % OF DAILY VALUE: <1%   FAT: <1 gm
PROTEIN: 3 gm   CARBOHYDRATES: 40 gm
CALCIUM: 47 mg   IRON: 1 mg   SODIUM: 72 mg
DIETARY FIBER: 4 gm

POACHED SECKEL PEARS
(Serves 6)

Seckel pears are the tiny, sugar-sweet pears that appear in late fall. Poaching them in cranberry juice or wine imparts flavor and also a lovely pink blush. Choose ripe, but not overly ripe, fruit for this spiced dessert; for variety, you can substitute peaches or apples. Then, use any leftover poaching liquid for fruit soups, or serve as a warm or chilled beverage.

2 pounds seckel pears, peeled, stems left on
3 cups cranberry juice or a combination of juice and red wine
1 tablespoon lemon juice
1 cinnamon stick
Several cloves

In saucepan, combine all ingredients. Heat to boiling, then reduce heat and simmer about 10 minutes.

Remove from heat and let cool. Refrigerate until ready to serve, at least 3 hours.

To serve, place pears in dessert cups. Spoon some of spiced mixture over pears.

TOTAL CALORIES PER SERVING: 162
TOTAL FAT AS % OF DAILY VALUE: 2%   FAT: 1 gm
PROTEIN: 1 gm   CARBOHYDRATES: 41 gm
CALCIUM: 21 mg   IRON: 1 mg   SODIUM: 6 mg
DIETARY FIBER: 4 gm

MANGO MANNA
(Serves 4)

Mangoes are a luscious, creamy fruit that need little or no preparation to turn them into something special.

3 ripe mangoes, peeled and cut into bite-size pieces
3/4 cup orange juice
1/2 teaspoon almond extract

Combine all ingredients. Refrigerate at least 1 hour before serving.

Variation: Substitute 3 tablespoons almond liqueur for 3 tablespoons of the orange juice. Omit the almond extract.

TOTAL CALORIES PER SERVING: 122
TOTAL FAT AS % OF DAILY VALUE: <1%   FAT: <1 gm
PROTEIN: 1 gm   CARBOHYDRATES: 31 gm
CALCIUM: 20 mg   IRON: <1 mg   SODIUM: 3 mg
DIETARY FIBER: 4 gm

Mary Clifford is a Registered Dietitian and lives in Roanoke, Virginia.

BERRY DELICIOUS IDEAS FOR SPRING

By Bobbie Hinman

Along with the blooming of flowers and the lengthening of days, the appearance of strawberries is a sure sign that summer is near. There's no other flavor that can rival that of a sweet, juicy, fresh strawberry. And if you've ever been lucky enough to sit in a strawberry patch on a warm, sunny day and taste these luscious gems as fresh as fresh can be, then you've had an experience that can't be equaled.

Other than tasting delicious, strawberries are a rich source of fiber, vitamin C, and several other vitamins and minerals. And their versatility makes them adaptable to any meal. Use them to add a flavor boost to breakfast, add them to fruit salads, or use them to create truly "enlightened" desserts. They're great alone or in combination with other fruits.

When selecting strawberries, let color be your guide. Good color indicates ripeness. Be sure to choose berries that are firm, dry, glossy and dark red in color with fresh green caps. If you are not planning to use them right away, it's preferable to store strawberries, unwashed, in the refrigerator. At best, they will keep for 3 to 5 days. However, in most households these delicious treats don't seem to last that long.

Strawberries are well adapted to freezing, so why not stock up while they are plentiful and prices are low. For the best values, look for those familiar "U-Pick" signs along country roads and take advantage of bulk savings. Although there are several different recommended freezing methods, I prefer to wash and hull the berries, spread them on paper towels to dry and just seal them in airtight plastic freezer bags. It's so nice to defrost them "out of season" and serve them over cereal or add them to your favorite dessert or fruit salad.

If you have a sweet tooth (and who doesn't?), what better way is there to make healthy desserts than to make ones that highlight fruits as their main ingredient. And at only 45 calories per cup and no saturated fat, there's no better choice than strawberries.

Following are some of my family's favorite strawberry recipes. I hope you'll try them and enjoy them.

STRAWBERRY DESSERT CRISPS

(Serves 6)

Prepare the topping and the sauce ahead of time and assemble these cool, refreshing crisps just before serving. They're a perfect summer dessert.

6-1/2 cups sliced or quartered fresh strawberries

TOPPING:
3/4 cup rolled oats
1/4 cup oat bran
1 Tablespoon firmly-packed brown sugar
1/2 teaspoon ground cinnamon
2 teaspoons vegetable oil
2 Tablespoons apple juice

SAUCE:
1 cup plain soy yogurt
1/4 cup plus 2 Tablespoons fruit-only strawberry jam
1 teaspoon maple or rice syrup

To prepare topping: Preheat oven to 350 degrees. Lightly oil a 10 X 15-inch shallow baking pan.

In a small bowl, combine oats, oat bran, brown sugar, and cinnamon. Mix well. Add oil and apple juice. Mix until all ingredients are moistened. Spread in prepared pan.

Bake 10 to 12 minutes at 350 degrees, until lightly browned. Stir several times while baking, breaking up any large lumps with the back of a spoon.

Cool in pan and place in a covered jar or plastic bag until serving time.

To prepare sauce: Combine all sauce ingredients in a small bowl. Mix well. Chill several hours or overnight.

At serving time: Divide strawberries evenly into 6 serving bowls or tall-stemmed sherbet glasses. Spoon sauce over berries. Sprinkle with oat topping.

TOTAL CALORIES PER SERVING: 202
TOTAL FAT AS % OF DAILY VALUE: 6%   FAT: 4 gm
PROTEIN: 5 gm   CARBOHYDRATES: 38 gm
CALCIUM: 45 mg   IRON: 2 mg   SODIUM: 24 mg
DIETARY FIBER: 4 gm

VERY BERRY BREAD PUDDING

(Serves 8)

This eggless, dairyless version of an old American tradition is our very favorite. It's delicious by itself or topped with Tofu Creme Topping (see recipe on next page).

2 cups blueberries
1/4 cup liquid sweetener
1 teaspoon vanilla extract
1/4 teaspoon ground cinnamon
1/2 cup orange juice
5 cups whole wheat bread cubes
2 cups strawberries, coarsely chopped

In a medium saucepan, combine blueberries, sweetener, vanilla, cinnamon, and orange juice. Bring to a boil over medium heat. Lower heat and simmer gently 5 minutes. Remove from heat.

Gently fold in bread cubes and strawberries, mixing until all bread is moistened. Transfer to an 8-inch square baking pan. Press pudding down into pan with the back of a spoon. Cover and chill.

TOTAL CALORIES PER SERVING: 109
TOTAL FAT AS % OF DAILY VALUE: 2%   FAT: 1 gm
PROTEIN: 2 gm   CARBOHYDRATES: 24 gm
CALCIUM: 32 mg   IRON: 1 mg   SODIUM: 123 mg
DIETARY FIBER: 4 gm

STRAWBERRY SHORTCAKE

(Makes 10 biscuits)

This classic dessert is made up of shortcake biscuits, cream topping and fresh or frozen strawberries. To assemble, simply split the biscuits, spoon on topping and berries, add the top of the biscuit, and more berries if desired.

WHOLE WHEAT BISCUITS

1 cup whole wheat flour
1 cup unbleached or all-purpose flour
1/4 teaspoon salt
1 Tablespoon baking powder
1/4 cup vegetable oil
1 Tablespoon liquid sweetener
2/3 cup soy milk

Preheat oven to 450 degrees.

In a large bowl, combine flours, baking powder, and salt. Mix well.

Add oil. Mix with a fork or a pastry blender until mixture resembles coarse crumbs. Add sweetener and milk. Stir until dry ingredients are moistened.

Place dough on a floured surface and knead a few times until dough holds together in a ball. Place a sheet of wax paper over dough and roll to 1/2-inch thick. Carefully remove wax paper. Using a 3-inch biscuit cutter or a glass, cut 10 biscuits. (Scraps can be put together and rolled again.)

Place biscuits on a lightly oiled baking sheet. Bake 10 minutes at 450 degrees until bottoms of biscuits are lightly browned. Remove to a wire rack to cool. Serve warm.

TOFU CREME TOPPING

(Makes 1 Cup)

This delicious topping can be varied by adding a few drops of your favorite extract, such as almond, orange or coconut. It makes a great topping for any type of fruit.

9 ounces soft tofu
1/4 cup liquid sweetener
2 teaspoons vanilla extract

Combine all ingredients in a blender container. Blend until smooth. Chill several hours to blend flavors.

STRAWBERRY SHORTCAKE (1 biscuit, 1/10 cup tofu creme topping, and 1/4 Cup strawberries)
TOTAL CALORIES PER SHORTCAKE SERVING: 199
TOTAL FAT AS % OF DAILY VALUE: 11%   FAT: 7 gm
PROTEIN: 6 gm   CARBOHYDRATES: 30 gm
CALCIUM: 152 mg   IRON: 2 mg   SODIUM: 221 mg
DIETARY FIBER: 2 gm

STRAWBERRY FRUIT SHERBET

(Serves 2)

This sherbet is cool and refreshing and makes a great snack. Add more juice and you have a delicious drink.

1 cup frozen strawberries
1/2 ripe medium banana
1/4 cup orange juice
1 teaspoon maple or rice syrup

Combine all ingredients in a blender container. Blend until smooth, stopping blender several times to stir mixture.

TOTAL CALORIES PER SERVING: 71
TOTAL FAT AS % OF DAILY VALUE: <1%   FAT: <1 gm
PROTEIN: 1 gm   CARBOHYDRATES: 17 gm
CALCIUM: 18 mg   IRON: <1 mg   SODIUM: 2 mg
DIETARY FIBER: 2 gm

Bobbie Hinman is the author of several cookbooks including The Meatless Gourmet *and* Oat Cuisine, *published by Prima Publishing Company. These books are available in bookstores nationwide.*

BAKED TREATS

Reed Mangels, Ph.D., R.D., contributed the following recipes. During December many of us are invited to office parties, family gatherings, and other end of the year activities. The following desserts would certainly add to the festivities.

ORANGE DATE MUFFINS
(Makes 12 medium muffins)

Everyone will enjoy these delicious muffins!

1-3/4 cups whole wheat pastry flour
1 Tablespoon baking powder
1/2 teaspoon cinnamon
1 Tablespoon Ener-G Egg Replacer
1/4 cup ~~vegetable oil~~ *applesauce*
1 cup orange juice
1 teaspoon grated orange or lemon
   rind
1 cup chopped, pitted dates tossed
   with 2 teaspoons flour

Preheat oven to 400 degrees. Stir together flour, baking powder, cinnamon, and egg replacer. Beat together oil, orange juice, and grated rind, and add to flour mixture. Fold in dates. Stir only until blended.
   Fill 8-12 greased muffin cups with batter. Bake for 20 to 25 minutes at 400 degrees.

TOTAL CALORIES PER MUFFIN: 151
TOTAL FAT AS % OF DAILY VALUE: 8%   FAT: 5 gm
PROTEIN: 3 gm   CARBOHYDRATES: 26 gm
CALCIUM: 80 mg   IRON: 1 mg   SODIUM: 124 mg
DIETARY FIBER: 4 gm

SHOO FLY CAKE
(Serves 8)

A moist, sweet cake I have taken to several parties.

2-1/2 cups whole wheat pastry flour
3/4 cup brown sugar or other
   sweetener
1 teaspoon baking soda
1/2 teaspoon salt
1/3 cup soft margarine
1 cup hot water
1/2 cup molasses (not blackstrap)

Preheat oven to 350 degrees. Stir together dry ingredients. Cut in margarine until mixture resembles fine crumbs. Remove 1/3 cup of crumbs and set aside. Stir together hot water and molasses, and add to crumb mixture in bowl. Stir just until blended.
   Turn into a greased 9-inch round cake pan. Sprinkle reserved crumbs on top. Bake at 350 degrees for 25 to 30 minutes or until done.

TOTAL CALORIES PER SERVING: 288
TOTAL FAT AS % OF DAILY VALUE: 12%   FAT: 8 gm
PROTEIN: 5 gm   CARBOHYDRATES: 53 gm
CALCIUM: 88 mg   IRON: 3 mg   SODIUM: 395 mg
DIETARY FIBER: 5 gm

ANN'S HERMIT COOKIES
(Makes six dozen cookies)

These cookies will be a big hit at any party.

1/2 cup soft margarine
2 cups brown sugar or other
   sweetener
1 Tablespoon Ener-G Egg Replacer
3-1/2 cups whole wheat pastry flour
1 teaspoon baking powder
1 teaspoon baking soda
2 teaspoons cinnamon
1 teaspoon nutmeg
1/2 cup soy milk and 2 Tablespoons
   lemon juice (let sit 5 minutes so
   it sours)
1/4 cup water
1 cup chopped pecans or walnuts
1/2 cup raisins
1/2 cup dates

Preheat oven to 375 degrees. Cream margarine and sugar. Mix egg replacer, flour, baking powder, baking soda, and spices. Add to the creamed mixture alternately with sour milk. Add 1/4 cup water as needed to make cookie dough. Add nuts, raisins, and dates. Mix well.

Drop by teaspoon on greased cookie sheet. Bake at 375 degrees about 12 to 15 minutes.

TOTAL CALORIES PER COOKIE: 64
TOTAL FAT AS % OF DAILY VALUE: 3%   FAT: 2 gm
PROTEIN: 1 gm   CARBOHYDRATES: 10 gm
CALCIUM: 12 mg   IRON: <1 mg   SODIUM: 43 mg
DIETARY FIBER: 1 gm

APPLE BUTTER PULL APARTS
(Makes 16 sweet rolls)

Good for a holiday breakfast.

2 cups whole wheat pastry flour
4 teaspoons baking powder
1 Tablespoon sweetener (optional)
1/2 teaspoon salt
1/2 cup soft margarine
2/3 cup water or apple juice
1 Tablespoon margarine
1/2 cup apple butter
1/2 cup raisins
1/4 cup apple butter
1/2 teaspoon cinnamon

Preheat oven to 375 degrees. Stir together flour, baking powder, optional sweetener, and salt. Cut in margarine. Add water or apple juice, stirring just until moistened.

Knead dough on lightly floured board 8-10 strokes. Roll dough out to 16 x 18-inch rectangle. Spread with 1 Tablespoon margarine. Combine 1/2 cup apple butter and raisins, and spread over dough. Roll up evenly starting with long side. Seal seam well. Cut into sixteen 1-inch slices.

Place, cut side down, in a greased 8 x 8 x 2-inch pan. Spread with 1/4 cup apple butter and sprinkle with cinnamon. Bake at 375 degrees for 35 to 40 minutes.

TOTAL CALORIES PER SWEET ROLL: 150
TOTAL FAT AS % OF DAILY VALUE: 11%   FAT: 7 gm
PROTEIN: 2 gm   CARBOHYDRATES: 22 gm
CALCIUM: 80 mg   IRON: 1 mg   SODIUM: 270 mg
DIETARY FIBER: 2 gm

**Please note: These baked treats
are not lowfat and should
be served on special occasions only.**

CINDY'S GOURMET PIE

THIS RECIPE RECEIVED RAVE REVIEWS WHEN DEMONSTRATED AT A VRG CONFERENCE IN BALTIMORE

STRAWBERRY CREAM PIE

(Serves 8)

Guests will absolutely love this pie!

2 cups apple juice concentrate
1 cup whole wheat couscous
Dash of cinnamon
3 Tablespoons agar agar
1-1/2 cups water
2 cups fresh strawberries
1/3 cup fructose or other granular
    sweetener
1 cup soy yogurt cheese (1/2 recipe
    below)

Take one 12-ounce can of frozen apple juice and mix with 12 ounces of water. This is your concentrate. Cook couscous with 2 cups of the apple juice concentrate until liquid is absorbed. Add a dash of cinnamon. Let cool until couscous can be handled comfortably. Press into a 9-inch pie pan.

Soak agar agar in water (the leftover apple juice concentrate plus water may be used). Place agar agar and water in a saucepan and heat until agar agar is dissolved, stirring constantly. Cut strawberries in half and place in food processor; sprinkle fructose over strawberries. Blend strawberries with soy yogurt and add agar agar mixture. Pour into pie shell and chill.

TOTAL CALORIES PER SERVING: 245
TOTAL FAT AS % OF DAILY VALUE: 2%   FAT: 1 gm
PROTEIN: 6 gm   CARBOHYDRATES: 55 gm
CALCIUM: 46 mg   IRON: 1 mg   SODIUM: 72 mg
DIETARY FIBER: 5 gm

HOW TO MAKE SOY YOGURT AND SOY YOGURT "CHEESE"

(Makes about 2 cups)

Use this soy yogurt "cheese" to make the strawberry cream pie or other pies with a creamy texture that you prepare at home.

1 liter soy milk
2 Tablespoons commercial soy
    yogurt

Heat soy milk in a saucepan over medium heat until soy milk is body temperature. (Test by placing a drop on wrist; it should not feel cold or hot.) Place in a clean container (I use a glass jar) and stir in 2 Tablespoons commercial soy yogurt. Place in a warm spot to incubate for 8 hours. (I use my oven since I have a pilot light.) Any warm, draft-free place will do. Refrigerate when done.

Soy yogurt "cheese" is made by placing soy yogurt in a colander lined with muslin and allowing the excess water to drain for at least 1 hour. I have allowed my "cheese" to drain overnight, resulting in a product similar in texture to cream cheese.

(Note: I have been totally unsuccessful in culturing lite or reduced fat soy milks.)

Cindy Blum resides in Westminster, Maryland. She is a part-time organic farmer and a professional opera singer.

CAN A "REAL" BIRTHDAY CAKE BE VEGAN?

By Judith Grabski Miner

In my contacts as a founder of the *Vermont Vegetarian Society*, I find that a big concern of people who either are vegans or are considering becoming vegans is what to do about family celebrations. The solution I propose is certainly not acceptable to all, but it has worked well for me. It is one way out of the dilemma.

You have adopted a vegan diet and are enjoying your kinder, gentler lifestyle. That is, until the day that little Janey comes home and announces that she wants a "real" cake for her birthday party with her fourth-grade friends. You and she have already settled on a menu of Tofu Pups, potato chips, and apple cider. What to do about the cake?

You could take the absolutist position: "We don't eat cakes in our house. They are unhealthy -- too sweet, too much fat." The result? A crying child, who may forever associate vegetarianism with deprivation. You could offer to bake a "health-food" cake, full of whole wheat flour, tofu, and molasses, maybe with dried fruits and nuts. Again, Janey cries. "The other kids will think it's yukky! I want a real birthday cake." You reach for your *Betty Crocker Cookbook*. Is this an appropriate time to forget about vegan principles and get out the butter, eggs, and milk?

If we are just talking nutrition, maybe yes. Dr. John McDougall (a vegetarian medical lecturer) assures us that it is eating royally three times a day which does us in, not the rare feast. However, the issue of animal exploitation is not so simple to resolve. Birthday or not, when we buy eggs and dairy products we are supporting the slaughter and suffering which inevitably accompany these animal industries. We do not give a good message to Janey if we ignore cruelty for our (and her) convenience and comfort.

There is another alternative. We can make a sweet, rich, gooey, unhealthy, but *real* birthday cake using all vegan ingredients. I have made several of these cakes for family birthday celebrations. In every case, the cakes were enthusiastically eaten by militant non-vegetarians. None suspected the cakes were vegan until I told them.

If you had a favorite "butter cake" recipe in your pre-vegan days, you can probably adapt that. Standard chocolate cakes, yellow cakes, spice cakes, and so forth lend themselves well to a vegan version.

SUBSTITUTES FOR ANIMAL INGREDIENTS

The non-vegan ingredients in such cakes are usually butter, eggs, and milk. White flour may be a nutritional loser, but is not an animal product. White sugar is a close call. It is normally considered vegan, but actually it is often whitened in a process that uses animal bones. Try using other sweeteners such as rice syrup. Use vegan soy margarine in place of shortening or butter, soy milk in place of dairy milk, and Ener-G Egg Replacer (available in natural foods stores) for eggs.

If your recipe calls for buttermilk, just put one tablespoon of vinegar in your measuring cup, and add soy milk as required. Mix the Ener-G Egg Replacer with water as directed on the box, according to the number of eggs in the cake recipe. If I am making a traditional cake, where the margarine and sugar are creamed first, I add the mixed Ener-G with the last addition of liquid (while adding the flour and liquid near the end of mixing). If the recipe is a Quick-Mix (not cake mix) cake, I add the Ener-G Egg Replacer whenever the recipe says to add the eggs. I usually bake a two-layer cake in 8-inch pans, in order to have higher layers. For frosting, I use a standard buttercream (confectioners sugar) recipe, substituting soy margarine and soy milk for the animal ingredients.

Doubtless, some will be horrified at the notion of serving such a nutritional disaster to one's loved family and guests. We need to remember that no one course of action is perfect for everybody. If you have a family of committed vegetarians, everybody may actually prefer a healthy cake, or no cake at all. If, however, you are dealing with a reluctant child (or grown-up child) to whom "birthday" means cake and "cake" means only one thing, upholding your pristine principles may lead to resentment and anger. I find it life-affirming that I can produce an unmistakable real birthday cake without contributing to the exploitation of farm animals.

VEGAN SUBSTITUTIONS FOR ANIMAL PRODUCTS IN CAKES

SHORTENING OR BUTTER: Use soy margarine. Make sure there is no whey or other dairy product in the soy margarine.

DAIRY MILK: Try soy milk. This is available in your local health food store, food co-op, Asian store, and some supermarkets.

EGGS: Use Ener-G Egg Replacer. If this binder is not available in your local health food store, write to Ener-G Foods, Box 84487, Seattle, WA 84487, and ask for their mail-order catalog. (There may be other brands of egg replacer you may like better.)

BUTTERMILK: Place 1 tablespoon of vinegar in your measuring cup and add soy milk as required.

FROSTING: You can use a sugarless apple butter.

SWEETENER: Because white sugar may be whitened using animal bones, some people may not want to use it. Try a sweet juice instead of water called for in the recipe. For an even sweeter taste, use juice concentrate in the mixture. Also, try rice syrup.

On the following page are two recipes I have used successfully. If you cannot tolerate using white flour, you could probably substitute whole wheat pastry flour for some of the white flour. I have not tried this, and so cannot guarantee the results.

ALL-IN-ONE VEGAN CHOCOLATE CAKE
(Serves 8)

This is sure to be a party pleaser!

1/2 cup soft soy margarine
1 Tablespoon vinegar
1 cup soy milk
1-2/3 cups all-purpose white flour
2/3 cup unsweetened cocoa powder
1-1/2 cups sweetener
1-1/2 teaspoons baking soda
1 teaspoon salt
2 teaspoons Ener-G Egg Replacer
1/4 cup water
1 teaspoon vanilla
1/2 cup water

Put vinegar in cup and add soy milk. Preheat oven to 350 degrees. Spray 2 round layer pans, 8" x 1-1/2", with Pam, or lightly oil and flour.

Place flour, cocoa, sweetener, baking soda, and salt in large bowl of electric mixer, and mix together well with spoon. Mix Ener-G Egg Replacer and 1/4 cup water until smooth. Add margarine, vanilla, soured soy milk, 1/2 cup water, and mixed egg replacer to dry ingredients in bowl. Beat with electric mixer for 3 minutes at medium speed, scraping bowl frequently. Pour into prepared pans.

Bake for 30 to 35 minutes at 350 degrees, or until wooden toothpick inserted in center of cake comes out clean. Remove from oven and let cool in pans for 5 minutes. Remove from pans and cool on cake rack until cold. Frost as desired.

TOTAL CALORIES PER SERVING (without frosting): 250
TOTAL FAT AS % OF DAILY VALUE: 12%   FAT: 8 gm
PROTEIN: 3 gm   CARBOHYDRATES: 44 gm
CALCIUM: 20 mg   IRON: 3 mg   SODIUM: 456 mg
DIETARY FIBER: 1 gm

VANILLA CAKE
(Serves 8)

Here's a simple white cake recipe.

1/2 cup soft soy margarine
2-3/4 cups all-purpose white flour
2-1/2 teaspoons baking powder
1/2 teaspoon salt
2 teaspoons Ener-G Egg Replacer
1/4 cup water
3/4 cup soy milk
1/2 cup water
1-3/4 cups sugar
1-1/2 teaspoons vanilla extract

Spray two round 8" x 1-1/2" pans with Pam, or lightly oil and flour. Preheat oven to 375 degrees.

Combine flour, baking powder, and salt and set aside. Mix Egg Replacer and 1/4 cup water and set aside. Mix soy milk and 1/2 cup water, and set aside.

In large bowl of electric mixer, beat soy margarine until it is creamy, about a minute. Gradually add sugar until well creamed. Beat in vanilla. Add mixed dry ingredients and mixed soy milk/water alternately to creamed margarine, sugar, and vanilla, beating after each addition. Begin and end with flour mixture. (Add flour in 4 steps, liquids in three.) Add mixed Ener-G along with the third addition of liquid. Turn evenly into pans.

Bake at 375 degrees for 30 to 35 minutes, or until done (wooden pick inserted into cake comes out clean). Remove from oven and let cool on cake rack for 10 minutes. Remove from pans and let cool on rack until cold. Frost as desired.

TOTAL CALORIES PER SERVING (without frosting): 295
TOTAL FAT AS % OF DAILY VALUE: 12%   FAT: 8 gm
PROTEIN: 5 gm   CARBOHYDRATES: 54 gm
CALCIUM: 69 mg   IRON: 2 mg   SODIUM: 298 mg
DIETARY FIBER: 1 gm

SOME LIKE IT COLD

-- VEGAN FROZEN DESSERTS --

By Nanette Blanchard

Nothing is as refreshing as a frozen dessert. By making your own icy creations, you can cut down on fat as well as save money. Experimenting with homemade ices and "ice creams" is fun, and even your worst mistakes quickly disappear.

There are two basic types of ice cream makers: freezer canister models that contain a chemical coolant and "old-fashioned" ice cream makers that require salt and ice. Both machines freeze and beat air simultaneously and are available in either electric or hand-crank models.

The freezer canister-type ice cream makers produce softer "ice creams;" the mixture should already be thick before freezing for best results. Because the freezer canisters need to be put in your freezer about 24 hours before attempting to make "ice cream," this type of ice cream maker requires some pre-planning. The old-fashioned ice cream makers are generally noisier and require adding salt and ice during the freezing process. Both types of machines take about 30 minutes to freeze a batch of "ice cream."

If you don't have an ice cream maker, you can still make your own "ice cream." Chill the mixture and pour in a shallow tray or baking pan and freeze. About every twenty minutes, remove the pan from the freezer and stir the mixture. Return to freezer and continue this process until entirely frozen.

To make perfect "ice cream" every time, make sure to chill all your ingredients well before mixing and freezing. Remember that cold numbs taste buds, and so the mixture will taste sweeter and more intense before freezing.

Add chopped nuts, cereal, or whole pieces of fruit near the end of the freezing process or they will sink to the bottom of the container and not get incorporated into the mixture. For a firmer textured "ice cream," let the frozen mixture "ripen" in a covered container for an hour in the freezer before serving. If the frozen mixture is too hard to scoop, put it in the refrigerator for about 20 minutes to soften enough to remove from container.

CHERRY ICE MILK
(Makes about 3-1/2 cups)

This is a simple yet delicious frozen dessert. It is an attractive color and the intense flavor of the cherries stands up well to freezing.

3 cups pitted fresh or frozen sweet
    cherries
1/4 cup unsweetened apple juice
1 cup lite soy milk
1 teaspoon vanilla extract

Stir together cherries and apple juice in a bowl. Let stand for several hours at room temperature, stirring occasionally. Purée cherry and apple juice mixture until smooth in a food processor or blender. Add soy milk and vanilla extract and process until mixed. Chill mixture. Freeze in an ice cream maker according to manufacturer's instructions.

TOTAL CALORIES PER HALF CUP SERVING: 64
TOTAL FAT AS % OF DAILY VALUE: 2%   FAT: 1 gm
PROTEIN: 1 gm   CARBOHYDRATES: 14 gm
CALCIUM: 21 mg   IRON: <1 mg   SODIUM: 14 mg
DIETARY FIBER: 1 gm

PINEAPPLE FROZEN
SOY YOGURT
(Makes 4 cups)

This creamy dessert is delicious topped with a mixture of sliced oranges and strawberries. For a tropical treat, top with fresh coconut and sliced bananas.

One 20-ounce can unsweetened
    crushed pineapple in its own juice
Two 6-ounce containers vanilla low-
    fat soy yogurt (fruit juice
    sweetened)
1/2 teaspoon vanilla extract

Mix ingredients together well and chill. Freeze in ice cream maker according to manufacturer's instructions. Let mixture "ripen" in the freezer in a covered container for an hour before serving.

TOTAL CALORIES PER HALF CUP SERVING: 62
TOTAL FAT AS % OF DAILY VALUE: <1%   FAT: <1 gm
PROTEIN: 1 gm   CARBOHYDRATES: 13 gm
CALCIUM: 16 mg   IRON: 1 mg   SODIUM: 12 mg
DIETARY FIBER: 1 gm

BANANA-RASPBERRY
"ICE CREAM"
(Makes about 3-1/2 cups)

Mashed bananas add an appealing texture and creaminess to frozen desserts. Garnish this ice cream with additional raspberries.

4 bananas
3/4 cup lite soy milk
1/2 cup frozen raspberries, thawed
    and drained
1/4 cup unsweetened apple juice

Peel and slice bananas and purée with remaining ingredients in a food processor. Freeze in ice cream maker according to manufacturer's instructions.

TOTAL CALORIES PER HALF CUP SERVING: 71
TOTAL FAT AS % OF DAILY VALUE: 2%   FAT: 1 gm
PROTEIN: 1 gm   CARBOHYDRATES: 19 gm
CALCIUM: 15 mg   IRON: <1 mg   SODIUM: 12 mg
DIETARY FIBER: 2 gm

Editor's note: Another terrific way to make vegan frozen desserts is to take fresh fruit and cut it up into small pieces and freeze it. Once frozen, put the fruit through a peanut butter maker, and the result is creamy and delicious.

HONEYDEW ICE
(Makes about 4-1/2 cups)

This simple, healthful treat is refreshing and can be prepared with a variety of melons. Try substituting watermelon for the honeydew melon. Garnish bowls with lime slices.

4 cups peeled, seeded, and cubed
   honeydew melon
2 Tablespoons fresh lime juice
1 teaspoon grated lime zest

Put ingredients in a food processor with steel blade or blender and process until puréed. Freeze in an ice cream maker according to manufacturer's instructions. Let mixture "ripen" in the freezer in a covered container for an hour before serving.

TOTAL CALORIES PER HALF CUP SERVING: 27
TOTAL FAT AS % OF DAILY VALUE: <1%   FAT: <1 gm
PROTEIN: <1 gm   CARBOHYDRATES: 7 gm
CALCIUM: 55 mg   IRON: <1 mg   SODIUM: 8 mg
DIETARY FIBER: 1 gm

ORANGE SHERBET
(Makes about 3-1/2 cups)

This lowfat sherbet has a fresh orange flavor and scent. For an attractive presentation, serve in a hollowed-out orange half. When squeezing the oranges, try to include some pulp.

1-1/2 cups fresh orange juice (about
   5 oranges)
1 Tablespoon grated orange zest
1-1/2 cups lite soy milk
1/4 cup unsweetened orange juice
   concentrate

Combine all ingredients and chill. Freeze in ice cream maker according to manufacturer's directions. Let mixture "ripen" in the freezer in a covered container for an hour before serving.

TOTAL CALORIES PER HALF CUP SERVING: 60
TOTAL FAT AS % OF DAILY VALUE: <1%   FAT: <1gm
PROTEIN: 1 gm   CARBOHYDRATES: 13 gm
CALCIUM: 28 mg   IRON: <1 mg   SODIUM: 21 mg
DIETARY FIBER: 1 gm

FROZEN BLUEBERRY TOFU
(Makes 4 cups)

Puréeing soft tofu with fruit makes a quick and simple frozen dessert. If desired, extra whole blueberries can be added about 15 minutes after putting mixture in ice cream maker.

4 cups fresh or frozen blueberries,
   thawed
1/4 cup lite soy milk
1/2 cup unsweetened apple juice
1 teaspoon vanilla extract
1/2 pound soft tofu

Purée all ingredients in a food processor or blender until smooth. Freeze in ice cream maker according to manufacturer's instructions.

TOTAL CALORIES PER HALF CUP SERVING: 74
TOTAL FAT AS % OF DAILY VALUE: 3%   FAT: 2 gm
PROTEIN: 3 gm   CARBOHYDRATES: 13 gm
CALCIUM: 38 mg   IRON: 2 mg   SODIUM: 10 mg
DIETARY FIBER: 2 gm

Nanette J. Blanchard is the author of a vegetarian Christmas cookbook published in 1995. She resides in Durango, Colorado.

ONLINE RESOURCES FOR VEGETARIANS

By Bobbi Pasternak
<NurseBobbi@aol.com>
(Copyright Bobbi Pasternak)

While vegetarians are not regarded with as much suspicion as we were in the past, it is not unusual for us to find ourselves feeling isolated. We may be the only vegetarian in the family or the community or at work. I was the only vegetarian I knew for seven years. Then I discovered cyberspace, that place between you and whoever you communicate with via telecommunications. To participate, all you need is a computer, a modem, a telephone line, and the appropriate software. There's some money involved too, but connecting to the Information Highway is becoming less costly.

There are abundant resources available online for vegetarians. This article provides a sampling of those currently available. The areas discussed will be commercial online services, the Internet, bulletin board systems, and electronic mail.

Please bear in mind that things change quickly in the online world. Electronic mailing lists come and go. Resources change addresses. If you have a problem accessing a resource listed in this article, please let me know so that I can let you know its status or check on it and make a correction in the next revision. On WWW, the latest version of this article is always available at http://www.clark.net/pub/bobbi/online.html

COMMERCIAL ONLINE SERVICES

Commercial online services include America Online (AOL), CompuServe (CIS), Delphi, Genie, eWorld, Microsoft Network (MSN), and Prodigy. Their pricing structures and available services vary. All services offer electronic mail, enabling subscribers to exchange e-mail messages within the service and with people who have an Internet e-mail address. Special interest areas contain message boards where members may post messages, read and respond. Real time conferencing or "chat" allows users to carry on "conversations" with others online at the same time. Real time conferences may be informal gatherings or formal meetings. A feature available on all services except Prodigy is the file library which allows users to place (upload) or retrieve (download) text files and software.

In deciding which service is right for you, consider the time of day you will be online, how much time you will be online, what services you will use, and your comfort level with the service's interface. The best way to determine all of this is to call the service and ask a lot of questions. If it sounds good, find out about free or reduced rate trials, go online, and see how you like it. Once you're on a service, here's what you'll find available for vegetarians.

Vegetarians on **America Online** can be found in several places, but most of AOL's vegetarian activity is centered in the Cooking Club's "Vegetarians Online" area. To get to there, use AOL Keyword: VEGAN. Vegetarians Online contains the following areas:

- Information On Vegetarian Living -- basic info for beginners
- Vegetarian Dialogue - a message base with a wide variety of topics
- Vegetarian Library -- numerous vegetarian files
- Vegetarian Sites on World Wide Web -- links to the best veggie web sites
- Vegetarian and Special Diets Recipes -- recipe message base

There is a weekly live chat for vegetarians in the Cooking Club Kitchen conference room on Wednesdays at 9:00 p.m. Eastern time. To get to the chat, use Keyword: Cookclub, then choose Kitchen Conference Room.

America Online's Pet Care Forum Message Center has a section dedicated to discussion of Animals and Society. In this section, several folders deal with animal rights and animal welfare topics.

On **CompuServe**, the Vegetarian Forum is home to a core of friendly and supportive members who came to the new forum from their former gathering place in Cooks Online Forum's Vegetarian section. (That section closed with the opening of the new forum.) To get there, GO VEGETARIAN. CIS is international in scope and there are vegetarians from Germany and the UK who participate in the forum on a regular basis. On CIS, the message sections and libraries are searchable by keywords, making it easier to find exactly what you're looking for.

The Vegetarian Forum includes a variety of message and library sections dedicated to vegetarian topics as well as a chat area. In addition to the sections dedicated to various vegetarian foods, there are sections titled Nutrition & Health, Vegetarian Children, The New Vegetarian, Outreach & Resources, Lifestyles, VRG (Vegetarian Resource Group) Online, Vegetarian Times Magazine, and In Print & On Disk. Monthly conferences are held at noon Eastern Standard Time (in the US) on the first Sunday of each month.

Delphi has at least two areas of potential interest for vegetarians: Custom Forum 112, Animal Rights and Vegetarian Living, and Custom Forum 39, Hearth and Home. These areas offer message boards, file libraries, and have live chat capabilities. If you plan on spending time online during Monday through Friday business hours, though, beware of the significant prime time surcharges.

Apple's **eWorld** boasts "The Natural Connection" with many features for the health-conscious public. A holistic "mini-mall" offers catalog shopping and classified advertising. The Holistic Resource Center contains directories of holistic product and service providers, a Reference Library, and publications. There are discussion areas and real-time conferences. The Natural Connection includes a special Institutes and Organizations area where vegetarian and health-related organizations can publish their newsletters and hold meetings. Currently, eWorld is only available to Mac users, but DOS and Windows software is planned.

GEnie's Food and Wine Roundtable has two vegetarian areas with messaging, file libraries and real-time conferences. One is a general vegetarian area, and the other is specifically for individuals following the McDougall Plan.

Microsoft Network is available to individuals running Windows95. A Vegetarian sub-Forum is included in What's Cooking... Online! Forum. The Vegetarian subForum currently includes the following sections:

- Chatter -- general introductions and discussion
- Organizations & Events -- Information about international, national, and local groups and events
- Health & Nutrition
- Issues & Information
- Vegetarian Journal -- excerpt files of the bi-monthly Vegetarian Journal and the quarterly Foodservice Update, both published by The Vegetarian Resource Group
- Vegetarian Food & Cooking Discussion
- Vegetarian Recipes
- Vegetarian Society -- files from the Vegetarian Society of the United Kingdom

The forum will be restructured according to the needs and interests of its membership. MSN's structure allows for the different sections to contain both messages and file downloads.

MSN's Vegetarian Chats will take place in the What's Cooking...Online! chat room. Upcoming chats are posted in the Chatter section of the subforum. To find the Vegetarian subForum, GO VEGETARIAN.

Prodigy boasts a friendly and active message board section for vegetarians. The Vegetarian section of the Food Bulletin Board is hosted by Member Reps Cath and Rona who set the tone and provide an abundance of helpful information and recipes. Prodigy has added live chat capability, USENET newsgroups and a World Wide Web browser in the past year.

THE INTERNET

The Internet has long been accessible from universities, businesses, government agencies and military sites. There has recently been a boom in usage by individuals from their home PCs due to the availability of "dial-up" services which connect your home PC via modem to the service's mainframe computer on the Internet. The commercial online services have been adding Internet access to their services. Features and the fees for using them vary from service to service, so call them for current information.

To receive an e-mail containing information about providers of dial-up Internet access, send an e-mail to: info-deli-server @netcom.com The message should include this line and nothing else: send PDIAL

The Internet's answer to message boards is USENET, consisting of thousands of special interest newsgroups where participants can read and post messages. Of interest to vegetarians are rec.food.veg and its spin-off rec.food.veg.cooking. The latter is restricted

to discussion of cooking only, but the former is open to any topic related to vegetarianism and discussion there is often heated. Another newsgroup alt.food.fat-free is for discussion of very low fat diets (less than 15% calories from fat), generally vegetarian and following the writings of Drs. Dean Ornish or John Mc-Dougall. Alt.food.low-fat has just been introduced. It is for discussion of diets which derive less than 30% calories from fat. Vegetarian topics are frequently addressed in sci.med.nutrition, the general nutrition newsgroup as well. For discussions about animal rights, check the newsgroup talk.politics.animals. USENET newsgroups can often be accessed via private Bulletin Board Services (BBS) and are also available through most commercial services.

On the Internet, real time chat occurs in International Relay Chat or IRC. The hundreds of channels are each devoted to a particular topic. One evening I found myself on channel #Veggies, teaching a woman in the midwest how to make the perfect pot of brown rice.

Several Internet features offer users access to information and files: file transfer protocol (ftp), Gopher, and World Wide Web (WWW). File transfer protocol allows you to visit another computer and retrieve files. Some examples of ftp sites with vegetarian documents and the subdirectories in which the documents are found are listed below. Commercial services providing ftp access are CompuServe, Delphi, and America Online.

ftp.informatik.uni-hamburg.de: /pub/doc/ vegetarian. This site, at the University of Hamburg, Germany, houses the collection of materials available electronically fromThe Vegetarian Resource Group. In addition to the text files, the DOS compatible "Vegetarian Game" is available here. Also available is the World Guide to Vegetarianism. Compiled by Internet vegetarians all over the world, the guide geographically lists vegetarian restaurants, vegetarian-friendly rest-aurants, natural foods stores and vegetarian organizations. The rec.food.veg newsgroup's FAQ (frequently asked questions file) is also here, providing the information most commonly requested in that newsgroup.

ftp.geod.emr.ca.:/pub/doc/Vegetarian/ Articles/and /pub/doc/Vegetarian/Recipes/. This site has the VRG material and also boasts thousands of vegetarian and vegan recipes.

sunsite.unc.edu: /pub/academic/ medi-cine/alternative-healthcare contains health articles from the USENET newsgroups.

Gopher is a menu based system that allows you to search by topic. One gopher site with vegetarian information is gopher.geod.emr.ca. Look under the section titled "Vegetarian Info." This site houses the same files as the ftp site ftp.geod.emr.ca. Gopher gives you a different way to look for them.

World Wide Web (WWW or the Web) creates links between many of the Internet's resources. An exciting Web resource for vegetarians, the Vegetarian Pages, has been developed by Geraint "Gedge" Edwards. To get to the Vegetarian Pages, go to http:// www.veg.org/veg. This takes you to the Vegetarian Pages and from there, you can choose a number of directions. There is information about vegetarian electronic mailing lists and USENET newsgroups. You can peruse the World Guide to Vegetar-ianism at your leisure. You can be taken directly to the vegetarian ftp sites where you can view, save or print the documents while online. The Vegetarian Pages will link you with information from the Vegetarian Society of the UK, Veggies Unite!, the Animal Rights Resource Site (ARRS), and others. You can look up recipes, environmental articles, nutritional data, and more. WWW tech-nology is still under development, so if you

find something doesn't work, don't be discouraged. Just go back and try again later.

To access the home page of the Vegetarian Resource Group, the address is: http://envirolink. org/arrs/VRG/home.html This site contains all of the VRG's electronically available material.

To access the Animal Rights Resource Site (ARRS) directly, use this address: http:// envirolink.org/arrs/index.html

For a searchable database of vegetarian recipes, visit Veggies Unite! at: http://www. honors.indiana.edu/~veggie/recipes.cgi Another searchable recipe database is avail-able at the FATFREE Mailing List Archives at http://www.fatfree.com/ This site offers a searchable database of very low fat vegetarian recipes from the popular email list.

ELECTRONIC MAIL

Whether you're on the Internet or on a commercial service, you will have electronic mail. There are also e-mail services which give you that capability without allowing access to the other features of the Internet. All commercial services now have Internet e-mail gateways, allowing e-mail to go between services or anywhere else on the 'Net. Cost involved in sending and receiving e-mail will vary, as will the ease with which you can manage your mail.

Even if e-mail is your only link to the information highway, you still have a number of options for exchanging information with other vegetarians and receiving vegetarian resources. The most popular of these is the electronic mailing list. A list is much like a message board except that it comes to you via e-mail and its use is restricted to its subscribers. Subscribers post messages, sending them to a central computer which then distributes the messages to all subscribers. Upon receiving a message, you can read it and reply if you like. Usually, each message is sent to each subscriber as it is received at the central computer, but this can become overwhelming on a busy list with 50 or more messages daily. An option is the Digest. When you subscribe to the digest format of a list, you receive one mailing per day which contains the previous day's posts. I highly recommend the digest format for those first subscribing to a list. The following are electronic mailing lists of interest to vegetarians with directions for subscribing to the list in digest form. Do not include the <>'s when placing your name in the space indicated.

VEGLIFE is for general vegetarian discussion. To subscribe, address e-mail to: listserv@vtvm1.bitnet The message should read: sub veglife <your first & last name> set veglife digest This is an alternate email address for subscribing to VEGLIFE: listserv@vtvm1.cc.vt.edu

VEGGIE is also a general list. It is a manually run list, so there will be a person reading your message rather than a computer. Mail your subscription request to: veggie-request@maths.bath.ac.uk In the message, explain briefly that you'd like to subscribe to the list in its digest form. The Veggie digest appears every few days rather than daily.

VEGAN-L is a list for vegans and aspiring vegans. To subscribe, address e-mail to: listserv@templevm.bitnet The message should read: sub vegan-l <your first & last name> set vegan-l digest An alternate email address for VEGAN-L is: listserv@vm.temple.edu

FATFREE is a list for those interested in a very low fat vegetarian diet according to the guidelines of Drs. Dean Ornish or John McDougall. To subscribe, send e-mail to: fatfree-request@fatfree.com. The Subject should read: SUBSCRIBE

VEGFOOD offers detailed discussion on vegetarian food preparation. According to Darrell A. Early, the list will also include, to a minor degree, discussion of cookbooks, cookware, spices, wines/spirits and so forth. There will be no discussion of ethical issues. To subscribe, send email to: listproc@cadserv.cadlab.vt.edu The message should read: sub vegfood <your full name>

Two e-mail lists are available for those interested in discussion or information about animal rights issues. AR-TALK is a discussion list and AR-NEWS is a news wire. (With AR-NEWS, you receive the e-mail but can not contribute posts to the list. To subscribe to AR-TALK, send e-mail to ar-talk-request@cygnus.com. The message should read: sub ar-talk <your email address> For AR NEWS, follow the same directions, but substitute "news" for "talk".

A variety of vegetarian e-mail lists have recently been launched covering such topics as vegetarian singles, vegetarian parents, and vegetarianism and religion. In addition, regional e-mailing lists are being developed all over the United States. For information on these lists, write the Vegetarian Resource Center at vrc@tiac.com.

You can obtain files by e-mail by using either a mail server or an archive server. One example of each follows.

The World Guide to Vegetarianism and the rec.food.veg FAQ file may be obtained by sending e-mail to: mail-server@rtfm.mit.edu Include any of the following lines (and nothing but those lines) in the message:

    send usenet/news.answers/vegetarian/guide/canada1

    send usenet/news.answers/vegetarian/guide/canada2

    send usenet/news.answers/vegetarian/guide/california1

    send usenet/news.answers/vegetarian/guide/california2

    send usenet/news.answers/vegetarian/guide/california3

    send usenet/news.answers/vegetarian/guide/usa1

    send usenet/news.answers/vegetarian/guide/usa2

    send usenet/news.answers/vegetarian/guide/usa3

    send usenet/news.answers/vegetarian/guide/usa4

    send usenet/news.answers/vegetarian/guide/usa5

    send usenet/news.answers/vegetarian/guide/europe1

    send usenet/news.answers/vegetarian/guide/europe2

    send usenet/news.answers/vegetarian/guide/other1

    send usenet/news.answers/vegetarian/guide/other2

    send usenet/news.answers/vegetarian/faq

The FatFree mailing list has an extensive recipe archive, available via archive server for those who can not access it by ftp or WWW. To get started, send a message to: archive-server@halcyon.com The message should read: help You will then get information for further use of the archive server. Using it will allow you to receive a listing of the available recipes then to request the recipes you want.

If e-mail is your only access to the Internet, there are ways in which you can access World Wide Web pages and Gopher sites via e-mail. To request a WWW page, you must know the exact name of the WWW page you want. Send an e-mail to listproc@ www0.cern.ch. In the body of your message, type the name of the Web page you want. For example, to retrieve the Vegetarian Pages' home page, the body of the message should read: http://www.veg.org/veg.

To learn more about accessing Gopher databases via e-mail, send an e-mail message to gopher@nips.ac.jp and it will send you the GopherMail home page with further instructions.

If you are interested in the Vegetarian Resource Group's electronically available material but have no access to file libraries or ftp, the VRG will send material via e-mail. For a list of available material, write to TheVRG@aol.com.

BULLETIN BOARD SYSTEMS

A bulletin board system (BBS) operates in a similar fashion to a commercial online service, but on a smaller scale. A BBS is generally local. While it could be accessed outside the local calling area, such usage would incur long distance phone charges for those outside the local dialing area. Sometimes a BBS is free and sometimes a membership fee is required. This information will be provided when you first sign on. A few bulletin board systems with areas of interest to vegetarians are listed below.

Perry Lowell (rollerskate@delphi.com) runs the BBS, SKATEboard (Fidonet 1:333/359, Echonet 50:5016/359, or (508) 788-1603). SKATEboard has specialty areas for vegetarians and vegans and can also be used to access USENET newsgroups of interest as well as Fidonet and Echonet echoes in which vegetarians participate. Perry says to look for Fidonet echoes INTERCOOK, GOURMET, COOKING and HOME_COOKING and Echonet's RECIPE_CORNER. For further information, contact Perry Lowell.

SALATA BBS is operated in Redondo Beach, CA. The phone number is 1-310-543-0439 and the telecomm parameters are 8N1. Salata supports connections up to 14,400 bps (V.32bis). It contains an online database of vegan recipes and many vegetarian/vegan files are available for downloading. Access to Fidonet and USENET conferences are available as is e-mail. All services are free of charge. For further information, send e-mail to Karen Mintzias <km@salata.com>.

HealthMate Wellness System BBS is operated by the San Diego Knowledge Network. The modem phone number is 619-745-HLTH and the voice number is 619-739-1912. HealthMate supports connections up to 14,400 bps. It offers conferences, e-mail and a database of text and software files covering a broad range of health and fitness topics. Additionally there's a Buyer's Club and classified section. There is no fee for the basic membership. For information via e-mail, contact Lorraine Harris <sdknownet@aol.com>.

ONLINE ETIQUETTE

No matter what method you use for tele-communications, there are some basic rules of behavior to keep in mind. When they are followed, cyberspace is a more pleasant place. Every commercial service, BBS and dial-up Internet provider has terms of service governing online behavior. Mailing lists will send you rules for posting. Read them and abide by them. It's best to read a message board, list or newsgroup for awhile prior to posting your first message. This will help prevent potentially embarrassing situations. Remember that your words are all others will see of you. There is no body language and no vocal intonation to help explain your meaning. If you are unsure about posting something, don't do it. Never post anything you would mind seeing come back at you next week or in the next millennium. Do not publicly post private e-mail you have received without the author's permission. Do treat others with respect and be non-judgmental. When you disagree with someone, be sure to respond in a manner that does not attack the person. If you're presenting something as fact rather than your opinion, have the resources to support your statements. There are those online who seem to exist only to annoy everyone else -- they are best ignored. Most people online exhibit behavior consistent with these suggestions.

VEGETARIAN KIDS ONLINE

Vegetarian teens and preteens are often encountered online. AOL's Vegetarians Online has a folder specifically intended for vegetarian kids' input, located in the Vegetarian Dialogue section. Vegetarian Teens now have their own section in CIS Vegetarian Forum.

There is a folder in AOL's Kids Online (KO) in the Clubs and Hobbies section called "Mission: Animal Rights". It's hosted by a pre-teen named Mike, and topics include both animal rights/animal welfare and vegetarianism in general. Mike also hosts another folder with the same title on eWorld.

RESOURCES
Phone numbers for the commercial online services are:

America Online	800-827-6364
CompuServe	800-848-8199
Delphi	800-695-4005
GEnie	800-638-9636
Microsoft Network	800-386-5550
Prodigy	800-776-3449
eWorld	800-775-4556

To learn more about the Internet, the following books are recommended.

The Whole Internet User's Guide and Catalog, Ed Krol, O'Reilly and Associates, Inc., 1992. ISBN: 1-56592-025-2

The Internet Guide for New Users, Daniel P. Dern, McGraw-Hill, Inc., 1994. ISBN: 0-07-016511-4 (PBK)

If you are online and having a problem finding your way around, I'd be glad to help you or send you to someone else who can. You can contact me via e-mail at the following addresses:

America Online:	NurseBobbi
Microsoft Network:	Bobbi_Dave
CompuServe:	70302,3442
Internet:	NurseBobbi@aol.com OR bobbi@clark.net

Those on Prodigy, Delphi, eWorld, or GEnie may write to me at an Internet address.

This article is published by Bobbi Pasternak and the Vegetarian Resource Group and may be freely distributed for non-commercial purposes, provided it is not altered.

The Vegetarian Resource Group, P.O. Box 1463, Baltimore, MD 21203 Phone: (410) 366-8343, Fax: (410) 366-8804, E-mail: TheVRG@aol.com

WHAT IS THE VEGETARIAN RESOURCE GROUP?
Our health professionals, activists, and educators work with businesses and individuals to bring about healthy changes in your school, workplace, and community. Registered dietitians and physicians aid in the development of nutrition-related publications and answer member and media questions about vegetarian diets. The Vegetarian Resource Group is a non-profit organization. Financial support comes primarily from memberships, contributions, and book sales.

Bobbi Pasternak is a nurse in Virginia and volunteers to put materials from The Vegetarian Resource Group on the Internet.

HOW MANY VEGETARIANS ARE THERE?
THE VEGETARIAN RESOURCE GROUP ASKS IN A 1994 NATIONAL ROPER POLL

By Charles Stahler

How many vegetarians are there in the United States? After "What do I eat?", this is one of the questions most commonly asked of The Vegetarian Resource Group.

At least once a day, a reporter, a student doing a paper, a market researcher, or a curious member calls VRG to ask us the number of vegetarians living in the United States. Americans (and we suspect also Canadians and other people in western cultures) worship statistics and exactness. Even though there will be one answer this week and another answer next week, people like specifics.

However, the answer to "How many vegetarians are there?" has to be given in general terms. We can relate the different pieces of information known and then the answer can be interpreted according to the specific need(s) of the person inquiring.

Unfortunately, statements are often taken out of context and repeated until they become truth. Because one person may be allergic to a certain food, people will then expand that to the idea that no one should eat that food. We caution readers not to do this. Please understand that in science and life, though we generalize to give us guidance, one has to look at the details of each situation, and then make a judgment as to what the answer is under those circumstances.

The attitude towards vegetarianism in the last twenty years has certainly changed. In the 1970's and early 1980's when we did outreach booths, often people would ask us, "Why be a vegetarian?"

We almost never hear that question now. Instead, people come by and say, "I wish I could do that." They are looking for information on how to eat more vegetarian meals. Working at a booth today, we often have pleasant conversations with lawyers, bankers, C.P.A.s, construction workers, or men and women in motorcycle jackets with tattoos.

Proof of this trend toward vegetarianism can be found in the grocery store. Where Heinz used to be the only vegetarian baked beans available, now there are several varieties on the shelf, from Campbell's to store brands. As we previously informed our readers, Archer Daniels Midland and Green Giant (Pillsbury) has introduced the vegetarian (vegan) Harvest burger in supermarkets across the country this year. Where before you couldn't find Mexican food, cakes, or breads without lard, almost all supermarkets now have choices which are free of animal ingredients. If you think back a few years, you will realize the magnitude of this change.

For those readers over age 30, could you imagine eating yogurt as a child? Did you even know what it was? Though probably not one of their best sellers, most stores in major metropolitan areas also carry tofu today. And some supermarkets even have their own brand of dairy-free ice cream.

Businesses will supply products which customers buy. The changes that have been happening are due to the public's demand for more vegetarian foods. According to a 1991 Gallup Poll conducted for the National Restaurant Association, about twenty percent of the population looks for a restaurant with vegetarian items when they eat out. About one-third of the public would order non-meat items if they were listed on the menu. This twenty to thirty percent of people interested in eating vegetarian food is fueling businesses' need to add vegetarian items to their offerings. Any company thinking about introducing new products will need to look at this population.

For specialty products and options in restaurants and supermarkets, we can see there is a pretty hefty customer base. This is probably why so many businesses are jumping on the bandwagon to add meatless selections. On the other hand, this number is still far from the majority. That is why a fast food place may be hesitant to add a vegetarian burger, or why a centerpiece of an advertising campaign may still not be vegetarian oriented.

When making a marketing decision, a business will have to decide whether this vegetarian-oriented population is their customer base and if they want their business. If the answer is yes, they will cater to them. If the answer is no, they may make different decisions. In a similar fashion, though most of the population still eats animal products, many natural foods stores decline to carry meat because the purchase of meat does not fit into the buying habits of most of their customers.

In a 1977-1978 United States Department of Agriculture Nationwide Food Consumption Survey, of 37,135 people surveyed, 1.2% answered yes to "Are you a vegetarian?" However some of these people also reported eating flesh during the three days on which dietary information was obtained.

This twenty to thirty percent of the population interested in vegetarian foods is consistent with the findings of different polls. For example, in a Gallup Poll done for *Hippocrates*

magazine in 1989, when asked to describe themselves, about 34% of people said they were a "chicken and broccoli type;" 12% "brown rice and vegetables type;" and 10% "pasta and salad type." Only 35% said they were "meat and potatoes type." Five percent were "burgers and fries type," while 3% were "pizza and soda type."

If you add the brown rice and vegetables people with the pasta and salad folks, about 22% would actually be looking for vegetarian items. This is close to the 20% figure in The National Restaurant Association Poll. If you note that only 35% were meat and potatoes people, it is no wonder food companies are adding so many new "light" options.

Yet on the other hand, the majority of these people with an interest in vegetarianism are still consuming mostly animal-based diets. So there are numerous markets for businesses. They need to figure out which market to concentrate on, and how they will reach it. For enterprising businesses, there is no question that there is money to be made by marketing vegetarian products if done in the right way to reach that audience.

BEYOND MARKETING

For marketing purposes, as explained above, there is poll information available about the number of vegetarian-interested people. But The Vegetarian Resource Group wanted to know how many actual vegetarians are out there. This will give us a baseline to follow trends over the next hundred years and more. Past polls have given some indication, but because of the way the questions were asked, we didn't have an accurate answer.

Most polls have asked people whether they consider themselves vegetarian. In a 1977-1978 United States Department of Agriculture Nationwide Food Consumption Survey, of 37,135 people surveyed, 1.2% answered yes to "Are you a vegetarian?" However some of these people also reported eating flesh during the three days on which dietary information was obtained. Recent answers from other sources have been around three to five percent or above. *Vegetarian Times* magazine reported 7%, or 12.4 million vegetarians, after asking people, "Do you consider yourself a vegetarian?"

These polls about the trends of the number of people being vegetarian are important because they indicate that there is currently a very positive image about vegetarianism. More and more people want to be called a vegetarian. The drawback in these types of polls is leaving it to the respondents to define vegetarian. So the answer is not really indicative of the people who do not eat meat, fish, or fowl and are actually vegetarian.

In one major poll, a question started, "Most people eat quite a lot of meat. But some people are vegetarian..." Another question stated, "During the 1960's and 1970's many young people got involved with alternative lifestyles and activities. Regarding the following list, which activities did you participate in?" Among the answers were smoked marijuana, dressed like a hippie, or became a vegetarian. So another problem associated with past polls was how the question was asked. Certainly there was a bias.

The Vegetarian Resource Group wanted to find out the number of people in the country who are vegetarians -- that is, do not eat meat, fish, and fowl.

POLL RESULTS

Marketing purposes aside, The Vegetarian Resource Group wanted to find out the number of people in the country who are vegetarians -- that is, do not eat meat, fish, and fowl. We already have an idea of the number of people who consider themselves vegetarians. In our Roper Poll question, we asked, "Please call off the items on this list, if any, that you

never eat. Meat. Poultry. Fish/Seafood. Dairy Products. Eggs. Honey. Eat Them All. Don't Know."

Please note that the key word is *never*. Our numbers could be very different if we omitted the word never. Instead, our results were mostly as we suspected.

The most surprising aspect of our survey is that up to one half million people in the country *may* be vegan. That is, they never eat meat, fish, fowl, milk, dairy, or eggs. It is astounding that this number could be so high in our animal-product-based society with daily messages to eat some type of animal product.

The most surprising aspect of our survey is that up to one half million people in the country may be vegan.

Please note that because this is a poll, and we could not ask every person in the country, we are not saying there are 500,000 vegans. We can have some confidence in saying there are between negligible vegans and 700,000 vegans in the country. Rather than a specific number, what the poll tells us is that though vegans are not yet a major percentage of the country's population, there is quite an interest in veganism. The Vegetarian Resource Group has some proof of this since we have sold over 40,000 copies of our *Simply Vegan* book. However, remember these figures are not for marketing purposes, as many more people may have a vegan-style diet, but may not be strict vegans.

We can be 95% sure that .3% to 1% of the population is vegetarian. That is, they **never** eat meat, fish or fowl. This is much lower than the three to seven percent who consider themselves vegetarians, or the 20 - 30% who buy vegetarian products, but still a pretty high number, which translates into approximately one half million to two million vegetarians, as we suspected. Taking into account other polls we have looked at, we believe this figure as reflective of the number of people who *never* eat meat, fish, and fowl, and is probably accurate.

We can be 95% sure that .3% to 1% of the population is vegetarian.

Though the number of vegans as a percentage of vegetarians seems potentially high, we have been warned against using the statistic in this way. Because of the numbers we are dealing with, at this time we would probably have to do a prohibitively expensive poll to really find out that information. However, our educated guess is that if you only define vegetarians as people who **never** eat meat, fish, and fowl, and vegans as individuals who **never** eat meat, fish, fowl, dairy, or eggs, there could be a high percentage of vegans in there (5% - 20%), since most people don't fall into the *never* category.

About 6% of the population never eats red meat; 3% never eat poultry; 3% never eat dairy products; 4% never eat eggs; and 4% never eat fish/seafood. As would be expected, the figures for not eating these foods among "influential" people are greater. (Influential people being politically and/or socially active.) For example, while 6% of the general population never eat red meat, 10% of "influential" people never eat

red meat. We suspect the "influential" category being a higher percentage would also pertain to vegan versus vegetarians. Among the leaders in the vegetarian movement we know, there is a higher number of vegans versus what might be in the general vegetarian population.

As far as numbers for never eating red meat, the percentages were pretty close between male and female, and black and white. The biggest difference was between the South (4%) and The West (10%); Conservatives (5%) and Liberals (9%).

However, the difference is not as great as you may think. You can't assume just because a person is vegetarian-oriented they will have a certain political ideology.

This Roper poll was a nationwide cross section of 1,978 men and women 18 years old or over. Individuals were interviewed face-to-face in respondents' homes. The sample interviewed in this study is a representative sample of the population of the Continental United States, age 18 and up -- exclusive of institutionalized segments of the population (Army camps, nursing homes, prisons, etc.). Validations were conducted by telephone on all interviewers' work.

VEGETARIAN RESOURCE GROUP 1994 ROPER POLL STATISTICS

Never Eat:	TOTAL	MALE	FEMALE	BLACK	INFLUENTIAL
Meat	6%	5%	7%	6%	10%
Poultry	3%	3%	3%	1%	6%
Fish/Seafood	4%	3%	5%	3%	4%
Eggs	4%	4%	5%	4%	5%
Honey	15%	15%	15%	20%	12%
Eat Them All	75%	77%	74%	70%	71%

Vegetarian Resource Group Conducts Roper Poll On Eating Habits of Youths

The Vegetarian Resource Group conducted a Roper poll of 8- to 17-year-olds in 1995 to find out the number of young vegetarians in the United States. There were a few surprises, with some of the numbers being higher than would be expected.

For comparison purposes, we asked the same question as in our adult poll (See *Vegetarian Journal* July/August, 1994.) "Please call off the items on this list, if any, that you never eat: Meat. Poultry. Fish/Seafood. Dairy Products. Eggs. Honey." Note that in most polls, respondents are asked if they consider themselves vegetarian. We used the word <u>never</u> which should give us a lower but more accurate figure.

A whopping 11% of girls 13 to 17 said they don't eat meat. This compares to 7% of adult females. This may be a trend. However, generally teenage females answer food questions differently from adults because of greater interest in their weight and appearance. Based on information we received over the Internet, our American figures here correspond with British figures. A 1993 Trent survey of children in England aged 11 to 16 indicated 12% of girls claimed to be vegetarian. Also in Great Britain, in *The Daily Telegraph* Gallup Poll in May 1993, 11% of 15- to 19-year-olds described themselves as vegetarian.

Back to the United States, about 5% of male teenagers don't eat meat, exactly the same as adult men. What's fascinating is that the opposite figures appeared for 8- to 12-year-olds. Eleven percent of boys say they don't eat meat, while only 6% of girls don't eat meat. Is this an inaccurate glitch in the figures or a sign of something to come? Is the meat industry being successful in their campaigns aimed towards males and bringing boys back into the fold? We'll be very curious to see the figures next time we conduct this poll.

Overall, 7% of youngsters say they don't eat poultry, with only 3% of adults abstaining. Gender doesn't affect the figures that much. Not eating fish or seafood is the most surprising finding, with 18% of kids saying they don't eat it. The children's age and gender don't have great impact. Only 4% of adults say they don't eat fish.

The high number of children and teens who do not eat fish can be explained only by postulating. We would have expected many children to eat tuna or fish sticks. Are parents no longer serving this? Do the kids not realize they are fish products? Do children just not like fish? This possible trend will also be fascinating to watch the next time The Vegetarian Resource Group does a poll.

Most other figures are in line with our adult poll. As to vegetarians, almost two percent of 8- to 12-year-olds say they don't eat meat, fish, or fowl. This is consistent with the adult poll, which came up with 1%, although more females than males are vegetarian among adults. A little over one percent of teens are vegetarian. Our adult figures are close to those reported by the National Livestock and Meat Board from research conducted by MRCA Information Services.

Because we are dealing with a small percentage of the population, it's hard to be sure that we have an accurate picture of vegans. But it appears that, as with adults (disregarding the use of honey), 1/3 to 1/2 of the teen vegetarians are vegan. We wouldn't have predicted this before doing the adult poll, but it makes sense. Many polls give the number of vegetarians as 6 to 10 percent. These are people who call themselves vegetarian. This is closer to our figure for people who don't eat meat. Of course many in this 6 to 10 percent figure probably eat meat sometimes. It seems that once a person "truly" becomes vegetarian, that is they don't eat meat, fish, or fowl, they probably continue towards veganism and thus don't consume dairy and eggs. The implication for marketing is that if you are producing a product for vegetarians, you might as well make it vegan (no animal products).

Another confusing result to us is that 4% of teens in the northeast don't eat meat, while the highest number of abstainers from meat are in the central part of the country, with 11%. The west is an average of 8%. As far as vegetarians, the highest number also came out of the midwest, though with the small num-

> *T he implication for marketing is that if you are producing a product for vegetarians, you might as well make it vegan.*

bers we may want to avoid making conclusions too quickly. Racial status doesn't affect the numbers. Percent of vegetarians are somewhat lower among the upper class than in middle or lower economic situations. Parents having attended college pushes figures up a little, but not too much. Other factors, such as households owning a personal computer or parents working don't have much of an impact.

One thousand and twenty-three children and teens ages 8 to 17 participated in this poll, which was conducted by interviewing youths at their homes. The margin of sampling error is plus or minus 4%. Because of the uncertainty inherent in doing all polls and because we are gathering data about a subset of the population, conclusions have to be put in perspective with other information, trends, and past and future surveys.

	8-12 year olds	13-17 year olds	13-17 FEMALE	ADULTS
DO NOT EVER EAT:				
MEAT	8%	8%	11%	6%
POULTRY	8%	6%	6%	3%
FISH/SEAFOOD	19%	17%	18%	4%
EAT NONE OF THE ABOVE	1.9%	1.4%	1.6%	1%
DAIRY PRODUCTS	4%	3%	3%	3%
EGGS	9%	8%	9%	4%

The Diversity of Gums in Food Products

By Stuart Cantor

Vegetable gums, or hydrocolloids, as they are technically called, have a diverse variety of applications and properties. In addition to their use in the cosmetic, pharmaceutical, and paint industries, they are also widely used in the food and beverage industry.

Gums help foods stay moist and prevent baked goods, such as cookies, cakes, and breads, from going stale. In salad dressings, they are used as thickening agents and as emulsifiers to prevent oil separation. Gums give jams and jellies a spreadable texture and give candies a gummy texture. They add body and creamy texture to cheese and ice cream. They also act as thickeners in syrups, frostings, and icings. In vegetarian burgers, gums act as binders to produce a moist and juicy product. Gums can replace fats as carriers of flavor. They help seasoning blends or salt stick to lowfat snack foods. They also can give lowfat foods a creamy, rich taste and texture without the fat.

The gums most widely used to produce vegetarian foods include guar, carrageenan, locust (carob) bean, CMC (cellulose gum), and xanthan gum.

The focus of this article is on the use of gums in lowfat or non-fat products. Fortunately, today there are many healthier alternatives to the high-fat, low-fiber foods of the past. These healthy foods mimic exactly the taste, texture, and flavor of their high-fat counterparts.

Gums are complex molecules, high in soluble dietary fiber, and virtually fat-free. Gums are polysaccharides (complex carbohydrates) and each gum is composed of different sugars, linked together in different proportions. Gums come from a variety of sources including trees, seeds, and marine plants. They can also be synthesized either chemically or via microbial fermentation. Typically, only small quantities of gum are necessary for most food applications. Different gums can also perform very similar functions in food products. There are currently fifteen gums approved by the Food and Drug Administration (FDA) in use today and others are being considered. The ones most widely used for vegetarian foods include guar, carrageenan, locust (carob) bean, CMC (cellulose gum), and xanthan gum.

GUAR GUM is derived from the seeds of plants cultivated in India and Pakistan. It can form fairly thick solutions in cold water but has no gelling or emulsifying properties. Guar can provide body in soy milk beverages and prevent separation of ingredients. It contributes smoothness in ice cream by promoting small ice crystals during the freezing process and also gives a more uniform texture to cheese products. Guar is also used in dry cake mixes and breads.

CARRAGEENAN is extracted from marine plants in the Philippines, Korea, and China. There are several types with differing chemical characteristics. Carrageenans are protein reactive and can form strong gels. They are currently used widely in the meat industry. Other uses include gel formation in lowfat cheeses, ice cream, and non-dairy toppings. In pie fillings, carrageenan prevents a "runny" fruit filling.

CELLULOSE GUM or CMC is a chemically modified natural gum. It is derived from either wood pulp or cotton fiber and can be prepared in a wide range of viscosity. This gum is noncaloric, since it is unable to be metabolized by humans. CMC functions to prevent ice crystal formation in ice cream and other frozen desserts, prevents sugar crystallization leading to grittiness in syrups, and acts as an effective stabilizer in acidified milk beverages. It is also used in tortilla products to retain moisture, retard staling, and maintain flexibility.

LOCUST BEAN or CAROB BEAN GUM has been utilized since ancient times. Locust bean gum functions in cheese products by controlling water loss and results in a firm, homogeneous, and spreadable product. This gum can also form dessert gels. While the gum is derived from the seeds, the pods that surround them are used in the manufacture of carob. The carob pods are naturally sweet and aromatic and are used as a substitute for chocolate.

XANTHAN GUM is produced by a microbial fermentation. It is cold water soluble, acid- and heat-stable, and although solutions appear gel-like, xanthan mixes and pours readily. Highly viscous solutions can be prepared using a low-gum concentration. Xanthan gum is used widely in the baking industry. It improves the freeze-thaw stability of frozen dough and is used in bakery fillings. In salad dressings, xanthan gum helps to stabilize the oil emulsion and provides thickness as well as particle-suspending abilities.

The applications of gums are very diverse, and they improve the quality of a wide variety of products. Recently, their use as fat replacers have paved the way for a whole new line of nutritious, delicious, and appetizing food products. Through greater consumer awareness of the health benefits of a vegetarian diet and more publicity about such foods, we should anticipate greater visibility of these products in the marketplace.

EXAMPLES OF VEGETARIAN PRODUCTS CONTAINING VEGETABLE GUMS*

GUAR: Nasoya's Nayonaise, Nasoya's Vegi-Dressings, Whitewave's Dairyless (non-dairy yogurt), Yves' Veggie Pepperoni, Yves' Veggie Wiener

CARRAGEENAN: Hain's SuperFruits, Imagine Foods' Dream Pudding, Lightlife's Smart Dogs

CELLULOSE GUM or CMC: Chef Garcia Corn Tortillas

LOCUST BEAN or CAROB BEAN GUM: Barbara's Fat Free Cereal Bars, Farm Foods' Ice Bean, Rice Dream's Vanilla Non-Dairy Dessert, Sweet Nothing's Vanilla Non-Dairy Dessert

XANTHAN GUM: Hain's Eggless Mayonnaise, San-J's Thai Peanut Sauce

*Note: Several items listed above contain more than one type of vegetable gum. Also, often natural foods products list vegetable gum as an ingredient; however, the specific type of gum used is not listed.

Stuart Cantor is a vegetarian and works for a gum company in Maryland.

WHOLE WHEAT BREAD

SUSAN'S WHOLE WHEAT BREAD
(Makes 2 medium loaves)

This recipe was created by Susan Meyers.

2-1/2 cups hot water
1/4 cup molasses
4 Tablespoons soft margarine
1 scant Tablespoon salt (optional)
1 package yeast
1/4 cup hot water
3-1/2 cups whole wheat flour
4 cups unbleached white flour

Place 2-1/2 cups hot water, molasses, margarine, and salt in a bowl and stir well.

Dissolve yeast in 1/4 cup hot water and add to above mixture. Add whole wheat flour and stir. Gradually add white flour while stirring. Reserve a little flour for board.

When dough is stiff and has absorbed flour, turn onto floured board and let rest 10 minutes. Then knead dough 10 minutes, adding flour as necessary to keep it from being too sticky.

Lightly oil a large bowl. Put dough in it. Turn over so the top is oiled. Cover with a warm damp towel. Let rise in warm place 1-1/2 hours or until dough doubles. Punch down and form two balls. Let rest 10 minutes. Lightly oil two 9 x 5 x 3-inch pans. Form oblongs of dough, and place in pans. Cover with wet towel. Let rise 1-1/4 hours.

Preheat oven 375 degrees (for Pyrex pans, 350 degrees). Bake 45 minutes.

TOTAL CALORIES PER SERVING: 241
TOTAL FAT AS % OF DAILY VALUE: 6%   FAT: 4 gm
PROTEIN: 7 gm   CARBOHYDRATES: 46 gm
CALCIUM: 30 mg   IRON: 3 mg   SODIUM: 37 mg
DIETARY FIBER: 4 gm

KAREN'S WHOLE WHEAT BREAD
(Makes 2 large or 3 medium loaves)

Many people have written to us requesting bread recipes. The following recipe has worked very well for Karen Lazarus, M.D.

3-1/2 cups apple juice
4 Tablespoons yeast
1-2 Tablespoons sweetener (I have used turbinado sugar or molasses at various times. Sugar works better.)
1 teaspoon salt
4 teaspoons olive oil
10 cups whole wheat flour

Warm apple juice. Add yeast, sweetener, salt, and oil, and mix. Allow to sit until yeast begins to rise.

Add flour. Knead for approximately 10 minutes. Place in large bowl in warm place, and let rise until double (about 60 to 90 minutes).

Deflate dough. Divide into 2 large or 3 medium loaf pans. Let rise until double, about 30 minutes.

Bake in preheated 350 degree oven for 30 to 35 minutes. Loaves should be golden brown and should sound hollow when tapped on the bottom.

TOTAL CALORIES PER SERVING: 200
TOTAL FAT AS % OF DAILY VALUE: 3%   FAT: 1 gm
PROTEIN: 8 gm   CARBOHYDRATES: 41 gm
CALCIUM: 21 mg   IRON: 2 mg   SODIUM: 101 mg
DIETARY FIBER: 6 gm

WILD FLOURS

Cooking with non-wheat flours

By Mary Clifford, R.D.

You might think that baking without wheat would make for a pretty limited diet. If so, you'd be wrong. "No wheat" doesn't mean no bread, no cake, no pasta, no goodies. Buckwheat, spelt, rice flour, oat flour, and many more wheat alternatives can add different flavors and textures to familiar foods.

HOW TO USE OTHER FLOURS

Traditional dough-containing wheat is elastic, with spongy, tender, high yields. For those with wheat or gluten allergies, eliminating these flours can be tricky, and often leads to products with a different texture from what you may be used to.

Are there any hard and fast rules for substituting for wheat? Not really. There are a number of cookbooks on the market that deal with using flours other than wheat, but it seems that they all offer a different formula for substitution. It also depends on whether you're using flour to bread, thicken, or bake.

Perhaps the best point to keep in mind is that most non-wheat flours do not substitute cup for cup for wheat flour. It's also a good idea to work with combinations of flours, since the flavor of one might be acceptable, but result in a too-crumbly or too-dense product by itself. The best way to come up with wheat-free dishes you enjoy is to experiment. Start with the following wheat-free recipes.

GUIDE TO NON-WHEAT FLOURS

Amaranth: mild flavor, good for baking.

Barley flour: mild, good for baking.

Brown rice flour: sweet, mild flavor, excellent for desserts. Use in combination with other flours as a binding agent (such as egg substitutes or mashed bananas) to avoid crumbly baked goods.

Buckwheat flour: strong flavor, best used in small quantities in combination with other flours.

Chickpea flour: perfect for savory goods because of its heartier, but mild, flavor. Can also be used in baking.

Oat flour: makes dense but flavorful and tender baked goods.

Rye flour: lacks elasticity, but adds a characteristic heartiness.

Spelt: recognized for its ease in baking (results are similar to using whole wheat flour).

BISCUITS

(Makes 1 dozen)

A melt-in-your mouth texture will make these a favorite breakfast treat. Experiment with adding basil, dried onion, and oregano for herbed biscuits, or raisins, chopped nuts, and orange juice (instead of soy milk) for a sweet version.

1-3/4 cups spelt flour
1 Tablespoon baking powder
Pinch of salt
1/4 cup soft margarine, chilled
1/2 cup lite soy milk
1/2 teaspoon melted margarine

Heat oven to 450 degrees. Grease a large baking sheet. In large bowl, mix together flour, baking powder, and salt. With pastry cutter or two knives, cut in margarine until mixture resembles fine crumbs.

Stir in soy milk until a soft dough forms and mixture pulls away from sides of bowl; do not overmix.

Turn dough out onto generously floured board. Knead gently (about 10 times). Pat dough out to between 1/4- and 1/2-inch thick. Cut with 2-1/2-inch biscuit cutter. Re-roll and cut scraps until remaining dough is used. Place on baking sheet and brush with melted margarine.

Bake biscuits about 10 minutes or until very lightly browned. Serve warm.

TOTAL CALORIES PER BISCUIT: 98
TOTAL FAT AS % OF DAILY VALUE: 6%   FAT: 4 gm
PROTEIN: 2 gm   CARBOHYDRATES: 14 gm
CALCIUM: 95 mg   IRON: 1 mg   SODIUM: 152 mg
DIETARY FIBER: 2 gm

SPELT BREAD

(Makes 1 pound loaf -- Serves 8)

Many people are hesitant to make their own bread, thinking that it's far too complex and fussy to bother with. But really, homemade bread is one of the simpler things to learn how to make. If you've only done it with an automatic bread machine, try this simple loaf as your first introduction to baking.

2 cups spelt flour
1 package quick-rising dry yeast
2 Tablespoons sugar or other
    granular sweetener
Pinch of salt
2/3 cup very warm soy milk
2 Tablespoons melted soft margarine

In large bowl, combine flour, yeast, sugar, and salt. Stir in soy milk and 1 Tablespoon melted margarine until dough forms. Turn dough out onto floured board and knead about 3 minutes or until smooth.

Grease mixing bowl and place dough in bowl, turning to coat lightly. Cover and place in warm spot away from drafts. Let rise about 30 minutes.

Heat oven to 350 degrees. Place dough on greased baking sheet, or, if desired, bake in greased 8- x 4-inch loaf pan. Brush with remaining tablespoon of melted margarine and bake about 25 minutes or until golden and loaf sounds hollow when tapped on top.

TOTAL CALORIES PER SERVING: 155
TOTAL FAT AS % OF DAILY VALUE: 5%   FAT: 3 gm
PROTEIN: 5 gm   CARBOHYDRATES: 28 gm
CALCIUM: 18 mg   IRON: 1 mg   SODIUM: 52 mg
DIETARY FIBER: 4 gm

PINEAPPLE UPSIDE-DOWN CAKE

(Serves 8)

This dense, moist cake is simple to make but looks festive enough for a special occasion.

1-1/2 teaspoons soft margarine
1 Tablespoon sugar or other granular
    sweetener
6 pineapple slices
1/4 cup soft margarine
1/4 cup sugar or other granular
    sweetener
3/4 cup brown rice flour
3/4 cup rye flour
Pinch of salt
1 Tablespoon baking powder
1 cup apple juice
1/2 cup crushed pineapple or
    applesauce for garnish

Heat oven to 375 degrees. Grease an 8-inch round baking pan. Melt 1-1/2 teaspoons margarine in bottom of pan. Sprinkle with 1 Tablespoon sugar. Place pineapple slices in pan. Set aside.

In large bowl, beat together 1/4 cup margarine and 1/4 cup sugar until light and fluffy. Combine flours, salt, and baking powder. Stir in flour mixture and apple juice alternately, until mixture is well combined. Pour over pineapple slices.

Bake cake about 20 minutes or until knife inserted in center comes out clean. Run spatula around edge of pan to loosen cake and invert onto serving platter. Serve warm or cool. Garnish with crushed pineapple or applesauce.

TOTAL CALORIES PER SERVING: 217
TOTAL FAT AS % OF DAILY VALUE: 11%   FAT: 7 gm
PROTEIN: 2 gm   CARBOHYDRATES: 38 gm
CALCIUM: 142 mg   IRON: 1 mg   SODIUM: 231 mg
DIETARY FIBER: 2 gm

SPOON CAKE

(Serves 6)

Although this comforting, old-fashioned cake is just as good served warm or at room temperature, there's something irresistible about freshly baked, still-hot-from-the-oven desserts.

2 cups mixed dried fruit
2 cups apple juice
1 Tablespoon lemon juice
1 teaspoon cinnamon
1/4 teaspoon nutmeg
2 Tablespoons maple syrup
1 cup oat flour
2 Tablespoons baking powder
Pinch of salt
1 Tablespoon soft margarine
2/3 cup lite soy milk

In small saucepan, combine dried fruit, apple juice, lemon juice, cinnamon, nutmeg, and maple syrup. Heat to boiling over high heat. Reduce heat to low and simmer about 15 minutes, or until mixture is reduced by about half, and is thick and syrupy.

Heat oven to 400 degrees. Grease a 2-quart baking dish. In medium bowl, combine flour, baking powder, and salt. Cut in margarine until well combined. Stir in soy milk until soft batter forms.

Pour fruit mixture into greased baking dish. Pour batter over fruit. Bake about 15 minutes or until knife inserted in cake portion only comes out clean.

TOTAL CALORIES PER SERVING: 270
TOTAL FAT AS % OF DAILY VALUE: 5%   FAT: 3 gm
PROTEIN: 5 gm   CARBOHYDRATES: 60 gm
CALCIUM: 395 mg   IRON: 3 mg   SODIUM: 429 mg
DIETARY FIBER: 5 gm

POTATO PANCAKES
(Serves 4)

These are similar to a Polish dish called kluski, which are like dumplings. Make them into large pancakes, as called for here, or silver-dollar sized pancakes to serve as appetizers.

2 cups mashed potatoes
3/4 cup oat flour
1 Tablespoon dried minced onion
Salt and pepper to taste
2 teaspoons soft margarine

In medium bowl, stir together all ingredients except margarine. Dough will be soft and sticky.

Melt margarine in non-stick saucepan over medium heat. With floured hands, form dough into four large pancakes. Fry, turning occasionally, until golden. Serve immediately.

TOTAL CALORIES PER SERVING: 195
TOTAL FAT AS % OF DAILY VALUE: 5%   FAT: 3 gm
PROTEIN: 5 gm   CARBOHYDRATES: 37 gm
CALCIUM: 18 mg   IRON: 1 mg   SODIUM: 27 mg
DIETARY FIBER: 4 gm

GARBANZO GRAVY
(Makes 2 cups)

The distinctive taste of garbanzos makes a toothsome change of pace when you turn it into gravy for rice, mashed potatoes, or casseroles.

3/4 cup garbanzo (chickpea) flour
1/3 cup nutritional yeast (found in health food stores)
2 Tablespoons dried minced onion
1/4 teaspoon garlic powder
Salt and pepper to taste
3 cups vegetable broth
2 Tablespoons steak sauce or vegetarian Worcestershire sauce

In 2-quart saucepan, combine all ingredients except broth and steak sauce. Toast over medium heat, stirring, about 2 minutes.

Gradually whisk broth and steak sauce or Worcestershire into flour mixture. Cook, stirring, until smooth and thickened. Serve immediately.

TOTAL CALORIES PER 2 TABLESPOON SERVING: 28
TOTAL FAT AS % OF DAILY VALUE: <1%   FAT: <1 gm
PROTEIN: 2 gm   CARBOHYDRATES: 4 gm
CALCIUM: 8 mg   IRON: <1 mg   SODIUM: 165 mg
DIETARY FIBER: <1 gm

Mary Clifford, R.D., is a dietitian in Roanoke, Virginia and co-author of Simple, Lowfat & Vegetarian.

COOKING WITH GLUTEN

By Dez Figueira

Gluten has been around for centuries. The Asians use it, the Seventh-day Adventists use it, all bakers know about it, and there are a number of technical papers in print about it. Many vegans and vegetarians, and even my cats, love it. Gluten is in a lot of foods, disguised as "wheat protein." Worthington Farms makes several delicious products based on gluten. I have been a gluten maven for about fifteen years, developing and refining its cookery.

Gluten is made from wheat flour. Wheat is a grass of the *Graminae* Family of the Genus *Triticum*, and was probably the first grain to be intentionally cultivated by humankind, dating back to Neolithic times, about seven thousand years ago. A bushel of wheat, weighing 60 pounds, will yield about 42 pounds of flour, which can produce 20 to 25 pounds of gluten.

Gluten is the protein substance that is obtained by manipulating dough under running water so that the starch is removed by a rinsing and kneading process, causing the starch to run off in a milky slurry. The word gluten is related to agglutinate, meaning hold together, which is what it does. As you work with it, you will notice its tendency to draw together.

Raw gluten is a cream-gray colored, iridescent, coherent, rubber-like, tenacious, ductile, elastic mass that is stretchy and slightly pearly in appearance. It sort of looks like used chewing gum. Properly developed gluten has a squeaky feel. Nutritionally speaking, gluten is relatively low in calories, fat, and cholesterol. It is also low in most vitamins and minerals, but can be served with vegetables and grains to make a lowfat dish rich in vitamins and minerals. The sodium content of gluten is quite variable. Gluten cooked in soy sauce or a salty broth will be high in sodium.

You can use a commercial gluten mix, purchase prepared gluten, or make it from scratch. Vital Wheat Gluten (VWG) is a gluten mix distributed by Arrowhead Mills and is made from hard winter wheat. VWG is found in health food stores and on the health food shelf at the supermarket. VWG is produced by making gluten in the usual way, drying it, and then powdering it. Vital Wheat Gluten does not require kneading or washing and it has the added advantage of being quick to prepare. When using VWG, note that one cup powder plus one cup liquid equals one pound gluten. Kneading time is one minute, and there is no washing involved. This is because you are actually reconstituting "instant" dried gluten that has already been made. You can add seasoning to the powder, and use oil and liquid seasoning or sauces, instead of or in addition to water, for the reconstituting liquid. Gluten produced from VWG must still be cooked in the usual ways.

	4 oz. purchased gluten	4 oz. prepared Vital Wheat Gluten
calories	157	132
protein (grams)	24	15
fat (grams)	0.2	0.7
carbohydrate (gm)	16	17
cholesterol	0	0

Gluten is also called seitan. This is cooked, ready-to-eat gluten that has been marinated in tamari and spices. Ready-to-eat gluten (seitan) is available in the refrigerator case in most health food stores. It usually comes in a plastic container similar to tofu. Some health food stores carry seitan in bottles on the shelf. In Asian stores, ready-to-eat gluten (seitan) is available in cans. It is usually half to one-third the price of seitan in the health food store. Names on cans in these stores may include mock duck, Mun Chai Ya, or Chai Pow Yu (mock abalone). Gluten is sometimes also called wheat meat. The packaged or canned items can be quickly warmed up and then served with bread, rice, or pasta. For a super fast meal, while warming up the gluten, add some frozen peas and corn.

TO MAKE GLUTEN

To make 3-1/2 to 5 pounds of gluten from scratch.

1. Mix 12 cups of flour with 7 cups of water until all the flour is moistened. Gather dough into a ball. After the dough begins to hold together, knead twenty minutes. The dough should be smooth and springy.

2. Place dough in a large bowl, cover completely with water and let rest one hour.

3. Place a large bowl of cool water in the sink. Adjust faucet so that a continuous trickle of cool water runs into the bowl.

4. Break off an apple-sized piece of dough and put it in the water in the bowl, stretch and squeeze the dough in the water so that the milky starch begins to separate. It takes about 15 minutes of washing for each piece of dough. Keep replacing water in bowl, keeping the dough under water as much as possible. Properly developed gluten is slightly iridescent and feels squeaky. When washing is complete, the rinse water should be clear.

5. Place the washed gluten in a container of cold water. Repeat step 4 until all gluten has been washed.

6. Raw gluten can be boiled for 20 minutes in water or a flavored broth, roasted slowly in broth, shaped into patties and fried, ground, and pan fried, or mixed with peanut butter and tomato paste and baked. Boiled

gluten can also be frozen and thawed for a different texture.

MAKING GLUTEN FROM SCRATCH

FLOUR: Any wheat flour will produce gluten (except self-rising). My flour of choice is stone ground, whole, hard red winter wheat from Arrowhead Mills, preferably Tascosa, or other hard red winter wheat varieties. Refined, bleached white flour probably has the lowest yield. It is okay to mix several different types of flour. Any type of wheat flour you have on hand will make gluten.

Stone ground whole wheat flour has the bran still in it, which adds dimension to the gluten texture and fiber to your diet. Some of the bran will be lost in the washing process. Another good flour to try is red durum which produces a golden creamy gluten.

Protein in wheat flour does vary according to the type of wheat it is made from. Hard spring wheat is about 12 to 18% protein. Hard winter wheat is about 10 to 15% protein.

WATER: The ratio of water to flour should be 0.7 parts water to 1 part flour, although the flour/water ratio can vary from 0.6:1 to 0.85:1, depending on the type of flour used. Hard water is preferable to soft water. Water temperature also matters. The ideal water temperature should be 15 degrees to 20 degrees centigrade (59 to 68 degrees Fahrenheit). If you have soft water and/or soft flour, sodium chloride will help make the gluten firmer. Your ideal combination is cool hard water and hard flour.

| Hard water/hard flour = high protein yield, strong gluten |
| Soft water/soft flour = low protein yield, weak gluten |
| Too cold water = low protein and aching hands |
| Too warm water = weak gluten |

AMOUNT	PRODUCES
1 cup unbleached white flour plus 1/3 cup water, kneaded for 20 minutes, washed for 15 minutes	1/3 cup raw gluten
1 cup stone ground whole wheat flour plus 3/8 cup water, kneaded for 20 minutes, washed for 15 minutes	3/8 cup raw gluten
1/2 cup whole wheat flour mixed with 1/2 cup Vital Wheat Gluten plus 5/8 cup water, kneaded for 5 minutes, washed for 10 minutes	1 cup raw gluten
2 cups whole wheat flour mixed with 2 cups Vital Wheat Gluten plus 2 cups water, kneaded for 5 minutes, washed for 10 minutes	3-3/4 cups raw gluten

GLUTEN PRODUCTION: In making gluten from any kind of flour, it is necessary to knead the dough. Kneading is what develops the gluten. Twenty minutes is usually sufficient. There is no difference in the kneading time from one type of flour to another. The main difference in flours is the ratio of gluten to starch -- the yield.

It is okay to soak the dough ball in water for up to eight hours without losing any to disintegration. Many factors can affect the finished gluten, but it is not possible to "ruin" a batch no matter how many liberties you take. Hardness/softness of water, water/flour ratio, type of flour, water temperature, resting time of dough, and kneading time, are probably the most significant factors.

It takes fifteen minutes to wash all the starch out of a hunk of gluten, no matter if you are doing a wad the side of a tennis ball or one as big as a cantaloupe.

GLUTEN TIPS

- Raw gluten can only be stored frozen.
- Raw gluten holds for up to 3 - 4 hours in water, if frequently rewashed.
- If not kept cold, it will ferment.
- Raw gluten may be frozen but when thawed must be briefly rewashed right away. It will "melt" away. Gluten that has had seasoning worked into it should be cooked or frozen immediately or it will draw up into a ball with all the "goodies" on the outside. This does not happen with Vital Wheat Gluten.
- Do not try to boil raw gluten that has been seasoned. You will waste all the seasoning. Same applies to Vital Wheat Gluten.
- Boiled and kept in water, gluten will keep indefinitely, if you change the water every day.
- More kneading = denser product.
- For tough, chewy gluten, or to make ground gluten, use extra flour, knead longer, boil finished gluten 30 minutes in plain water, then drain, cool, squeeze and freeze. Freezing makes it more fibrous.
- For soft, tender gluten, simmer shreds in a broth containing margarine and seasoning.
- There are eight basic ways to process gluten, and these apply to Vital Wheat Gluten as well as "scratch" gluten: raw, fried; raw, baked; raw, fried, then simmered; boiled, fried, processed; boiled, frozen, thawed, fried, processed; roasted from raw state with oils and spices and seasonings; roasted flat, plain, for grinding (granola); and boiled, then ground, then fried, for use in sauces.
- Gluten, in its raw state, can be pan roasted into a delicious meal in about 20 minutes, using a seasoning broth. Raw gluten can be torn into chunks and baked for ten minutes in a hot oven for a crunchy snack.

One way to avoid a lot of deep frying is to bake cubed gluten in a slow oven until it is dried, brown, and hard. Used in stews and soups it will absorb flavor and soften up when added in the last five minutes of cooking. Try this with plain boiled as well as thawed gluten, for different textures. Experiment with seasoned soy sauces. While your cubes are baking, be generous with the soy sauce, or try other sauces. Freeze your cubes in quantity and save time on recipes using fried cubes.

ONE WAY TO MAKE GROUND GLUTEN

Boil one pound of raw gluten in salted, oiled water for 45 minutes. When using Vital Wheat Gluten (VWG), reconstitute 1 cup VWG powder to 7/8 cup water for a denser product.

When the boiled gluten is cool enough to handle, cut it into small pieces and process through a grinder or food processor. A blender works well, also.

You can freeze it or use it immediately. At this point, you can season it with soy sauce or liquid smoke and bake it. You can also fry it in olive oil and spices before freezing.

ANOTHER WAY TO MAKE GROUND GLUTEN

Roll out raw gluten very thin. Bake at 400 degrees on well-oiled cookie sheet until brown and crispy. Roll again after baking to crumble it into pieces. Put the crumbled pieces into a cloth bag and pound it with a wooden mallet or heavy mug. Raw gluten will puff up in the oven; you will need to poke it to break the bubbles.

EASY BAKED BEANS
(Serves 5)

Ground gluten adds a unique touch to these baked beans.

1 cup fresh or frozen corn
1 cup cooked pinto beans
1 cup cooked wild rice
3 cloves garlic, minced
1/2 cup bell pepper, chopped
1-1/2 teaspoons oregano
2 Tablespoons tamari or soy sauce
1 cup ground gluten
1 cup low-sodium canned tomatoes
1 cup low-sodium V8 Juice or
    tomato sauce
1-1/2 teaspoons paprika
1/2 cup chopped scallions
1 Tablespoon maple syrup
1-1/2 teaspoons molasses

Preheat oven to 350 degrees. Combine all the ingredients together in a large bowl. Mix well, then pour into a large casserole dish. Bake at 350 degrees for 45 minutes. Serve warm.

TOTAL CALORIES PER SERVING: 179
TOTAL FAT AS % OF DAILY VALUE: 2%   FAT: 1 gm
PROTEIN: 9 gm   CARBOHYDRATES: 28 gm
CALCIUM: 57 mg   IRON: 2 mg   SODIUM: 428 mg
DIETARY FIBER: 5 gm

DEFINITION OF TERMS
BOILED GLUTEN: has not yet been frozen.
RAW GLUTEN: made from scratch or reconstituted Vital Wheat Gluten (VWG).
THAWED GLUTEN: has been boiled, cooled, frozen, then thawed.
GROUND GLUTEN: see method above.

DIRTY RICE
(Serves 4-6)

Serve as a main or side dish.

1 vegetable bouillon cube
3/4 cup hot water
1 cup shallots, chopped
2 teaspoons olive oil
1/4 cup celery, chopped
1/2 cup carrots, shredded
1/4 cup mushrooms, sliced
1 pound ground gluten
2 cups cooked brown rice

Melt the bouillon cube in the hot water and set it aside. Meanwhile, sauté the shallots and oil in a large frying pan until transparent. Add the celery and carrots. Sauté 6 minutes longer. Stir in the mushrooms and stir-fry 1 more minute. Fold in the gluten, mixing well. Cover pan and simmer for 2 minutes. Add the cooked rice and pour the liquid bouillon quickly into skillet and cover immediately. Turn off the heat and do not uncover for 1 minute. Serve warm.

TOTAL CALORIES PER SERVING: 214
TOTAL FAT AS % OF DAILY VALUE: 5%   FAT: 3 gm
PROTEIN: 10 gm   CARBOHYDRATES: 35 gm
CALCIUM: 32 mg   IRON: 2 mg   SODIUM: 68 mg
DIETARY FIBER: 2 gm

PATATAS VASCONGADAS
(Serves 6)

This is a hearty potato dish your friends will enjoy.

6 large red potatoes, well scrubbed
Water
1/2 cup low-sodium V8 Juice or
    tomato sauce
2 cloves, whole or 1/2 Tablespoon
    clove powder
1 tiny shallot, minced
1 cup ground gluten
1 Tablespoon chives

Cut potatoes into thick slices. Place the potatoes in a pot and cover them half way with water. Add V8 juice, cloves, and shallot. Bring to a boil, then reduce heat. Simmer covered until potatoes are almost done. Add gluten and simmer until the potatoes are tender. Remove from heat. Sprinkle dish with chives before serving warm.

TOTAL CALORIES PER SERVING: 312
TOTAL FAT AS % OF DAILY VALUE: <1%   FAT: <1 gm
PROTEIN: 10 gm   CARBOHYDRATES: 67 gm
CALCIUM: 29 mg   IRON: 4 mg   SODIUM: 25 mg
DIETARY FIBER: 6 gm

STUFFED ONIONS
(Serves 6)

Here's a unique stuffed onion recipe.

1/8 cup soft tofu
1 cup cream style corn
1 Tablespoon paprika
1 cup celery, finely chopped
1 cup ground gluten
6 giant onions (preferably Vidalia)
1 cup vegetable broth
1 Tablespoon soft margarine

Blend tofu, corn, and paprika together in a large bowl. Add the celery and gluten and mix well. Set the bowl aside.

Preheat oven to 350 degrees. Peel the onions carefully. Boil onions in a pot with the vegetable broth for 10 minutes. Carefully remove the centers of each onion and chop very finely. Add chopped onion to the stuffing mixture that had been set aside.

Stuff onion with stuffing and arrange them in a baking dish. Dot onions with margarine and bake at 350 degrees for 20 minutes. Serve warm.

TOTAL CALORIES PER SERVING: 162
TOTAL FAT AS % OF DAILY VALUE: 5%   FAT: 3 gm
PROTEIN: 9gm   CARBOHYDRATES: 25 gm
CALCIUM: 90 mg   IRON: 1 mg   SODIUM: 202 mg
DIETARY FIBER: 3 gm

STUFFED PEPPERS WITH SAUCE

(Serves 6 - two peppers each)

These peppers are stuffed with a mixture of gluten, vegetables, and quinoa (a delicious grain found in natural food stores and some super-markets).

12 bell peppers
1 onion, chopped fine
1 Tablespoon olive oil
4 cloves garlic, minced
3-1/2 cups ground gluten
1 teaspoon fresh parsley, finely
    chopped
1/2 teaspoon basil
1/2 cup celery, chopped
3 cups cooked quinoa
12 small button mushrooms, stems
    removed

Remove and dice tops of bell peppers. Clean peppers out and set them aside.

Sauté onion and olive oil in a frying pan for 3 minutes. Add garlic and continue stir-frying for 3 more minutes. Add gluten, parsley, basil, and celery. Cover frying pan and simmer over low heat for 5 minutes.

Combine fried mixture with the cooked quinoa in a large bowl. Stuff each pepper halfway with the mixture. Place one mush-room in center of each pepper. Fill peppers up with remaining mixture, packing tightly.

Place stuffed peppers in a roasting pan, standing up. Bake at 350 degrees for 45 minutes until peppers start to change color. While the peppers are baking, prepare the following sauce.

STUFFED PEPPER SAUCE
Diced pepper tops from above
1 small onion, peeled and chopped
2 cloves garlic, minced
1 teaspoon olive oil
Two 15-ounce cans whole tomatoes
6-ounce can V8 Juice or tomato
    sauce
1 small bayleaf
Pinch of oregano
Salt and pepper to taste

Sauté diced pepper tops, onion, garlic, and olive oil in a frying pan for 5 minutes. Crush tomatoes into saucepan. Add V8 juice and seasonings. Cover pan and simmer for 40 minutes, stirring frequently. Serve on soup plates with sauce poured over baked stuffed peppers.

TOTAL CALORIES PER SERVING: 307
TOTAL FAT AS % OF DAILY VALUE: 9%   FAT: 6 gm
PROTEIN: 16 gm   CARBOHYDRATES: 50 gm
CALCIUM: 92 mg   IRON: 6 mg   SODIUM: 259 mg
DIETARY FIBER: 7 gm

Dez Figueira is a freelance writer from Miami Beach, Florida.

VEGETARIAN CROCKPOT IDEAS

By Marilyn Haldane

Vegetables are primary candidates for the convenience of the crockpot (slow cooker); however, there are some basic rules of crockpot cooking. For instance, you should use less liquid when slow-cooking because less water is lost from steam. Also, you should use a light hand when seasoning because the long cooking times allow the flavors to develop fully, and they become more potent than with regular cooking. This is a guide I hope you will find helpful.

GRAINS

Whole grains may be cooked for 3 to 4-1/2 hours on high or 8 to 10 hours on low. Rolled grains (oats, rye, wheat, triticale) may also be cooked on low heat overnight, but they tend to get a little over-cooked and, besides, they cook quickly on the stove.

Other grains such as grits, cracked wheat and rye, bulgur, and smaller grains such as millet, quinoa, amaranth, and teff take less time to cook (6-8 hours on low). Use your own judgment as to whether these smaller grains are worth using the crockpot. Some take only 20-35 minutes to cook on the stove anyway, but if you are looking to create a soup or entrée and want the grains to absorb the seasonings, by all means use the crockpot to develop the flavor.

It is also wonderful to put grains in the crockpot with water and some dried fruit and spices at night for a warm, hearty breakfast the next morning.

Pasta can also be added to dishes made in the crockpot. It should not be added until 2 hours (at most) before serving. Pasta will cook on high in 30 to 45 minutes.

VEGETABLES

It is better to cook vegetables on low because they retain more color and texture than when cooked on high. To ensure even cooking, cut vegetables in equal sizes. Root vegetables (carrots, potatoes, parsnips, yams, beets, turnips, etc.), onions, and some squash (winter varieties) will take longer to cook than other vegetables (2-3 hours, chopped; 5-6 hours, chunk; 6-8 hours, whole -- except larger vegetables like potatoes which take 8-10 hours), so add them first.

Other vegetables (not including leafy greens) will take less time to cook, about 2-3 hours or less (45 minutes on high). For leafy greens, add them just before serving (as in a soup or stew) and stir in to warm. The leftover heat will cook them just right.

For cooking single vegetables, add a little water (you don't need to cover them in water) and cook. Frozen vegetables do not need added water and will cook in 2-3 hours or in 45 minutes on high.

You can also bake potatoes and other vegetables whole. Just wash (do not dry) and put them in the crockpot for 8-10 hours. Artichokes can also be cooked whole. Add some water to cover the bottom of the crockpot and cook 2-3 hours or 45 minutes on high.

If you are cooking a stew or soup that uses root and other vegetables, put the longer cooking vegetables in the crockpot in the morning. When you get home from work or 30-45 minutes before you want to eat, add the other vegetables (which you could have chopped in the morning to save time). Just before serving, add greens if desired.

Vegetables may be kept warm in the crockpot for 1-2 hours after the crockpot has been turned off.

from over-cooking (they will start to break up and fall apart). You may season the broth with onion and garlic if you like or cook them in plain water, drain and rinse, and freeze for use later. Do not add salt until the beans are as tender as you desire because the salt will inhibit any more softening of the beans.

Lentils, split peas, and black-eyed peas don't require the long cooking time of other beans, but do well in the crockpot when used for soups.

FRUIT

For dried fruit, add the minimum amount of water (usually just enough to cover) and cook on low 7-8 hours or on high 3-4 hours. Try adding a slice or two of lemon to prunes before cooking; after cooking, remove the lemon (don't squeeze it out) and remove pits if necessary. Blend in blender until smooth, and chill. This makes a wonderful fruit pudding. I haven't tried anything but prunes, but I imagine other dried fruits would work also.

For baked fresh fruit such as pears and apples, fill or season as desired, and cook on low with 1/2 cup water in bottom of crockpot for 6-8 hours (or overnight for a breakfast treat). If you stack the fruit, it will get tender and may sink a little, but unless it gets over-cooked, it won't mash down.

BEANS

The crockpot is wonderful for cooking beans! Use 4 cups water to 1 cup beans (soaked or unsoaked). Cook on low for 8-10 hours (pre-soaked) or 12-14 hours (unsoaked). Cooking on high (at a steady boil) takes about 4-6 hours, but watch closely after 3 to 4 hours to prevent the beans

Marilyn Haldane resides in Albuquerque, New Mexico and teaches cooking classes.

THE PRESSURE'S ON!

By Nanette J. Blanchard

In today's fast-paced society, an old-fashioned appliance has recently been rediscovered as a tool for getting healthy meals to the table in just minutes. Modern pressure cookers are safer than ever and easier to use than many other kitchen appliances. When the lid is locked in place, the steam produced by boiling liquid builds pressure, raising the cooking temperature and producing foods much more quickly than conventional methods.

This higher cooking temperature is especially helpful at higher altitudes and produces tender-cooked beans and whole grains in minutes. Foods prepared in pressure cookers also retain nutrients that would otherwise be lost in the steam from other methods of cooking.

Always be sure to follow your pressure cooker's manufacturer's instructions and use caution when removing the lid after cooking. Several pressure cooker models feature a quick steam-release valve; if not, pressure can be released quickly by placing it under cold running water. When pressure is dropped naturally, it takes about an additional 10 to 15 minutes before you can open the lid. The following recipes were all tested in a Presto 6-quart stainless steel pressure cooker.

HERBED BROWN RICE
(Serves 4)

The pressure cooker can steam grains, giving them a fluffy, light texture in just minutes.

1 cup long-grain brown rice
3 cups water, divided
2 Tablespoons Italian flat-leaf parsley
4 scallions, diced

Mix brown rice with 1-1/2 cups water in a metal bowl which fits loosely into pressure cooker. Place bowl in pressure cooker along with an additional 1-1/2 cups water for the bottom of the pressure cooker (not in bowl). Lock lid in place, and bring to medium pressure. Cook for 10 minutes. Let pressure drop naturally. Remove lid and stir in parsley and scallions and let rice steam uncovered an additional 5 minutes.

TOTAL CALORIES PER SERVING: 173
TOTAL FAT AS % OF DAILY VALUE: 2%   FAT: 1 gm
PROTEIN: 4 gm   CARBOHYDRATES: 36 gm
CALCIUM: 16 mg   IRON: 1 mg   SODIUM: 4 mg
DIETARY FIBER: 3 gm

EASY CURRIED GARBANZOS
(Serves 4)

Here is a simple bean dish that you can make at the last minute in under an hour. No pre-soaking is required.

1 Tablespoon oil
2 teaspoons curry powder
1-1/2 cups dried garbanzo beans
4 cups water
Hot pepper sauce

Heat oil in pressure cooker and stir in curry powder. Add garbanzo beans and water and lock lid in place. Bring to high pressure and continue cooking for 35 minutes. Let pressure drop naturally. Drain off excess liquid and add hot pepper sauce to taste.

TOTAL CALORIES PER SERVING: 300
TOTAL FAT AS % OF DAILY VALUE: 11%   FAT: 7 gm
PROTEIN: 15 gm   CARBOHYDRATES: 46 gm
CALCIUM: 112 mg   IRON: 5 mg   SODIUM: 20 mg
DIETARY FIBER: 9 gm

SAVORY VEGETABLE STEW

(Serves 4)

This hearty stew laced with mustard and cinnamon can also be added to a whole wheat pie crust or topped with a whole wheat baking mix and baked for a vegetable pot pie.

1 large onion, diced
3 cloves garlic, minced
3 carrots, chopped
3 red potatoes, peeled and diced
1 cup fresh or frozen corn kernels
2 cups vegetable broth
2 Tablespoons prepared mustard
1/2 teaspoon ground cinnamon
1 teaspoon liquid sweetener
1 teaspoon salt (optional)

Stir all ingredients together in pressure cooker. Lock lid in place and bring to pressure over high heat. Cook for 4 minutes. Release pressure by a quick-release method. For a thicker stew, stir 1 Tablespoon cornstarch into 1 Tablespoon cold water until smooth. Add to cooked stew and cook uncovered, stirring constantly, for 2 minutes or until thickened.

TOTAL CALORIES PER SERVING: 178
TOTAL FAT AS % OF DAILY VALUE: 3%   FAT: 2 gm
PROTEIN: 5 gm   CARBOHYDRATES: 31 gm
CALCIUM: 40 mg   IRON: 1 mg   SODIUM: 233 mg
DIETARY FIBER: 5 gm

SMOKY BEAN SOUP

(Serves 6)

This unusual soup gains its smoky flavor from chipotle chili peppers (jalapenos that are smoke-dried). The pressure cooker really saves time in this recipe because the pinto beans are added dry without any pre-soaking or pre-cooking. If you like spicy dishes, add 2 chipotle peppers.

2 Tablespoons oil
1 onion, chopped
3 cloves garlic, minced
1-2 chipotle chili peppers
1 bay leaf
1 teaspoon ground cumin
3 stalks celery, diced
1 cup dry pinto beans
One 9-ounce package frozen cut
   green beans
5 cups water

Put all ingredients into pressure cooker and stir. Lock lid in place and bring to high pressure. Continue cooking for 35 minutes. Release pressure by the quick-release method. Remove lid and test beans for softness. If additional cooking is necessary, lock lid in place again, bring to high pressure and continue cooking at high pressure for several more minutes. Serve hot.

TOTAL CALORIES PER SERVING: 269
TOTAL FAT AS % OF DAILY VALUE: 12%   FAT: 8 gm
PROTEIN: 10 gm   CARBOHYDRATES: 40 gm
CALCIUM: 123 mg   IRON: 5 mg   SODIUM: 154 mg
DIETARY FIBER: 10 gm

EASY MUSHROOM BARLEY SOUP

(Serves 6)

Enjoy this simple soup.

1 Tablespoon oil
3 cloves garlic, minced
1 large red onion, chopped
8 ounces mushrooms, sliced
1/2 cup pearl barley
1 cup frozen baby lima beans
6 cups vegetable broth
1 bay leaf
Freshly ground black pepper

Sauté onion and garlic in oil in pressure cooker over medium heat. Add mushrooms, and continue cooking, stirring another 5 minutes. Add remaining ingredients (except pepper) and lock lid in place. Cook on high pressure for 20 minutes and let pressure drop naturally. Season with pepper.

TOTAL CALORIES PER SERVING: 150
TOTAL FAT AS % OF DAILY VALUE: 6%   FAT: 4 gm
PROTEIN: 5 gm   CARBOHYDRATES: 26 gm
CALCIUM: 22 mg   IRON: 2 mg   SODIUM: 228 mg
DIETARY FIBER: 6 gm

AMARANTH WITH APRICOTS AND CURRANTS

(Serves 4)

If you've never tried amaranth, here is a simple recipe highlighting the grain's corn-like flavor. Top this cereal with some plain soy yogurt.

1 cup amaranth
2 cups water
2 teaspoons oil
1/4 teaspoon salt
1/2 cup dried currants
1/4 cup chopped dried apricots
1 teaspoon grated orange rind
1/4 teaspoon cinnamon

In pressure cooker with lid locked into place, bring all ingredients to high pressure and cook for 6 minutes. Release pressure by quick-release method and stir well. If all liquid is not absorbed, continue cooking and stirring mixture for several more minutes.

TOTAL CALORIES PER SERVING: 272
TOTAL FAT AS % OF DAILY VALUE: 9%   FAT: 6 gm
PROTEIN: 8 gm   CARBOHYDRATES: 51 gm
CALCIUM: 95 mg   IRON: 5 mg   SODIUM: 156 mg
DIETARY FIBER: 2 gm

For additional information about pressure cookers, please contact these manufacturers.

1. All-American Pressure Cookers and Pressure Canners, Wisconsin Aluminum Foundry Co., Inc., 838 South 16th Street, P.O. Box 246, Manitowoc, WI 54221-0246; (414) 682-8627

2. Cuisinart Quick Cuisine Pressure Cooker/ Steamers, Cuisinarts Corp., 77 Havemeyer Lane, Stamford, CT 06902; (203) 975-4600

3. Presto Stainless Steel and Aluminum Pressure Cookers and Pressure Canners, National Presto Industries, Eau Claire, WI 54703-3703; (715) 839-2121

4. Mirro Speed Cookers and Canners, Mirro Company, 1512 Washington Street, P.O. Box 1330, Manitowoc, WI 54221-1330; (414) 684-4421

Nanette J. Blanchard is a systems operator for the Cooks Online Forum of CompuServe Information Services. She conducts weekly electronic conferences on food and cooking topics.

BOOK CATALOG
RESOURCES FROM
THE VEGETARIAN RESOURCE GROUP

If you are interested in purchasing any of the following VRG titles, please send a check or money order made out to *The Vegetarian Resource Group* (Maryland residents must add 5% sales tax) and mail it along with your order to *The Vegetarian Resource Group, P.O. Box 1463, Baltimore, MD 21203*. Make sure you include your shipping address. Or call (410) 366-8343 to order with a Visa or Mastercard credit card. Price given includes postage in the United States. Outside the USA please pay in US funds by credit card or money order and add $2.00 per book for postage.

SIMPLY VEGAN
Quick Vegetarian Meals, 2nd Edition
By Debra Wasserman & Reed Mangels, Ph.D., R.D.

Simply Vegan is an easy-to-use vegetarian guide that contains over 160 kitchen-tested vegan recipes (no meat, fish, fowl, dairy, or eggs). Each recipe is accompanied by a nutritional analysis.

Reed Mangels, Ph.D., R.D., has included an extensive vegan nutrition section on topics such as Protein, Fat, Calcium, Iron, Vitamin B12, Pregnancy and the Vegan Diet, Feeding Vegan Children, and Calories, Weight Gain, and Weight Loss. A Nutrition Glossary is provided, along with sample menus, meal plans, and a list of the top recipes for Iron, Calcium, and Vitamin C.

Also featured are food definitions and origins, and a comprehensive list of mail-order companies that specialize in selling vegan food, natural clothing, cruelty-free cosmetics, and ecologically-based household products. **TRADE PAPERBACK $13**

THE LOWFAT JEWISH VEGETARIAN COOKBOOK
Healthy Traditions From Around The World
By Debra Wasserman

The Lowfat Jewish Vegetarian Cookbook contains over 150 lowfat, vegan international recipes. Savor potato knishes, Polish plum and rhubarb soup, Indian curry and rice, Greek pastries, and Spinach Pies. Feast on Romanian apricot dumplings, North African barley pudding, Pumpernickel and Russian flat bread, sweet fruit kugel, Czechoslovakian noodles with poppy seeds, and Russian blini. Celebrate with eggless challah, hamentashen for Purim, Chanukah latkes, mock "chopped liver," Russian charoset, eggless matzo balls, and Syrian wheat pudding.

Breakfast, lunch, and dinner menus are provided, as well as 33 unique Passover dishes and Seder ideas, and Rosh Hashanah Dinner suggestions. Each recipe is accompanied by a nutritional analysis.
TRADE PAPERBACK $15

MEATLESS MEALS FOR WORKING PEOPLE
Quick and Easy Vegetarian Recipes
By Debra Wasserman & Charles Stahler

Vegetarian cooking can be simple or complicated. *The Vegetarian Resource Group* recommends using whole grains and fresh vegetables whenever possible. However, for the busy working person, this isn't always possible. **Meatless Meals For Working People** contains over 100 delicious fast and easy recipes, plus ideas which teach you how to be a vegetarian within your hectic schedule using common convenient vegetarian foods. This handy guide also contains a spice chart, party ideas, information on fast food chains, and much, much more. **TRADE PAPERBACK, $6**

SIMPLE, LOWFAT & VEGETARIAN
By Suzanne Havala, M.S., R.D. & Mary Clifford, R.D.

This 368-page book is an easy-to-use guide to lowfat eating that shows you how to reduce the fat in your meals with a few simple changes, but allows you to continue enjoying dining in Chinese, Mexican, fast food, Indian, natural foods, and other restaurants. You'll also learn what to order when flying, traveling on Amtrak, going to the movies, or visiting an amusement park. Good food choices, before and after menu magic, fat content of foods, and helpful charts are presented for these and many other situations. The book also contains suggestions for 30 days of quick lowfat meals, tips on how to modify your own recipes, sample menus, weekly shopping lists, plus 50 vegan recipes. **TRADE PAPERBACK $15**

NO CHOLESTEROL PASSOVER RECIPES
100 Vegan Recipes
By Debra Wasserman & Charles Stahler

For many, low-calorie Passover recipes are quite a challenge. Here is a wonderful collection of Passover dishes that are non-dairy, no-cholesterol, eggless, and vegetarian. It includes recipes for eggless blintzes, dairyless carrot cream soup, festive macaroons, apple latkes, sweet and sour cabbage, knishes, broccoli with almond sauce, mock "chopped liver," no oil lemon dressing, eggless matzo meal pancakes, and much more. **TRADE PAPERBACK $9**

VEGETARIAN QUANTITY RECIPES
From The Vegetarian Resource Group

Here is a helpful kit for people who must cook for large groups and institutional settings. It contains 28 vegetarian recipes including main dishes, burgers, sandwich spreads, side dishes, soups, salads, desserts, and breakfast. Each recipe provides a serving for 25 and 50 people, and a nutritional analysis. The kit also contains a listing of over 140 companies offering vegetarian food items in institutional sizes and "Tips for Introducing Vegetarian Food Into Institutions." **PACKET $15**

VEGETARIAN JOURNAL'S FOOD SERVICE UPDATE NEWSLETTER
Edited by The Vegetarian Resource Group staff

This quarterly newsletter is for food service personnel and others working for healthier food in schools, restaurants, hospitals, and other institutions. **Vegetarian Journal's Food Service Update** offers advice, shares quantity recipes, and spotlights leaders in the industry who are providing the healthy options being looked for by consumers. **NEWSLETTER $25 includes both** *Vegetarian Journal* **and** *Vegetarian Journal's FoodService Update*

VEGETARIAN JOURNAL'S GUIDE TO NATURAL FOODS RESTAURANTS IN THE U.S. & CANADA

For the health-conscious traveler, this is the perfect traveling companion to insure a great meal or the ideal lodgings when away from home or if you are looking for a nearby vegetarian place. There has been a delightful proliferation of restaurants designed to meet the growing demand for healthier meals. To help locate these places, there is now a single source for information on over 2,000 restaurants, vacation resorts, and more.

    The Vegetarian Journal's Guide to Natural Foods Restaurants (Avery Publishing Group, Inc.) is a helpful guide listing eateries state by state and province by province. Each entry not only describes the house specialties, varieties of cuisine, and special dietary menus, but also includes information on ambiance, attire, and reservations. It even tells you whether or not you can pay by credit card. And there's more. Included in this guide are listings of vegetarian inns, spas, camps, tours, travel agencies, and vacations spots. **TRADE PAPERBACK $14**

LEPRECHAUN CAKE AND OTHER TALES
A Vegetarian Story-Cookbook
By Vonnie Winslow Crist and Debra Wasserman

This vegan story-cookbook is for children ages 8 through 11. The book includes a glossary of cooking terms, clean-up and preparation instructions, and safety tips. Children will love preparing and eating the delicious recipes. Sit down and enjoy learning about a leprechaun in the kitchen, a baby dragon down the block, friendly forest deer from South America, and the Snow Queen's Unicorn teach children and adults who love them, about friendship, caring, and healthy cooking. **TRADE PAPERBACK $11**

THE VEGETARIAN GAME

This computer software educational game contains 750 questions. Learn while having fun. Categories include health/nutrition, how food choices affect the environment, animals and ethical choices, vegetarian foods, famous vegetarians, and potluck. Three age levels: 5-9; 10 or older/adults new to vegetarianism; and individuals with advanced knowledge of vegetarianism or anyone looking for a challenge. **IBM PC compatible with CGA or better or Hercules graphics; MS DOS 2.0 or higher. SOFTWARE $20** *When ordering, indicate 3.5" or 5.25" disk.*

INDEX

To order additional copies of
VEGAN HANDBOOK,
send $20 (postage included) per book to
The Vegetarian Resource Group, PO Box 1463, Baltimore, MD 21203.
(Outside the USA, pay in US funds only and add $3 per book for additional postage.)

WHAT IS THE VEGETARIAN RESOURCE GROUP?

Our health professionals, activists, and educators work with businesses and individuals to bring about healthy changes in your school, workplace, and community. Registered dietitians and physicians aid in the development of practical nutrition related publications and answer member or media questions about the vegetarian lifestyle.

Vegetarian Journal **is one of the benefits members enjoy.** Readers receive practical tips for vegetarian meal planning, articles on vegetarian nutrition, recipes, natural food product reviews, and an opportunity to share ideas with others. All nutrition articles are reviewed by a registered dietitian or medical doctor.

The Vegetarian Resource Group also publishes books and special interest newsletters such as *Vegetarian Journal's Food Service Update* and *Tips for Vegetarian Activists.*

To Join **The Vegetarian Resource Group**

and Receive the Bimonthly **Vegetarian Journal** for One Year
Send $20.00 to The Vegetarian Resource Group
P.O. Box 1463, Baltimore, MD 21203.
(Mexico/Canada send $30 and other foreign countries send $42 in US funds only.)
Orders can be charged over the phone by calling (410) 366-8343
or faxed by calling (410) 366-8804. Our e-mail address is TheVRG@aol.com